TEACHER'S GUIDE

SIDE by SIDE

THIRD EDITION

BOOK 2

Steven J. Molinsky
Bill Bliss

Contributing Authors

Sarah Lynn
Mary Ann Perry

with

John Kopec

Longman

W9-ATL-212

Side by Side, 3rd edition
Teacher's Guide 2

Pearson Education, 10 Bank Street, White Plains, NY 10606

Vice president, director of publishing: *Allen Ascher*
Editorial manager: *Pam Fishman*
Vice president, director of design and production: *Rhea Banker*
Associate director of electronic production: *Aliza Greenblatt*
Production manager: *Ray Keating*
Director of manufacturing: *Patrice Fraccio*
Digital layout specialists: *Kelly Tavares, Paula Williams, Wendy Wolf*
Interior design: *Wendy Wolf*
Interior art: *Judy A. Wolf*
Cover design: *Elizabeth Carlson*
Cover art: *Richard E. Hill*
Copyediting: *Janet Johnston*

The authors gratefully acknowledge the contribution
of Tina Carver in the development of the original
Side by Side program.

ISBN 0-13-027289-2

2 3 4 5 6 7 8 9 10 – CRK – 05 04 03 02

CONTENTS

INTRODUCTION

Side by Side is an English language program for young-adult and adult learners from beginning to high-intermediate levels. The program consists of Student Books 1 through 4 and accompanying Activity Workbooks, Teacher's Guides, Communication Games Books, an Audio Program, a Video Program, a Picture Program, and a Testing Program.

Side by Side offers learners of English a dynamic, communicative approach to learning the language. Through the methodology of guided conversations, *Side by Side* engages students in meaningful conversational exchanges within carefully structured grammatical frameworks, and then encourages students to break away from the textbook and use these frameworks to create conversations on their own. All the language practice that is generated through the texts results in active communication between students . . . practicing speaking together "side by side."

The Guided Conversation lessons serve as the "anchor" for the presentation of the grammatical and functional language core of the program. These lessons are followed by a variety of reading, writing, listening, pronunciation, role-playing, and discussion activities that reinforce and expand upon this conversational core.

A special feature of this third edition are the "*Side by Side* Gazette" pages that appear periodically throughout the texts. These magazine-style pages contain feature articles, fact files, vocabulary expansion, cross-cultural topics, authentic listening activities, e-mail exchanges, and cartoon springboards for interactive role-playing activities.

The goal of *Side by Side* is to engage students in active, meaningful communicative practice with the language. The aim of the *Side by Side* Teacher's Guides is to offer guidelines and strategies to help achieve that goal.

Student Text Overview

CHAPTER OPENING PAGES

The opening page of each chapter provides an overview of the grammatical structures and topics that are treated in the chapter. A Vocabulary Preview depicts some of the key vocabulary words that students will encounter within the chapter. Some teachers may wish to present and practice these words before beginning the chapter. Other teachers may prefer to wait until the words occur in the particular lesson in which they are introduced.

GUIDED CONVERSATION LESSONS

Grammatical Paradigms

A new grammatical structure appears first in the form of a grammatical paradigm, or "grammar box"—a simple schema of the structure. (Grammar boxes are in a light blue tint.) These paradigms are meant to be a

reference point for students as they proceed through a lesson's conversational activities. While these paradigms highlight the structures being taught, they are not intended to be goals in themselves. Students are not expected to memorize or parrot back these rules. Rather, we want students to take part in conversations that show they can *use* these rules correctly.

Model Guided Conversations

Model conversations serve as the vehicles for introducing new grammatical structures and many communicative uses of English. Because the model becomes the basis for all the exercises that follow, it is essential that students be given sufficient practice with it before proceeding with the lesson.

Side by Side Exercises

In the numbered exercises that follow the model, students pair up and work "side by side," placing new content into the given conversational framework. These exercises form the core learning activity of each conversation lesson.

FOLLOW-UP EXERCISES AND ACTIVITIES

- **Reading** selections offer enjoyable reading practice that simultaneously reinforces the grammatical and thematic focus of each chapter.

- **Reading Check-Up** exercises provide focused practice in reading comprehension.

- **Listening** exercises enable students to develop their aural comprehension skills through a variety of listening activities.

- **Pronunciation** exercises provide models of authentic pronunciation and opportunities for student listening and speaking practice.

- **How to Say It!** activities expose students to key communication strategies.

- **Talk About It!** and **Think About It!** activities offer additional opportunities for conversational practice.

- **In Your Own Words** activities provide topics and themes for student compositions and classroom discussions in which students write about their friends, families, homes, schools, and themselves.

- *Side by Side* **Journal** activities provide the opportunity for students to write about things that are meaningful to them.

- **Role Play**, **Interactions**, and **Interview** activities provide opportunities for dynamic classroom interaction.

- **On Your Own** and **How About You?** activities give students valuable opportunities to apply lesson content to their own lives and experiences and to share opinions in class. Through these activities, students bring to the classroom new content based on their interests, their backgrounds, and their imaginations.

SIDE BY SIDE GAZETTE

- **Feature Articles** provide interesting and stimulating content.

- **Fact Files** present facts about the world for class discussion.

- **Build Your Vocabulary!** sections provide enrichment in key vocabulary areas.

- **Around the World** sections offer rich opportunities for cross-cultural comparison.

- **Global Exchange** activities give students experience with online communication.

- **Listening** sections offer students authentic listening opportunities.

- **What Are They Saying?** cartoons serve as springboards for interactive role-playing activities.

SUPPORT AND REFERENCE SECTIONS

- The **Chapter Summary** at the end of each chapter provides charts of the grammar structures presented in the chapter along with a listing of key vocabulary words. This summary is useful as a review and study guide after students have completed the chapter.

- An **Appendix** contains Listening Scripts, a Thematic Vocabulary Glossary, and a list of Cardinal Numbers and Past Tense Irregular Verbs.

- An **Index** provides a convenient reference for locating grammatical structures in the text.

Ancillary Materials

ACTIVITY WORKBOOKS

The Activity Workbooks offer a variety of exercises for reinforcement, fully coordinated with the student texts. A special feature of the Activity Workbooks is the inclusion of GrammarRaps for practice with rhythm, stress, and intonation and GrammarSongs from the *Side by Side TV* videos. Periodic check-up tests are also included in the workbooks.

AUDIO PROGRAM

The Student Text audios are especially designed to serve as a student's speaking partner, making conversation practice possible even when the student is studying alone. In addition to the guided conversation models and exercises, the audios contain the vocabulary preview words at the beginning of each chapter, the listening and pronunciation exercises, the reading selections, and the *Side by Side* Gazettes.

The Activity Workbook audios contain the listening and pronunciation exercises, along with the GrammarRaps and GrammarSongs.

VIDEO PROGRAM

The *Side by Side TV* videos and accompanying Video Workbooks are designed to serve as a video accompaniment to the series. These innovative videos offer original comedy sketches, on-location interviews, rap numbers, music videos, and other popular TV formats. The *Side by Side TV* videos are fully coordinated with the *Side by Side* student texts.

COMMUNICATION GAMES BOOKS

This innovative teacher resource provides a wealth of interactive language games designed to serve as enjoyable and motivating reinforcement of key grammatical structures presented in the student texts. All of the games are accompanied by reproducible activity masters for ease of classroom use.

PICTURE PROGRAM

Side by Side Picture Cards illustrate key concepts and vocabulary items. They can be used for introduction of new material, for review, for enrichment, and for role-playing activities. Suggestions for their use are included in the Teacher's Guide. Also, the Appendix to the Teacher's Guide contains a triple listing of the Picture Cards: numerically, alphabetically, and by category.

TESTING PROGRAM

The *Side by Side* Testing Program consists of a placement test and individual chapter tests, mid-book tests, and final tests for each level of the program.

Format of the Teacher's Guide

CHAPTER OVERVIEW

The Chapter Overview provides the following:

- Functional and grammatical highlights of the chapter

- A listing of new vocabulary and expressions

CHAPTER OPENING PAGE

The Teacher's Guide offers suggestions for presenting and practicing the words depicted in the Vocabulary Preview.

STEP-BY-STEP LESSON GUIDE

Conversation Lessons

Included for each conversation lesson are the following:

- **FOCUS:** the grammatical and topical focus of the lesson
- **CLOSE UP:** short grammar explanations accompanied by examples from the lesson
- **GETTING READY:** suggestions for introducing the new concepts in the lesson
- **INTRODUCING THE MODEL:** steps for introducing model conversations
- **SIDE BY SIDE EXERCISES:** suggestions for practicing the exercises, as well as a listing of new vocabulary
- **LANGUAGE NOTES, CULTURE NOTES,** and **PRONUNCIATION NOTES**
- **WORKBOOK:** page references for exercises in the Activity Workbook that correspond to the particular lesson
- **EXPANSION ACTIVITIES:** optional activities for review and reinforcement of the content of the lesson

Reading Lessons

Included for each reading lesson are the following:

- **FOCUS** of the reading
- **NEW VOCABULARY** contained in the reading
- **READING THE STORY:** an optional preliminary preview stage before students begin to read the selection, along with suggestions for presenting the story and questions to check students' comprehension
- **READING CHECK-UP:** answer keys for the reading comprehension exercises
- **READING EXTENSION:** additional questions and activities that provide additional skill reinforcement of the reading selection

Other Follow-Up Lessons

Included for other follow-up lessons are the following:

- **LISTENING** scripts and answer keys for the listening exercises
- Strategies for presenting and practicing the *How to Say It!, How About You?, On Your Own, In Your Own Words, Role Play, Interactions, Interview, Talk About It!, Think About It!, Pronunciation,* and *Side by Side Journal* activities

Chapter Summary

Included for each Chapter Summary are the following:

- **GRAMMAR SUMMARY** tasks
- **KEY VOCABULARY** reinforcement and expansion activities
- **END-OF-CHAPTER EXPANSION ACTIVITIES** that review and reinforce the grammar structures and vocabulary presented in the chapter

Side by Side Gazette

Included for the *Side by Side* Gazette pages are the following:

- Strategies for introducing, practicing, and expanding upon the *Feature Articles, Fact Files, Build Your Vocabulary!, Around the World, Global Exchange, Listening,* and *What Are They Saying?* sections of the Gazette

WORKBOOK ANSWER KEYS AND LISTENING SCRIPTS

Answers and listening scripts for all exercises contained in the Activity Workbooks are provided at the end of each chapter of the Teacher's Guide.

General Teaching Strategies

VOCABULARY PREVIEW

You may wish to introduce the words in the Vocabulary Preview before beginning the chapter, or you may choose to wait until they first occur in a specific lesson. If you choose to introduce them at this point, the Teacher's Guide offers these suggestions:

1. Have students look at the illustrations and identify the words they already know.

2. Present the vocabulary. Say each word and have the class repeat it chorally and individually. Check students' understanding and pronunciation of the words.

3. Practice the vocabulary as a class, in pairs, or in small groups. Have students cover the word list and look at the pictures. Practice the words by saying a word and having students tell the number of the illustration and/or giving the number of the illustration and having students say the word.

GUIDED CONVERSATION LESSONS

Introducing Model Conversations

Given the importance of the model conversation, it is essential that students practice it several times in a variety of ways before going on to the exercises.

This Teacher's Guide offers the following comprehensive 8-step approach to introducing the model:

1. Have students look at the model illustration. This helps establish the context of the conversation.

2. Set the scene.

3. *Present the model.* With books closed, have students listen as you present the model or play the audio one or more times. To make the presentation of the model as realistic as possible, you might draw two stick figures on the board to represent the speakers in the dialog. You can also show that two people are speaking by changing your position or by shifting your weight from one foot to the other as you say each speaker's lines.

4. *Full-Class Repetition.* Model each line and have the whole class repeat in unison.

5. Have students open their books and look at the dialog. Ask if there are any questions, and check understanding of new vocabulary.

6. *Group Choral Repetition.* Divide the class in half. Model line A and have Group 1 repeat. Model line B and have Group 2 repeat. Continue with all the lines of the model.

7. *Choral Conversation.* Have both groups practice the dialog twice, without a teacher model. First Group 1 is Speaker A and Group 2 is Speaker B; then reverse.

8. Call on one or two pairs of students to present the dialog.

In steps 6, 7, and 8, encourage students to look up from their books and *say* the lines rather than read them. (Students can of course refer to their books when necessary.)

The goal is not memorization or complete mastery of the model. Rather, students should become familiar with the model and feel comfortable saying it.

At this point, if you feel that additional practice is necessary before going on to the exercises, you can do Choral Conversation in small groups or by rows.

Alternative Approaches to Introducing Model Conversations

Depending upon the abilities of your students and the particular lesson you're teaching, you might wish to try the following approaches to vary the way in which you introduce model conversations.

- **Pair Introduction**

  Have a pair of students present the model. Then practice it with the class.

- **Trio Introduction**

  Call on *three* students to introduce the model. Have two of them present it while the third acts as the *director*, offering suggestions for how to say the lines better. Then practice the dialog with the class.

- **Cloze Introduction**

  Write a cloze version of the model conversation on the board for student reference as you introduce the model. For lessons that provide a skeletal framework of the model (for example, Book 2 pp. 6, 55, 112, 119, 132), you can use that as the cloze version. For other lessons, you can decide which words to delete from the dialog.

- **Scrambled Dialog Introduction**

  Write each line of the dialog on a separate card. Distribute the cards to students and have them practice saying their lines, then talk with each other to figure out what the correct order of the lines should be. Have them present the dialog to the class, each student in turn reading his or her line. Have the class decide if it's in the correct order. Then practice the dialog with the class.

  Warning: Do a scrambled dialog introduction *only* for conversations in which there is only one possible sentence order!

- **Disappearing Dialog Introduction**

  Write the dialog on the board and have students practice saying it. Erase a few of the words and practice again. Continue practicing the dialog several times, each time having erased more of the words, until the dialog has completely *disappeared* and students can say the lines without looking at them.

- **Eliciting the Model**

  Have students cover up the lines of the model and look only at the illustration. Ask questions based on the illustration and the situation. For example: *Who are these people? Where are they? What are they saying to each other?* As a class, in groups, or in pairs, have students suggest a possible dialog. Have students present their ideas and then compare them with the model conversation in the book. Then practice the dialog with the class.

Side by Side Exercises

The numbered exercises that follow the model form the core learning activity in each conversation lesson. Here students use the illustrations and word cues to create conversations based on the structure of the model. Since all language practice in these lessons is conversational, you will always call on a pair of students to do each exercise. Your primary role is to serve as a resource to the class — to help students with new structures, new vocabulary, intonation, and pronunciation.

The Teacher's Guide recommends the following three steps for practicing the exercises. (Students should be given thorough practice with the first two exercises before going on.)

1. **Exercise 1:** Introduce any new vocabulary in the exercise. Call on two students to present the dialog. Then do Choral Repetition and Choral Conversation practice.

2. **Exercise 2:** Same as for Exercise 1.

3. For the remaining exercises, there are two options: either Full-Class Practice or Pair Practice.

   Full-Class Practice: Call on a pair of students to do each exercise. Introduce new vocabulary one exercise at a time. (For more practice, you can call on other pairs of students or do Choral Repetition or Choral Conversation.)

   Pair Practice: Introduce new vocabulary for all the exercises. Next have students practice all the exercises in pairs. Then have pairs present the exercises to the class. (For more practice, you can do Choral Repetition or Choral Conversation.)

The choice of Full-Class Practice or Pair Practice should be determined by the content of the particular lesson, the size and composition of the class, and your own teaching style. You might also wish to vary your approach from lesson to lesson.

- **Suggestions for Pairing Up Students**

  Whether you use Full-Class Practice or Pair Practice, you can select students for pairing in various ways.

  - You might want to pair students by ability, since students of similar ability might work together more efficiently than students of dissimilar ability.

  - On the other hand, you might wish to pair a weaker student with a stronger one. The slower student benefits from this pairing, while the more advanced student strengthens his or her abilities by helping a partner.

You should also encourage students to look at each other when speaking. This makes the conversational nature of the language practice more realistic. One way of ensuring this is *not* to call on two students who are sitting next to each other. Rather, call on students in different parts of the room and encourage them to look at each other when saying their lines.

- **Presenting New Vocabulary**

  Many new words are introduced in each conversation lesson. The illustration usually helps to convey the meaning, and the new words are written for students to see and use in these conversations. In addition, you might:

  - write the new word on the board or on a word card.

  - say the new word several times and ask students to repeat chorally and individually.

  - help clarify the meaning with visuals.

  Students might also find it useful to keep a notebook in which they write each new word, its meaning, and a sentence using that word.

- **Open-Ended Exercises**

  In many lessons, the final exercise is an open-ended one. This is indicated in the text by a *blank box*. Here students are expected to create conversations based on the structure of the model, but with vocabulary that they select themselves. This provides students with an opportunity for creativity, while still focusing on the particular structure being practiced. These open-ended exercises can be done orally in class and/or assigned as homework for presentation in class the following day. Encourage students to use dictionaries to find new words they want to use.

General Guiding Principles for Working with Guided Conversations

- *Speak*, not *Read* the Conversations

  When doing the exercises, students should practice *speaking* to each other, rather than *reading* to each other. Even though students will need to refer to the text to be able to practice the conversations, they should not read the lines word by word. Rather, they should scan a full line and then look up from the book and *speak* the line to the other person.

- **Intonation and Gesture**

  Throughout, you should use the book to teach proper intonation and gesture. (Capitalized words are used to indicate spoken emphasis.) Students should be encouraged to truly *act out* the dialogs in a strong and confident voice.

- **Student-Centered Practice**

  Use of the texts should be as student-centered as possible. Modeling by the teacher should be efficient and economical, but students should have every opportunity to model for each other when they are capable of doing so.

- **Vocabulary in Context**

  Vocabulary can and should be effectively taught in the context of the conversation being practiced. Very often it will be possible to grasp the meaning from the conversation or its accompanying illustration. You should spend time drilling vocabulary in isolation only if you feel it is absolutely essential.

- **No "Grammar Talk"**

  Students need not study formally or be able to produce grammatical rules. The purpose of the texts is to engage students in active communication that gets them to *use* the language according to these rules.

Relating Lesson Content to Students' Lives and Experiences

- **Personalize the Exercises**

  While doing the guided conversation exercises, whenever you think it is appropriate, ask students questions that relate the situations in the exercises to their own lives and personal experiences. This will help make the leap from practicing language in the textbook to using the language for actual communication.

- **Interview the Characters**

  Where appropriate, as students are presenting the exercises to the class, as a way of making the situations come alive and making students feel as though they really *are* the characters in those situations, ask questions that students can respond to based on their imaginations.

If you wish, preview the story by having students talk about the story title and/or illustrations. You may choose to introduce new vocabulary beforehand, or have students encounter the new vocabulary within the context of the reading.

Have students read silently, or follow along silently as the story is read aloud by you, by one or more students, or on the audio program. Ask students if they have any questions and check understanding of new vocabulary. Then do the Reading Check-Up exercises.

How to Say It!

How to Say It! activities are designed to expose students to important communication strategies. Present the conversations the same way you introduce model guided conversations: set the scene, present the model, do full-class and choral repetition, and have pairs of students present the dialog. Then divide the class into pairs and have students practice other conversations based on the *How to Say It!* model and then present them to the class.

How About You?

How About You? activities are intended to provide students with additional opportunities to tell about themselves. Have students do these activities in pairs or as a class.

 ON YOUR OWN

On Your Own activities offer students the opportunity to contribute content of their own within the grammatical framework of the lesson. You should introduce these activities in class and assign them as homework for presentation in class the next day. In this way, students will automatically review the previous day's

grammar while contributing new and inventive content of their own.

These activities are meant for simultaneous grammar reinforcement and vocabulary building. Students should be encouraged to use a dictionary when completing the *On Your Own* activities. In this way, they will use not only the words they know but also the words they would *like* to know in order to really bring their interests, backgrounds, and imaginations into the classroom.

As a result, students will teach each other new vocabulary as they share a bit of their lives with others in the class.

 IN YOUR OWN WORDS

Have students do the activity as written homework, using a dictionary for any new words they wish to use. Then have students present and discuss what they have written, in pairs or as a class.

 ROLE PLAY

Have pairs of students practice role-playing the activity and then present their role plays to the class.

 INTERACTIONS

Divide the class into pairs and have students practice conversations based on the skeletal models. Then call on students to present their conversations to the class.

 INTERVIEW

Have students circulate around the room to conduct their interviews and then report back to the class.

TALK ABOUT IT!

Call on a few different pairs of students to present the model dialogs. Then divide the class into pairs and have students take turns using the models to ask and answer questions about the characters and situations depicted on the page. Then call on pairs to present conversations to the class.

THINK ABOUT IT!

Divide the class into pairs or small groups. Have students discuss the questions and then share their thoughts with the class.

PRONUNCIATION

Pronunciation exercises provide students with models of natural English pronunciation. The goal of these exercises is to enable learners to improve their own pronunciation and to understand the pronunciation of native speakers using English in natural conversational contexts.

Have students first focus on listening to the sentences. Say each sentence in the left column or play the audio one or more times and have students listen carefully and repeat. Next, focus on pronunciation. Have students say each sentence in the right column and then listen carefully as you say it or play the audio. If you wish, you can have students continue practicing the sentences to improve their pronunciation.

JOURNAL

The purpose of the *Side by Side Journal* activity is to show students how writing can become a vehicle for communicating thoughts and feelings. Have students begin a journal in a composition notebook. In these journals, students have the opportunity to write about things that are meaningful to them.

Have students write their journal entries at home or in class. Encourage students to use a dictionary to look up words they would like to use. They can share their written work with other students if appropriate. Then as a class, in pairs, or in small groups, have students discuss what they have written.

If time permits, you may want to write a response in each student's journal, sharing your own opinions and experiences as well as reacting to what the student has written. If you are keeping portfolios of students' work, these compositions serve as excellent examples of students' progress in learning English.

CHAPTER SUMMARY

- **Grammar**

  Divide the class into pairs or small groups, and have students take turns forming sentences from the words in the grammar boxes. Student A says a sentence, and Student B points to the words from each column that are in the sentence. Then have students switch: Student B says a sentence, and Student A points to the words.

- **Key Vocabulary**

  Have students ask you any questions about the meaning or pronunciation of the vocabulary. If students ask for the pronunciation, repeat after the student until the student is satisfied with his or her own pronunciation.

- **Key Vocabulary Check**

  When completing a chapter, as a way of checking students' retention of the key vocabulary depicted on the opening page of the chapter, have students open their books to the first page of the chapter and cover the list of vocabulary words. Either call out a number and have students tell you the word, or say a word and have students tell you the number.

 FEATURE ARTICLE

Have students read silently, or follow along silently as the article is read aloud by you, by one or more students, or on the audio program. You may choose to introduce new vocabulary beforehand, or have students encounter it within the context of the article. Ask students if they have any questions, and check understanding of vocabulary.

 FACT FILE

Present the information and have the class discuss it.

 BUILD YOUR VOCABULARY!

Have students look at the illustrations and identify any words they already know. Then say each word and have the class repeat it chorally and individually. Check students' understanding and pronunciation of the words.

 AROUND THE WORLD

Divide the class into pairs or small groups and have students react to the photographs and answer the questions. Then have students report back to the class.

 GLOBAL EXCHANGE

Have students read silently or follow along silently as the message is read aloud by you, by one or more students, or on the audio program.

For additional practice, you can have students write back to the person and then share their writing with the class. You may also wish to have students correspond with a keypal on the Internet and then share their experience with the class.

 WHAT ARE THEY SAYING?

Have students talk about the people and the situation in the cartoon, and then create role plays based on the scene. Students may refer back to previous lessons as a resource, but they should not simply reuse specific conversations. You may want to assign this exercise as written homework, having students prepare their role plays, practice them the next day with other students, and then present them to the class.

EXPANSION ACTIVITIES

This Teacher's Guide offers a rich variety of optional Expansion Activities for review and reinforcement. Feel free to pick and choose or vary the activities to fit the particular needs and learning styles of students in your class. These ideas are meant to serve as a springboard for developing your own learning activities.

We encourage you to try some of the teaching approaches offered in this Teacher's Guide. In keeping with the spirit of *Side by Side*, these suggestions are intended to provide students with a language learning experience that is dynamic . . . interactive . . . and fun!

Steven J. Molinsky
Bill Bliss

GRAMMAR

SIMPLE PRESENT TENSE

I We You They	cook.
He She It	cooks.

LIKE TO

I We You They	like to / don't like to	
He She It	likes to / doesn't like to	cook.

PRESENT CONTINUOUS TENSE

(I am)	I'm	
(He is) (She is) (It is)	He's She's It's	cooking.
(We are) (You are) (They are)	We're You're They're	

SIMPLE PAST TENSE

I He She It We You They	cooked.

FUTURE: GOING TO

I'm He's She's It's We're You're They're	going to cook.

Am	I	
Is	he she it	going to cook?
Are	we you they	

Yes,	I	am.
	he she it	is.
	we you they	are.

No,	I'm	not.
	he she it	isn't.
	we you they	aren't.

INDIRECT OBJECT PRONOUNS

He gave	me him her it us you them	a present.

PAST TIME EXPRESSIONS

yesterday
yesterday morning / afternoon / evening
last night
last week / weekend / month / year
last Sunday / Monday / . . . / Saturday
last January / February / . . . / December
last spring / summer / fall (autumn) / winter

IRREGULAR VERBS

drive – drove
give – gave
go – went
lend – lent
lose – lost
sell – sold
send – sent
swim – swam
write – wrote

FUNCTIONS

INQUIRING ABOUT INTENTION

Are you going to *cook spaghetti this week*?

What are you going to *give your wife for her birthday*?

EXPRESSING LIKES AND DISLIKES

Do you like *spaghetti*?
    Yes, I do.
    No, I don't.

Do you like to *ski*?
    Yes, I do.
    No, I don't.

I don't like to *cook spaghetti* very often.

EXPRESSING INABILITY

I can't *give her a necklace*.

SUGGESTING

How about *flowers*?

EXPRESSING UNCERTAINTY

I don't know.

NEW VOCABULARY

Past Tense Verbs

bought (buy)
gave (give)
lent (lend)
lost (lose) *his* job
sent (send)
sold (sell)
swam (swim)

Places Around the U.S.

California
Florida
New Jersey
Wisconsin

East Coast
West Coast

up north
down south

Directions

east
north
south
west

Common Gifts

CD
CD player
doll
painting (n)
perfume
plant (n)
present (n)

Communication

chat online
communicate
Internet
message
send

Foods

cheese
oranges
pancakes

Miscellaneous

advice
ago
anniversary
coast
condominium
far apart
give advice
go hiking
into
like to
van

Text Page 1: Chapter Opening Page

VOCABULARY PREVIEW

You may want to present these words before beginning the chapter, or you may choose to wait until they first occur in a specific lesson. If you choose to present them at this point, here are some suggestions:

1. Have students look at the illustrations on text page 1 and identify the words they already know.

2. Present the vocabulary. Say each word and have the class repeat it chorally and individually. Check students' understanding and pronunciation of the words.

3. Practice the vocabulary as a class, in pairs, or in small groups. Have students cover the word list and look at the pictures. Practice the words in the following ways:

   - For days of the week and months of the year, say a word and have students point to the abbreviation in the calendar. For seasons, say a season and have students point to the illustration.

   - For days of the week and months of the year, point to an abbreviation on the calendar and have students say the word. For seasons, point to an illustration and have students name the season.

FOCUS

- Like to
- Simple Present Tense: Review
- Leisure Activities

CLOSE UP

RULE: The verb *like* is followed by the infinitive form of the verb.

EXAMPLES: What do you **like to do** on the weekend?
I **like to read.**

GETTING READY

Introduce *like to.*

1. Tell about yourself and a friend. For example:

   I like to go to the beach.
   My friend Bob likes to write letters.

2. Make sentences with forms of *like to.* Have students repeat. For example:

   I like to *(swim).*
   You like to *(study English).*
   She likes to *(drive).*
   He likes to *(dance).*
   We like to *(ski).*
   They like to *(play soccer).*

INTRODUCING THE MODELS

There are two model conversations. Introduce and practice each model before going on to the next. For each model:

1. Have students look at the model illustration.

2. Set the scene: "Two friends are talking."

3. With books closed, have students listen as you present the model or play the audio one or more times.

4. **Full-Class Repetition:** Model each line and have students repeat.

5. Have students open their books and look at the dialog. Ask students if they have any questions.

6. **Group Choral Repetition:** Divide the class in half. Model line A and have Group 1 repeat. Model line B and have Group 2 repeat.

7. **Choral Conversation:** Groups 1 and 2 practice the dialog twice, without teacher model. First, Group 1 is Speaker A and Group 2 is Speaker B. Then reverse.

8. Call on one or two pairs of students to present the dialog.

   (For additional practice, do Choral Conversation in small groups or by rows.)

SIDE BY SIDE EXERCISES

Examples

1. A. What do Mr. and Mrs. Johnson like to do on the weekend?
   B. They like to watch TV.

2. A. What does Tom like to do on the weekend?
   B. He likes to play basketball.

1. **Exercise 1:** Call on two students to present the dialog. Then do Choral Repetition and Choral Conversation practice.

2. **Exercise 2:** Same as above.

3. **Exercises 3–5:**

New Vocabulary

4. chat online
5. go hiking

Culture Note

When people *chat online*, they send messages back and forth to each other instantaneously over the Internet.

Either

Full-Class Practice: Call on a pair of students to do each exercise. Introduce the new vocabulary before doing Exercises 4 and 5. (For more practice, call on other pairs of students, or do Choral Repetition or Choral Conversation.)

or

Pair Practice: Introduce the new vocabulary. Next, have students in pairs practice all the exercises. Then have pairs present the exercises to the class. (For more practice, do Choral Repetition or Choral Conversation.)

4. **Exercise 6:** Have students use the model as a guide to create their own conversations, using vocabulary of their choice. Encourage students to use dictionaries to find new words they want to use. This exercise can be done orally in class or for written homework. If you assign it for homework, do one example in class to make sure students understand what's expected. Have students present their conversations in class the next day.

WORKBOOK

Page 2

EXPANSION ACTIVITIES

1. **Beanbag Toss**

   Have students toss a beanbag back and forth. The student to whom the beanbag is tossed names an activity he or she likes to do. For example:

   Student 1: I like to swim.
   Student 2: I like to ski.
   Student 3: I like to watch TV.
        etc.

2. **Grammar Chain**

   a. Start the chain game:

       Teacher: I like to go to the beach on the weekend.
       (to Student A): What do you like to do?

   b. Student A must answer and ask Student B, who then continues the chain. For example:

       Student A: I like to play baseball.
       (to Student B): What do you like to do?

   Student B: I like to ride my bicycle.
   (to Student C): What do you like to do?
        etc.

3. **Common Interests**

   a. Put the following on the board:

   I like to _____ on the weekend.
   He/She likes to _____ on the weekend.
   We both like to _____ on the weekend.
   ---

   b. Divide the class into pairs.

   c. Have students interview each other about what they like to do on the weekend. The object is for students to find two things that are different and one thing they have in common and then report back to the class. For example:

       I like to go to the beach on the weekend.

She likes to go hiking on the weekend.
We both like to go jogging on the weekend.

4. Telephone

   a. Divide the class into large groups. Have each group sit in a circle.

   b. Whisper a short story to one student in each group. For example:

      "Sally likes to go to the beach. She likes to sit in the sun and swim. Then she likes to take a shower and relax in her yard."

   c. The first student whispers the story to the second student, and so forth around the circle.

   d. When the story gets to the last student, that person says it aloud. Is it the same story you started with? The group with the most accurate story wins.

5. Memory Chain

   a. Divide the class into groups of 5 or 6 students each.

   b. Tell each student to think of something that he or she likes to do on the weekend.

   c. One group at a time, have Student 1 begin. For example:

   I like to work in my garden.

   d. Student 2 repeats what Student 1 said and adds a statement about himself or herself. For example:

      Maria likes to work in her garden. I like to wash my car.

   e. Student 3 continues in the same way. For example:

      Maria likes to work in her garden. Tom likes to wash his car. I like to go jogging.

   f. Continue until everyone has had a chance to play the *memory chain*.

6. Which One Isn't True?

   a. Tell students to write three true statements and one false statement about things they like to do. For example:

      I like to go dancing every Friday night.
      I like to clean my house every day.
      I like to call my friends on the telephone.
      I like to study English.

   b. Have students take turns reading their statements to the class, and have the class guess which statement isn't true.

TALK ABOUT IT! *What Do They Like to Do?*

FOCUS

> • Review: Simple Present Tense, Past Tense, Present Continuous Tense, Future: Going to
>
> • Daily Activities

GETTING READY

1. Write the following on the board:

2. Point to *Bill* on the board and tell the class that this is your friend Bill, and he really likes to study.

   a. Point to *every day* on the board and ask: "What does he do every day?" (Students answer: "He studies.")

   b. Point to *yesterday* on the board and ask: "What did he do yesterday?" (Students answer: "He studied.")

   c. Point to *right now* on the board and ask: "What's he doing right now?" (Students answer, "He's studying.")

   d. Point to *tomorrow* on the board and ask: "What's he going to do tomorrow?" (Students answer: "He's going to study.")

3. Point to *Jane* on the board and tell the class that this is your friend Jane, and she really likes to drink milk.

   a. Point to *every day* on the board and ask:

"What does she do every day?" (Students answer: "She drinks milk.")

   b. Point to *yesterday* on the board and ask: "What did she do yesterday?" (Students answer: "She drank milk.")

   c. Point to *right now* on the board and ask: "What's she doing right now?" (Students answer: "She's drinking milk.")

   d. Point to *tomorrow* on the board and ask: "What's she going to do tomorrow?" (Students answer: "She's going to drink milk.")

INTRODUCING THE PEOPLE

1. Have students read silently or follow along silently as the description of the characters is read aloud by you, by one or more students, or on the audio program.

2. Ask students if they have any questions. Check understanding of vocabulary. Introduce the irregular past tense form *swam.*

CONVERSATION PRACTICE

There are two sets of questions at the bottom of the page. The questions on the left are singular. The questions on the right are plural.

1. Have pairs of students use these questions to talk about the people on the page. This can be done as either Full-Class Practice or Pair Practice.

2. Then, have students ask and answer questions about other people they know.

3. If you do the activity as Pair Practice, call on pairs to present their conversations to the class.

WORKBOOK

Page 3

EXPANSION ACTIVITIES

1. True or False?

a. Have students open their books to text page 3.

b. Make statements about the characters on text page 3, and have students tell you *True or False*. If the statement is false, have students correct it. For example:

> Teacher: Irene likes to play the piano.
> Student: True.
>
> Teacher: Robert is going to read a book tomorrow.
> Student: False. He's going to cook.

Variation: Call on students to make statements about the characters, and have other students respond.

2. Category Dictation

a. Have students draw three columns on a piece of paper and label them <u>Every Day</u>, <u>Right Now</u>, and <u>Yesterday</u>.

b. Dictate verb phrases and have students write them in the appropriate column. For example:

> They study.
> They're getting up.
> They studied.
> They're studying.
> They got up.
> They get up.

3. Sentence Cues

a. On separate cards, write key words that can be put together to form sentences. Clip together the cards for each sentence. For example:

I	like	watch TV	every night
Peter	ride	bicycle	yesterday
Betty	see	movie	tomorrow
Richard	swim	beach	every weekend
Carmen	work	bank	right now
My friends	go	sailing	yesterday

b. Divide the class into small groups and give a clipped set of cards to each group.

c. Have each group write sentences based on the cards.

d. Have one member of each group write that group's sentences on the board, and compare everybody's sentences.

4. What's Wrong?

a. Divide the class into pairs or small groups.

b. Write several sentences such as the following on the board or on a handout. Some of the sentences should be correct, and others incorrect. For example:

> Barbara likes play tennis.
> My brother ride his bicycle yesterday.
> We sat in the clinic all night.
> David work right now.
> They're going to go dancing tomorrow.
> My parents live in Florida.
> Sally write letters to her friends very week.
> Frank swim at the beach yesterday.

c. The object of the activity is for students to identify which sentences are incorrect and then correct them.

d. Have students compare their answers.

Variation: Do the activity as a game with competing teams. The team that successfully completes the task in the shortest time is the winner.

Text Pages 4–5: Are You Going to Cook Spaghetti This Week?

FOCUS

- Review: Simple Past Tense, Future: Going to, Like to
- Time Expressions

GETTING READY

1. Review past time expressions.

   a. Have students practice saying the days of the week, months of the year, and seasons. If you did not present these as part of the Vocabulary Preview on text page 1, refer to the teaching suggestions on Teacher's Guide page 4.

   b. Have students looks at the calendar illustrations on text page 1 as you review the words *week, weekend, month,* and *year.* Also, review the expressions *yesterday morning, yesterday afternoon, yesterday evening,* and *last night.*

2. Review the past tense forms of the regular verbs: *watch, plant,* and *clean,* and the irregular verbs: *drive, make, go,* and *write.* Say the base form, and have students tell you the past tense form.

INTRODUCING THE MODEL

1. Have students look at the model illustration.

2. Set the scene: "Two friends are talking."

3. With books closed, have students listen as you present the model or play the audio one or more times.

4. **Full-Class Repetition:** Model each line and have students repeat.

   ### Pronunciation Note

   The pronunciation focus of Chapter 1 is **Contrastive Stress** (text page 9). You should model this pronunciation at this point and encourage students to incorporate it into their language practice.

I cooked spaghetti LÁST week.
I watched videos YÉSTERDAY.

5. Have students open their books and look at the dialog. Ask students if they have any questions. Check understanding of vocabulary.

6. **Group Choral Repetition:** Divide the class in half. Model line A and have Group 1 repeat. Model line B and have Group 2 repeat.

7. **Choral Conversation:** Groups 1 and 2 practice the dialog twice, without teacher model. First Group 1 is Speaker A and Group 2 is Speaker B. Then reverse.

8. Call on one or two pairs of students to present the dialog.

   (For additional practice, do Choral Conversation in small groups or by rows.)

SIDE BY SIDE EXERCISES

Examples

1. A. Are you going to watch videos today?
   B. No, I'm not. I watched videos YESTERDAY, and I don't like to watch videos very often.

2. A. Are you going to drive downtown this weekend?
   B. No, I'm not. I drove downtown LAST weekend, and I don't like to drive downtown very often.

1. **Exercise 1:** Call on two students to present the dialog. Then do Choral Repetition and Choral Conversation practice.

2. **Exercise 2:** Same as above.

3. **Exercises 3–9:**

New Vocabulary
4. pancakes

Language Note

Exercises 5, 6, and 9: The expression *going to* is commonly used to mean *going to go*. For example: Are Mr. and Mrs. Jenkins going (to go) to the mall this Saturday? Are you and your friends going (to go) skiing this December? Are you and your family going (to go) to WonderWorld this year?

Either

Full-Class Practice: Call on a pair of students to do each exercise. Introduce the new vocabulary before doing Exercise 4. (For more practice, call on other pairs of students, or do Choral Repetition or Choral Conversation.)

or

Pair Practice: Introduce the new vocabulary. Next, have students practice all of the exercises in pairs. Then have pairs present the exercises to the class. (For more practice, do Choral Repetition or Choral Conversation.)

4. **Exercise 10:** Have students use the model as a guide to create their own conversations, using vocabulary of their choice. Encourage students to use dictionaries to find new words they want to use. This exercise can be done orally in class or for written homework. If you assign it for homework, do one example in class to make sure students understand what's expected. Have students present their conversations in class the next day.

WORKBOOK

Pages 4–7

EXPANSION ACTIVITIES

1. Find the Right Person!

   a. Before you do this exercise, have each student write a true statement about himself or herself.

   b. Put the information on a handout in the following form:

   > Find someone who . . .
   >
   > 1. has two sisters.   _____
   > 2. went to London last fall. _____
   > 3. likes to go jogging.   _____
   > 4. works in a bank.   _____
   > 5. is going to study music   _____
   >   next year.

   c. Have students circulate around the room, asking each other questions to identify the above people. For example:

   > Do you have two sisters?
   > Did you go to London last fall?

   d. The first student to find all the people, raise his or her hand, and tell the class who they are is the winner of the game. For example:

   > Maria has two sisters.
   > Robert went to London last fall.
   > Carla likes to go jogging.
   > David works in a bank.
   > Rita is going to study music next year.

2. Category Dictation

   a. Have students draw two columns on a piece of paper. At the top of one column, have students write Things I Like to Do, and at the top of the other column, have them write Things I Don't Like to Do.

   b. Dictate various activities and have students write them in the appropriate column. For example:

   (continued)

Things I Like to Do	Things I Don't Like to Do
go to the beach	drive downtown
watch videos	clean my room
read novels	wash my windows

3. Expand the Sentence!

Tell students that the object of the activity is to build a long sentence on the board, one word at a time.

a. Call on a student to write a pronoun or someone's name on the far left side of the board. For example:

George

b. Have another student come to the board and add a word. For example:

George isn't

c. Have a third student add a third word. For example:

George isn't going

d. Continue until each student in the class has had one or more turns to add a word to expand the sentence into the longest one they can think of. For example:

George isn't going to clean his apartment this weekend because he cleaned his apartment last weekend, and he doesn't like to clean his apartment very often.

4. Information Gap Handouts

a. Tell students that your friend John is going to have a very busy week next week. He has a lot of things to do. Make up a schedule for John's week, but divide the information between two different schedules. For example:

Schedule A:

SUN	MON	TUE	WED	THU	FRI	SAT
wash his windows		plant flowers in his garden		wash the floors and vacuum the carpets		relax and watch TV

Schedule B:

SUN	MON	TUE	WED	THU	FRI	SAT
	paint his kitchen		cook spaghetti and bake apple pies		fix his broken front steps	

b. Divide the class into pairs. Give each member of the pair a different schedule. Have students share their information and fill in their schedules. For example:

Student A: John is going to wash his windows on Sunday.

Student B: Okay. [writes the information in Schedule B] On Monday he's going to paint his kitchen.

c. The pairs continue until each has a filled calendar.

d. Have students look at their partner's schedule to make sure that they have written the information correctly.

How to Say It!

> **Talking About Likes and Dislikes:**
> When making small talk, it is common for people to discuss their likes and dislikes.

1. Write on the board:

2. Set the scene: "These people are talking about things they like and things they don't like."

3. Present the first two conversations, while pointing to the word *like* on the board.

4. Full-Class Repetition.

5. Ask students if they have any questions.

6. Group Choral Repetition.

7. Choral Conversation.

8. Call on one or two pairs to present the dialogs.

9. Set the scene: "These people are talking about things they like to do and things they don't like to do."

10. Present the next two conversations, while pointing to *like to* on the board and practice as above.

11. Divide the class into pairs, and have students practice conversations using *like* and *like to*. To inspire students' conversations, list the following categories on the board:

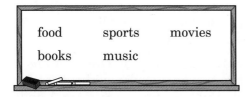

12. Call on pairs to present their conversations to the class.

EXPANSION ACTIVITY

Class Survey

1. Have the class brainstorm different weekend activities. Write their ideas on the board.

2. Have students write down these activities on a sheet of paper with columns for *yes* and *no* responses. For example:

Weekend Activities	Yes	No
see a movie plant flowers clean the house go shopping read		

3. Have students circulate around the room, interviewing each other and marking the responses in the *Yes* or the *No* columns.

4. Have students report their findings to the class. What are the most popular weekend activities in the class?

Option: If you wish, you can have students organize the results of the survey as a bar graph or pie chart.

Variation: Have students also interview friends and family members and report to the class.

FOCUS

- Indirect Object Pronouns: *him, her*

CLOSE UP

RULE: Direct and indirect object pronouns follow the verb. The direct and indirect object pronouns for *he* and *she* are *him* and *her*.

EXAMPLES: What are you going to give **your husband** for his birthday?
I don't know. I can't give **him** a watch.

What are you going to give **your grandmother** for her birthday?
I don't know. I can't give **her** flowers.

GETTING READY

1. Make sentences with indirect objects, using names of students in your class. For example:

    I'm going to give *(Carol)* a pencil.
    I'm going to give her a pencil.

    I'm going to give *(Robert)* a pencil.
    I'm going to give him a pencil.

2. Say a sentence with an indirect object noun and have students say the sentence with a pronoun. For example:

    Teacher: I'm going to give *(David)* a book.
    Students: I'm going to give him a book.

    Other possible sentences:

    I'm going to give *(Maria)* a dictionary.
    I'm going to give *(Michael)* a pen.
    I'm going to give *(George)* a calculator.
    I'm going to give *(Jane)* a watch.

3. Read the sentences in the box at the top of text page 6, and have students repeat.

INTRODUCING THE MODEL

1. Have students look at the model illustration.

2. Set the scene: "Two friends are talking. One doesn't know what to give his wife for her birthday."

3. With books closed, have students listen as you present the model or play the audio one or more times.

4. **Full-Class Repetition:** Model each line and have students repeat.

5. Have students open their books and look at the dialog. Ask students if they have any questions. Check understanding of new vocabulary: *present, ago.*

    ### Culture Note

    In the United States people usually give gifts to family members and close friends on their birthdays. Birthdays are also often celebrated with a party.

6. **Group Choral Repetition:** Divide the class in half. Model line A and have Group 1 repeat. Model line B and have Group 2 repeat, and so on.

7. **Choral Conversation:** Groups 1 and 2 practice the dialog twice, without teacher model. First, Group 1 is Speaker A and Group 2 is Speaker B. Then reverse.

8. Call on one or two pairs of students to present the dialog.

    (For additional practice, do Choral Conversation in small groups or by rows.)

SIDE BY SIDE EXERCISES

Examples

> 1. A. What are you going to give your husband for his birthday?
>   B. I don't know. I can't give him a watch. I gave him a watch last year.
>   A. How about a briefcase?
>   B. No. I can't give him a briefcase. I gave him a briefcase two years ago.
>   A. Well, what are you going to give him?
>   B. I don't know. I really have to think about it.
>
> 2. A. What are you going to give your girlfriend for her birthday?
>   B. I don't know. I can't give her perfume. I gave her perfume last year.
>   A. How about a bracelet?
>   B. No. I can't give her a bracelet. I gave her a bracelet two years ago.
>   A. Well, what are you going to give her?
>   B. I don't know. I really have to think about it.

1. **Exercise 1:** Call on two students to present the dialog. Then do Choral Repetition and Choral Conversation practice.

2. **Exercise 2:** Introduce the new word *perfume*. Same as above.

3. **Exercises 3–5:**

> **New Vocabulary**
> 5. doll

Either

Full-Class Practice: Call on a pair of students to do each exercise. Introduce the new vocabulary before doing Exercise 5. (For more practice, call on other pairs of students or do Choral Repetition or Choral Conversation.)

   or

Pair Practice: Introduce the new vocabulary. Next, have students practice all of the exercises in pairs. Then have pairs present the exercises to the class. (For more practice, do Choral Repetition or Choral Conversation.)

4. **Exercise 6:** Have students use the model as a guide to create their own conversations, using vocabulary of their choice. Encourage students to use dictionaries to find new words they want to use. This exercise can be done orally in class or for written homework. If you assign it for homework, do one example in class to make sure students understand what's expected. Have students present their conversations in class the next day.

WORKBOOK

Page 8

EXPANSION ACTIVITIES

1. Sentences Alive!

a. Make up several sentences based on this lesson. For example:

> I gave him a new briefcase last year.
> We gave her flowers two years ago.
> What are you going to give your husband for his birthday?
> I'm going to give him a watch.
> I can't give her a bicycle.
> He gave her perfume last year.

b. Write the words to each of these sentences on separate cards.

c. One sentence at a time, distribute the cards randomly to students in the class.

d. Have students decide on the correct word order of the sentence and then come to the front of the room, and make the sentence *come alive* by standing in order while holding up their cards and saying the sentence aloud one word at a time.

e. Repeat with other sentences and other students.

2. The Perfect Present!

a. Put on the board:

> 1. friend / 45 years old / likes to eat
> 2. aunt / 65 / likes to read
> 3. roommate / 25 / likes to go jogging
> 4. little sister / 10 / likes to paint
> 5. cousin / 18 / likes to listen to music
> 6. friend / 17 / lazy / doesn't like to work
> 7. _____

b. Tell your students:

> This month, many people I know are going to have birthdays. My friend Albert is 45 years old. He likes to eat. What can I give him?

Have students answer by suggesting any gift they wish. For example:

> How about candy?

c. Tell about the other people on the board, and have students suggest gifts.

d. For Number 7 on the board, have students make up information about someone who is having a birthday. Other students in the class then suggest gifts.

3. Class Discussion

a. Divide the class into pairs or small groups.

b. Write the following on the board:

> Some good presents for a man are _____, _____, and _____.
> Some good presents for a woman are _____, _____, and _____.

c. Have students complete the sentences in pairs or small groups and then discuss their responses as a class.

d. Then, dictate the following sentence and have students write it on a piece of paper:

> Good presents are always very expensive.

e. As a class, in pairs, or in small groups, have students discuss the statement.

4. Guess the Present!

a. Tell the class: "Somebody gave me a very nice present. Can you guess what the person gave me?"

b. Students try to guess the present by asking Yes/No questions. For example:

> Student: Can you wear it?
> Teacher: No, I can't.
>
> Student: Is it large?
> Teacher: No, it isn't.
>
> Student: Do you write with it?
> Teacher: No, I don't.
>
> Student: Do you listen to it?
> Teacher: Yes, I do.
>
> Student: Is it a tape?
> Teacher: No, it isn't.
>
> Student: Is it a CD?
> Teacher: Yes, it is.

Variation: Have students take turns beginning the activity.

Text Page 7: What Did Your Parents Give You?

FOCUS

- Indirect Object Pronouns: *me, us, you, them*

CLOSE UP

RULE:	Direct and indirect object pronouns follow the verb. The direct and indirect object pronouns for *I, you, we* and *they* are *me, you, us,* and *them*.
EXAMPLES:	They gave **me** a CD player. They gave **us** a plant. I gave **you** a blouse. I gave **them** a painting.

GETTING READY

1. Write the following on the board:

I	me
he	him
she	her
we	us
you	you
they	them

2. Make sentences with indirect objects, and have students repeat. As you speak, gesture to yourself or students in the class as appropriate. For example:

   I'm going to give **them** a book.
   (Teacher points to two students.)

   I'm going to give **you** a book.
   (Teacher points to all the students.)

   They're going to give **me** a book.
   (Teacher points to himself/herself.)

   He's going to give **us** a book.
   (Teacher points to himself/herself and another student.)

3. Create situations where people give books to each other, and each time ask what happened. For example:

(Teacher gives a book to a few students and asks other students)

   Teacher: What did I do?
   Students: **You** gave **them** a book.

(Teacher gives a book to a few students and asks those students)

   Teacher: What did I do?
   Students: **You** gave **us** a book.

(Teacher instructs a male student to give a book to a female student and then asks the female student)

   Teacher: What did he do?
   Student: **He** gave **me** a book.

   etc.

INTRODUCING THE MODEL

1. Have students look at the model illustration.

2. Set the scene: "Two friends are talking about birthday presents."

3. With books closed, have students listen as you present the model or play the audio one or more times.

4. **Full-Class Repetition:** Model each line and have students repeat.

5. Have students open their books and look at the dialog. Ask students if they have any

questions. Check understanding of the word *CD player*.

6. **Group Choral Repetition:** Divide the class in half. Model line A and have Group 1 repeat. Model line B and have Group 2 repeat.

7. **Choral Conversation:** Groups 1 and 2 practice the dialog twice, without teacher model. First, Group 1 is Speaker A and Group 2 is Speaker B. Then reverse.

8. Call on one or two pairs of students to present the dialog.

   (For additional practice, do Choral Conversation in small groups or by rows.)

SIDE BY SIDE EXERCISES

Examples

> 1. A. What did you give your parents for their anniversary?
>   B. I gave them a painting.
> 2. A. What did Mr. Lee's grandchildren give him for his birthday?
>   B. They gave him a computer.

1. **Exercise 1:** Introduce the new words *anniversary* and *painting*. Call on two students to present the dialog. Then do Choral Repetition and Choral Conversation practice.

2. **Exercise 2:** Same as above.
3. **Exercises 3–4:**

> **New Vocabulary**
> 3. plant

Either

Full Class Practice: Call on a pair of students to do each exercise. Introduce the new vocabulary before doing Exercise 3. (For more practice, call on other pairs of students, or do Choral Repetition or Choral Conversation.)

or

Pair Practice: Introduce the new vocabulary. Next, have students in pairs practice all the exercises. Then have pairs present the exercises to the class. (For more practice, do Choral Repetition or Choral Conversation.)

WORKBOOK

Pages 9–11

EXPANSION ACTIVITIES

1. Listen Carefully!

   a. Put the following on the board:

   b. Read sentences such as the following, and have students say the number of the indirect object pronoun they can substitute for the noun in each sentence.

   I gave *my wife* a sweater. *(2)*
   She's going to buy *her husband* a watch. *(1)*
   They bought *their daughter* a CD player. *(2)*
   I didn't give *my parents* a painting. *(3)*
   I can't send *my uncle* flowers. *(1)*
   She always gives *her sister* clothes. *(2)*
   He always gives *his children* candy. *(3)*

2. True or False?

   Point to characters in the illustrations on text page 7 and make statements. Have students tell you if a statement is *True or False.* If a statement is false, have students correct it. For example:

(pointing to the model)
Teacher: He gave his parents a CD player.
Student: False. His parents gave him a CD player.

(pointing to Exercise 3)
Teacher: Their children gave these people a plant.
Student: True.

(pointing to Exercise 2)
Teacher: Mr. Lee gave his grandchildren a computer.
Student: False. They gave him a computer.

3. Giving Game

a. Have a small group of students volunteer to stand in front of the class and exchange possessions (for example: *pens, pencils, books, notebooks*).

b. Ask the class: "What happened?" Have the class recount who gave what to whom. For example:

Student 1:   John gave Maria his pen.
Student 2:   Maria gave John her book.
Student 3:   Carla gave Robert her pencil.
Student 4:   Robert gave Carla his notebook.

4. Memory Chain

a. Divide the class into groups of 5 or 6 students each.

b. Have students answer the question *What did your family give you on your last birthday?*

c. One group at a time, have Student 1 begin. For example:

My family gave me a CD.

d. Student 2 repeats what Student 1 said and adds a statement about himself or herself. For example:

Dave's family gave him a CD. My family gave me a plant.

e. Student 3 continues in the same way. For example:

Dave's family gave him a CD. Sally's family gave her a plant. My family gave me a book.

f. Continue until everyone has had a chance to play the *memory chain*.

5. Indirect Object Match Game

a. Make a set of cards with Speaker A's and Speaker B's lines:

Our children gave my husband and me a book.	They gave us a book.
My daughter gave my son a book.	She gave him a book.
My brother gave my sister a book.	He gave her a book.
My wife and I gave our children a book.	We gave them a book.
My parents gave my boyfriend a book.	They gave him a book.
My girlfriend gave my parents a book.	She gave them a book.
My brother and I gave our mother a book.	We gave her a book.
You gave our grandchildren a book.	You gave them a book.
My brother and sister gave you a book.	They gave you a book.

b. Distribute the cards to students.

c. Have students memorize the sentence on their cards and then walk around the room, saying their sentence until they find their match.

d. Then have pairs of students say their matched sentences aloud to the class.

How to Read a Date

1. Review months of the year. Write abbreviations for months on the board, and have students say the name of the month.

2. Introduce ordinal numbers.

   a. Have students look at the list of ordinal numbers on page 154 of the Student Book.

   b. Say each number and have students repeat chorally and individually. Point out the abbreviations: *-st, -nd, -rd,* and *-th.*

   c. Explain that dates are read as ordinal numbers, even though they are often written as cardinal numbers. For example, January 10 is read as "January tenth."

   d. Write different dates on the board and have students say them.

3. Practice conversations with dates.

   a. Present conversations with the dates that are listed, and have students repeat:

      A. When is your birthday?
      B. My birthday is January twenty-third.

      A. When is your birthday?
      B. My birthday is November sixteenth.

      A. When is your birthday?
      B. My birthday is December thirty-first.

   b. Divide the class into pairs, and have students practice conversations in which they ask and answer about their birthdays.

   c. Call on students to report about their partner's birthday.

EXPANSION ACTIVITY

Class Survey

1. Have students circulate around the room, interviewing each other and asking each other about their birthdays.

2. Have students report their findings to the class to determine the following:

   What month has the most birthdays?
   Whose birthday is next?
   Who just had a birthday?
   Who is going to have a birthday while in this class?

Option: Keep all the birthday information so that you can acknowledge each student's birthday.

 JOURNAL

Have students write their journal entries at home or in class. Encourage students to use a dictionary to look up words they would like to use. Students can share their written work with other students if appropriate. Have students discuss what they have written as a class, in pairs, or in small groups.

Have students keep a journal of their written work. If time permits, you may want to write a response in each student's journal, sharing your own opinions and experiences as well as reacting to what the student has written. If you are keeping portfolios of students' work, these compositions serve as excellent examples of students' progress in learning English.

READING *Very Good Friends: East and West /*
Very Good Friends: North and South

FOCUS

- Review of Tenses: Simple Present, Simple Past
- Indirect Object Pronouns

NEW VOCABULARY

Story 1	Story 2
advice	cheese
California	communicate
CD	condominium
East Coast	down south
far apart	Florida
give advice	Internet
lent (lend)	into
lost (lose *his* job)	message
New Jersey	oranges
sent (send)	sold (sell)
West Coast	up north
	van
	Wisconsin

READING THE STORIES

Optional: Preview the stories by having students talk about the story titles and/or illustrations. You may choose to introduce new vocabulary beforehand, or have students encounter the new vocabulary within the context of the reading.

1. Have students read silently or follow along silently as the stories are read aloud by you, by one or more students, or on the audio program.

2. Ask students if they have any questions. Check understanding of vocabulary.

3. Check students' comprehension, using some or all of the following questions:

   Story 1:
   What does he write her letters about?
   What does she write him letters about?
   What did he send her last year on her birthday?
   What did she send him last year on his birthday?
   How did he help her last year?
   How did she help him last year?

   Story 2:
   What do we send them messages about?
   What do they send us messages about?
   What did we send them last year on their anniversary?
   What did they send us last year on our anniversary?
   How did we help them last year?
   How did they help us last year?

✓ READING *CHECK-UP*

TRUE OR FALSE?

1. False
2. True
3. False
4. True
5. True
6. True
7. False
8. True
9. False

READING EXTENSION

Tic Tac Question Formation

1. Draw a tic tac grid on the board and fill it with the following question words:

How?	Who?	Where?
What?	Was?	Did?
When?	Why?	Is?

2. Divide the class into two teams. Give each team a mark: *X* or *O*.

3. Choose one of the stories, and have each team ask a question about the story that begins with one of the question words and then provide the answer to the question. If the question and answer are correct, the team gets to put its mark in that space. For example:

> X Team: How do Carlos and Maria communicate with their friends? On the Internet.

X?	Who?	Where?
What?	Was?	Did?
When?	Why?	Is?

4. The first team to mark out three boxes in a straight line—vertically, horizontally, or diagonally—wins.

 **LISTENING**

Listen and choose the correct answer.

1. What are you going to do tomorrow?

2. What do you do in the summer?

3. When did you clean your apartment?

4. What did you give your parents for their anniversary?

5. Where did you and your friends go yesterday?

6. How often do they send messages to each other?

7. What did he give her?

8. When are you going to make pancakes?

Answers

1. b	5. a
2. b	6. b
3. a	7. a
4. a	8. b

 IN YOUR OWN WORDS

1. Make sure students understand the instructions.

2. Have students do the activity as written homework, using a dictionary for any new words they wish to use.

3. Have students present and discuss what they have written, in pairs or as a class.

 PRONUNCIATION

> **Contrastive Stress:** When we make a contrast, the new information receives more stress than the old information, which is already understood. For example:
>
> I'm not going to clean my room this week. I cleaned my room LÁST week.

Focus on Listening

Practice the sentences in the left column. Say each sentence or play the audio one or more times. Have students listen carefully and repeat.

Focus on Pronunciation

Practice the sentences in the right column. Have students say each sentence and then listen carefully as you say it or play the audio.

If you wish, have students continue practicing the sentences to improve their pronunciation.

Text Page 10

✓ CHAPTER SUMMARY

GRAMMAR

1. Divide the class into pairs or small groups.
2. Have students take turns forming sentences from the words in the grammar boxes. Student A says a sentence, and Student B points to the words from each column that are in the sentence. Then have students switch: Student B says a sentence, and Student A points to the words.

KEY VOCABULARY

Have students ask you any questions about the meaning or pronunciation of the vocabulary. If students ask for the pronunciation, repeat after the student until the student is satisfied with his or her own pronunciation.

EXPANSION ACTIVITIES

1. Do You Remember the Words?

   Check students' retention of the vocabulary depicted on the opening page of Chapter 1 by doing the following activity:

   a. Have students open their books to page 1.

   b. For days of the week and months of the year, say a word and have students point to the abbreviation in the calendar, or point to an abbreviation in the calendar and have students say the word.

   c. For seasons, point to an illustration and have students name the season, or say a season and have students point to the illustration.

   Variation: You can also do this activity as a game with competing teams.

2. Student-Led Dictation

   a. Tell each student to choose a word or phrase from the Key Vocabulary list on text page 10 and look at it very carefully.

   b. Have students take turns dictating their words to the class. Everybody writes down that student's word.

   c. When the dictation is completed, call on different students to write each word on the board to check the spelling.

3. Beanbag Toss

   a. Call out a topic from the chapter—for example: *Months of the Year.*

   b. Have students toss a beanbag back and forth. The student to whom the beanbag is tossed must name a word in that category. For months, days of the week, and seasons, have students name them in order. For example:

      Student 1: January
      Student 2: February
      Student 3: March

   c. Continue until all the words in the category have been named.

END-OF-CHAPTER ACTIVITIES

1. Question Game

a. Write the following sentence on the board:

> Mrs. Miller isn't going to cook spaghetti this week because she cooked spaghetti last week, and she doesn't like to cook spaghetti very often.

b. Underline different elements of the sentence, and have students create a question based on that portion of the sentence. For example:

> <u>Mrs. Miller</u> isn't going to cook spaghetti this week because she cooked spaghetti last week, and she doesn't like to cook spaghetti very often.

Who isn't going to cook spaghetti?

> Mrs. Miller isn't going to cook spaghetti this week <u>because she cooked spaghetti last week, and she doesn't like to cook spaghetti very often</u>.

Why isn't Mrs. Miller going to cook spaghetti this week?

> Mrs. Miller isn't going to cook spaghetti this week because she cooked spaghetti <u>last week</u>, and she doesn't like to cook spaghetti very often.

When did Mrs. Miller cook spaghetti?

c. Continue with other sentences.

2. Board Game

a. On poster boards or on manila file folders, make up game boards with a pathway consisting of separate spaces. You may use any theme or design you wish.

b. Divide the class into groups of two to four students, and give each group a game board, a die, and each student something to be used as a playing piece.

c. Give each group a pile of cards face-down with questions written on them. For example:

> What are the days of the week?
> What months are in the summer?
> What months are in the winter?
> What months are in the spring?
> What months are in the fall?
> What are the months of the year starting with *January*?
> What are the abbreviations for the days of the week?
> What are the abbreviations for the months of the year?

d. Each student in turn rolls the die, moves the playing piece along the game path, and after landing on a space, picks a card, reads the question, and answers it. If the student is correct, that student takes an additional turn.

e. The first student to reach the end of the pathway is the winner.

WORKBOOK PAGE 2

A. WHAT DO THEY LIKE TO DO?

1. likes to watch TV
2. like to play soccer
3. likes to write letters
4. like to listen to music
5. like to go dancing
6. likes to chat online
7. likes to go hiking
8. like to go to the mall
9. likes to go to the beach

B. LISTENING

Listen and choose the correct response.

1. What do your friends like to do on the weekend?
2. What does your sister like to do on the weekend?
3. What does your brother like to do on the weekend?
4. What do you and your friends like to do on the weekend?
5. What does your son like to do on the weekend?
6. What do you like to do on the weekend?
7. What does your next-door neighbor like to do on the weekend?
8. What does your cousin Sue like to do on the weekend?

Answers

1. b   5. a
2. b   6. b
3. a   7. b
4. b   8. a

WORKBOOK PAGE 3

C. WHAT DO THEY LIKE TO DO?

1. watch
   He watches
   He watched
   He's going to watch
2. listen
   I listen
   I listened
   I'm going to listen
3. ride
   She rides
   She rode
   She's going to ride
4. sing
   They sing
   They sang
   They're going to sing
5. bake
   We bake
   We baked
   We're going to bake
6. go
   He goes
   He went
   He's going to go

WORKBOOK PAGE 4

D. LIKES AND DISLIKES

1. likes to cook   2. doesn't like to take
3. like to feed   4. don't like to eat
5. likes to read   6. doesn't like to wait
7. like to watch   8. don't like to drive
9. likes to clean   10. don't like to go

WORKBOOK PAGES 5–6

F. DAY AFTER DAY

1. washes
   He washed
   He's going go wash
2. gets up
   She got up
   She's going to get up
3. go
   They went
   They're going to go
4. study
   I studied
   I'm going to study
5. plays
   He played
   He's going to play
6. makes
   She made
   She's going to make
7. plant
   We planted
   We're going to plant
8. writes
   He wrote
   He's going to write
9. visits
   She visited
   She's going to visit
10. do
   We did
   We're going to do

WORKBOOK PAGE 8

I. WHAT'S PAULA GOING TO GIVE HER FAMILY?

1. She's going to give him gloves.
2. She's going to give her a dog.
3. She's going to give him a watch.
4. She's going to give them a CD player.
5. She's going to give her a sweater.
6. She's going to give him a novel.
7. She's going to give them a plant.
8. She's going to give him a cell phone.

J. PRESENTS

1. gave, I'm going to give him
2. gave, he's going to give her
3. gave, she's going to give him
4. gave, we're going to give them
5. gave, I'm going to give her
6. gave, we're going to give him

WORKBOOK PAGE 9

K. MORE PRESENTS

1. I, her	**2.** They, me
3. He, them	**4.** They, us
5. She, me	**6.** We, him
7. I, you	**8.** You, me

WORKBOOK PAGE 10

L. MATCHING

1. b	**5.** h
2. d	**6.** f
3. a	**7.** e
4. c	**8.** g

M. WHAT'S THE NUMBER?

1. 50th	**6.** 1st
2. 99th	**7.** 16th
3. 15th	**8.** 65th
4. 12th	**9.** 84th
5. 77th	**10.** 36th

N. LISTENING

Listen and write the ordinal number you hear.

Many people live and work in this large apartment building in New York City.

1. There's a barber shop on the second floor.
2. The Wong family lives on the twelfth floor.
3. The Acme Internet Company is on the thirtieth floor.
4. Bob Richards lives on the thirteenth floor.
5. There's a bank on the third floor.
6. There's a dentist's office on the ninth floor.
7. There's a flower shop on the first floor.
8. The Martinez family lives on the nineteenth floor.
9. Louise Lane works on the seventeenth floor.
10. There's a computer store on the fourth floor.
11. There's an expensive French restaurant on the forty-eighth floor.
12. My apartment is on the fifth floor.
13. The Park family lives on the thirty-fourth floor.
14. Dr. Jacobson has an office on the twenty-sixth floor.
15. The Walker family lives on the sixty-second floor.
16. There's a health club on the eighteenth floor.

Answers

1. 2nd	**9.** 17th
2. 12th	**10.** 4th
3. 30th	**11.** 48th
4. 13th	**12.** 5th
5. 3rd	**13.** 34th
6. 9th	**14.** 26th
7. 1st	**15.** 62nd
8. 19th	**16.** 18th

WORKBOOK PAGE 11

O. RICHARD'S BIRTHDAYS

1. had	**14.** wanted
2. made	**15.** had
3. baked	**16.** cooked
4. gave	**17.** ate
5. loved	**18.** played
6. played	**19.** enjoyed
7. give	**20.** talk
8. went	**21.** have
9. swam	**22.** went
10. went	**23.** had
11. liked	**24.** give
12. like	**25.** cook
13. gave	**26.** danced

P. MATCHING

1. b
2. d
3. a
4. c

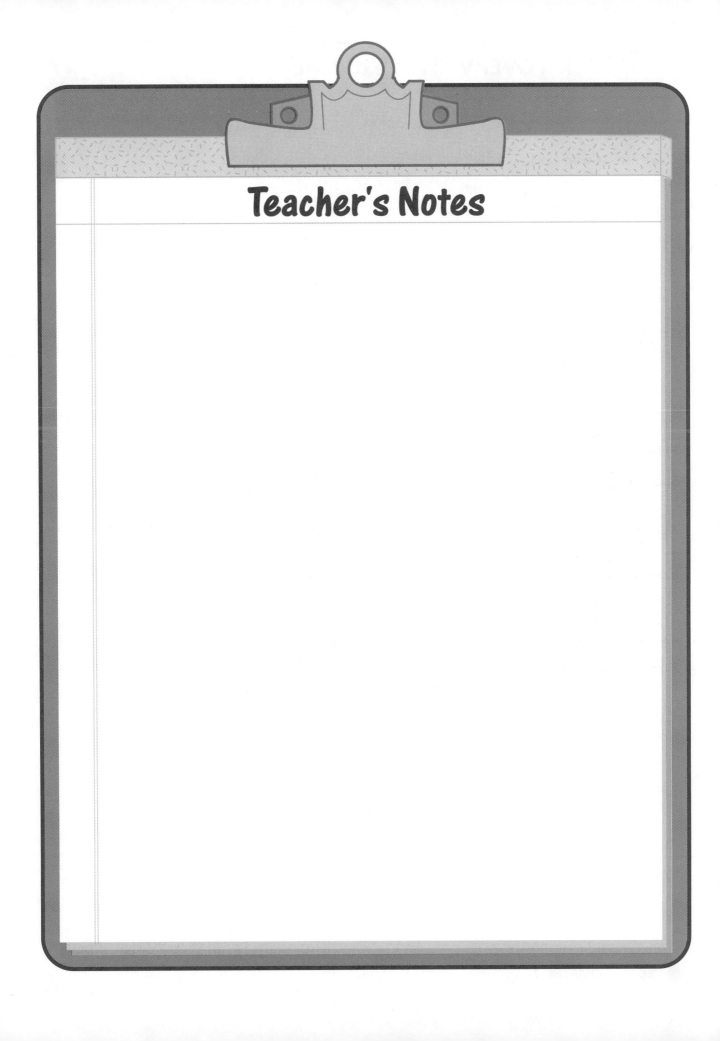

Teacher's Notes

GRAMMAR

COUNT / NON-COUNT NOUNS

There isn't any	bread. lettuce. flour.

There aren't any	apples. eggs. lemons.

How much	milk cheese ice cream	do you want?
How many	cookies french fries meatballs	

Not too	much. many.

Just	a little. a few.

FUNCTIONS

SUGGESTING

Let's *make sandwiches for lunch*!

ASKING FOR AND REPORTING INFORMATION

There isn't any *bread*.
There aren't any *apples*.

My doctor says that *too many cookies are bad for my health*.

INQUIRING ABOUT WANT–DESIRE

How much *milk* do you want?
How many *cookies* do you want?

INQUIRING ABOUT SATISFACTION

How do you like *the potatoes*?

EXPRESSING SATISFACTION

I think it's *delicious*.
I think they're *delicious*.

OFFERING

Would you care for some more?

EXPRESSING INABILITY

We can't.

EXPRESSING GRATITUDE

Thanks.

COMPLIMENTING

This *chicken* is *delicious*!
    I'm glad you like it.
These *potatoes* are *fantastic*!
    I'm glad you like them.

NEW VOCABULARY

Foods

apple
apple pie
banana
bread
butter
cake
carrot
chicken
chocolate cake
coffee
cookie
egg
fish
flour
french fries
grapes
hamburger
ice cream
ketchup
lemon
lettuce
mayonnaise
meat
meatballs
milk
mustard
omelet
onion
orange
orange juice
pear
pepper
pizza
potato
rice

salad
salt
sandwich
soda
soy sauce
sugar
tea
tomato
vegetable
yogurt

Adjectives

delicious
excellent
fantastic
fresh

Kitchen

cabinet
counter
freezer
refrigerator

Determiners

a few
a little
many
more
much

WH-Questions

How many?
How much?

Miscellaneous

bag
care
groceries
health
just
spend (spent)
taste
walk out

EXPRESSIONS

bad for my health
good for *him*
Here you are.
Just a few.
Just a little.
Let's
Not too many.
Not too much.
think so
Would you care for some more?

Text Page 11: Chapter Opening Page

VOCABULARY PREVIEW

You may want to introduce these words before beginning the chapter, or you may choose to wait until they first occur in a specific lesson. If you choose to introduce them at this point, here are some suggestions:

1. Have students look at the illustrations on text page 11 and identify the words they already know.

2. Present the vocabulary. Say each word and have the class repeat it chorally and individually. Check students' understanding and pronunciation of the words.

3. Practice the vocabulary as a class, in pairs, or in small groups. Have students cover the word list and look at the pictures. Practice the words in the following ways:

   • Say a word and have students tell the number of the illustration.

   • Give the number of an illustration and have students say the word.

Text Page 12

  TALK ABOUT IT! *Where Are the Cookies? / Where's the Cheese?*

FOCUS

- Count/Non-Count Nouns

CLOSE UP

RULE:	There are two groups of nouns—count and non-count.
	Count nouns are nouns you can count. Count nouns have a singular and a plural form.
EXAMPLE:	I have an apple. She has five **apples**.
RULE:	Non-count nouns are nouns you cannot count. Non-count nouns have only one (singular) form.
EXAMPLE:	Where's the **flour**? The **flour** is on the counter.

GETTING READY

Note: The following food items from text page 11 were not included in the Vocabulary Preview on text page 11: *butter, coffee, cookies, flour, ice cream, milk, orange juice, rice, soda, sugar, tea, yogurt.* If you previewed the words on text page 11, review them at this point. If you did not preview the words on text page 11, introduce all the words at this point.

1. Use *Side by Side* Picture Cards 163–198, the illustrations on text page 11, or your own visuals, or bring products from home to introduce the following food items:

Count Nouns

apples	lemons
bananas	onions
carrots	pears
cookies	potatoes
eggs	tomatoes
grapes	

Non-Count Nouns

bread	meat
butter	milk
cake	mustard
cheese	orange juice
chicken	pepper
coffee	rice
fish	salt
flour	soda
ice cream	soy sauce
ketchup	sugar
lettuce	tea
mayonnaise	yogurt

2. Introduce the concept of count and non-count nouns.

   a. Write on the board:

   > There are _____ in my kitchen.
   > There's _____ in my kitchen.

   b. Hold up a visual of a count noun and say:

   There are *(apples)* in my kitchen.

   Have students repeat.

   c. Continue with three or four other count nouns.

   d. Hold up a visual of a non-count noun and say:

   There's *(milk)* in my kitchen.

   Have students repeat.

   e. Continue with three or four other non-count nouns.

INTRODUCING THE MODELS

There are four model conversations. Introduce and practice each before going on to the next. For each model:

1. Have students look at the model illustration.

2. Set the scene: "Family members are talking."

3. With books closed, have students listen as you present the model or play the audio one or more times.

4. **Full-Class Repetition:** Model each line and have students repeat.

5. Have students open their books and look at the dialog. Ask students if they have any questions. Check understanding of new vocabulary:

> 1st model: *cabinet*
> 3rd model: *counter*
> 4th model: *ice cream, freezer*

6. **Group Choral Repetition:** Divide the class in half. Model line A and have Group 1 repeat. Model line B and have Group 2 repeat.

7. **Choral Conversation:** Groups 1 and 2 practice the dialog twice, without teacher model. First, Group 1 is Speaker A and Group 2 is Speaker B. Then reverse.

8. Call on one or two pairs of students to present the dialog.

   (For additional practice, do Choral Conversation in small groups or by rows.)

CONVERSATION PRACTICE

1. Have pairs of students use the model conversations to ask and answer questions about the foods depicted on the page. This exercise can be done as either Full-Class Practice or Pair Practice.

2. Call on pairs to present conversations to the class.

WORKBOOK

Pages 12–13

EXPANSION ACTIVITIES

1. True or False?

   a. Have students open their books to text page 12.

   b. Make statements about the food items on text page 12, and have students tell you *True or False*. If the statement is false, have students correct it. For example:

   > Teacher: The bananas are on the counter.
   > Student: True.

   > Teacher: The ketchup is in the cabinet.
   > Student: False. The ketchup is in the refrigerator.

   Variation: Call on students to make true or false statements about the foods in the illustrations, and have other students respond.

2. Drawing Game

   a. Write down on two sets of cards as many of the following food vocabulary items as you wish:

bananas	bread	carrots	milk
onions	cheese	soda	oranges
lettuce	apples	butter	eggs
tomatoes	lemons	pears	grapes
rice	potatoes	cake	cookies
chicken	fish	meat	salt

   b. Divide the class into two teams. Have each team sit together in a different part of the room.

   c. Place each set of cards on a table or desk in front of the room. Also place a pad of paper and pencil next to each team's set of cards.

   d. When you say "Go!", a person from each team comes to the table, picks a card from that team's pile, draws the item on the card, and shows the drawing to the rest of the team. The team then guesses what the word is.

e. When a team correctly guesses a word, another team member picks a card and draws the word written on that card.

f. Continue until each team has guessed all the words in their pile.

g. The team that guesses the words in the shortest time wins the game.

3. Clap in Rhythm

a. Have students sit in a circle.

b. Establish a steady, even beat—one-two-three-four, one-two-three-four—by having students clap their hands to their laps twice and then clap their hands together twice. Repeat throughout the game, maintaining the same rhythm.

c. The object is for each student in turn to name a food each time the hands are clapped together twice. Nothing is said when students clap their hands on their laps.

Note: The beat never stops! If a student misses a beat, he or she can either wait for the next beat or pass to the next student.

4. Chain Game

a. Begin the game by saying:

"In my kitchen there's milk."

b. Have each student take a turn in which he or she repeats what the person before said and adds a new food item. For example:

"In my kitchen, there's milk and there's bread."
"In my kitchen, there's milk, there's bread, and there are tomatoes."

5. Likes and Dislikes

a. Have students draw two columns on a piece of paper. At the top of one column, have students write <u>I like</u>. At the top of the other column, have them write <u>I don't like</u>.

b. Dictate various food items from the text and have students write them in either the left or right column, depending on whether they *like* or *don't like* them.

<u>I like</u>	<u>I don't like</u>
apples	lemons
cheese	fish
bananas	yogurt

c. At the end of the dictation, have students compare their lists to see which food items people *like* and *don't like*.

6. Dictation Game

a. Make up a list of 6–10 food items. Write the list in large print on a piece of paper. For example:

onions	yogurt
potatoes	cheese
flour	lemons
bananas	eggs

b. Put the paper on the far side of the room or out in the hallway so that students can't read it from their seats.

c. Divide the class into pairs. One student from each pair runs to read the list and then returns to dictate the list to their partner. The runner may go back and forth as many times as necessary. The first pair to finish the list wins.

 Make a List!

Assign this as homework. Encourage students to use dictionaries to find new words they want to use. In class, have students compare their lists.

Text Page 13: Let's Make Sandwiches for Lunch!

FOCUS

- Count/Non-Count Nouns

CLOSE UP

RULE:	The word *any* is used in negative statements with plural count and non-count nouns.
EXAMPLES:	There isn't **any** bread. There aren't **any** apples.

INTRODUCING THE MODELS

There are two model conversations. Introduce and practice each separately. For each model:

1. Have students look at the model illustration.

2. Set the scene: "People are talking about food they want to make."

3. With books closed, have students listen as you present the model or play the audio one or more times.

4. **Full-Class Repetition:** Model each line and have students repeat.

   Pronunciation Note

   The pronunciation focus of Chapter 2 is **Reduced *for*** (text page 18). You may wish to model this pronunciation at this point and encourage students to incorporate it into their language practice.

   Let's make sandwiches for lunch!
   Let's make an apple pie for dessert!

5. Have students open their books and look at the dialog. Ask students if they have any questions. Check understanding of new vocabulary:

   1st model: *let's, make, sandwich, for lunch*

   2nd model: *for dessert*

6. **Group Choral Repetition:** Divide the class in half. Model line A and have Group 1 repeat. Model line B and have Group 2 repeat, and so on.

7. **Choral Conversation:** Groups 1 and 2 practice the dialog twice, without teacher model. First, Group 1 is Speaker A and Group 2 is Speaker B. Then reverse.

8. Call on one or two pairs of students to present the dialog.

   (For additional practice, do Choral Conversation in small groups or by rows.)

SIDE BY SIDE EXERCISES

Examples

1. A. Let's make pizza for lunch!   B. Sorry, we can't. There isn't any cheese.
2. A. Let's make some fresh lemonade!   B. Sorry, we can't. There aren't any lemons.

1. **Exercise 1:** Introduce the new word *pizza*. Call on two students to present the dialog. Then do Choral Repetition and Choral Conversation practice.

2. Exercise 2: Introduce the new word *fresh*. Same as above.

3. Exercises 3–8:

> **New Vocabulary**
>
> 3. salad
> 4. omelet
> 7. french fries
>   hamburger
> 8. meatballs

Either

Full-Class Practice: Call on a pair of students to do each exercise. Introduce the new vocabulary before doing Exercises 3, 4, 7, 8. (For more practice, call on the other pairs of students, or do Choral Repetition or Choral Conversation.)

or

Pair Practice: Introduce the new vocabulary. Next, have students in pairs practice all the exercises. Then have pairs present the exercises to the class. (For more practice, do Choral Repetition or Choral Conversation.)

4. Exercise 9: Have students use the model as a guide to create their own conversations, using vocabulary of their choice. (They can use any foods they wish.) Encourage students to use dictionaries to find new words they want to use. This exercise can be done orally in class or for written homework. If you assign it for homework, do one example in class to make sure students understand what's expected. Have students present their conversations in class the next day.

WORKBOOK

Pages 14–15

EXPANSION ACTIVITIES

1. Guided Conversation Match Game

   a. Make a set of cards with Speaker A's and Speaker B's lines from the following conversations:

Let's make sandwiches for lunch!	Sorry, we can't. There isn't any bread.
Let's make an apple pie for dessert!	Sorry, we can't. There aren't any apples.
Let's make pizza for lunch!	Sorry, we can't. There isn't any cheese.
Let's make some fresh lemonade!	Sorry, we can't. There aren't any lemons.
Let's make a salad for dinner!	Sorry, we can't. There isn't any lettuce.
Let's make an omelet for breakfast!	Sorry, we can't. There aren't any eggs.

Let's bake a cake for dessert!	Sorry, we can't. There isn't any flour.
Let's make some fresh orange juice for breakfast!	Sorry, we can't. There aren't any oranges.
Let's have french fries with our hamburgers!	Sorry, we can't. There aren't any potatoes.
Let's have meatballs with our spaghetti!	Sorry, we can't. There isn't any meat.

   b. Distribute the cards to students.

   c. Have students memorize the sentences on their cards and then walk around the room, saying their sentences until they find their match.

   d. Then have pairs of students say their matched sentences aloud to the class.

2. Sense or Nonsense?

   a. Divide the class into four groups.

   (continued)

b. Make four sets of the cards from Expansion Activity 1.

c. Mix up the cards and distribute sets of cards to each group, keeping Speaker A's and Speaker B's cards in different piles.

d. Have students take turns picking up one card from each pile and reading the sentence to the group. For example:

Let's make some fresh lemonade!	Sorry, we can't. There isn't any cheese.

e. That group decides if the sentence makes sense or is nonsense.

f. After all the cards have been picked, have the groups lay out all the cards and put together all the sentence combinations.

3. Finish the Sentence!

Begin a sentence and have students add appropriate endings to the sentence. For example:

Teacher:	We can't make a salad because
Students:	. . . there isn't any lettuce.
	. . . there aren't any tomatoes.
	. . . there aren't any carrots.
Teacher:	We can't make an apple pie because
Students:	. . . there aren't any apples.
	. . . there isn't any flour.
	. . . there isn't any butter.

4. What Came Before?

a. Divide the class into pairs.

b. Write on the board the final line of a conversation. For example:

Sorry, we can't. There isn't any cheese.

c. Have each pair create a conversation ending with that line.

d. Call on pairs to present their conversations to the class, and compare everybody's versions.

5. Associations

a. Divide the class into pairs or small groups.

b. Name a meal, and have students write down all the foods they associate with that meal. For example:

lunch: hamburger, french fries, sandwich, pizza, salad

c. Have a student from each pair or group come to the board and write their words.

Variation: Do the activity as a game in which you divide the class into teams. The team with the most number of associations is the winner.

6. Do You Remember?

a. Divide the class into pairs.

b. Find a picture from a magazine and show it to the class for one minute. The picture should depict a scene with foods.

c. Put away the picture and have students write down what foods they remember in the scene.

d. Have students compare their lists with their partner and then look at the picture to see how much they remembered.

7. What Are the Ingredients?

a. Write the following foods on the board:

french fries	cake
salad	ice cream
pizza	apple pie
sandwich	pancakes

b. Have students in small groups write a list of the ingredients for each food.

c. Have students compare their lists with the class.

8. Role Play

Use the following conversational model and word cards as cues to role play ordering food in a restaurant.

a. Write on the board:

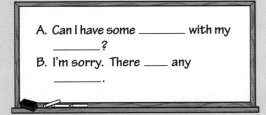

A. Can I have some _____ with my
   _____?
B. I'm sorry. There ____ any
   _____.

b. Set the scene: "A customer is ordering food in a restaurant."

c. Hold up a word card showing two food items often eaten together. For example:

rice / chicken	ice cream / apple pie
ketchup / french fries	cheese / bread
butter / bread	soda / pizza
bananas / yogurt	french fries / hamburger

d. Have pairs of students create conversations based on the model. For example:

cue: rice / chicken

A. Can I have some rice with my chicken?
B. I'm sorry. There isn't any rice.

cue: bananas / yogurt

A. Can I have some bananas with my yogurt?
B. I'm sorry. There aren't any bananas.

Text Page 14: How Much Milk Do You Want?

FOCUS

- *Much/A Little* with Non-Count Nouns
- *Many/A Few* with Count Nouns

CLOSE UP

RULE: Count and non-count nouns take different determiners. The determiners *much* and *a little* are used with non-count nouns.

EXAMPLES: How **much** milk do you want?
Just **a little** (milk).

The determiners *many* and *a few* are used with count nouns.

EXAMPLES: How **many** cookies do you want?
Just **a few** (cookies).

GETTING READY

1. Introduce non-count noun determiners.

   a. Write the following conversation on the board, and have students repeat after you:

   > A. Do you want some milk?
   > B. Okay, but just a little.

   b. Put the following non-count nouns on the board or on word cards for students to use as cues for creating similar conversations: *ice cream, bread, orange juice.*

2. Introduce count noun determiners.

   a. Write the following conversation on the board, and have students repeat after you:

   > A. Do you want some cookies?
   > B. Okay, but just a few.

   b. Put the following count nouns on the board or on word cards for students to use as cues for creating similar conversations: *carrots, eggs, potatoes.*

INTRODUCING THE MODELS

There are two model conversations. Introduce and practice each separately. For each model:

1. Have students look at the model illustration.

2. Set the scene:

   1st model: "A mother and daughter are talking."
   2nd model: "Two friends are talking."

3. Present the model.

4. Full-Class Repetition.

5. Ask students if they have any questions. Check understanding of new vocabulary:

   1st model: *how much, too much, just, a little, Here you are.*
   2nd model: *how many, too many, a few*

6. Group Choral Repetition.

7. Choral Conversation.

8. Call on one or two pairs of students to present the dialog.

(For additional practice, do Choral Conversation in small groups or by rows.)

Examples

> 1. A. How much rice do you want?
>   B. Not too much. Just a little.
>   A. Okay. Here you are.
>   B. Thanks.
>
> 2. A. How many french fries do you want?
>   B. Not too many. Just a few.
>   A. Okay. Here you are.
>   B. Thanks.

1. **Exercise 1:** Call on two students to present the dialog. Then do Choral Repetition and Choral Conversation practice.

2. **Exercise 2:** Same as above.

3. **Exercises 3–5:** Either Full-Class Practice or Pair Practice.

4. **Exercise 6:** Have students use the model as a guide to create their own conversations, using vocabulary of their choice. (They can use any foods they wish.) Encourage students to use dictionaries to find new words they want to use. This exercise can be done orally in class or for written homework. If you assign it for homework, do one example in class to make sure students understand what's expected. Have students present their conversations in class the next day.

WORKBOOK

Pages 16–17

EXPANSION ACTIVITIES

1. **How Many? How Much?**

   Say the nouns below. After each word have students respond either "How much?" (for noncount) or "How many?" (for count).

french fries	(How many?)
rice	(How much?)
sugar	(How much?)
hamburgers	(How many?)
sandwiches	(How many?)
flour	(How much?)
mayonnaise	(How much?)
butter	(How much?)
orange juice	(How much?)
grapes	(How many?)
apples	(How many?)
eggs	(How many?)
bread	(How much?)
onions	(How many?)

2. **A Little/A Few**

   a. Write the following conversational model on the board:

   > A. Do you want some _____?
   > B. Thanks. Just (a little/a few).
   > A. Are you sure?
   > B. Yes.
   > A. Okay. { Here's a little _____.
   >   { Here are a few _____.

   b. Hold up word cards or *Side by Side* Picture Cards for different foods to use as cues for creating conversations based on the model. For example:

   > (rice)
   > A. Do you want some rice?
   > B. Thanks. Just a little.
   > A. Are you sure?
   > B. Yes.
   > A. Okay. Here's a little rice.
   >
   > (cookies)
   > A. Do you want some cookies?
   > B. Thanks. Just a few.
   > A. Are you sure?
   > B. Yes.
   > A. Okay. Here are a few cookies.

   (continued)

3. Too Much/Too Many

Use the conversational model below and word cues to have students create conversations.

a. Write on the board:

> A. You look terrible! What's the matter?
> B. I have a very bad _____.
> A. Why?
> B. Because I _____ too (much/many)
>   _____ last night.

b. Set the scene: "Two friends are talking. One of them feels terrible."

c. Hold up a word card showing key words such as those below. Call on two students to create a conversation.

Key words:

headache read/books	stomachache eat/chicken and rice
sore throat sing/songs at a party	backache plant/flowers in the yard
earache listen to/CDs	toothache eat/cake

For example:

> A. You look terrible! What's the matter?
> B. I have a very bad headache.
> A. Why?
> B. Because I read too many books last night.

d. Call on pairs of students to create similar conversations, using any vocabulary they wish.

4. Category Dictation

a. Have students draw two columns on a piece of paper. At the top of one column, have students write <u>Things I eat</u>. At the top of the other column, have them write <u>Things I drink</u>.

b. Dictate various food items from the text, and have students write them in the appropriate column. For example:

Things I eat	Things I drink
ice cream	milk
rice	soda
cookies	tea

Variation:

a. Have students draw two columns on a piece of paper. At the top of one column, have students write <u>How Much?</u>. At the top of the other column, have them write <u>How Many?</u>.

b. Dictate various food items from the text and have students write them in the appropriate column. For example:

How Much?	How Many?
milk	bananas
cheese	apples
flour	potatoes

5. Match the Cards

a. Make duplicate sets of cards such as the following:

three bananas two carrots a lot of cheese a lot of salad	three bananas two carrots a lot of cheese a lot of salad
two bananas one carrot a lot of cheese a lot of salad	two bananas one carrot a lot of cheese a lot of salad
two bananas one carrot a lot of cheese a little salad	two bananas one carrot a lot of cheese a little salad
two bananas five carrots a little cheese a little salad	two bananas five carrots a little cheese a little salad

two bananas five carrots a little cheese a lot of salad	two bananas five carrots a little cheese a lot of salad
two bananas a lot of cheese a few carrots a little salad	two bananas a lot of cheese a few carrots a little salad
one banana a few carrots a little cheese a lot of salad	one banana a few carrots a little cheese a lot of salad

b. Distribute a card to each student.

c. Have students walk around the room, trying to find their corresponding match without looking at each others' cards. They can ask the following questions:

How many bananas do you have?
How many carrots do you have?
How much cheese do you have?
How much salad do you have?

ROLE PLAY *Would You Care for Some More?*

FOCUS

- Review: Count/Non-Count Nouns

INTRODUCING THE MODEL

Introduce the role play model with the first two food items depicted on text page 15.

Answer Key

> A. How do you like the chocolate cake?
> B. I think it's delicious.
> A. I'm glad you like it. Would you care for some more?
> B. Yes, please. But not too much. Just a little. My doctor says that too much chocolate cake is bad for my health.
>
> A. How do you like the cookies?
> B. I think they're delicious.
> A. I'm glad you like them. Would you care for some more?
> B. Yes, please. But not too many. Just a few. My doctor says that too many cookies are bad for my health.

For each conversation:

1. Have students look at the illustration.

2. Set the scene: "Some friends are having dinner. The hostess is talking to one of the guests about the food."

3. With books closed, have students listen as you present the model or play the audio one or more times.

4. Full-Class Repetition.

5. Have students open their books and look at the dialog. Ask students if they have any questions. Check understanding of new vocabulary: *How do you like?, delicious, Would you care for some more?, bad for my health, chocolate*

6. Group Choral Repetition.

7. Choral Conversation.

8. Call on one or two pairs of students to present the dialog.

9. In pairs, have students practice the conversation with the third illustrated food item *(ice cream)*.

10. For homework, have students use the model as a guide to write two dinner table conversations: one using a non-count noun, and the other using a count noun. Encourage students to expand the conversation any way they wish. Have students present their conversations in class the next day without referring to their written homework. (For added realism, you can set up a dinner table in front of the class with glasses and plates, silverware and cups.)

WORKBOOK

Pages 18–20

EXPANSION ACTIVITIES

1. Table Talk

   Use *Side by Side* Picture Cards 163–198, your own visuals, or word cards of count and non-count food items.

   a. Write on the board:

   > A. Would you like some more _____?
   > B. Just (a little/a few), please. (It's/They're) delicious.

   b. Set the scene: "A friend is having dinner at your house."

   c. Hold up a visual or word card, and call on two students to create a conversation. For example:

(cake)
 A. Would you like some more cake?
 B. Just a little, please. It's delicious.

d. Practice this way with other food items.

2. Dictate and Discuss

a. Divide the class into pairs or small groups.

b. Dictate sentences about food and have students decide whether they agree or disagree:

> Eggs are bad for your health.
> Fish is bad for your health.
> Coffee is bad for your health.
> Butter is bad for your health.
> Salad is bad for your health.
> Orange juice is bad for your health.
> Salt is bad for your health.

c. Call on students to share their opinions with the rest of the class.

How to Say It!

Complimenting About Food: In the United States it is appropriate to compliment the cook on the food.

There are two model conversations. Introduce and practice each separately. For each model:

1. Set the scene: "Two people are eating and talking about the food."

2. Present the conversation.

3. Full-Class Repetition.

4. Ask students if they have any questions. Check understanding of new vocabulary: *excellent, fantastic*

5. Group Choral Repetition.

6. Choral Conversation.

7. Call on one or two pairs to present the dialog.

8. Have students practice conversations in which they compliment someone about the food. To inspire students' conversations, you might list the following suggestions on the board:

pizza	hamburgers
sandwich	cake
french fries	fresh lemonade
meatballs	bread

READING *Two Bags of Groceries*

FOCUS

- Count/Non-Count Nouns

NEW VOCABULARY

bag
groceries
spent (spend)
walk out

READING THE STORY

Optional: Preview the story by having students talk about the story title and/or illustration. You may choose to introduce new vocabulary beforehand, on have students encounter the new vocabulary within the context of the reading.

1. Have students read silently or follow along silently as the story is read aloud by you, by one or more students, or on the audio program.

2. Ask students if they have any questions. Check understanding of vocabulary.

3. Check students' comprehension:

   Why is Henry upset?
   What did he buy?

✓ READING *CHECK-UP*

Q & A

1. Call on a pair of students to present the model.

2. Have students work in pairs to create new dialogs.

3. Call on pairs to present their new dialogs to the class.

READING EXTENSION

Have students answer the following questions:

   Did Henry buy healthy food?
   Did Henry buy expensive food?
   Why is Henry upset?
   Do you think his groceries were expensive?
   How can Henry save money on his groceries?

How About You?

Have students do the activity in pairs or as a class. Have students compare what they bought.

 LISTENING

Listen and choose what the people are talking about.

1. A. How much do you want?
   B. Just a little, please.

2. A. Do you want some more?
   B. Okay. But just a few.

3. A. These are delicious!
   B. I'm glad you like them.

4. A. I ate too many.
   B. How many did you eat?

5. A. They're bad for my health.
   B. Really?

6. A. It's very good.
   B. Thank you.

7. A. Would you care for some more?
   B. Yes, but not too much.

8. A. There isn't any.
   B. There isn't?!

Answers

1. a   5. a
2. b   6. a
3. a   7. b
4. b   8. a

READING *Delicious! / Tastes Terrible!*

FOCUS

- Count/Non-Count Nouns

NEW VOCABULARY

Story 1
think so

Story 2
care
good for
taste
vegetable

READING THE STORIES

Optional: *Preview the stories by having students talk about the story titles and/or illustrations. You may choose to introduce new vocabulary beforehand, or have students encounter the new vocabulary within the context of the reading.*

1. Have students read silently or follow along silently as the stories are read aloud by you, by one or more students, or on the audio program.

2. Ask students if they have any questions. Check understanding of vocabulary.

3. Check students' comprehension, using some or all of the following questions:

   Story 1
   What does Lucy like?
   How do you know?
   What do her friends often tell her?
   Does Lucy think so?

   What does Fred like?
   How do you know?
   What does his doctor often tell him?
   Does Fred think so?

Story 2
Does Daniel like vegetables?
How do you know?
What do his parents often tell him?
Does Daniel care?

Does Alice like yogurt?
How do you know?
What do her children often tell her?
Does Alice care?

READING EXTENSION

Discuss the following with the class:

   Are ice cream and french fries good for your health?
   What are some delicious foods that are bad for your health?
   What foods are good for your health?
   What are some healthy foods that taste terrible?
   What are some healthy foods that taste delicious?

EXPANSION ACTIVITY

Class Survey

1. Have the class tell their favorite foods. Make a list of the foods on the board.

2. Have students write the list on a sheet of paper with columns for *yes* and *no* responses. For example:

Favorite Foods	Yes	No
chocolate ice cream spaghetti pizza		

3. Have students circulate around the room, interviewing each other and marking the responses in the *yes* or the *no* columns.

4. Have students report their findings to the class. What are the most popular foods in the class? Then have students discuss:

   Are these foods good for you, or are they bad for you?

Variation: Have students also interview friends and family members and report to the class.

Divide the class into pairs or small groups and have them discuss the questions. Then have students report back to the class.

PRONUNCIATION

> **Reduced *for*:** In daily English usage, the word *for* is usually pronounced "fr."

Focus on Listening

Practice the sentences in the left column. Say each sentence or play the audio one or more times. Have students listen carefully and repeat.

Focus on Pronunciation

Practice the sentences in the right column. Have students say each sentence and then listen carefully as you say it or play the audio.

If you wish, have students continue practicing the sentences to improve their pronunciation.

 JOURNAL

Have students write their journal entries at home or in class. Encourage students to use a dictionary to look up words they would like to use. Students can share their written work with other students if appropriate. Have students discuss what they have written as a class, in pairs, or in small groups.

 CHAPTER SUMMARY

GRAMMAR

1. Divide the class into pairs or small groups.
2. Have students take turns forming sentences from the words in the grammar boxes. Student A says a sentence, and Student B points to the words from each column that are in the sentence. Then have students switch: Student B says a sentence, and Student A points to the words.

KEY VOCABULARY

Have students ask you any questions about the meaning or pronunciation of the vocabulary. If students ask for the pronunciation, repeat after the student until the student is satisfied with his or her own pronunciation.

EXPANSION ACTIVITIES

1. **Do You Remember the Words?**

   Check students' retention of the vocabulary depicted on the opening page of Chapter 2 by doing the following activity:

   a. Have students open their books to page 11 and cover the list of vocabulary words.

   b. Either call out a number and have students tell you the word, or say a word and have students tell you the number.

   Variation: You can also do this activity as a game with competing teams.

2. **Student-Led Dictation**

   a. Tell each student to choose a word from the Key Vocabulary list on text page 18 and look at it very carefully.

   b. Have students take turns dictating their words to the class. Everybody writes down that student's word.

   c. When the dictation is completed, call on different students to write each word on the board to check the spelling.

3. **Beanbag Toss**

   a. Call out the topic: *Foods.*

   b. Have students toss a beanbag back and forth. The student to whom the beanbag is tossed must name a food item. For example:

      Student 1: cake
      Student 2: bread
      Student 3: butter

   (continued)

EXPANSION ACTIVITIES (Continued)

   c. Continue until all the words have been named.

   Variation: You can also do this activity as a game with competing teams.

4. Letter Game

   a. Divide the class into teams.

   b. Say, "I'm thinking of a food that starts with a."

   c. The first person to raise his or her hand and guess correctly [apple] wins a point for his or her team.

   d. Continue with other letters of the alphabet and food items.

   The team that gets the most correct answers wins the game.

5. Movable Categories

   a. On separate cards, write out the names of food items from the list on text page 18.

   b. Give each student a card.

   c. Call out one of the following categories:

   > foods for breakfast
   > foods for lunch
   > foods for dinner
   > foods for dessert
   > foods to drink

   d. All those students whose food items are appropriate for that category go to the right side of the room. All the other students go to the left side.

   e. Those who are in the right group call out their words for the class to verify.

   f. Continue with other categories.

1. Board Game

a. On poster boards or on manila file folders, make up game boards with a pathway consisting of separate spaces. You may use any theme or design you wish.

b. Divide the class into groups of 2 to 4 students and give each group a game board and a die, and each student something to be used as a playing piece.

c. Give each group a pile of cards face-down with food questions written on them. For example:

> Name three vegetables.
> Name three foods that are good for your health.
> Name three foods that are bad for your health.
> Name three breakfast foods.
> Name three lunch foods.
> Name three dinner foods.
> Name three dessert foods.
> What food can you make with flour, tomatoes, and cheese?
> What food can you make with flour, eggs, sugar, butter, and milk?
> What food can you make with eggs, butter, cheese or vegetables?
> What food can you make with meat, bread, ketchup, and mustard?

d. Each student in turn rolls the die, moves the playing piece along the game path, and after landing on a space, picks a card, reads the question, and answers it. If the student is correct, that student takes an additional turn.

e. The first student to reach the end of the pathway is the winner.

2. Telephone

a. Divide the class into large groups. Have each group sit in a circle.

b. Whisper a short story to one student in each group. For example:

> "Yesterday Lucy bought some groceries. She bought a few apples, a little cheese, a few bananas, a little rice, and a few oranges. She spent thirty dollars."

c. The first student whispers the story to the second student, and so forth around the circle.

d. When the story gets to the last student, that person says it aloud. Is it the same story you started with? The group with the most accurate story wins.

3. What Are They Talking About?

a. Write the two words on the board

cake
cookies

b. Say one of the following phrases in random order and ask students whether the person is talking about *cake* or *cookies*.

> How much do you want?
> How many do you want?
> There aren't any.
> There isn't any.
> It's bad for my health.
> They're bad for my health.
> Just a little.
> Just a few.
> I'm glad you like them.
> I'm glad you like it.
> They're delicious.
> It's delicious.

WORKBOOK ANSWER KEY AND LISTENING SCRIPTS

WORKBOOK PAGE 12

A. WHAT'S THE FOOD?

1. tomatoes
2. carrots
3. grapes
4. potatoes
5. ice cream
6. apples
7. lettuce
8. bread
9. cake
10. flour
11. onions
12. ketchup
13. mustard
14. eggs
15. meat
16. oranges
17. soy sauce
18. pepper
19. cheese
20. mayonnaise

WORKBOOK PAGE 13

B. WHAT ARE THEY SAYING?

1. Where's, It's
2. Where are, They're
3. Where's, It's
4. Where are, They're
5. Where are, They're
6. Where's, It's
7. Where are, They're
8. Where's, It's

C. LISTENING

Listen and choose the correct response.

1. Where's the tea?
2. Where are the oranges?
3. Where's the fish?
4. Where are the cookies?
5. Where's the cake?
6. Where's the rice?
7. Where are the pears?
8. Where's the cheese?

Answers

1. a   5. a
2. b   6. a
3. a   7. b
4. b   8. a

WORKBOOK PAGE 14

D. I'M SORRY, BUT . . .

1. there aren't any french fries
2. there isn't any tea
3. there isn't any chicken
4. there aren't any cookies
5. there isn't any cake
6. there aren't any sandwiches
7. there isn't any orange juice
8. there aren't any meatballs

WORKBOOK PAGE 15

E. THERE ISN'T/THERE AREN'T

1. isn't any mayonnaise, mustard
2. aren't any bananas, grapes
3. isn't any meat, fish
4. aren't any apples, pears
5. isn't any ice cream, yogurt
6. isn't any milk, orange juice
7. aren't any tomatoes, onions
8. aren't any potatoes, rice

F. LISTENING

Listen and put a check under the correct picture.

1. Let's have some pizza!
2. Where are the eggs?
3. Let's make some fresh orange juice!
4. Let's bake a pie!
5. Where are the potatoes?
6. Let's have a sandwich for lunch!

Answers

1. ___ ✔   2. ✔ ___   3. ✔ ___
4. ✔ ___   5. ___ ✔   6. ___ ✔

WORKBOOK PAGE 16

G. WHAT'S THE WORD?

1. How many, too many, a few
2. How much, too much, a little
3. How much, too much, a little
4. How many, too many, a few
5. How much, too much, a little
6. How many, too many, a few

H. WHAT'S THE PROBLEM?

1. too many
2. too much
3. too much
4. too many

J. WHATS THE WORD?

1. little, much
2. few, many
3. This, is, it, little
4. These, are, them, few
5. little, it's
6. them, few
7. it's, it
8. many, they're, few

K. MATCHING

1. e
2. j
3. h
4. c
5. i
6. g
7. b
8. d
9. f
10. a

L. LISTENING

Listen and put a check under the correct picture.

1. A. Would you care for some more?
   B. Yes, please. But not too much.

2. A. Do you like them?
   B. Yes, but my doctor says that too many are bad for my health.

3. A. These are wonderful!
   B. I'm glad you like them. I bought them this morning.

4. A. How much did you eat?
   B. I ate too much!

5. A. I bought it this morning, and it's very good. Would you like a little?
   B. Yes, please.

6. A. I really don't like them.
   B. But they're good for you!

7. A. How do you like them?
   B. They're wonderful.

8. A. Would you care for some more?
   B. Yes, please. But not too much.

9. A. Hmm. This is delicious. Would you care for some more?
   B. Yes, please. But just a little.

10. A. This is delicious!
    B. I'm glad you like it. I made it this morning.

Answers

1.	___	✔	2.	✔	___
3.	✔	___	4.	___	✔
5.	___	✔	6.	✔	___
7.	___	✔	8.	___	✔
9.	___	✔	10.	✔	___

GRAMMAR

COUNT / NON-COUNT NOUNS

| Lettuce Butter Milk | is | |
| Apples Carrots Onions | are | very expensive. |

| Add | a little | salt. sugar. honey. |
| | a few | potatoes. nuts. raisins. |

| I recommend our | chocolate ice cream. scrambled eggs. |

| It's They're | delicious. |

IMPERATIVES

Please **give me** a dish of ice cream.
Put a little butter into a saucepan.
Cook for 3 hours.

PARTITIVES

a bag of flour	**a dozen** eggs	**a jar of** jam	**a bowl of** chicken soup
a bottle of ketchup	**a gallon of** milk	**a loaf of** bread	**a cup of** hot chocolate
a box of cereal	**a half pound (half a pound) of** cheese	**a pint of** ice cream	**a dish of** ice cream
a bunch of bananas		**a pound of** meat	**a glass of** milk
a can of soup	**a head of** lettuce	**a quart of** orange juice	**an order of** scrambled eggs
			a piece of apple pie

FUNCTIONS

INQUIRING ABOUT WANT-DESIRE

Do we need anything from *the supermarket*?

What would you like *for dessert*?

EXPRESSING WANT-DESIRE

We need *a loaf of bread*.

I'm looking for *a head of lettuce*.

Please give me a *dish of chocolate ice cream*.
I'd like *a glass of tomato juice*.

ASKING FOR AND REPORTING INFORMATION

How much does *a head of lettuce* cost?
A dollar ninety-five.

Lettuce is very *expensive this week*.
Apples are very *expensive this week*.

There isn't any more *lettuce*.
There aren't any more *bananas*.

Everybody says *it's delicious*.

EXPRESSING SURPRISE-DISBELIEF

A DOLLAR NINETY-FIVE?! That's a lot of money!

ASKING FOR A RECOMMENDATION

What do you recommend?
What do you recommend for *breakfast*?

MAKING A RECOMMENDATION

I recommend *our chocolate ice cream*.

I recommend the *pancakes*.

INQUIRING ABOUT SATISFACTION

How is *the vegetable soup*?

EXPRESSING SATISFACTION

It's *delicious*.

INSTRUCTING

Put a little butter into a saucepan.
Chop up a few onions.

CHECKING UNDERSTANDING

A loaf of bread?
There isn't?
There aren't?

NEW VOCABULARY

Foods

baking soda
cereal
chicken soup
chocolate ice cream
fruitcake
honey
hot chocolate
jam
mushroom
nuts
raisin
scrambled eggs
soup stew
strawberry
Swiss cheese
tomato juice
vanilla ice cream
vegetable soup
vegetable stew
water
white bread
whole wheat bread

Adjectives

magnificent
out of this world
romantic
tasty

Partitives

bottle of
bowl of
box of
bunch of
can of
cup of
dish of
gallon of
glass of
half a pound of
half pound of
head of
jar of
loaf/loaves of
order of
piece of
pint of
pound of
quart of

dozen

Cooking Verbs

add
chop up
cut up
mix (in)
pour
put (into)
slice

Miscellaneous

appetite
appetizer
baked (adj)
broiled (adj)
cents
cost
decide
disappointed
get home
get there
main course
menu
mixing bowl
need
order (v)
recipe
saucepan
shopping list
sit down
suggest
table
wedding anniversary

EXPRESSIONS

Anything else?
lost *her* appetite
What would you like for *dessert*?

Text Page 19: Chapter Opening Page

VOCABULARY PREVIEW

You may want to introduce these words before beginning the chapter, or you may choose to wait until they first occur in a specific lesson. If you choose to introduce them at this point, here are some suggestions:

1. Have students look at the illustrations on text page 19 and identify the words they already know.

2. Present the vocabulary. Say each word and have the class repeat it chorally and individually. Check students' understanding and pronunciation of the words.

3. Practice the vocabulary as a class, in pairs, or in small groups. Have students cover the word list and look at the pictures. Practice the words in the following ways:

   • Say a food item and have students tell the number of the illustration.

   • Give the number of an illustration and have students say the food item.

Text Page 20: Do We Need Anything from the Supermarket?

FOCUS

- Introduction of Partitives

a bag of	*a jar of*
a bottle of	*a loaf of (two loaves of)*
a bunch of	*a pint of*
a box of	*a pound (lb.) of*
a can of	*a half pound of/half a pound of*
a gallon of	*a quart of*
a head of	*a dozen*

- Making a Shopping List

CLOSE UP

RULE:	Non-count nouns cannot be *counted*, but they may be measured. *Partitives* measure specific quantities of non-count nouns. Partitives can be counted.
EXAMPLES:	a **head** of lettuce two **heads** of lettuce a **can** of soup three **cans** of soup

RULE:	Partitives can measure by weight or size.
EXAMPLES:	a **pound** of cheese a **gallon** of milk a **quart** of orange juice a **pint** of ice cream

RULE:	Partitives can measure by describing the container.
EXAMPLES:	a **box** of cereal a **jar** of jam a **bag** of flour a **bottle** of ketchup a **can** of soup

RULE:	Partitives can measure by describing the shape.
EXAMPLES:	a **head** of lettuce a **bunch** of carrots a **loaf** of bread

RULE:	English measurements are different from the metric system.
EXAMPLES:	1 pound = 0.45 kilograms 1 quart (2 pints) = 0.95 liters 1 pint = 0.475 liters 1 gallon (4 quarts) = 3.8 liters

GETTING READY

1. Check students' understanding of what a *shopping list* is.

2. Introduce or review the partitive constructions in the shopping list on text page 20, using *Side by Side* Picture Cards 163–198, the illustrations on text page 19, or real food items you bring to class. Refer to the suggestions for presenting the vocabulary on Teacher's Guide page 000.

   ### Language Notes

   A *dozen* means a group of twelve. Like other determiners, it is used with count nouns, but it is not followed by the word *of* —for example: *a dozen eggs, a dozen apples.*

   1/2 pound may be expressed as *a half pound* or *half a pound.*

   On price labels and in advertisements, weight measurements are usually abbreviated as follows: *pt.* for *pint, qt.* for *quart, gal.* for *gallon,* and *lb.* for *pound.*

3. Practice plural forms.

   a. Model singular and plural partitives, and have students repeat. For example:

      a can of soup
      two cans of soup

      a jar of jam
      two jars of fam

   b. Give the singular form of the other items on the shopping list, and have students give the plural.

INTRODUCING THE MODEL

1. Have students look at the model illustration.

2. Set the scene: "A husband and wife are talking."

3. Present the model.

4. Full-Class Repetition.

Pronunciation Note

The pronunciation focus of Chapter 3 is *Of Before Consonants and Vowels* (text page 26). You may wish to model this pronunciation and encourage students to incorporate it into their language practice.

   a jar of jam

   a head of lettuce

   a pound of oranges

   a dish of ice cream

5. Ask students if they have any questions. Check understanding of new vocabulary: *loaf, need, anything else.*

   ### Culture Note

   Supermarket: Most people in the United States shop for food in supermarkets, where they can buy all their groceries in one store. Supermarkets typically have separate departments for foods, such as baked goods, meat, fruit, and vegetables.

6. Group Choral Repetition.

7. Choral Conversation.

8. Call on one or two pairs of students to present the dialog.

   (For additional practice, do Choral Conversation in small groups or by rows.)

SIDE BY SIDE EXERCISES

Examples

1. A. Do we need anything from the supermarket?
   B. Yes. We need a box of cereal.
   A. A box of cereal?
   B. Yes.
   A. Anything else?
   B. No. Just a box of cereal.

2. A. Do we need anything from the supermarket?
   B. Yes. We need a jar of jam.
   A. A jar of jam?
   B. Yes.
   A. Anything else?
   B. No. Just a jar of jam.

1. **Exercise 1:** Call on two students to present the dialog. Check understanding of *box, cereal*. Then do Choral Repetition and Choral Conversation practice.

2. **Exercise 2:** Check understanding of *jar, jam*. Same as above.

3. **Exercises 3–9:** Either Full-Class Practice or Pair Practice.

New Vocabulary

3. bottle	6. loaves
4. bunch	7. bag
5. can	8. quart
soup	9. gallon

4. **Exercise 10:** Have students use the model as a guide to create their own conversations, using vocabulary of their choice. (They can use any food products they wish.) Encourage students to use dictionaries to find new words they want to use. This exercise can be done orally in class or for written homework. If you assign it for homework, do one example in class to make sure students understand what's expected. Have students present their conversations in class the next day.

WORKBOOK

Pages 21–23

EXPANSION ACTIVITIES

1. Clap in Rhythm

   a. Have students sit in a circle.

   b. Establish a steady, even beat—one-two-three-four, one-two-three-four—by having students clap their hands to their laps twice and then clap their hands together twice. Repeat throughout the game, maintaining the same rhythm.

   c. The object is for each student in turn to name a food item with a partitive each time the hands are clapped together twice. Nothing is said when students clap their hands on their laps.

   Note: The beat never stops! If a student misses a beat, he or she can either wait for the next beat or pass to the next student.

2. Shopping List Chain Game

   a. Begin the game by saying:

   "We're going shopping and we need a can of soup."

   b. Call on a student to repeat what you said and add another food item to the list. For example:

   "We're going shopping and we need a can of soup and a bag of flour."

   c. Have each student take a turn in which he or she repeats what the person before said and adds a new food item to the shopping list. For example:

   "We're going shopping and we need a can of soup, a bag of flour, and a loaf of bread."

3. Bleep!

   a. Write the following vocabulary words on cards, mix up the cards, and put them face-down in a pile on a table or desk in front of the room:

can	jar	bottle	box
bag	loaf	bunch	head
pound	quart	dozen	

   b. Divide the class into pairs.

   c. Have each pair come to the front of the room, pick two cards from the pile, and create a conversation in which they use those two words.

(continued)

d. Call on the pairs to present their conversations to the class. However, instead of saying the two words when they come up in the conversations, students should say the word *bleep* instead!

e. Other students then try to guess the *bleeped* words. For example:

> A. Do we need anything from the supermarket?
> B. Yes. We need a *bleep* of flour.
> A. Do we need anything else?
> B. Yes. We also need two *bleeps* of soup.

4. Dictation Game

a. Make up a list of 6–10 food items. Write the list in large print on a piece of paper. For example:

> a loaf of bread
> a jar of jam
> a bag of flour
> a bunch of bananas
> a pint of ice cream
> a pound of cheese
> a gallon of milk
> a dozen eggs

b. Put the paper on the far side of the room or out in the hallway so that students can't read it from their seats.

c. Divide the class into pairs. One student from each pair runs to read the list and then returns to dictate the list to the partner. The runner may go back and forth as many times as necessary. The first pair to finish the list wins.

5. Partitive Match

a. Make a set of split sentence cards such as the following:

We need a bunch of . . .	bananas.

We need a bag of . . .	flour.
We need a loaf of . . .	bread.
We need a jar of . . .	jam.
We need a bottle of . . .	ketchup.
We need a quart of . . .	orange juice.
We need a dozen . . .	eggs.
We need a can of . . .	soup.
We need a box of . . .	cereal.
We need a pint of . . .	ice cream.
We need a pound of . . .	cheese.
We need a head of . . .	lettuce.

b. Distribute a card to each student.

c. Have students memorize the sentence portion on their cards, then walk around the room trying to find their corresponding match.

d. Then have pairs of students say their completed sentences aloud to the class.

6. Sense or Nonsense?

a. Divide the class into four groups.

b. Make four copies of the cards from the previous activity.

c. Mix up the cards and distribute sets of cards to each group, keeping the beginning and endings cards in different piles.

d. Have students take turns picking up one card from each pile and reading the sentence to the group. For example:

We need a bottle of . . .	bananas.

e. That group decides if the sentence makes sense or is nonsense.

f. After all the cards have been picked, have the groups lay out all the cards and put together all the sentence combinations that make sense.

7. Expanding Shopping List

a. Establish a chain game in which students add new items to a shopping list in increasing quantities. For example:

Teacher: Do we need anything from the supermarket?

Student A: Yes. We need a box of cereal. (to Student B)
Do we need anything from the supermarket?

Student B: Yes. We need a box of cereal and two quarts of milk. (to Student C)
Do we need anything from the supermarket?

Student C: Yes. We need a box of cereal, two quarts of milk, and three loaves of bread.

b. Continue the chain with other students.

Note: If your class is large, you might want to divide the class into groups of 6 to 8 students for this activity.

8. What Will I Make?

a. Set the scene:

"Tomorrow my friends are going to eat lunch at my house. Tonight I'm going to the supermarket. Here's what I'm going to buy."

b. Then dictate the following food items.

1. a head of lettuce
2. a bunch of carrots
3. three tomatoes

c. After the dictation, review the shopping list. Call out each number and have students tell you the food item.

d. Have students look at the list and guess what you're going to make for lunch (*a salad*).

e. Repeat with other shopping lists of ingredients. For example:

1. a quart of milk
2. a bag of flour
3. a dozen eggs
4. a bag of sugar
(*a cake*)

1. a pound of meat
2. a loaf of bread
3. a bag of onions
4. a bottle of ketchup
5. a jar of mustard
(*hamburgers*)

 Make a Shopping List!

Assign this activity as homework. Encourage students to use dictionaries to find new words they want to use. In class, have students compare their shopping lists.

EXPANSION ACTIVITY

What Do We Need to Buy?

1. Divide the class into four groups.

2. Have each group make a *menu* of what they would like to make for breakfast, for lunch, and for dinner.

3. Have each group give their list to another group. That group must then make a list of the foods they would need to buy at the supermarket in order to make the things on the other group's menu.

4. Have students share their *shopping lists* with the whole class.

FOCUS

- Partitives
- Asking About Prices

CLOSE UP

RULE:	Cent prices are written in two ways: with a cent sign (¢), or with a dollar sign ($) and a decimal point.
EXAMPLES:	10¢ = $0.10 75¢ = $0.75

RULE:	There are two ways of expressing prices: *formal* and *informal*.
EXAMPLES:	$1.25 = *(formal)* one dollar and twenty-five cents *(informal)* a dollar twenty-five $10.50 = *(formal)* ten dollars and fifty cents *(informal)* ten fifty

GETTING READY

1. Review numbers from 1 to 100.

   a. Count together as a class from 1 to 100.

   b. Write different numbers on the board and call on students to say the number.

2. Have students look at the box at the top of text page 21.

   a. Introduce the cent (¢) symbol and the dollar ($) symbol. Read the prices aloud and have students repeat chorally and individually.

   b. Write more prices on the board and have students repeat chorally and individually.

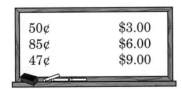

50¢	$3.00
85¢	$6.00
47¢	$9.00

c. On the board, write prices with dollars and cents. For example:

$1.75
$3.50
$2.29

Model the two different ways of saying them and have students repeat:

   one dollar and seventy-five cents
   a dollar seventy-five

   three dollars and fifty cents
   three fifty

   two dollars and twenty-nine cents
   two twenty-nine

d. Write other prices on the board and have students say each of them in two different ways.

INTRODUCING THE MODELS

There are two model conversations. Introduce and practice each separately. For each model:

1. Have students look at the model illustration.

2. Set the scene: "A customer is talking to a clerk in a supermarket."

3. Present the model.

4. Full-Class Repetition.

5. Ask students if they have any questions. Check understanding of new vocabulary: *cost, cents, You're right.*

6. Group Choral Repetition

7. Choral Conversation.

8. Call on one or two pairs of students to present the dialog.

   (For additional practice, do Choral Conversation in small groups or by rows.)

SIDE BY SIDE EXERCISES

In these exercises, students can use any prices they wish.

Examples

1. A. How much does a loaf of bread cost?
   B. Three seventy-five.
   A. Three seventy-five?! That's a lot of money!
   B. You're right. Bread is very expensive this week.

2. A. How much does a bunch of carrots cost?
   B. A dollar ten.
   A. A dollar ten?! That's a lot of money!
   B. You're right. Carrots are very expensive this week.

1. **Exercise 1:** Call on two students to present the dialog. Then do Choral Repetition and Choral Conversation practice.

2. **Exercise 2:** Same as a above.

3. **Exercises 3–7:** Either Full-Class Practice or Pair Practice.

New Vocabulary

7. Swiss cheese

---

4. **Exercise 8:** Have students use the model as a guide to create their own conversations, using vocabulary of their choice. (They can use any foods and prices they wish.) Encourage students to use dictionaries to find new words they want to use. This exercise can be done orally in class or for written homework. If you assign it for homework, do one example in class to make sure students understand what's expected. Have students present their conversations in class the next day.

WORKBOOK

Page 24

EXPANSION ACTIVITIES

1. Dictation

Dictate prices, and have students write them with a dollar sign and decimal point. For example:

Teacher: three dollars and twenty-eight cents
Students: [write] $3.28

Teacher: two forty-five
Students: [write] $2.45

Variation: Have students dictate the prices.

2. Associations

a. Divide the class into pairs or small groups.

b. Call out the name of a unit of measurement, and tell students to write down all the words they associate with that unit of measurement. For example:

a gallon of: milk, ice cream, water
a bag of: onions, potatoes, flour
a box of: cereal, cookies, rice

c. Have a student from each pair or group come to the board and write their words.

Variation: Do the activity as a game in which you divide the class into teams. The team with the most number of associations is the winner.

3. Tic Tac Grammar

a. Have students draw a tic tac grid and fill it in with any nine of the following words:

bag	head
bottle	jar
box	loaf
bunch	pound
can	quart
dozen	

b. Call out the name of a food item. If a student has written on his or her grid a container or quantity that the item you have named comes in, the student should write "of" and the name of the item in the appropriate box. For example: *butter.*

box	jar	head
loaf	bunch	quart
bottle	bag	pound *of* butter

c. The first student to write three items in a straight line—either horizontally, vertically, or diagonally—wins the game.

d. Have the winner call out the words to check for accuracy.

4. Tic Tac Partitive

a. Have students draw a tic tac grid and fill it in with any nine of the following food items:

soup	jam
ketchup	cereal
sugar	bread
carrots	lettuce
eggs	ice cream
oranges	milk

b. Make statements about food items such as the following:

A can costs eighty cents.
A bunch costs a dollar nineteen.
A pint costs two twenty-five.

c. Students should cross out a food item on their grid that comes in that container.

d. The first student to cross out three items in a straight line—either horizontally, vertically, or diagonally—wins the game.

e. Have the winner call out the words to check for accuracy.

5. Price Concentration

a. Write 12 prices in words and numbers. For example:

$1.25	one twenty-five

(continued)

$10.25	ten twenty-five
$12.25	twelve twenty-five
$120.25	one twenty twenty-five
$112.25	one twelve twenty-five
$125.25	one twenty-five twenty-five

b. Shuffle the cards and place them face-down in three rows of 4 each.

c. Divide the class into two teams. The object of the game is for students to find the matching cards. Both teams should be able to see all the cards, since *concentrating* on their location is an important part of playing the game.

d. A student from Team 1 turns over two cards. If they match, the student picks up the cards, that team gets a point, and the student takes another turn. If the cards don't match, the student turns them face-down, and a member of Team 2 takes a turn.

e. The game continues until all the cards have been matched. The team with the most matches wins the game.

Variation: This game can also be played in groups and pairs.

6. Compare the Prices

a. Cut out several supermarket advertisements from the newspaper and bring them to class.:

b. Divide the class into pairs or small groups.

c. Have students compare the prices of the same food items in different supermarkets.

7. Dialog Builder

a. Divide the class into pairs.

b. Write the following line on the board:

Ten dollars!? That's a lot of money!

c. Have each pair create a conversation incorporating that line. Students can begin and end their conversations any way they wish, but they must include that line in their dialogs.

d. Call on students to present their conversations to the class.

8. Supermarket Role Play

Bring a variety of food items to class. You can also use *Side by Side* Picture Cards for foods (163–198) or your own visuals. Have students create role plays, using the conversational model below and the food items or visuals as *props.* Students can use any prices they wish.

a. Write on the board:

A. How much does _____ cost?
B. _____.
A. _____ ?! { That's a lot of money!
                 That's a bargain! }
B. You're right.

_____ is/are very { expensive
                      cheap } this week.

b. Introduce the word *bargain.* Then call on pairs of students to role play the conversation, using visuals or real food items.

9. Guess the Prices!

a. Brainstorm with the class a short list of common foods and write students' suggestions on the board.

b. As a class, in pairs, or in small groups, have students guess how much each of these food items costs.

c. Then have students go to a supermarket and find out the actual cost of these foods.

d. Have everybody report back to the class and see how accurate the predictions were.

READING *Nothing to Eat for Dinner*

FOCUS

- Partitives
- Count/Non-Count Nouns

NEW VOCABULARY

> appetite
> disappointed
> get home
> get there
> lost (lose) her appetite
> sat (sit) down

READING THE STORY

Optional: Preview the story by having students talk about the story title and/or illustration. You may choose to introduce new vocabulary beforehand, or have students encounter the new vocabulary within the context of the reading.

1. Have students read silently or follow along silently as the story is read aloud by you, by one or more students, or on the audio program.

2. Ask students if they have any questions. Check understanding of vocabulary.

3. Check students' comprehension, using some or all of the following questions:

    Why was Joan upset when she opened her refrigerator?
    What did she need from the supermarket?
    Why was she disappointed when she got to the supermarket?
    How did Joan feel?
    What did Joan do?

✔ READING *CHECK-UP*

Q & A

1. Call on a pair of students to present each model.

2. Have students work in pairs to create new dialogs.

3. Call on pairs to present their new dialogs to the class.

READING EXTENSION

Dictate the following sentences. Have students decide whether the sentences are *true* or *false*, or *we don't know*, based on the story. Have students explain their reasoning.

> Joan lives alone.
> Joan works very hard.
> Joan has a car.
> Joan doesn't spend much time at home.
> Joan shops at the supermarket very often.
> The supermarket had a lot of food.

 ### LISTENING

Listen and choose what the people are talking about.

1. A. How much does a gallon cost?
   B. Two seventy-nine.

2. A. They're very expensive this week.
   B. You're right.

3. A. How many loaves do we need?
   B. Three.

4. A. Sorry. There aren't any more.
   B. There aren't?!

5. A. I need two pounds.
   B. Two pounds? Okay.

6. A. How much does the large box cost?
   B. Five thirty-nine.

7. A. How many cans do we need?
   B. Three.

8. A. I bought too much.
   B. Really?

Answers

1. b

2. a

3. b

4. a

5. b

6. a

7. b

8. b

Text Page 23: What Would You Like?

FOCUS

- Introduction of Partitives:

  a bowl of   *a glass of*
  a cup of   *an order of*
  a dish of   *a piece of*

- Ordering Food in a Restaurant

INTRODUCING THE MODELS

There are two model conversations. Introduce and practice each separately. For each model:

1. Have students look at the model illustration.

2. Set the scene:

    1st model: "A waiter is talking to a customer in a restaurant."
    2nd model: "A waitress is talking to a customer in a restaurant."

3. Present the model.

4. Full-Class Repetition.

5. Ask students if they have any questions. Check understanding of new vocabulary:

    1st model: *What would you like?, decide, a dish of*
    2nd model: *scrambled eggs, out of this world, an order of*

    ### Language Note

    The expression *an order of* refers to servings of food in a restaurant—for example, *an order of pancakes, an order of french fries.*

6. Group Choral Repetition.

7. Choral Conversation.

8. Call on one or two pairs of students to present the dialog.

9. Introduce the new expressions *magnificent, out of this world.* Have pairs of students practice the model again, using different expressions in place of *delicious* (1st model) and *out of this world* (2nd model).

(For additional practice, do Choral Conversation in small groups or by rows.)

SIDE BY SIDE EXERCISES

Examples

In the exercises, students can choose any adjectives for describing the food.

1. A. What would you like for lunch?
   B. I can't decide. What do you recommend?
   A. I recommend our chicken soup. Everybody says it's (delicious).
   B. Okay. Please give me a bowl of chicken soup.

2. A. What would you like for breakfast?
   B. I can't decide. What do you recommend?
   A. I recommend our pancakes. Everybody says they're (fantastic).
   B. Okay. Please give me an order of pancakes.

1. **Exercise 1:** Introduce the new expression *a bowl of chicken soup.* Call on two students to present the dialog. Then do Choral Repetition and Choral Conversation practice.

2. **Exercise 2:** Same as above.

3. **Exercises 3–7:** Either Full Class Practice or Pair Practice.

New Vocabulary

3. a piece of
4. a glass of
5. strawberries
6. a cup of
   hot chocolate
7. vanilla ice cream

4. Exercise 8: Have students use the model as a guide to create their own conversations, using vocabulary of their choice. (They can use any foods they wish.) Encourage students to use dictionaries to find new words they want to use. This exercise can be done orally in class or for written homework. If you assign it for homework, do one example in class to make sure students understand what's expected. Have students present their conversations in class the next day.

WORKBOOK

Pages 25–26

EXPANSION ACTIVITIES

1. Concentration

a. Write the following on cards:

a bowl of	cereal
a piece of	pie
a cup of	hot chocolate
a dish of	ice cream
a glass of	milk
an order of	pancakes

b. Shuffle the cards and place them face-down in three rows of 4 each.

c. Divide the class into two teams. The object of the game is for students to find the matching cards. Both teams should be able to see all the cards, since *concentrating* on their location is an important part of playing the game.

d. A student from Team 1 turns over two cards. If they match, the student picks up the cards, that team gets a point, and the student takes another turn. If the cards don't match, the student turns them face-down, and a member of Team 2 takes a turn.

e. The game continues until all the cards have been matched. The team with the most matches wins the game.

Variation: This game can also be played in groups and pairs.

2. Match the Sentences

a. Make a set of split sentence cards such as the following:

Please give me a dish of . . .	ice cream.
Please give me an order of . . .	pancakes.
Please give me a bowl of . . .	strawberries
Please give me a piece of . . .	pie.

| Please give me a glass of . . . | milk. |
| Please give me a cup of . . . | tea. |

b. Distribute a card to each student.

c. Have students memorize the sentence portion on their cards, then walk around the room trying to find their corresponding match.

d. Then have pairs of students say their completed sentences aloud to the class.

3. Sense or Nonsense?

a. Divide the class into four groups.

b. Make four copies of the cards from the previous activity.

c. Mix up the cards and distribute sets of cards to each group, keeping the beginning and endings cards in different piles.

d. Have students take turns picking up one card from each pile and reading the sentence to the group. For example:

| Please give me a glass of . . . | pancakes. |

e. That group decides if the sentence makes sense or is nonsense.

f. After all the cards have been picked, have the groups lay out all the cards and put together all the sentence combinations that make sense.

4. Telephone

a. Divide the class into large groups. Have each group sit in a circle.

b. Whisper a sentence to one student in each group. For example:

"I'd like a bowl of chicken soup, an order of pancakes, a dish of strawberries, and a cup of hot chocolate."

c. The first student whispers the sentence to the second student, and so forth around the circle. The student listening may ask for clarification by saying, "I'm sorry. Could you repeat that?"

d. When the message gets to the last student, that person says it aloud. Is it the same message you started with? The group with the most accurate message wins.

5. Restaurant Role Play

a. Write on the board:

A. What would you like $\begin{Bmatrix} \text{for} \\ \text{to} \end{Bmatrix}$ _____?

B. I don't know. What do you recommend?

A. How about a/an _____ of _____?

B. No, thank you. I don't really like _____.

A. Well, how about a/an _____ of _____?

B. Okay. That's fine.

b. Call on two students to create a conversation using word cues such as those below. Student A is the waiter or waitress. Student B is the customer.

Give the waiter/waitress a word card with appropriate cues. Sample word cards:

| breakfast
pancakes
cereal | drink
orange juice
milk | dessert
vanilla ice cream
apple pie |
| breakfast
yogurt
eggs | drink
hot chocolate
tea | dessert
chocolate cake
strawberry ice cream |

Example:

A. What would you like for breakfast?

B. I don't know. What do you recommend?

A. How about an order of pancakes?

B. No, thank you. I don't really like pancakes.

A. Well, how about a bowl of cereal?

B. Okay. That's fine.

(continued)

6. Dialog Builder!

a. Divide the class into pairs.

b. Write the following line on the board:

> I can't decide.

c. Have each pair create a conversation incorporating that line. Students can begin and end their conversations any way they wish, but they must include that line in their dialogs.

d. Call on students to present their conversations to the class.

7. Recommending Restaurants

Have students use the following conversational model to talk about favorite places to eat in their community.

a. Write on the board:

> A. Tell me, where do you like to eat?
> B. I like to eat at _____.
> A. Oh, really? What do you recommend?
> B. I recommend the _____.
>   (It's/They're) _____. How about you?
>   Where do you like to eat?
> A. I like to eat at_____. The _____
>   there (is/are) _____.

b. Have pairs of students create conversations. Encourage students to expand the dialog any way they wish. This can be done as Full-Class Practice or Pair Practice.

Example:

A. Tell me, where do you like to eat?
B. I like to eat at Stanley's Restaurant.
A. Oh, really? What do you recommend?
B. I recommend the pizza. It's excellent. How about you? Where do you like to eat?
A. I like to eat at Mr. Burger. The hamburgers there are out of this world.

8. Ranking Restaurants

a. Brainstorm with the class several good local restaurants.

b. Have students rank these restaurants from *very expensive* to *not very expensive*, with the first being *very expensive*.

c. As a class, in pairs, or in small groups, have students compare their lists.

d. Then try other rankings, such as:

> good for your health — bad for your health
> fun for a family — not fun for a family
> romantic — not romantic

How to Say It!

Making a Recommendation About Food: When recommending food, people say "I recommend/I suggest the _____." The use of the definite article *the* refers to that particular dish on the menu.

1. Set the scene: "Two friends are talking in a restaurant."

2. Present the conversation.

3. Full-Class Repetition.

4. Ask students if they have any questions. Check understanding of new vocabulary: *suggest*.

5. Group Choral Repetition.

6. Choral Conversation.

7. Call on one or two pairs to present the dialog.

8. Have pairs of students practice conversations in which they recommend foods. To inspire students' conversations, you may want to display *Side by Side* Picture Cards for foods, food products from your home, or pictures of foods. You should also encourage students to expand the conversations to include other recommendations. Have pairs present their conversations to the class.

FOCUS

- Imperatives
- Review of *a little* and *a few*
- Recipes

CLOSE UP

RULE: The *imperative* is the base form of the verb, with *you* as the understood subject. The imperative is used to give introductions.

EXAMPLES: *(You)* **Chop up** a few onions.
(You) **Add** a little salt.

GETTING READY

1. Introduce the new word *mushrooms*.
2. Practice saying *a little* or *a few* with the foods below:

mushrooms	potatoes	salt
butter	flower	tomatoes
onions	carrots	pepper

Say each word and have students form expressions with *a little* or *a few*. For example:

Teacher	Students
mushrooms	a few mushrooms
butter	a little butter

STANLEY'S FAVORITE RECIPES

1st Recipe

1. Have students follow along in the book as you read the introduction to the recipe at the top of the page.

2. Ask students if they have any questions. Check understanding of new vocabulary: *recipe, vegetable stew.*

3. **Step 1:** Introduce the new words *put (into), saucepan.* Read the sentence and have students repeat.

4. **Step 2:** Introduce the new expression *chop up.* Same as above.

5. **Steps 3–10:**

New Vocabulary
3. cut up
4. pour in, water
5. slice
6. add

For each:

a. Introduce any new words.

b. Call on a student to say the sentence, filling in either *a little* or *a few*.

Answer Key for 3–9:

3. Cut up a few potatoes.
4. Pour in a little water.
5. Slice a few carrots.
6. Add a little salt.
7. Chop up a few mushrooms.
8. Slice a few tomatoes.
9. Add a little pepper.

2nd Recipe

1. Have students follow along in the book as you read the introduction to the recipe.

2. Check understanding of the word *fruitcake*.

3. **Steps 1 and 2:** Introduce the new expression *mixing bowl*. Then read each sentence and have students repeat.

4. **Steps 3–10:**

New Vocabulary

5. honey
6. baking soda
7. nuts
9. mix in
   raisins

For each:

a. Introduce any new words.

b. Call on a student to say the sentence, filling in either *a little* or *a few*.

Answer Key for 3–9:

3. Slice a few apples.
4. Cut up a few oranges.
5. Pour in a little honey.
6. Add a little baking soda.
7. Chop up a few nuts.
8. Add a little salt.
9. Mix in a few raisins.

WORKBOOK

Page 27

EXPANSION ACTIVITIES

1. True or False?

   a. Have students open their books to text page 24.

   b. Make statements about the recipes and have students tell you *True* or *False*. If the statement is false, have students correct it. For example:

   Recipe 1

   Teacher: Cut up a few potatoes.
   Student: True.

   Teacher: Slice a few onions.
   Student: False. Slice a few tomatoes.

Variation: You can call on students to make true or false statements about the recipe, and have other students respond.

2. Miming

   a. Write down on cards the following verbs from Stanley's recipes:

chop	cut up
slice	add
pour	put
mix in	cook

(continued)

b. Have students take turns picking a card from the pile and pantomiming the action on the card.

c. The class must guess what the person is doing.

Variation: This can be done as a game with competing teams.

3. Let's Make a Recipe!

a. Have students sit in a circle.

b. Distribute to the class *Side by Side* Picture Cards 163–198 or your own visuals of food items.

c. Begin by saying: "Put a little butter into a saucepan."

d. Student 1 repeats what you said and adds the item in the visual. For example:

> Student 1: *[holding a visual of onions]* Put a little butter into a saucepan. Chop up a few onions.
>
> Student 2: *[holding a visual of carrots]* Put a little butter into a saucepan. Chop up a few onions. Slice a few carrots.

e. Continue around the room in this fashion, with each student repeating what the previous one said and adding another sentence. To help their classmates remember the long recipe, students may pantomime their cooking action as well as hold up the visual.

f. You can do the activity again, beginning and ending with different students.

If the class is large, you may want to divide students into groups to give students more practice.

4. Two-Way Dictation

a. Make up a short recipe. Divide the information on two recipe cards. For example:

Card A:

> **Stanley's Special Apple Dessert**
>
> 1. Slice 8 apples.
> 2. _____ .
> 3. Chop up some butter in a mixing bowl.
> 4. _____ .
> 5. Put the flour and the butter on top of the apples and the sugar.
> 6. _____ .

Card B:

> **Stanley's Special Apple Dessert**
>
> 1. _____ .
> 2. Mix in some sugar.
> 3. _____ .
> 4. Add some flour to the butter.
> 5. _____ .
> 6. Bake for 45 minutes.

b. Divide the class into pairs. Give each member of the pair a different recipe card. Have students dictate their lines to each other to complete the recipe.

c. Have students look at their partner's recipe card to make sure that they have written the information correctly.

5. Telephone

a. Divide the class into large groups. Have each group sit in a circle.

b. Whisper the following recipe instructions to one student in each group:

> "Slice a few apples, add a little sugar, chop up a few nuts, add a little salt, pour in a little honey, and mix in a few raisins."

c. The first student whispers the instructions to the second student, and so forth around the circle. The student listening may ask for clarification by repeating the phrases: "Slice a few apples?"

d. When the recipe gets to the last student, that person says it aloud. Is it the same recipe you started with? The group with the most accurate recipe wins.

6. **What Is It?**

Have students use word cues to present recipes to the class. Other students must then guess what the recipe is for.

a. Write the ingredients for recipes on word cards. Put the name of the recipe in parentheses at the bottom of each card. For example:

a quart/cold water lemon juice sugar (lemonade)	5 eggs pepper milk butter salt cheese (omelet)
lettuce tomatoes carrots (salad)	hot milk chocolate sugar (hot chocolate)

butter milk flour salt eggs chocolate baking sugar powder (chocolate cake)	butter salt onions mushrooms water tomatoes carrots pepper (vegetable stew)

b. Give the cards to students and have them present the recipes, using vocabulary on text page 24. For example:

Student 1: Pour in a quart of cold water. Add a little lemon juice. Mix in a little sugar. What is it?

Student 2: Lemonade.

Student 3: Put five eggs in a bowl. Add a little milk. Add a little salt and pepper. Cook it in a little butter for five minutes. Put a little cheese on it. What is it?

Student 4: An omelet.

 Project

1. For homework, have students write their favorite recipes, using the models on text page 24 as a guide. Encourage students to use dictionaries if necessary.

2. Have students present their recipes in class the next day. Students should write any new words on the board and introduce them to the class.

READING *At the Continental Restaurant*

FOCUS

- Partitives
- Count/Non-Count Nouns

NEW VOCABULARY

appetizer
baked chicken
broiled fish
date
main course
menu
order (v)
romantic
tasty
tomato juice
vegetable soup
wedding anniversary

READING THE STORY

Optional: *Preview the story by having students talk about the story title and/or illustration. You may choose to introduce new vocabulary beforehand, or have students encounter the new vocabulary within the context of the reading.*

1. Have students read silently or follow along silently as the story is read aloud by you, by one or more students, or on the audio program.

2. Ask students if they have any questions. Check understanding of vocabulary.

3. Check students' comprehension, using some or all of the following questions:

   Where did Sherman and Dorothy Johnson go for dinner?
   Why?
   Where did they sit?
   What did they order?
   How was the food?

READING EXTENSION

Dictate the following sentences. Have students decide whether the sentences are true or false, then explain the reasoning for their answers.

1. The Johnsons are married.

2. The Continental Restaurant is new.

3. The Johnsons like noisy and crowded restaurants.

4. The Johnsons were not hungry.

5. The Continental Restaurant is a good restaurant.

6. The Johnsons go to the Continental Restaurant every year on their anniversary.

 ROLE PLAY

1. Divide the class into groups of three.

2. Have each group use the conversational frameworks on text page 25 to create a conversations between Sherman and Dorothy Johnson and their waiter or waitress.

3. Call on different groups to present their role plays to the class.

PRONUNCIATION

> ***Of* Before Consonant and Vowels:** In informal English, the /v/ in the word *of* is dropped before words beginning with a consonant. The final /v/ sound is pronounced when the following word begins with a vowel. For example:
>
>   a bowl of soup
>
>   a pound of oranges

Focus on Listening

Practice the sentences in the left column. Say each sentence or play the audio one or more times. Have students listen carefully and repeat.

Focus on Pronunciation

Practice the sentences in the right column. Have students say each sentence and then listen carefully as you say it or play the audio.

If you wish, have students continue practicing the sentences to improve their pronunciation.

 ## JOURNAL

Have students write their journal entries at home or in class. Encourage students to use a dictionary to look up words they would like to use. Students can share their written work with other students if appropriate. Have students discuss what they have written as a class, in pairs, or in small groups.

WORKBOOK

Check-Up Test: Pages 28–29

CHAPTER SUMMARY

GRAMMAR

1. Divide the class into pairs or small groups.
2. Have students take turns forming sentences from the words in the grammar boxes. Student A says a sentence, and Student B points to the words from each column that are in the sentence. Then have students switch: Student B says a sentence, and Student A points to the words.

KEY VOCABULARY

Have students ask you any questions about the meaning or pronunciation of the vocabulary. If students ask for the pronunciation, repeat after the student until the student is satisfied with his or her own pronunciation.

EXPANSION ACTIVITIES

1. Do You Remember the Words?

   Check students' retention of the vocabulary depicted on the opening page of Chapter 3 by doing the following activity:

   a. Have students open their books to page 19 and cover the list of vocabulary words.

   b. Either call out a number and have students tell you the food item, or say a food item and have students tell you the number.

   Variation: You can also do this activity as a game with competing teams.

2. Student-Led Dictation

   a. Tell each student to choose a word or phrase from the Key Vocabulary list on text page 26 and look at it very carefully.

   b. Have students take turns dictating their words to the class. Everybody writes down that student's word. *(continued)*

EXPANSION ACTIVITIES (Continued)

c. When the dictation is completed, call on different students to write each word on the board to check the spelling.

3. Beanbag Toss

a. Call out a topic—for example: *Describing Food.*

b. Have students toss a beanbag back and forth. The student to whom the beanbag is tossed must name a word in that category. For example:

    Student 1:   fantastic
    Student 2:   delicious
    Student 3:   out of this world

c. Continue until all of the words in the category have been named.

Variation: You can also do this activity as a game with competing teams.

4. Letter Game

a. Divide the class into teams.

b. Say: "I'm thinking of a food that starts with *h.*"

c. The first person to raise his or her hand and guess correctly *[honey]* wins a point for his or her team.

d. Continue with other letters of the alphabet and food items.

The team that gets the most correct answers wins the game.

5. Movable Categories

a. Write out the names of food items from the list on page 26 on separate cards.

b. Give each student a card.

c. Call out one of the following categories:

    foods you can slice
    foods you can chop up
    foods you can cook
    foods you can bake
    food you can pour

d. All those students whose food items are appropriate for that category go to the right side of the room. All the other students go to the left side.

e. Those who are in the right group call out their words for the class to verify.

f. Continue with other categories.

6. Category Dictation

a. Have students draw three columns on a piece of paper. Tell them to write <u>a cup of</u> at the top of the left column, <u>an order of</u> at the top of the middle column, and <u>a piece of</u> at the top of the right column.

b. Dictate various food items from the text. Have students write them in the appropriate column. For example:

<u>a cup of</u>	<u>an order of</u>	<u>a piece of</u>
hot chocolate	pancakes	pie
milk		pizza

c. At the end of the dictation, have students compare their lists.

END-OF-CHAPTER ACTIVITIES

1. Board Game

a. On poster boards or on manila file folders, make up game boards with a pathway consisting of separate spaces. You may use any theme or design you wish.

b. Divide the class into groups of two to four students. Give each group a game board, a die, and each student something to be used as a playing piece.

c. Give each group a pile of cards face-down with sentences written on them. Some sentences should be correct, and others incorrect. For example:

> Cut up a few oranges.
> Slice a little water.
> Chop up a few meat.
> Please give me an order of french fries.
> We need a bottle of jam.
> We need a gallon of flour.
> We need a box of cereal.
> I'm looking for a lettuce.
> There aren't any more cake.
> Add a little eggs.
> We need a bunch bananas.
> Please give me a piece of pancakes.

d. Each student in turn rolls the die, moves the playing piece along the game path, and after landing on a space, picks a card, reads the sentence, and says if it is *correct* or *incorrect*. If the sentence is incorrect and the student is able to give the correct version, that student takes an additional turn.

e. The first student to reach the end of the pathway is the winner.

2. Associations

a. Divide the class into pairs or small groups.

b. Call out cooking verbs and tell students to write down all the foods they associate with that verb. For example:

> slice: tomatoes, carrots, bananas
> cook: stew, soup, scrambled eggs
> bake: cookies, bread, cake, chicken

c. Have a student from each pair or group come to the board and write their words.

Variation: You can do the activity as a game in which you divide the class into teams. The team with the most number of associations is the winner.

3. Sense or Nonsense?

a. Make a set of split sentence cards such as the following:

Slice a few . . .	carrots.
Cook the stew . . .	in a saucepan.
Add a little . . .	salt.
Pour in a little . . .	water.
Bake the . . .	cake.
Chop up a little . . .	meat.
Mix in a few . . .	nuts.

b. Place the cards in two piles—one pile of verb phrases and the other of objects.

c. Have students take turns picking one card from each pile and reading the two phrases to the group. For example:

Mix in a few . . .	meat.

d. The group decides if the sentence makes *sense* or is *nonsense*.

e. After all the cards have been picked, have the group lay out all the cards and put together phrase combinations that *make sense*.

(continued)

END-OF-CHAPTER ACTIVITIES (Continued)

4. Dialog Builder!

a. Divide the class into pairs.

b. On the board, write a line from a conversation in Chapter 3, such as the following:

I'm glad you like them.

Other possible lines are:

I'm glad you like it.
What would you like?
There aren't any.
There isn't any.
Anything else?
That's a lot of money!

c. Have each pair create a conversation incorporating that line. Students can begin and end their conversations any way they wish, but they must include that line in their dialogs.

d. Call on students to present their conversations to the class.

WORKBOOK PAGE 21

A. SHOPPING LISTS

1. can of, head of, bottle of, pound of, bag of
2. box of, jar of, loaf of, bunch of, dozen
3. gallons of, boxes of, bunches of, pounds of, loaves of

WORKBOOK PAGE 22

B. WHAT ARE THEY SAYING?

1. jam
2. ice cream
3. bananas
4. cookies
5. onions
6. cheese

C. LISTENING

Listen to the conversations. Put a check under the foods you hear.

1. A. Do we need anything from the supermarket?
   B. Yes. We need a pound of apples, a bunch of bananas, and a head of lettuce.

2. A. What do we need at the supermarket?
   B. We need a pound of cheese, a box of rice, and a bottle of soda.

3. A. Do we need anything from the supermarket?
   B. Yes. We need a loaf of bread, a pound of onions, and a dozen oranges.

4. A. What do we need at the supermarket?
   B. We need a pound of potatoes, a pint of ice cream, and a jar of mustard.

Answers

1. ✔ __ ✔ __ ✔
2. __ ✔ ✔ ✔ __
3. ✔ __ ✔ __ ✔
4. __ ✔ ✔ __ ✔

WORKBOOK PAGE 24

E. SHOPPING FOR FOOD

1. much, quart, cost
   quart, milk costs
   money
   right, is
2. much, loaf of
   loaf, bread costs
   loaves
   loaves, of
   bread is

3. much does, pound
   pound of, costs
   much
   are
   are

F. LISTENING

Listen and circle the price you hear.

1. A box of cereal costs a dollar ninety-nine.
2. Two cans cost five dollars.
3. Three jars cost four dollars and seventy-nine cents.
4. It costs twenty-five cents.
5. A bottle costs two forty-seven.
6. Two boxes cost six dollars and sixty cents.
7. Three thirteen?! That's a lot of money!
8. A pound costs a dollar fifty.
9. Two dollars and ten cents?! That's cheap!

Answers

1. $1.99	4. 25¢	7. $3.13
2. $5	5. $2.47	8. $1.50
3. $4.79	6. $6.60	9. $2.10

WORKBOOK PAGE 25

G. WHAT'S THE WORD?

1. b
2. a
3. b
4. a
5. a
6. b

H. WHERE WOULD YOU LIKE TO GO FOR LUNCH?

1. is
2. it
3. order
4. of
5. is
6. glass
7. are
8. they
9. order
10. of
11. are
12. is
13. much
14. many
15. piece
16. of
17. bowl
18. of
19. dish
20. of
21. is
22. cup
23. of

WORKBOOK PAGE 27

K. WHAT'S THE WORD?

1. carrots
2. oranges
3. nuts
4. water
5. apples
6. bowl
7. Mix in
8. Cook

L. WHAT'S THE RECIPE?

1. a little
2. a few
3. a few, a little
4. a few
5. a little, a little
6. a few

M. LISTENING

Listen and circle the correct to complete the sentences.

1. Add a little . . .
2. Chop up a few . . .
3. Cut up a few . . .
4. Pour in a little . . .
5. Slice a few . . .
6. Mix in a little . . .

Answers

1. b	4. a
2. b	5. b
3. a	6. a

WORKBOOK PAGES 28–29

CHECK-UP TEST: Chapters 1-3

A.

1. bunch
2. can
3. bag
4. piece
5. boxes
6. loaves

B.

1. many
2. much
3. like to
4. much
5. few, them, they're
6. This, is, little

C.

1. drove, He's going to drive
2. went, I'm going to go
3. played, We're going to play
4. wrote, She's going to write
5. made, He's going to make

D.

1. he's going to give her
2. she's going to give him
3. we're going to give them

E.

Listen and circle the correct word.

Ex. I want some lemons.
1. I'd like some ice cream.
2. I need some tomatoes.
3. I'm looking for lettuce.
4. May I have some meatballs?
5. I want some whole wheat bread.

Answers

1. isn't
2. aren't
3. isn't
4. aren't
5. isn't

FEATURE ARTICLE
Food Shopping

PREVIEWING THE ARTICLE

1. Have students talk about the title of the article and the accompanying photographs.

2. You may choose to introduce the following new vocabulary beforehand, or have students encounter it within the context of the article:

> items
> open market
> past
> wholesale store

READING THE ARTICLE

1. Have students read silently or follow along silently as the article is read aloud by you, by one or more students, or on the audio program.

2. Ask students if they have any questions. Check understanding of new vocabulary.

3. Check students' comprehension. Have students read the text again and take notes on the differences between people's shopping habits in the past and today. For example:

In the Past	Today
There weren't any refrigerators.	People have refrigerators.
People shopped every day.	People shop once or twice a week.
People shopped at small food stores and at open markets.	People shop in small grocery stores, large supermarkets, wholesale stores, and on the Internet.

 FACT FILE
One Day's Food

1. Before reading the Fact File, ask students: "How many eggs do you think are produced every day? How many chocolate bars are made every day? How much rice is made every day?" Write students' ideas on the board.

2. Introduce the new vocabulary: *hens, produce (v), billion, enough, island, size, Cyprus, ton, cocoa beans, chocolate bars, amount, pyramid.* Have students read the Fact File and then check to see how accurate their predictions were.

Language Notes

A *billion* is the number 1,000,000,000.
A *ton* is 2,240 pounds.

 BUILD YOUR VOCABULARY!
Ordering Fast Food

hamburger	slice of pizza
hot dog	donut
sandwich	bagel
taco	muffin
bowl of chili	

1. Introduce the phrase *I'd like*. Explain that this expression is used in polite requests. Have the class repeat it chorally and individually.

2. Have students look at the illustrations of fast-food items and identify any words they already know.

Culture Note

These foods are extremely common in the United States, especially in *fast-food* restaurants, where food is prepared beforehand and served quickly.

3. Present the vocabulary. Say each word and have the class repeat it chorally and individually. Check students' understanding and pronunciation of the words.

4. To give students more practice with the words, you may wish to do the following:

a. Write this conversation on the board:

> A. May I help you?
>
> B. Yes. I'd like_____, please.

b. Have pairs of students practice the fast-food items, using the conversational model on the board.

c. Call on pairs to present their conversations to the class.

EXPANSION ACTIVITIES

1. Clap in Rhythm

Object: Once a clapping rhythm is established, students must continue naming different fast foods.

a. Have students sit in a circle.

b. Establish a steady even beat—one-two-three-four, one-two-three-four—by having students clap their hands to their laps twice and then clap their hands together twice. Repeat throughout the game, maintaining the same rhythm.

c. The object is for each student in turn to name a fast-food item each time the hands are clapped together twice. Nothing is said when students clap their hands on their laps.

Note: The beat never stops! If a student misses a beat, he or she can either wait for the next beat or pass to the next student.

2. Drawing Game

a. Write down on two sets of cards the food vocabulary items on text page 27.

b. Divide the class into two teams. Have each team sit together in a different part of the room.

c. Place each set of cards on a table or desk in front of the room. Also place a pad of paper and pencil next to each team's set of cards.

d. When you say "Go!", a person from each team comes to the table, picks a card from that team's pile, draws the item on the card, and shows the drawing to the rest of the team. The team then guesses what the word is.

e. When a team correctly guesses a word, another team member picks a card and draws the word written on that card.

f. Continue until each team has guessed all the words in their pile.

g. The team that guesses the words in the shortest time wins the game.

3. Category Dictation

a. Have students draw two columns on a piece of paper. At the top of one column, have students write <u>Breakfast</u>, and at the top of the other column have them write <u>Lunch</u>.

b. Dictate various food items from the text, and have students write them in the appropriate column. For example:

<u>Breakfast</u>	<u>Lunch</u>
muffin	sandwich
bagel	pizza
	hamburger

c. At the end of the dictation, have students compare their lists.

 AROUND THE WORLD
Where People Shop for Food

1. Have students read silently or follow along silently as the text is read aloud by you, by one or more students, or on the audio program.

2. Have students first work in pairs or small groups to respond to the questions. Then have students tell the class what they talked about. Write any new vocabulary on the board.

EXPANSION ACTIVITIES

1. Ranking

a. Have students brainstorm all the ways to shop for food. Write their ideas on the board.

b. Have students rank these ways to shop from *expensive* to *cheap*, with the first being the *most expensive*. For example:

1. small grocery store
2. Internet
3. supermarket
4. open market
5. wholesale food store

c. As a class, in pairs, or in small groups, have students compare their lists.

d. Then have students rank the items from *easy* to *difficult*, from *takes a little time* to *takes a long time*, and from *fun* to *not fun*.

2. Survey on Food Shopping Habits

a. Have students find out how their classmates shop for food. Have students conduct their surveys by circulating around the room, asking each other.

b. For homework, have students draw up the survey results in graph form (such as a bar graph or pie chart.) In class, have students share their graphs and report their results.

Variation: Instead of interviewing fellow classmates, have students interview friends, family members, or students in another English class.

3. Advantages and Disadvantages

a. Have students draw two columns on a piece of paper. At the top of one column, have students write <u>Good</u>. At the top of the other column, have them write <u>Bad</u>.

b. Say one of the ways to buy food, and have students brainstorm ways in which it is good and ways in which it is bad. Write their ideas in columns on the board and have students copy on their papers. For example:

Open Markets

<u>Good</u>	<u>Bad</u>
The food is fresh.	It's slow.
It's fun.	It can be expensive.

c. For homework, have students write a paragraph about where they like to buy food and why.

 GLOBAL EXCHANGE

1. Set the scene: "Two keypals, Glen25 and MariaV, are writing to each other."

2. Have students read silently or follow along silently as the message is read aloud by you, by one or more students, or on the audio program.

3. Ask students if they have any questions. Check understanding of new vocabulary: *middle, roll, snack, light, supper.*

4. Suggestions for additional practice:

- Have students write a response to Glen25 and share their writing in pairs.

- Have students correspond with a keypal on the Internet and then share their experience with the class.

 LISTENING *Attention, Food Shoppers!*

1. Set the scene: "You're listening to announcements on special food prices in different supermarkets."

2. Introduce new vocabulary: *on sale, price, section, special* (n), *flavor.*

Listen and match the products and the prices.

Attention, food shoppers! Thank you for shopping at Save-Rite Supermarket! Crispy Cereal is on sale this week. A box of Crispy Cereal is only three dollars and forty-nine cents. Three forty-nine is a very good price for Crispy Cereal. So buy some today!

Attention, shoppers! Right now in the bakery section, whole wheat bread is on sale. Buy a loaf of whole wheat bread for only two seventy-five. That's right! Just two seventy-five! The bread is hot and fresh. So come to the bakery section and get a loaf now!

Thank you for shopping at Sunny Supermarket! We have a special low price on orange juice today. A quart of orange juice is only a dollar seventy-nine. Orange juice is in Aisle 5, next to the milk.

Hello, food shoppers! It's 95 degrees today. It's a good day for Sorelli's Ice Cream! Sorelli's Ice Cream comes in vanilla, chocolate, and other delicious flavors. And today, a pint of Sorelli's Ice Cream is only three twenty-five!

Welcome to Bartley's Supermarket! We have a special today on bananas. You can buy bananas for only forty cents a pound. Bananas are good for you! So walk over to our fruit section and buy a bunch of bananas today!

Answers

1. d
2. a
3. e
4. c
5. b

WHAT ARE THEY SAYING?

FOCUS

- Ordering Fast Food

Have students talk about the people and the situation, and then create role plays based on the scene. Students may refer back to previous lessons as a resource, but they should not simply reuse specific conversations.

Note: You may want to assign this exercise as written homework, having students prepare their role plays, practice them the next day with other students, and then present them to the class.

Teacher's Notes

GRAMMAR

FUTURE TENSE: WILL

(I will)	I'll	
(He will)	He'll	
(She will)	She'll	
(It will)	It'll	work.
(We will)	We'll	
(You will)	You'll	
(They will)	They'll	

I	
He	
She	
It	won't work.
We	
You	
They	

Will	I he she it we you they	arrive soon?

Yes,	I he she it we you they	will.

No,	I he she it we you they	won't.

TIME EXPRESSIONS

The train will arrive	in	a few	days. minutes. hours. weeks. months.
		a week. an hour. half an hour. a little while. two or three days.	
	at seven o'clock.		

MIGHT

I He She It We You They	might clean it today.

FUNCTIONS

ASKING FOR AND REPORTING INFORMATION

Will *the train arrive* soon?
  Yes, *it* will. *It'll arrive in five minutes.*

INQUIRING ABOUT PROBABILITY

Do you think *it'll rain tomorrow?*

EXPRESSING PROBABILITY

Maybe *it* will, and maybe *it* won't.

EXPRESSING POSSIBILITY

I might *clean it today.*
You might *hurt your head.*

INQUIRING ABOUT INTENTION

When are you going to *clean your apartment?*

WARNING

Careful!
You might *hurt your head.*

I'm sorry. { What did you say?
Could you please repeat that?
Could you say that again?

EXPRESSING GRATITUDE

Thanks for *the warning*.

EXTENDING AN INVITATION

Would you like to *go swimming* with me?

ACCEPTING AN INVITATION

Okay. I'll *go swimming* with you.

DECLINING AN INVITATION

No, I don't think so.

NEW VOCABULARY

Health

catch a cold
flu
get seasick
get sick
measles
nauseous
pregnant
spots
sunburn

Body Parts

arm
feet
leg

Inquiries

break
drown
fall
get a shock
get hit
get hurt

Safety

helmet
safety glasses
warning

Simple Future Tense

will
won't

Modals of Possibility

might
might not

Beginnings and Endings

arrive
be back
begin
end
get home
return

Life Events

get married
grow up
move
name

Time Expressions

at *7:00*
half an hour
in a few hours
in a few minutes
in a little while
in an hour
in a week
in half an hour
in two or three days
some day

Miscellaneous

absolutely
all over
any more
bloom
come
company picnic
either
fall asleep
get out of
go for a walk
go outside

go sailing
go to work
grass
guest
idea
indoors
instead
machine
maybe
outdoors
puppy
ready
snow (n)
stay
step (v)
storm
take a walk
test
tired of
touch
winter coat
wires
you two

EXPRESSIONS

Careful!
Do you think . . . ?
Don't worry!
I can't wait
I'm positive!
Just think
sick and tired of
take chances
Thanks for *the warning*.
Watch your step!
We'll just have to wait and see.
What did you say?
Would you like to go swimming
    with me?

Text Page 29: Chapter Opening Page

VOCABULARY PREVIEW

You may want to present these words before beginning the chapter, or you may choose to wait until they first occur in a specific lesson. If you choose to present them at this point, here are some suggestions:

1. Have students look at the illustrations on text page 29 and identify the words they already know.

2. Present the vocabulary. Say each word and have the class repeat it chorally and individually. Check students' understanding and pronunciation of the words.

3. Practice the vocabulary as a class, in pairs, or in small groups. Have students cover the word list and look at the pictures. Practice the words in the following ways:

   - Say a word and have students tell the number of the illustration.
   - Give the number of an illustration and have students say the word.

Text Page 30: Will the Train Arrive Soon?

FOCUS

- Future Tense: *Will*
- Time Expressions:

  in a few minutes/hours
  in a week/in an hour/in half an hour/in a little while
  in five minutes/in two or three days
  at 7:00

CLOSE UP

RULE:	The simple future tense is used to make predictions for the future.
EXAMPLE:	**Will** the guests **be** here soon? 　　Yes, they **will**. They**'ll be** here in half an hour.

RULE:	The simple future tense is formed with *will* + the base form of the verb. In affirmative statements the auxiliary verb (also called the *helping verb*) contracts with subject pronouns.
EXAMPLES:	I **will arrive.**　　**I'll arrive.** He **will arrive.**　　He**'ll arrive.** She **will arrive.**　　She**'ll arrive.** It **will arrive.**　　It**'ll arrive.** We **will arrive.**　　We**'ll arrive.**

RULE:	*Will* does not contract with subject pronouns in short answers.
EXAMPLES:	Will you be ready soon? 　　Yes, **I will.** 　　(**I'll** be ready in a few minutes.) Will the storm end soon? 　　Yes, **it will.** 　　(**It'll** end in a few hours.)

GETTING READY

1. Introduce *will* by forming a few sentences with *will* that describe a regular, predictable event. For example:

   Every day school ends at 3:00.
   Tomorrow school will end at 3:00.

   Every day our class begins at 9:00.
   Tomorrow our class will begin at 9:00.

2. Practice the forms of *will* in the box at the top of text page 30.

   a. Form sentences with both the full forms and the contracted forms. Have students repeat. For example:

      I will work.
      I'll work.

      He will work.
      He'll work.

b. Read the following sentences with the full forms of *will*, and have students give the contracted forms:

Teacher	Students
I will arrive.	I'll arrive.
He will be home.	He'll be home.
She will work.	She'll work.
It will rain.	It'll rain.
We will eat.	We'll eat.
You will get up.	You'll get up.
They will arrive.	They'll arrive.

c. Practice short answers with *will*.

1.) Read the question and answer in the right-hand box at the top of the page, and have students repeat chorally:

> Teacher: Will he work?
> Students: Yes, he will.

2.) Replace with other pronouns in the question form, and have students respond with the appropriate short answer. For example:

> Teacher: Will she work?
> Students: Yes, she will.

> Teacher: Will it work?
> Students: Yes, it will.

INTRODUCING THE MODEL

1. Have students look at the model illustration.

2. Set the scene: "At the train station, a woman is asking for information about the train."

3. Present the model.

4. Full-Class Repetition.

5. Ask students if they have any questions. Check understanding of the time expression *in five minutes*.

6. Group Choral Repetition.

7. Choral Conversation.

8. Call on one or two pairs of students to present the dialog.

(For additional practice, do Choral Conversation in small groups or by rows.)

SIDE BY SIDE EXERCISES

Examples

> 1. A. Will the game begin soon?
>   B. Yes, it will. It'll begin at 7:00.
>
> 2. A. Will Ms. Lopez return soon?
>   B. Yes, she will. She'll return in an hour.

1. **Exercise 1:** Call on two students to present the dialog. Then do Choral Repetition and Choral Conversation practice.

2. **Exercise 2:** Introduce the new expressions: *return, in an hour*. Same as above.

3. **Exercises 3–8:** Either Full-Class Practice or Pair Practice.

New Vocabulary

3. ready
   in a few minutes
4. guests
   in half an hour
5. get home
   in a little while
6. be back
   in a week
7. storm
   end
   in a few hours
8. get out of
   in two or three days

Language Note

In a little while indicates a short but unknown length of time.

WORKBOOK

Page 30

EXPANSION ACTIVITIES

1. Can You Hear the Difference?

a. Write on the board:

A	B
I will return soon.	I'll return soon.
He will return soon.	He'll return soon.
She will return soon.	She'll return soon.
It will return soon.	It'll return soon.
We will return soon.	We'll return soon.
You will return soon.	You'll return soon.
They will return soon.	They'll return soon.

b. Choose a sentence randomly from one of the two columns and say it to the class. Have the class listen and say whether it's from Column A or Column B.

c. Have students continue the activity in pairs. One student pronounces a sentence, and the other identifies its column. Then have them reverse roles.

d. Write other similar sentences on the board and continue the practice.

2. Match the Conversations

a. Make a set of matching cards. For example:

Will the game begin soon?	Yes, it will. It'll begin in fifteen minutes.
Will the bus arrive soon?	Yes, it will. It'll arrive in half an hour.
Will Bob return soon?	Yes, he will. He'll return in a few minutes.
Will your brother be ready soon?	Yes, he will. He'll be ready in five or ten minutes.
Will your sister get home soon?	Yes, she will. She'll get home in an hour.

Will Susan be back soon?	Yes, she will. She'll be back in a few minutes.
Will the guests be here soon?	Yes, they will. They'll be here in a little while.
Will the employees get out of work soon?	Yes, they will. They'll get out in ten minutes.

b. Distribute a card to each student.

c. Have students memorize the sentences on their cards, and then have students walk around the room saying their sentences until they find their match.

d. Then have pairs of students say their matched sentences aloud to the class.

3. Ranking

a. Dictate the following time expressions to the class:

    in five minutes
    in an hour
    in a few minutes
    in half an hour
    in a week
    in a few hours
    in two or three days

b. Have students order these time expressions from *soon* to *later*, with the first being the soonest.

c. Have students compare their lists as a class, in pairs, or in small groups.

4. Telephone

a. Divide the class into large groups. Have each group sit in a circle.

b. Whisper a short prediction about the coming year to one student. For example:

"Next year the weather will be beautiful. It'll be warm in the winter and cool in the summer. It'll rain a little in the spring, but it'll be sunny every day in the summer."

(continued)

c. The first student whispers the prediction to the second student, and so forth around the circle.

d. When the prediction gets to the last student, that person says it aloud. Is it the same prediction you started with? The group with the most accurate message wins.

5. Role Play: A Business Call

a. Put the following conversational framework on the board:

> A. Hello. Can I speak to _____, please?
> B. I'm sorry. _____ isn't here right now.
> A. I see. When will ____ be back?
> B. ____ 'll be back in_____.
> A. In _____?
> B. Yes. That's right.
> A. Okay. I'll call back then. Thank you.
> B. You're welcome. Good-bye.

b. Set the scene: "This is a business telephone call. Speaker A is the caller, and Speaker B is the secretary."

c. Call on pairs of students to role play the telephone call, using any name and time expression. You can use Full-Class Practice or Pair Practice. For added realism, bring a telephone to class. Have the secretary sit in front of the class and *answer the phone.* For example:

> A. Hello. Can I speak to Ms. Montero, please?
> B. I'm sorry. Ms. Montero isn't here right now.
> A. I see. When will she be back?
> B. She'll be back in two hours.
> A. In two hours?
> B. Yes. That's right.
> A. Okay. I'll call back then. Thank you.
> B. You're welcome. Good-bye.

6. Role Play: Predicting the Future

Have students pretend to be fortune tellers and predict the future.

a. Divide the class into pairs. One person is the fortune teller, and the other is the client.

b. Write the following cues on the board:

> have a test
> get married
> find a good job
> this class end
> rain
> _____
> _____
> _____

c. Have the client ask the fortune teller a question, using one of the cues on the board or any other he or she wishes. The fortune teller should answer, using one of the time expressions from the lesson. For example:

> A. Will we have a test soon?
> B. Yes, you will. You'll have a test in a few days.
>
> A. Will I get married soon?
> B. Yes, you will. You'll get married in a few months.

7. What's Her Future?

a. Show a photograph of a young child. Have the class answer the following questions:

> How old do you think the child is?
> Where do you think this child lives?

b. Once the class has agreed on this information, divide the class into groups. Have each group make predictions about the child's future.

c. Have groups share their predictions with the class.

Text Page 31: What Do You Think?

FOCUS

- Future Tense: *Will / Won't*
- Expressing Possibility with *Maybe*

CLOSE UP

RULE: The negative in the simple future tense is formed with *not* after the auxiliary *will*. The auxiliary *will* often contracts with *not*. The contracted form of *will not* is *won't*.

EXAMPLE: Maybe it will, and maybe it (will not) **won't**.

GETTING READY

1. Review contractions with *will*. Say the full form of each pronoun, and have students give the contracted form. For example:

Teacher	Students
I will work.	I'll work.
He will work.	He'll work.

2. Introduce *won't*.

   a. Form sentences with the words in the box at the top of text page 31. Use each pronoun to make a sentence with *will* and then with *won't*. Have students repeat chorally. For example:

      I will work.
      I won't work.

      He will work.
      He won't work.

   b. Make statements with *will* and have students negate them. For example:

Teacher	Students
I'll go soon.	I won't go soon.
He'll work today.	He won't work today.
She'll arrive soon.	She won't arrive soon.

It'll be hot tomorrow.	It won't be hot tomorrow.
We'll be ready soon.	We won't be ready soon.
You'll be there.	You won't be there.
They'll be on time.	They won't be on time.

INTRODUCING THE MODEL

1. Have students look at the model illustration.

2. Set the scene: "Two co-workers are talking."

3. Present the model.

4. Full-Class Repetition.

5. Ask students if they have any questions. Check understanding of new vocabulary: *maybe, We'll just have to wait and see.*

6. Group Choral Repetition.

7. Choral Conversation.

8. Call on one or two pairs of students to present the dialog.

   (For additional practice, do Choral Conversation in small groups or by rows.)

SIDE BY SIDE EXERCISES

Examples

1. A. Do you think Mr. Lee will give us a test tomorrow?
   B. Maybe he will, and maybe he won't. We'll just have to wait and see.

2. A. Do you think your daughter will get married soon?
   B. Maybe she will, and maybe she won't. We'll just have to wait and see.

1. **Exercise 1:** Introduce the new word *test*. Call on two students to present the dialog. Then do Choral Repetition and Choral Conversation practice.

2. **Exercise 2:** Same as above.

3. **Exercises 3–8:** Either Full-Class or Pair Practice.

   New Vocabulary

   7. some day
   ---

4. **Exercise 9:** Have pairs of students create dialogs about any future events.

WORKBOOK

Pages 31–33

EXPANSION ACTIVITIES

1. Match the Conversations

a. Make a set of matching cards. For example:

Do you think I'll be rich some day?	Maybe you will, and maybe you won't.
Do you think your brother will get married soon?	Maybe he will, and maybe he won't.
Do you think (Jane) will be famous some day?	Maybe she will, and maybe she won't.
Do you think we'll have a lot of homework tonight?	Maybe we will, and maybe we won't.
Do you think you'll study English this weekend?	Maybe I will, and maybe I won't.
Do you think your friends will buy you a nice birthday present?	Maybe they will, and maybe they won't.

Do you think there will be a lot of traffic this weekend?	Maybe there will, and maybe there won't.

b. Distribute a card to each student.

c. Have students memorize the sentence on their cards, and then have students walk around the room saying their sentence until they find their match.

d. Then have pairs of students say their matched sentences aloud to the class.

2. Predictions

a. Have each student write a prediction about the future, using *will*. Students can make predictions about anything they wish. For example:

> (George) will buy a motorcycle.
> (Maria) will get a new job with a big salary.
> (Richard) and (Alice) will get married next year.
> I'll become a famous scientist some day.
> It will rain cats and dogs tonight.

b. Write the following conversational framework on the board:

```
A. Do you really think _____?
B. Yes. I think ____ will.
     or
   No. I'm sure ____ won't.
```

c. Have each student read his or her prediction. For each prediction, call on two other students to create a conversation, using the framework on the board. For example:

Student 1: George will buy a motorcycle.
Student 2: Do you really think George will buy a motorcycle?
Student 3: Yes. I think he will.
             or
           No. I'm sure he won't.

Note: You can do this activity as a class, or divide students into groups of three and have them take turns reading and talking about their predictions.

3. What Will Happen Next?

a. Select a dramatic photograph from a newspaper or magazine.

b. Show the picture to the class. Have students identify vocabulary in the picture. Write the vocabulary on the board for student reference.

c. Ask the class: "What will happen next?" Have students work in pairs to compose their predictions.

d. Have students share their predictions with the class.

4. Dictate and Discuss

a. Divide the class into pairs or small groups.

b. Dictate sentences such as the following, and then have students discuss them as a class, in pairs, or in small groups:

A woman will be the next president/prime minister of our country.
Families will spend a lot of time together in the future.
Computers will be very small in the future.
People won't use cars in the future.
Children will go to school twelve hours a day in the future.
The weather will be hot in the future.

c. Call on students to share their opinions with the rest of the class.

Variation: Have pairs or groups write predictions. Have them dictate their predictions to the class, and then have the class discusss them.

READING *I Can't Wait for Spring to Come!*

FOCUS

- Future Tense: *Will*

NEW VOCABULARY

any more	Just think . . .
bloom	outdoors
come	sick and tired of
go for a walk	snow (n)
go outside	stay
grass	tired of
I can't wait	winter coat
indoors	

READING THE STORY

Optional: Preview the story by having students talk about the story title and/or illustration. You may choose to introduce new vocabulary beforehand, or have students encounter the new vocabulary within the context of the reading.

1. Have students read silently or follow along silently as the story is read aloud by you, by one or more students, or on the audio program.

2. Ask students if they have any questions. Check understanding of vocabulary.

3. Check students' comprehension, using some or all of the following questions:

   What's this boy tired of?
   Will it be winter in a few weeks?
   Will it be cold?
   Will it snow?
   Will he have to stay indoors?

What will he do?
What will he and his friends do?
What will the neighborhood look like in a few weeks?
What will his father do outdoors?
What will his mother do outdoors?
What won't they do on weekends?
What will they do instead?

✓ READING *CHECK-UP*

TRUE, FALSE, OR MAYBE?

1. False
2. True
3. Maybe
4. False
5. Maybe
6. False
7. True
8. Maybe

READING EXTENSION

Have students read the story again and find all the words that describe *winter*. Then have students look for words that describe *spring*. Then have students compare their lists. For example:

Winter	Spring
snow	sunny
cold	warm
coats	outdoors
boots	flowers bloom
indoors	play with friends
sad	
gray	

How About You?

Have students answer the questions, in pairs or as a class.

Text Page 33: They Really Can't Decide

FOCUS

- *Might*

CLOSE UP

RULE:	The modal *might* is used to describe possibility in the present and future.
EXAMPLE:	When are you going to clean your room? I don't know. I **might** clean it today, or I **might** clean it next Saturday.

RULE:	The modal *might* is an auxiliary verb that combines with the base form of the verb. It doesn't contract with subject pronouns.
EXAMPLES:	I **might arrive.** He **might arrive.** She **might arrive.** It **might arrive.** We **might arrive.** You **might arrive.** They **might arrive.**

GETTING READY

1. Introduce *might*. Describe a possibility using *maybe*. Then describe the same possibility using *might*. For example:

    Maybe it'll rain tomorrow.
    It might rain tomorrow.

    Maybe I'll get married soon.
    I might get married soon.

2. Form sentences with the words in the box at the top of text page 32. Have students repeat. For example:

    I might clean it today.
    He might clean it today.
    She might clean it today.

INTRODUCING THE MODELS

There are two model conversations. Introduce and practice each separately. For each model:

1. Have students look at the model illustration.

2. Set the scene: "People can't decide what they're going to do."

3. Present the model.

4. Full-Class Repetition.

    ### Pronunciation Note

    The pronunciation focus of Chapter 4 is the informal pronunciation of ***Going to*** (text page 37). Tell students that this is very common in informal speech. You may wish to model this pronunciation at this point *(When are you going to clean your room? Where are you going to go for your vacation?)* and encourage students to incorporate it into their language practice.

5. Ask students if they have any questions. Check understanding of vocabulary.

6. Group Choral Repetition.

7. Choral Conversation.

8. Call on one or two pairs of students to present the dialog.

(For additional practice, do Choral Conversation in small groups or by rows.)

SIDE BY SIDE EXERCISES

In these exercises, students can answer the questions any way they wish, using the model as a guide.

Examples

1. A. What's he going to make for dinner tonight?
    B. He doesn't know. He might make (*spaghetti and meatballs*), or he might make (*chicken with rice*). He really can't decide.

2. A. What color is she going to paint her bedroom?
    B. She doesn't know. She might paint it (*yellow*), or she might paint it (*green*). She really can't decide.

3. A. What are they going to name their new daughter?
    B. They don't know. They might name her (*Ann*), or they might name her (*Louise*). They really can't decide.

Answer Key

4. We don't know. We might get married (*this summer*), or we might get married (*next winter*). We really can't decide.
5. I don't know. I might buy him (*a jacket*), or I might buy him (*a sweater*). I really can't decide.
6. They don't know. They might (*go to a play*), or they might (*see a movie*). They really can't decide.
7. I don't know. I might (*take the bus*), or I might (*ride my bicycle*). I really can't decide.
8. He doesn't know. He might name it (*Rover*), or he might name it (*Max*). He really can't decide.
9. I don't know. I might be (*a teacher*), or I might be (*a lawyer*). I really can't decide.

1. Exercise 1: Call on two students to present the dialog. Then do Choral Repetition and Choral Conversation practice.

2. Exercise 2: Same as above.

3. Exercises 3–9: Either Full-Class Practice or Pair Practice.

> **New Vocabulary**
> 3. name (v)
> 4. you two
> 8. puppy

Language Note

The expression *you two* (Exercise 4) is an informal way of saying *the two of you*.

WORKBOOK

Page 34

EXPANSION ACTIVITIES

1. Match the Conversations

a. Make the following set of matching cards:

When are you going to leave?	I might leave at nine, or I might leave at ten. I really can't decide.
Where are you going to live?	I might live in Easton, or I might live in Weston. I really can't decide.
What are you going to have?	I might have a pizza, or I might have a sandwich. I really can't decide.
How are you going to get there?	I might take the bus, or I might take the train. I really can't decide.
What are you going to get her?	I might get her a sweater, or I might get her a jacket. I really can't decide.
When are you going to get there?	I might get there today, or I might get there tomorrow. I really can't decide.
Who are you going to see?	I might see my sister, or I might see my brother. I really can't decide.
What are you going to be?	I might be a doctor, or I might be a teacher. I really can't decide.
Where are you going to meet me?	I might meet you in the park, or I might meet you at the zoo. I really can't decide.

b. Distribute a card to each student.

c. Have students memorize the sentences on their cards, and then have students walk around the room saying their sentences until they find their match.

d. Then have pairs of students say their matched sentences aloud to the class.

2. Dialog Builder!

a. Divide the class into pairs.

b. On the board write a line from a conversation such as the following:

> I really can't decide.

c. Have each pair create a conversation incorporating that line. Students can begin and end their conversations any way they wish, but they must include that line in their dialogs.

d. Call on students to present their conversations to the class.

3. Role Play: Harry Can Never Decide

a. Set the scene:

"My friend Harry can NEVER decide what to do. For example: What's he going to do tonight? He doesn't know. He might go to the movies, or he might watch TV at home. He can't decide."

b. Have students pretend to be *Harry* and answer questions using any vocabulary they wish. For example:

Teacher: Harry, what are you going to do this weekend?
Harry: I don't know. I might *(go swimming)*, or I might *(go sailing)*. I can't decide.

Possible questions for Harry:

What are you going to do this weekend?
Where are you going to go for your vacation?
What are you going to name your new cat?
What are you going to study next year?
When are you going to get married?
How many children are you going to have?

c. Have students think of other questions to ask Harry.

Text Page 34: Careful!

FOCUS

- Imperatives
- *Might*

INTRODUCING THE MODEL

1. Have students look at the model illustration.

2. Set the scene: "Two co-workers are talking."

3. Present the model.

4. Full-Class Repetition.

5. Ask students if they have any questions. Check understanding of new vocabulary: *Careful!, put on, helmet, What did you say?, Thanks for the warning.*

   ### Language Note

   In this conversation, *I'm sorry* has the meaning of *Excuse me*. In other contexts, *I'm sorry* can mean *I apologize*.

6. Group Choral Repetition.

7. Choral Conversation.

8. Call on one or two pairs of students to present the dialog.

   (For additional practice, do Choral Conversation in small groups or by rows.)

SIDE BY SIDE EXERCISES

Examples

1. A. Careful! Put on your safety glasses!
   B. I'm sorry. What did you say?
   A. Put on your safety glasses! You might hurt your eyes.
   B. Oh. Thanks for the warning.

2. A. Careful! Don't stand there!
   B. I'm sorry. What did you say?
   A. Don't stand there! You might get hit!
   B. Oh. Thanks for the warning.

1. **Exercise 1:** Introduce the new word *safety glasses*. Call on two students to present the dialog. Then do Choral Repetition and Choral Conversation practice.

2. **Exercise 2:** Introduce the new expression *get hit*. Same as above.

3. **Exercises 3–5:** Either Full-Class Practice or Pair Practice.

New Vocabulary

3. watch your step
   fall
4. touch
   machine
   get hurt
5. wires
   get a shock

4. **Exercise 6:** Have students use the model as a guide to create their own conversations, using vocabulary of their choice. Encourage students to use dictionaries to find new words they want to use. This exercise can be done orally in class or for written homework. If you assign it for homework, do one example in class to make sure students understand what's expected. Have students present their conversations in class the next day.

WORKBOOK

Page 35

EXPANSION ACTIVITIES

1. Pantomime Role Play

Have pairs of students come to the front of the room and pantomime one of the situations on text page 34. The class watches and guesses the situation and what the two characters are saying.

2. Warnings!

a. Write the following suggestions or warnings on the board:

> Take your umbrella!
> Don't touch that dog!
> Don't play your music too loud!
> Don't eat that!
> Don't pick up that box!
> Take ten dollars more!
> Don't touch that wire!
> Study every night!
> Don't ride your bicycle in traffic!

b. In another column on the board, write the following cues for possible responses.

> bite
> get a shock
> get hit
> need money
> get sick
> rain
> get angry
> hurt your back
> have a quiz

c. Have pairs of students take turns choosing a warning from the first column and an appropriate response from the second column. For example:

Student A: Don't play your music too loud!
Student B: Your neighbors might get angry.

Student A: Don't eat that!
Student B: You might get sick!

d. Have students create their own list of warnings and responses.

3. Safety Rules

a. Divide the class into pairs or small groups.

b. Call out different work environments and tell students to write down all the safety rules they can associate with that work environment.

c. Have students share their rules with the class as you write them on the board. Then have the class brainstorm reasons for each rule. For example:

> <u>restaurant kitchen</u>
>
> Don't touch the pots.   They might be hot.
> Watch your fingers.   You might get cut.
> Sweep the floor often.   You might fall.

4. Draw and Discuss

a. In small groups, have students draw several warning signs.

b. Have the groups show their signs to the class. Can the class understand what the sign means?

> What's the warning?
> Why is there danger?

As students interpret the signs, write their ideas on the board.

How to Say It!

1. Set the scene: "Someone is warning another person about a wet floor."

2. Present the conversation.

3. Full-Class Repetition.

4. Ask students if they have any questions. Check understanding of the new expressions.

5. Group Choral Repetition.

6. Choral Conversation.

7. Call on one or two pairs to present the dialog.

8. Divide the class into pairs, and have them practice other conversations on the page, using the different expressions for repetition.

9. Call on a few pairs to present their conversations to the class.

EXPANSION ACTIVITY

Telephone

1. Divide the class into large groups. Have each group sit in a circle.

2. Whisper a set of warnings to one student. For example:

   "Watch your step! I washed the floor. It's wet. You might fall."

3. The first student whispers the message to the second student, and so forth around the circle. The student listening may ask for clarification by saying, "I'm sorry. Could you please repeat that?"

4. When the message gets to the last student, that person says it aloud. Is it the same message you started with? The group with the most accurate message wins.

Text Page 35: I'm Afraid I Might Drown

FOCUS

- *Might*
- Future Tense: *Will*
- Extending Invitations

INTRODUCING THE MODEL

1. Have students look at the model illustration.

2. Set the scene: "Two friends are talking."

3. Present the model.

4. Full-Class Repetition.

5. Ask students if they have any questions. Check understanding of new vocabulary: *Would you like to _____ with me?, drown, Don't worry!, I'm positive.*

   ### Language Note

   Would you like to _____ with me? is a polite way to extend an invitation.

6. Group Choral Repetition.

7. Choral Conversation.

8. Call on one or two pairs of students to present the dialog.

   (For additional practice, do Choral Conversation in small groups or by rows.)

SIDE BY SIDE EXERCISES

Examples

1. A. Would you like to go skiing with me?
   B. No, I don't think so.
   A. Why not?
   B. I'm afraid I might break my leg.
   A. Don't worry! You won't break your leg.
   B. Are you sure?
   A. I'm positive!
   B. Okay. I'll go skiing with you.

2. A. Would you like to go to the beach with me?
   B. No, I don't think so.
   A. Why not?
   B. I'm afraid I might get a sunburn.
   A. Don't worry! You won't get a sunburn.
   B. Are you sure?
   A. I'm positive!
   B. Okay. I'll go to the beach with you.

1. **Exercise 1:** Introduce the new words *break, leg.* Call on two students to present the dialog. Then do Choral Repetition and Choral Conversation practice.

2. **Exercise 2:** Introduce the new word *sunburn.* Same as above.

3. **Exercises 3–8:** Either Full-Class Practice or Pair Practice.

   New Vocabulary

   3. step
      feet
   4. take a walk
      catch a cold
   5. fall asleep
   6. company picnic
   7. roller coaster
      get sick
   8. go sailing
      get seasick

4. **Exercise 9:** Have students use the model as a guide to create their own conversations, using vocabulary of their choice. (Students may use any activities they wish.) Encourage students to use dictionaries to find new words they want to use. This exercise can be done orally in class or for written homework. If you assign it for homework, do one example in class to make sure students understand what's expected. Have students present their conversations in class the next day.

WORKBOOK

Page 36–39

1. Disappearing Dialog

a. Write the model conversation on the board.

b. Ask for two student volunteers to read the conversation.

c. Erase a few of the words from each line of the dialog. Have two different students read the conversation.

d. Erase more words and call on two more students to read the conversation.

e. Continue erasing words and calling on pairs of students to say the model until all the words have been erased and the dialog has disappeared.

2. Scrambled Dialogs

a. Divide the class into three groups.

b. Make sets of conversations from three different exercises on text page 35, writing each line on a separate card.

c. Give each group one set of cards, and have the group members reorder the conversation.

d. Have each group read their conversation aloud while the others listen to check for accuracy.

Variation: Do the activity as a game with competing teams. The team that reorders its conversation in the shortest time is the winner.

3. Dialog Builder!

a. Divide the class into pairs.

b. Write a line on the board from a conversation such as the following:

I'm afraid I might get sick.

Other possible lines:

I'm afraid I'll have a terrible time.
I'm afraid I might get hurt.
I'm afraid I might fall.
I'm sure I'll fall asleep.

c. Have each pair create a conversation incorporating that line. Students can begin and end their conversations any way they wish, but they must include that line in their dialogs.

d. Call on students to present their conversations to the class.

4. Match the Conversations

a. Make a set of matching cards based on invitations and refusals. For example:

Would you like to play football with me?	No, I don't think so. I'm afraid I might break my leg.
Would you like to play in the snow with me?	No, I don't think so. I'm afraid I might catch a cold.
Would you like to go to a classical music concert with me?	No, I don't think so. I'm afraid I might fall asleep.
Would you like to go sailing with me?	No, I don't think so. I'm afraid I might get seasick.
Would you like to play in the yard?	No, I don't think so. I'm afraid your dog might bite me.
Would you like to plant flowers in the garden with me?	No, I don't think so. I'm afraid I might get dirty.
Would you like to ride your bicycle with me in the city?	No, I don't think so. I'm afraid I might get hit.
Would you like to go swimming with me?	No, I don't think so. I'm afraid a fish might bite me.

b. Distribute a card to each student.

c. Have students memorize the sentences on their cards, and then have students walk around the room saying their sentences until they find their match.

d. Then have pairs of students say their matched sentences aloud to the class.

5. Concentration

a. Use the cards from the above activity. Place them face down in four rows of 4 each.

b. Divide the class into two teams. The object of the game is for students to find the matching cards. Both teams should be able to see all the cards, since *concentrating* on their location is an important part of playing the game.

c. A student from Team 1 turns over two cards. If they match, the student picks up the cards, that team gets a point, and the student takes another turn. If the cards don't match, the student turns them face down, and a member of Team 2 takes a turn.

d. The game continues until all the cards have been matched. The team with the most correct matches wins the game.

Variation: This game can also be played in groups and pairs.

6. Tell-a-Story!

a. Write the following cues on the board:

> **might**
> watch too much TV
> eat too much/many _____
> drink too much/many _____
> forget to _____
> go _____ and get _____
>
> **might not**
> do _____
> feed _____
> _____ on time

b. Tell this story about Jack's parents, pointing to key words on the board and any vocabulary you wish to complete the sentences.

"Jack's parents really need a vacation, but they're afraid to go. They're worried about their teenage son, Jack. They don't want to leave him at home."

They're afraid he might watch too much TV.
They're afraid he might eat too much candy.
They're afraid he might drink too much soda.
They're afraid he might forget to brush his teeth.
They're afraid he might go to the beach and get a bad sunburn.
They're afraid he might not do his homework.
They're afraid he might not feed the dog.
They're afraid he might not get up on time for school.

c. Point to the word cues on the board, and call on students to retell each part of the story.

d. Have students brainstorm other reasons why Jack's parents might be afraid to go on vacation.

Possible Follow-up: Divide the class into pairs or small groups, and have students create a story about *Judy's parents,* who are afraid to go on vacation because of what might happen while they're away. Have students tell their stories to the class.

7. Information Gap Role Plays

a. Divide the class into groups of three.

b. Give cue cards to two of the students, and have them create role plays based on the following situations:

> Invite your friend to go swimming with you.

> You don't like the water.
> You're afraid _____ might _____.

(continued)

Invite your friend to go skiing with you.

You don't like to ski.
You're afraid _____ might _____.

Invite your friend to go dancing with you.

You never go dancing.
You're afraid _____ might _____.

Invite your friend to go to the beach with you.

You don't like to go to the beach.
You're afraid _____ might _____.

Invite your friend to go to the movies with you.

You don't like to go to the movies.
You're afraid _____ might _____.

c. Have the third student interrupt the conversation to find out what's wrong. For example:

   A. Do you want to go swimming with me?
   B. I don't think so. I'm afraid a fish might bite me.
   A. Don't worry! A fish won't bite you!
   C. Excuse me. What's the matter?
   A. I want to go swimming, but he doesn't want to go with me. He's afraid a fish might bite him.

Students should then continue the conversations any way they wish.

d. Call on the groups to present their role plays to the class.

READING *Just in Case*

FOCUS

- *Might*

NEW VOCABULARY

absolutely	go to work	nauseous
all over	idea	pregnant
arm	instead	spot
either	measles	take chances
flu	might not	

READING THE STORY

Optional: *Preview the story by having students talk about the story title and/or illustrations. You may choose to introduce new vocabulary beforehand, or have students encounter the new vocabulary within the context of the reading.*

1. Have students read silently, or follow along silently as the story is read aloud by you, by one or more students, or on the audio program.

2. Ask students if they have any questions. Check understanding of vocabulary.

3. Check students' comprehension, using some or all of the following questions:

> Did Larry go to work today?
> Will he go to work tomorrow?
> What might he do instead?

What's the matter with him?
What does he think?
Is he positive?

Did Mrs. Randall go to the office today?
Will she go to the office tomorrow?
What might she do instead?
What's the matter with her?
What does she think?
Is she positive?

Did Tommy and Julie Harris go to school today?
Will they go to school tomorrow?
What might they do instead?
What's the matter with them?
What do Mr. and Mrs. Harris think?
Are they positive?

✓ READING *CHECK-UP*

CHOOSE

1. can't
2. might
3. Are you
4. might
5. Will
6. might not

READING EXTENSION

Have students answer the following questions:

> Why does Larry think he has the flu?
> Why does Mrs. Randall think she might be pregnant?
> Why do Mr. and Mrs. Harris think their children might have the measles?

LISTENING

WHAT'S THE LINE?

Mrs. Harris (from the story on page 36) is calling Tommy and Julie's school. Listen and choose the correct lines.

1. Good morning. Park Elementary School.
2. Yes, Mrs. Harris. What can I do for you?
3. Oh? What's the matter?
4. That's too bad. Are you going to take them to the doctor?
5. Well, I hope Tommy and Julie feel better soon.

Answers

1. a
2. b
3. a
4. b
5. a

WHAT'S THE WORD?

Listen and choose the word you hear.

1. I might go to school tomorrow.
2. I want to come to work today.
3. Don't walk there!
4. We'll be ready in half an hour.
5. They'll go to school tomorrow.
6. Don't stand there! You might get hit!
7. I call the doctor when I'm sick.
8. Watch your step! There are wet spots on the floor.
9. I'm sick and tired of sailing.

Answers

1. b	4. a	7. a
2. a	5. a	8. b
3. b	6. b	9. a

Write a Note!

1. Make sure students understand the instructions.
2. Have students do the activity as written homework, using a dictionary for any new words they wish to use.
3. Have students present and discuss what they have written, in pairs or as a class.

PRONUNCIATION

> ***Going to:*** In daily English usage, the pronunciation of the phrase *going to* is often reduced to *gonna*.

Focus on Listening

Practice the sentences in the left column. Say each sentence or play the audio one or more times. Have students listen carefully and repeat.

Focus on Pronunciation

Practice the sentences in the right column. Have students say each sentence and then listen carefully as you say it or play the audio.

If you wish, have students continue practicing the sentences to improve their pronunciation.

JOURNAL

Have students write their journal entries at home or in class. Encourage students to use a dictionary to look up words they would like to use. Students can share their written work with other students if appropriate. Have students discuss what they have written as a class, in pairs, or in small groups.

CHAPTER SUMMARY

GRAMMAR

1. Divide the class into pairs or small groups.

2. Have students take turns forming sentences from the words in the grammar boxes. Student A says a sentence, and Student B points to the words from each column that are in the sentence. Then have students switch: Student B says a sentence, and Student A points to the words.

KEY VOCABULARY

Have students ask you any questions about the meaning or pronunciation of the vocabulary. If students ask for the pronunciation, repeat after the student until the student is satisfied with his or her own pronunciation.

EXPANSION ACTIVITIES

1. Do You Remember the Words?

   Check students' retention of the vocabulary depicted on the opening page of Chapter 4 by doing the following activity:

   a. Have students open their books to page 29 and cover the list of vocabulary words.

   b. Either call out a number and have students tell you the word, or say a word and have students tell you the number.

   Variation: You can also do this activity as a game with competing teams.

2. Student-Led Dictation

   a. Tell each student to choose a word or phrase from the Key Vocabulary list on text page 38 and look at it very carefully.

   b. Have students take turns dictating their words to the class. Everybody writes down that student's word or phrase.

   c. When the dictation is completed, call on different students to write each word on the board to check the spelling.

3. Beanbag Toss

   a. Call out the topic: *health words.*

   b. Have students toss a beanbag back and forth. The student to whom the beanbag is tossed must name a health word. For example:

   Student 1: the flu
   Student 2: the measles
   Student 3: get sick

   c. Continue until all the words in the category have been named.

   Variation: You can also do this activity as a game with competing teams.

4. Category Dictation

   a. Have students draw three columns on a piece of paper. Tell them to write <u>Injuries</u> at the top of the left column, <u>Life Events</u> at the top of the middle column, and <u>Beginnings and Endings</u> at the top of the right column.

   b. Dictate various words from the Key Vocabulary list, and have students write them in the appropriate column. For example:

<u>Injuries</u>	<u>Life Events</u>	<u>Beginnings and Endings</u>
get a shock	get married	return
fall	move	arrive

   c. At the end of the dictation, have students compare their lists.

END-OF-CHAPTER ACTIVITIES

1. Miming

a. Write on cards the following verbs presented in Chapter 4:

catch a cold	get a sunburn	get a shock	get married
fall	grow up	drown	return
feel nauseous	break a leg	fall asleep	move

b. Have students take turns picking a card from the pile and pantomiming the action on the card.

c. The class must guess the verb.

Variation: This can be done as a game with competing teams.

2. Question Game

a. Write the following sentences on the board:

> Richard won't go to the office tomorrow. He'll stay home instead because he thinks he might have the flu.

b. Underline different elements of the sentences, and have students create a question based on that portion of the sentence. For example:

> <u>Richard</u> won't go to the office tomorrow. He'll stay home instead because he thinks he might have the flu.

Who won't go to the office tomorrow?

> Richard won't go to the office tomorrow. He'll <u>stay home</u> instead because he thinks he might have the flu.

What will Richard do tomorrow?

> Richard won't go to the office tomorrow. He'll stay home instead <u>because he thinks he might have the flu.</u>

Why will Richard stay home?

c. Continue with other sentences.

3. Board Game

a. On poster boards or on manila file folders, make up game boards with a pathway consisting of separate spaces. You may use any theme or design you wish.

b. Divide the class into groups of 2 to 4 students and give each group a game board, a die, and each student something to be used as a playing piece.

c. Give each group a pile of cards face-down with sentences written on them. Some sentences should be correct, and others incorrect. For example:

> They'll be back soon.
> The guests will be here at a little while.
> Maybe she'll give us a test, and maybe she won't.
> He is get sick and tired of winter.
> We might go to Paris, or we might go to Tokyo.
> Careful! You put on your safety glasses.
> She'll might go to the doctor.
> I'm afraid I might break my leg.
> Would you like see a movie with me?
> When will you going to cut the grass?
> They won't watch TV in the spring.
> Thanks the warning.
> She doesn't want to take any chances.
> Watch you step!
> I'm positive you drown.

d. Each student in turn rolls the die, moves the playing piece along the game path, and after landing on a space, picks a card, reads the sentence, and says if it is *correct* or *incorrect*. If the sentence is incorrect and the student is able to give the correct version, that student takes an additional turn.

e. The first student to reach the end of the pathway is the winner.

4. Time Capsule

a. Tell students they're going to write predictions about themselves five years from now. Write the following questions on the board to help them think of predictions:

> Where will you live?
> What job will you have?
> Will you speak English well?
> Will you be married?
> Will you be happy?
> Will you be rich or famous?
> Will you have children?
> Will you still be friends with _____?

b. Have students write their predictions for homework.

c. After you have reviewed their writing, have students seal their predictions in an envelope and write on the front "Time Capsule: Open five years from *(today's date)*."

WORKBOOK ANSWER KEY AND LISTENING SCRIPTS

WORKBOOK PAGE 30

A. SOON

1. I will, I'll be back
2. it will, It'll begin
3. he will, He'll return
4. we will, We'll be ready
5. they will, They'll arrive
6. it will, It'll end
7. she will, She'll be here
8. I will, I'll get out

WORKBOOK PAGE 31

B. WE'LL JUST HAVE TO WAIT AND SEE

1. will, she will, she won't
2. will, he will, he won't
3. you'll, will, I won't
4. I'll, will, you won't
5. it'll, it will, it won't
6. there will, there will, there won't
7. will, we will, we won't
8. will, they will, they won't

WORKBOOK PAGE 32

C. WHAT DO YOU THINK?

1. he'll bake, he won't bake
2. she'll order, she won't order
3. they'll go, they won't go
4. I'll get, I won't get
5. it'll arrive, it won't arrive
6. we'll finish, we won't finish

D. LISTENING

Listen and circle the words you hear.

1. I want to have the chocolate ice cream.
2. They won't fax the letter this morning.
3. I want to recommend the fish today.
4. Peter and William won't go home this morning.
5. She won't eat meat.
6. They want to get married soon.
7. He won't buy a car this year.
8. We want to use our computer now.

Answers

1. want to
2. won't
3. want to
4. won't
5. won't
6. want to

7. won't
8. want to

E. DIFFERENT OPINIONS

1. it'll be
2. they'll arrive
3. she'll be
4. he'll buy
5. we'll have

WORKBOOK PAGE 34

G. THEY DON'T KNOW

1. He might make eggs
   he might make pancakes
2. She might get up at 10 o'clock
   she might get up at noon
3. They might clean it today
   they might clean it tomorrow
4. I might give them a plant
   I might give them a painting
5. We might watch game shows
   we might watch cartoons
6. They might go to Manila
   they might go to Bangkok
7. I might go to the beach
   I might go to a museum
8. He might name it Chester
   he might name it Fluffy

WORKBOOK PAGE 35

H. BE CAREFUL!

1. a
2. b
3. a
4. a
5. b
6. b

I. LOUD AND CLEAR

1. Wendy, walk, work, winter, weather
2. waiter, waitress won't walk, wet
3. Walter, wife want, wash, windows, weekend
4. We wanted, water wasn't warm

WORKBOOK PAGES 36–37

J. PESSIMISTS

1. she's afraid she might break her leg
2. he's afraid he might get a sunburn
3. I'm afraid I might drown
4. we're afraid we might miss our bus

5. they're afraid they might get sick
6. he's afraid he might step on her feet
7. we're afraid we might fall asleep
8. I'm afraid I might have a terrible time
9. he's afraid he might get a backache
10. she's afraid she might get seasick
11. I'm afraid I might get fat
12. she's afraid she might catch a cold
13. we're afraid it might rain
14. he's afraid he might look terrible

K. LISTENING

Listen and choose the correct answer.

1. I'm afraid I might get sick!
2. I'm afraid I might fall asleep!
3. I'm afraid I might step on your feet!
4. I'm afraid I might break my leg!
5. I'm afraid I might catch a cold!
6. I'm afraid I might drown!
7. I'm afraid I might get seasick!
8. I'm afraid I might get a sunburn!
9. I'm afraid I might have a terrible time!
10. I'm afraid I might look terrible!

Answers

1. a
2. b
3. b
4. a
5. b
6. a
7. b
8. b
9. a
10. a

M. GrammarSong

1. make
2. cake
3. wide
4. decide
5. go
6. Mexico
7. wide
8. decide
9. her
10. sweater
11. wide
12. decide

GRAMMAR

COMPARATIVES

| My new apartment is | colder
larger
bigger
prettier | than my old apartment. |
| | more comfortable
more attractive | |

SHOULD

| Should | I
he
she
it
we
you
they | study? |

| I
He
She
It
We
You
They | should study. |

POSSESSIVE PRONOUNS

| This dog is much friendlier than | mine.
his.
hers.
ours.
yours.
theirs. |

FUNCTIONS

DESCRIBING

It was *fast/large/comfortable/interesting*.
My new _____ is *faster/larger/more comfortable/more interesting*.

My dog isn't as *friendly* as *your dog*.
They aren't as *clean* as they used to be.

Bicycles are *safer* than *motorcycles*.
Yours is much *friendlier* than mine.

ASKING FOR ADVICE

Should I *buy a bicycle or a motorcycle*?

OFFERING ADVICE

I think you should *buy a bicycle*.

EXPRESSING AN OPINION

I think *Los Angeles is much more interesting than New York*.
In my opinion, *the weather in Honolulu is better than the weather in Miami*.

EXPRESSING AGREEMENT

That's right.

I agree.
I agree with you.
I think so, too.

EXPRESSING DISAGREEMENT

I disagree.
I disagree with you.
I don't think so.

ASKING FOR AND REPORTING INFORMATION

Why?
Why do you say that?

INITIATING A TOPIC

You know . . .

INQUIRING ABOUT CERTAINTY

Do you really think so?

EXPRESSING CERTAINTY

Definitely!

EXPRESSING DISSATISFACTION

I'm very upset about *the streets here in Brownsville*.

NEW VOCABULARY

Adjectives

attractive
better
capable
cute
exciting
fancy
fashionable
fast
friendly
honest
hospitable
intelligent
lazy
left
light
modern
neat
polite
powerful
rainy
real
reliable
right
safe
satisfied
smart
snowy
soft
spicy
sympathetic
talented
talkative
understanding
useful
wide

Computers

desktop computer
notebook computer
printer

Possessive Pronouns

mine
his
hers
ours
yours
theirs

Modal for Giving Advice

should

Miscellaneous

although
because of
bus system
changes (n)
change (v)
dishwasher
fan
fire (v)
fur
furniture
grades
hand
hard
hire
Latin
mayor
meatloaf

more
parrot
professor
pronunciation
rent (v)
rocking chair
roommate
sports car
tennis racket
used to
vote (for)
wig

EXPRESSIONS

Definitely!
Don't be ridiculous!
go out with
no matter how
on the air
take a course
take piano lessons
they say

Text Page 39: Chapter Opening Page

VOCABULARY PREVIEW

You may want to present these words before beginning the chapter, or you may choose to wait until they first occur in a specific lesson. If you choose to present them at this point, here are some suggestions:

1. Have students look at the illustrations on text page 39 and identify the words they already know.

2. Present the vocabulary. Say each word and have the class repeat it chorally and individually. Check students' understanding and pronunciation of the words.

3. Practice the vocabulary as a class, in pairs, or in small groups. Have students cover the word list and look at the pictures. Practice the words in the following ways:

   • Say a word and have students tell the number of the illustration.

   • Give the number of an illustration and have students say the word.

Text Page 40: My New Bicycle Is Faster

FOCUS

- Comparatives with -er

CLOSE UP

SPELLING RULE:	To form the comparative, -er is added to one-syllable adjectives.
EXAMPLES:	soft–soft**er** small–small**er**
SPELLING RULE:	For one-syllable adjectives that end in -e, only -r is added.
EXAMPLES:	large–large**r** safe–safe**r**
SPELLING RULE:	For one-syllable adjectives that end with a single consonant preceded by a single vowel, the final consonant is doubled, and -er is added.
EXAMPLES:	big–big**ger** hot–hot**ter**
SPELLING RULE:	For two-syllable adjectives that end in -y preceded by a consonant, the -y changes to i and -er is added.
EXAMPLES:	fancy–fanc**ier** pretty–prett**ier**

GETTING READY

1. Introduce comparative adjectives with -er endings.

   a. Draw 2 buildings and 2 people on the board:

   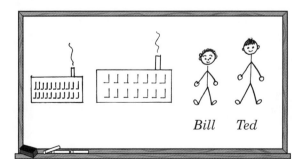

b. Point and say:

   This building is big.
   That building is bigger.

   Bill is tall.
   Ted is taller.

c. Say these sentences again and have students repeat chorally.

2. Read the adjectives in the boxes at the top of text page 40. Have students repeat chorally. Check understanding of the words *soft, safe*.

INTRODUCING THE MODEL

1. Have students look at the model illustration.

2. Set the scene: "Two friends are talking."

3. Present the model.

4. Full-Class Repetition.

5. Ask students if they have any questions. Check understanding of the word *fast*.

6. Group Choral Repetition.

7. Choral Conversation.

8. Call on one or two pairs of students to present the dialog.

   (For additional practice, do Choral Conversation in small groups or by rows.)

SIDE BY SIDE EXERCISES

Examples

1. A. I think you'll like my new rug.
   B. But I liked your OLD rug. It was soft.
   A. That's right. But my new rug is softer.

2. A. I think you'll like my new tennis racket.
   B. But I liked your OLD tennis racket. It was light.
   A. That's right. But my new tennis racket is lighter.

Answer Key to Comparative Adjectives 3–12:

3. larger	8. fancier
4. safer	9. quieter
5. bigger	10. prettier
6. hotter	11. smaller
7. friendlier	12. cuter

1. **Exercise 1:** Check understanding of the word *soft*. Call on two students to present the dialog. Then do Choral Repetition and Choral Conversation practice.

2. **Exercise 2:** Check understanding of the words *tennis racket, light*. Same as above.

3. **Exercises 3–12:** Either Full-Class Practice or Pair Practice.

New Vocabulary

4. safe
6. hot
7. friendly
8. sports car
9. dishwasher
10. wig
12. cute

Language Note

In Exercise 6, the adjective *hot* has the meaning *spicy*.

WORKBOOK

Page 40

1. Comparatively Speaking!

a. Put the following on the board:

Bob is tall.
Bill is taller.

Bob   Bill

b. Begin by saying: "I have two friends, Bob and Bill. They're very different. For example, Bob is tall. Bill is taller." Now I'm going to tell YOU about Bob, and you're going to tell ME about Bill.

c. Make statements about Bob and call on individual students to make statements about Bill in the comparative.

| Teacher: | Bob's car is fast. |
| Student: | Bill's car is faster. |

| Teacher: | Bob's apartment is big. |
| Student: | Bill's apartment is bigger. |

| Teacher: | Bob's neighborhood is safe. |
| Student: | Bill's neighborhood is safer. |

| Teacher: | Bob's dog is friendly. |
| Student: | Bill's dog is friendlier. |

| Teacher: | Bob's office is large. |
| Student: | Bill's office is larger. |

| Teacher: | Bob's car is shiny. |
| Student: | Bill's car is shinier. |

| Teacher: | Bob's neighbors are quiet. |
| Student: | Bill's neighbors are quieter. |

| Teacher: | Bob's new suit is fancy. |
| Student: | Bill's new suit is fancier. |

| Teacher: | Bob's cat is cute. |
| Student: | Bill's cat is cuter. |

2. Miming Game

a. Write on cards the following adjectives:

quiet	heavy	old	short
cute	big	friendly	loud
small	clean	soft	fast
tall	dirty	light	fancy

b. Have a pair of students take turns picking up a card from the pile. One student pantomimes the adjective on the card, and the other pantomimes its comparative.

c. The class must guess the adjective and its correct comparative.

Variation: This can be done as a game with competing teams.

3. Clap in Rhythm

a. Have students sit in a circle.

b. Establish a steady, even beat—one-two-three-four, one-two-three-four—by having students clap their hands to their laps twice and then clap their hands together twice. Repeat throughout the game, maintaining the same rhythm.

c. The object is for Student 1 to say an adjective and Student 2 to say its comparative, Student 3 to say another adjective, and Student 4 to say the comparative of that adjective, and so on, each time the hands are clapped together twice. Nothing is said when students clap their hands on their laps.

Note: The beat never stops! If a student misses a beat, he or she can either wait for the next beat or pass to the next student.

4. Role Play: I Remember

a. Put the following conversational model on the board:

(continued)

A. I remember your _____.
   _____ (was/were) very _____.
B. That's right. But YOUR _____
   (was/were) _____er.

b. Put these word cues on the board or on word cards:

house pretty	car fast	neighbors nice
dog ugly	cat friendly	office big

c. Set the scene: "Two old people are sitting in the park and talking about the past."

d. Call on pairs of students to role play the people, using the conversational model on the board and the word cues. This can be done as a class or in pairs. Examples:

   A. I remember your house. It was very pretty.
   B. That's right. But YOUR house was prettier.

   A. I remember your neighbors. They were very nice.
   B. That's right. But YOUR neighbors were nicer.

e. Encourage students to expand their conversations and add other comparisons.

5. Scrambled Comparative Game

a. Divide the class into teams.

b. Put some or all of these scrambled words on the board. With books closed, have students work together in their teams to unscramble the words. The first team to successfully unscramble them all wins.

fesra	(safer)
leidnfreri	(friendlier)
tirrepte	(prettier)
gibgre	(bigger)
egrarl	(larger)
fosret	(softer)
rasfte	(faster)
canifre	(fancier)
tohret	(hotter)
thiglre	(lighter)

6. Associations

a. Divide the class into pairs or small groups.

b. Call out an adjective, and tell students to write down all the different things that adjective can describe. For example:

fast:	car, bicycle, train, motorcycle
friendly:	boy, girl, dog, person, teacher
safe:	neighborhood, car, street
soft:	rug, hair, chair
easy:	homework, book, class, recipe
fancy:	car, dress, shoes
cute:	cat, dog, boy, girl

c. Have a student from each pair or group come to the board and write their words.

Variation: Do the activity as a game in which you divide the class into teams. The team with the most number of associations is the winner.

Text Page 41: My New Rocking Chair Is More Comfortable

FOCUS

- Comparatives with *more*
- Review of Comparatives with *-er*

CLOSE UP

RULE:	The comparative of adjectives that have three or more syllables is formed by placing *more* before the adjective.
EXAMPLES:	beautiful–**more** beautiful delicious–**more** delicious

RULE:	The comparatives of two-syllable adjectives that don't end in *-y* are less predictable. Some are formed with *more*, and some are formed with *-er*.
EXAMPLES:	honest–**more** honest simple–simpl**er** quiet–quiet**er**

GETTING READY

1. Introduce comparative adjectives with *more*.

   a. Draw 2 houses and 2 cups on the board:

   b. Point and say:

   > This house is beautiful.
   > That house is more beautiful.
   >
   > This coffee is delicious.
   > That coffee is more delicious.

   c. Say these sentences again and have students repeat chorally.

2. Read the adjectives in the boxes at the top of text page 41. Have students repeat chorally. Check understanding of the word *intelligent*.

INTRODUCING THE MODEL

1. Have students look at the model illustration.

2. Set the scene: "Two friends are talking."

3. Present the model.

4. Full-Class Repetition.

5. Ask students if they have any questions. Check understanding of the word *rocking chair*.

6. Group Choral Repetition.

7. Choral Conversation.

8. Call on one or two pairs of students to present the dialog.

   (For additional practice, do Choral Conversation in small groups or by rows.)

SIDE BY SIDE EXERCISES

Examples

1. A. I think you'll like my new apartment building.
   B. But I liked your OLD apartment building. It was beautiful.
   A. That's right. But my new apartment building is more beautiful.

2. A. I think you'll like my new roommate.
   B. But I liked your OLD roommate. She was interesting.
   A. That's right. But my new roommate is more interesting.

Answer Key to Comparative Adjectives 3–11:

3. more intelligent	8. smarter
4. more handsome	9. more delicious
5. more attractive	10. nicer
6. more powerful	11. more talkative
7. faster	

1. **Exercise 1:** Call on two students to present the dialog. Then do Choral Repetition and Choral Conversation practice.

2. **Exercise 2:** Introduce the new word *roommate*. Same as above.

3. **Exercises 3–11:** Either Full-Class Practice or Pair Practice.

New Vocabulary

3. intelligent
5. attractive
6. powerful
7. printer
8. smart
9. meatloaf
11. parrot
    talkative

---

4. **Exercise 12:** Have students use the model as a guide to create their own conversations, using vocabulary of their choice. (They can use any adjectives they wish.) Encourage students to use dictionaries to find new words they want to use. This exercise can be done orally in class or for written homework. If you assign it for homework, do one example in class to make sure students understand what's expected. Have students present their conversations in class the next day.

WORKBOOK

Pages 41–42

EXPANSION ACTIVITIES

1. Comparatively Speaking!

a. Put the following on the board:

Jean   *Jane*

Jean's apartment is beautiful.
Jane's apartment is more beautiful.

b. Begin by saying: "I have two friends, Jean and Jane. They're very different. For example, Jean's apartment is beautiful. Jane's apartment is more beautiful." Now I'm going to tell YOU about Jean, and you're going to tell ME about Jane.

c. Make statements about Jean, and call on individual students to make statements about Jane in the comparative.

> Teacher: Jean's new sofa is comfortable.
> Student: Jane's new sofa is more comfortable.

Teacher: Jean's friends are interesting.
Student: Jane's friends are more interesting.

Teacher: Jean's children are intelligent.
Student: Jane's children are more intelligent.

Teacher: Jean's husband is handsome.
Student: Jane's husband is more handsome.

Teacher: Jean's office is attractive.
Student: Jane's office is more attractive.

Teacher: Jean's new computer is powerful.
Student: Jane's new computer is more powerful.

Teacher: Jean's cakes and pies are delicious.
Student: Jane's cakes and pies are more delicious.

Teacher: Jean's parrot is talkative.
Student: Jane's parrot is more talkative.

2. Comparative Chain Game

a. Divide the class into small groups.

b. Start the chain game by making a statement about Helen's new car. For example:

Helen has a new car. Her old car was comfortable.

c. Student A must turn that statement into a comparative:

But her new car is more comfortable.

d. Student B continues the chain by making another statement about Helen's car. For example:

Her old car was fast.

e. Student C continues the chain by turning Student B's statement into a comparative:

But her new car is faster.

f. The chain continues until everybody has had a chance to tell about Helen's car.

g. Continue the activity with more comparative chain games about Helen. For example:

her new house
her new computer
her new recipe for chili
her new boyfriend

3. Miming Game

a. Write on cards the following adjectives:

beautiful	handsome	intelligent	powerful
delicious	talkative	comfortable	interesting

b. Have a pair of students take turns picking up a card from the pile. One student pantomimes the adjective on the card, and the other pantomimes its comparative.

c. The class must guess the adjective and its correct comparative

Variation: This can be done as a game with competing teams.

4. Category Dictation

a. Have students draw two columns on a piece of paper. At the top of one column, have students write <u>more</u>, and at the top of the other column, have them write <u>-er</u>.

b. Dictate adjectives from Chapter 5 and have students write them in the appropriate column. For example:

<u>more</u>	<u>-er</u>
interesting	softer
delicious	faster
comfortable	bigger
intelligent	cuter

5. Tic Tac Definitions

a. Have students draw a tic tac grid on their papers and fill in the grid with any nine of the following nouns from the exercises on text pages 40 or 41.

dog	office	sports car
recipe	wig	cell phone
cat	rug	roommate
briefcase	computer	printer
parrot	boss	neighborhood

(continued)

b. Give definitions of the words, and tell students to cross out any word on their grids for which you have given the definition.

c. The first person to cross out three words in a straight line—either vertically, horizontally, or diagonally—wins the game.

d. Have the winner call out the words to check the accuracy.

6. Role Play: I'll Never Forget

a. Put the following conversational model on the board:

> A. I'll never forget your _____.
> ____ (was/were) very _____.
> B. I know. But YOUR _____
> was/were _____.

b. Put these word cues on the board or on word cards:

grandfather energetic	wedding beautiful	neighbors interesting
dog intelligent	50th birthday party nice	house attractive

c. Set the scene: "Two old people are sitting in a restaurant and talking about the past."

d. Call on pairs of students to role play the people, using the conversational model on the board and the word cues. This can be done as a class or in pairs. Examples:

A. I'll never forget your grandfather. He was very energetic.

B. I know. But YOUR grandfather was more energetic.

A. I'll never forget your wedding. It was very beautiful.

B. I know. But YOUR wedding was more beautiful.

e. Encourage students to expand their conversations and add other comparisons.

7. What's the Comparative?

a. Divide the class into small groups.

b. Say the following adjectives in random order, and have students raise their hand and give the comparative forms:

attractive	intelligent
beautiful	interesting
big	large
comfortable	light
cute	nice
delicious	powerful
easy	pretty
fancy	quiet
fast	safe
friendly	smart
hot	soft

Variation: If you wish, you can do the activity as a game with competing teams. Each team gets a point for giving the correct form. The team with the most points wins the *comparative* game.

8. Associations

a. Divide the class into pairs or small groups.

b. Call out an adjective from text page 41, and tell students to write down all the different things that adjective can describe. For example:

comfortable:	chair, sofa
attractive:	house, man, person, woman
interesting:	book, movie, idea
powerful:	computer, car, person
delicious:	food, recipe, meatloaf

c. Have a student from each pair or group come to the board and write their words.

Variation: Do the activity as a game in which you divide the class into teams. The team with the most number of associations is the winner.

FOCUS

- Should
- Comparatives with *than*

CLOSE UP

RULE:	The modal *should* is used to give advice to someone.
EXAMPLE:	Should I buy a bicycle or a motorcycle? I think you **should** buy a bicycle.

RULE:	The modal *should* is an auxiliary verb that combines with the base form of the verb. It doesn't contract with subject pronouns.
EXAMPLES:	I **should buy** She **should buy** He **should buy** It **should buy** We **should buy** You **should buy** They **should buy**

RULE:	When comparing two items, the *comparative* is used with *than*.
EXAMPLES:	Bicycles are **safer than** motorcycles. English is **more useful than** Latin.

GETTING READY

1. Introduce *should*. Describe several problems and give advice using *should*. For example:

    Jane is very hungry.
    She should eat lunch.

    Bill is sick today.
    He should go to the doctor.

2. Form sentences using the words in the box at the top of text page 42, and have students repeat. For example:

    I should study.
    He should study.
    She should study.

INTRODUCING THE MODELS

There are two model conversations. Introduce and practice each separately. For each model:

1. Have students look at the model illustration.

2. Set the scene: "This person can't decide what to do."

3. Present the model.

4. Full-Class Repetition.

5. Ask students if they have any questions. Check understanding of new vocabulary:

    2nd model: *useful, Latin*

Pronunciation Note

The pronunciation focus of Chapter 5 is **Yes/No Questions with *or*** (text page 48). You may wish to model this pronunciation at this point and encourage students to incorporate it into their language practice.

Should I buy a bicycle or a motorcycle?

Should we buy this fan or that fan?

6. Group Choral Repetition.

7. Choral Conversation.

8. Call on one or two pairs of students to present the dialog.

SIDE BY SIDE EXERCISES

Examples

1. A. Should I buy a used car or a new car?
   B. I think you should buy a used car.
   A. Why?
   B. Used cars are cheaper than new cars.

2. A. Should he go out with Ellen or Helen?
   B. I think he should go out with Ellen.
   A. Why?
   B. Ellen is more interesting than Helen.

Answer Key to Comparative Adjectives 3–15:

3. friendlier
4. more honest
5. more intelligent
6. prettier
7. quieter
8. more attractive
9. more talented
10. fancier
11. warmer
12. more convenient
13. more capable
14. lazier
15. more exciting

1. **Exercise 1:** Call on two students to present the dialog. Then do Choral Repetition and Choral Conversation practice.

2. **Exercise 2:** Introduce the new expression *go out with*. Same as above.

3. **Exercises 3–15:** Either Full-Class Practice or Pair Practice.

New Vocabulary

4. vote for
   honest
5. take a course
   professor
7. fan
9. piano lesson
   talented
10. left hand
    right hand
11. fur
12. notebook computer
    desktop computer
13. hire
    capable
14. fire
    lazy
15. rent
    exciting

4. **Exercise 16:** Have students use the model as a guide to create their own conversations, using vocabulary of their choice. Encourage students to use dictionaries to find new words they want to use. This exercise can be done orally in class or for written homework. If you assign it for homework, do one example in class to make sure students understand what's expected. Have students present their conversations in class the next day.

WORKBOOK

Pages 43–46

EXPANSION ACTIVITIES

1. Match the Conversations

a. Make a set of matching cards based on giving advice. For example:

I'm hungry.	You should eat some food.
I'm thirsty.	You should drink some water.
I'm tired.	You should go to bed early tonight.
I think I have the flu.	You should call the doctor.
I'm bored.	You should go out with your friends.
I have a bad toothache.	You should call the dentist.
English is difficult to learn.	You should study more.
I need more money.	You should get another job.

b. Distribute a card to each student.

c. Have students memorize the sentences on their cards, and then have students walk around the room saying their sentences until they find their match.

d. Then have pairs of students say their matched sentences aloud to the class.

2. I Need Your Advice

a. Divide the class into pairs.

b. Put the following conversational model and word cues on the board:

A. Should I _____ or _____?
B. I think you should _____ because
_____ than _____.

wear:	old shoes	new shoes
take:	candy	flowers
wear:	jeans	jacket and tie/dress
take:	bus	subway
drink:	soda	lemonade

c. Set the scene: "You're going to a party, and you aren't sure what to do."

d. Have pairs of students create conversations in which they ask for and give advice, using the word cues and conversational model on the board. Students can use any vocabulary they wish in giving reasons for their answers. For example:

A. Should I wear my old shoes or my new shoes to the party?
B. I think you should wear your old shoes because they're more comfortable than your new shoes.
    or
I think you should wear your new shoes because they're more attractive than your old shoes.

e. Encourage students to expand the conversations any way they wish and also to think of other questions to ask.

f. Call on pairs to present their conversations to the class.

3. What Should They Do?

a. Write situations such as the following on index cards.

Timothy doesn't have any friends. What should he do?

(continued)

Peter and Carol can't find their dog.
What should they do?

Greta is very bored.
What should she do?

My fax machine is broken.
What should I do?

Our new neighbors are very noisy.
What should we do?

Barbara wants to be rich some day.
What should she do?

b. Have a student pick up a card and read the situation to the class.

c. Call on several students to give advice. Encourage students to be imaginative in their answers.

4. Key Word Comparisons

Have students make comparisons between different things they might buy or do. Write the key words below on the board and ask the following questions. Students can answer using the adjectives on the board or any others they wish.

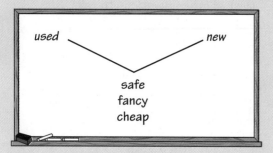

Should I buy a used car or a new car?

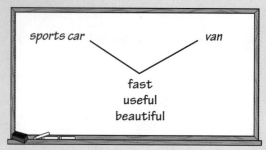

Should I buy a sports car or a van?

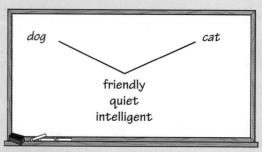

Should I get a dog or a cat?

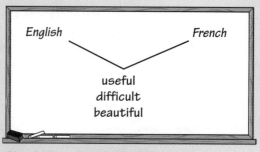

Should I study English or French?

Possible answers:

I think you should buy a new car because new cars are safer than used cars.

or

I think you should buy a new car because new cars are fancier than used cars.

or

I think you should buy a new car because used cars aren't as safe as new cars.

or

I think you should buy a used car because used cars are cheaper than new cars.

5. Sharing Good Advice

a. Write the following model on the board:

> Should I _____ or _____ ?

b. Have each student write a question asking for advice based on the model.

c. Write the following response model on the board:

> I think you should _____ because _____ (is/are) _____ than _____ .

d. Have students read their questions aloud, and have members of the class give advice. For example:

> Student 1: Should I see the movie *Love Lost* or *Seasick* this weekend?
>
> Student 2: I think you should see *Love Lost* because it's a better movie than *Seasick*.

6. Dictate and Discuss

a. Divide the class into pairs or small groups.

b. Dictate sentences such as the following and then have students discuss them:

> Dogs are friendlier than cats.
> Used cars are better than new cars.
> English is easier than _(other language)_ .
> Our city is more beautiful than _(other city)_ .

c. Call on students to share their opinions with the rest of the class.

7. Class Discussion

a. Divide the class into small groups.

b. Have each group write statements similar to those in Activity 6 above.

c. Have the groups read their sentences aloud for the class to discuss.

8. Let's Compare!

a. Divide the class into pairs or small groups.

b. Call out two related words. For example:

car	motorcycle
dog	cat
apartment	house
train	bus
New York	Paris
winter	summer

c. Have students compare the two items any way they wish.

d. Call on students to tell their ideas to the class in order to compare everybody's comparisons.

Variation: Have students think of additional word pairs for the class to compare.

9. Mystery Conversations

a. Divide the class into pairs.

b. Write the following sentence on the board:

> I think you should _____ because _____ .

c. Write roles such as the following on word cards, and give one to each pair of students:

a parent and a child	a boss and an employee
a teacher and a student	two friends
two neighbors	a doctor and a patient
a wife and a husband	a brother and a sister

d. Have each pair create a short dialog that incorporates the sentence on the board. The dialogs should be appropriate for the roles the students have on their cards.

e. Have each pair present their dialog to the class. Then have the other students guess who the people are.

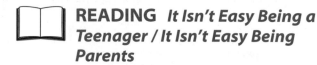

READING *It Isn't Easy Being a Teenager / It Isn't Easy Being Parents*

FOCUS

- Should
- Comparatives

NEW VOCABULARY

Story 1	Story 2
better	fashionable
grades	sympathetic
hard	understanding
neat	
no matter how	
satisfied	
You know, . . .	

READING THE STORIES

Optional: Preview the stories by having students talk about the story titles and/or illustrations. You may choose to introduce new vocabulary beforehand, or have students encounter the new vocabulary within the context of the reading.

1. Have students read silently, or follow along silently as the stories are read aloud by you, by one or more students, or on the audio program.

2. Ask students if they have any questions. Check understanding of vocabulary. Explain that *better* is the comparative form of *good*.

3. Check students' comprehension:

   Story 1: What do his parents think?
   Story 2: What do their children think?

✓ READING CHECK-UP

WHAT'S THE WORD?

1. healthy
2. nice
3. good
4. short
5. polite
6. fashionable
7. new
8. interesting
9. friendly

READING EXTENSION

Tic Tac Question Formation

1. Draw a tic tac grid on the board and fill it with question words. For example:

How?	Who?	Do?
What?	Should?	Are?
Does?	Why?	Is?

2. Divide the class into two teams. Give each team a mark: *X* or *O*.

3. Choose one of the stories, and have each team ask a question about the story that begins with one of the question words and then provide the answer to the question. If the question and answer are correct, the team gets to put its mark in that space. For example:

   X Team: Does the boy try to be a good son? Yes, he does.

How?	Who?	Do?
What?	Should?	Are?
X	Why?	Is?

4. The first team to mark out three boxes in a straight line—vertically, horizontally, or diagonally—wins.

 LISTENING

Listen and choose what the people are talking about.

1. A. I like it. It's fast.
   B. It is. It's much faster than my old one.

2. A. Is it comfortable?
   B. Yes. It's more comfortable than my old one.

3. A. I think it should be shorter.
   B. But it's very short now!

4. A. They aren't very polite.
   B. You're right. They should be more polite.

5. A. Is it safe?
   B. Yes. It's much safer than my old one.

6. A. Which one should I buy?
   B. Buy this one. It's more powerful than that one.

Answers

1. b

2. a

3. a

4. b

5. a

6. b

Text Page 45: Don't Be Ridiculous!

FOCUS

- Possessive Pronouns
- Comparative Expressions:

$$as \underline{\hspace{1cm}} as$$

$$much \left\{ \begin{array}{c} \underline{\hspace{1cm}}er \\ \hline more \underline{\hspace{1cm}} \end{array} \right\} than$$

CLOSE UP

RULE:	Possessive pronouns are nouns that indicate possession. Unlike possessive adjectives, they are used alone without a noun following.
EXAMPLES:	my dog **mine** his novel **his** her pronunciation **hers** our apartment **ours** your computer **yours** their house **theirs**
RULE:	To emphasize a comparison, *much* is placed before the comparative.
EXAMPLES:	Yours is **much friendlier** than mine. Yours are **much more interesting** than his.

GETTING READY

1. Introduce possessive pronouns.

   a. Make sentences with the words in the box at the top of text page 45. Have students repeat each sentence with a possessive pronoun. For example:

   > This is my book. This is mine.
   > This is his book. This is his.
   > This is her book. This is hers.

   b. Practice using possessive pronouns by asking about objects in the classroom and having students answer using possessive pronouns. For example, point to Student B's pencil and ask Student A:

Teacher: That pencil isn't mine. Is it yours?

Student A: No, it isn't mine. It's his/hers.

2. Introduce *as* _____ *as*.

   a. Put the following on the board:

Tim's house   Tom's house

b. Say:

> Tim's house is big.
> Tom's house is bigger.
> Tim's house isn't as big as Tom's house.

c. Put the following on the board:

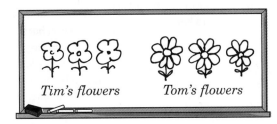

d. Say:

> Tim's flowers are pretty.
> Tom's flowers are prettier.
> Tim's flowers aren't as pretty as Tom's flowers.

INTRODUCING THE MODELS

There are two model conversations. Introduce and practice each separately. For each model:

1. Have students look at the model illustration.

2. Set the scene:

1st model: "Two people are taking a walk in the park with their dogs."

2nd model: "A husband and wife are talking. The husband is a writer, and he's talking about his books."

3. Present the model.

4. Full-Class Repetition.

5. Ask students if they have any questions. Check understanding of new vocabulary:

1st model: *as _____ as, Don't be ridiculous!, much _____ than*

2nd model: *Ernest Hemingway*

Culture Note

Ernest Hemingway was a famous 20th-century American author and journalist.

6. Group Choral Repetition.

7. Choral Conversation Practice.

8. Call on one or two pairs of students to present the dialog.

(For additional practice, do Choral Conversation in small groups or by rows.)

SIDE BY SIDE EXERCISES

Examples

> 1. A. You know, my apartment isn't as clean as your apartment.
>   B. Don't be ridiculous! Yours is MUCH cleaner than mine.
> 2. A. You know, my computer isn't as powerful as Bob's computer.
>   B. Don't be ridiculous! Yours is MUCH more powerful than his.

1. **Exercise 1:** Call on two students to present the dialog. Then do Choral Repetition and Choral Conversation practice.

2. **Exercise 2:** Same as above.

3. **Exercises 3–8:** Either Full-Class Practice or Pair Practice.

> **New Vocabulary**
> 4. furniture
> 6. pronunciation

4. **Exercise 9:** Have students use the model as a guide to create their own conversations, using vocabulary of their choice. Encourage students to use dictionaries to find new words they want to use. This exercise can be done orally in class or for written homework. If you assign it for homework, do one example in class to make sure students understand what's expected. Have students present their conversations in class the next day.

WORKBOOK

Pages 47–49

EXPANSION ACTIVITIES

1. What's the Possessive?

a. Write the following on the board:

Yes. It's/They're _____.

b. While holding up objects, make statements and have students respond with a possessive pronoun, using the model on the board. For example:

Teacher: Is this *(Robert's)* book?
Student: Yes, it's his.

Teacher: Are these *(Maria's)* pencils?
Student: Yes. They're hers.

Teacher: Is this my dictionary?
Student: Yes. It's yours.

2. Whose Is It?

a. Have a small group of students volunteer to stand in front of the class and exchange possessions (for example: pens, keys, bags, books).

b. Point to an object a student is holding and ask the class: "Whose is it?" Have the class identify the owner. Encourage students to use possessive pronouns. For example:

Student 1: That's Mario's pen.
Teacher: Is it Mario's?
Student 1: Yes. It's his.

Student 2: This is Maria's book.
Teacher: Is it Maria's?
Student 2: Yes. It's hers.

3. Match the Conversations

a. Make the following set of matching cards. For example:

My car isn't as fast as his car.	Don't be ridiculous! Yours is much faster than his.

My car isn't as fast as her car.	Don't be ridiculous! Yours is much faster than hers.
My car isn't as fast as their car.	Don't be ridiculous! Yours is much faster than theirs.
My car isn't as fast as your car.	Don't be ridiculous! Yours is much faster than mine.
Your car isn't as fast as his car.	Don't be ridiculous! Mine is much faster than his.
Your car isn't as fast as her car.	Don't be ridiculous! Mine is much faster than hers.
Your car isn't as fast as their car.	Don't be ridiculous! Mine is much faster than theirs.
Your car isn't as fast as my car.	Don't be ridiculous! Mine is much faster than yours.

b. Distribute a card to each student.

c. Have students memorize the sentences on their cards, and then have students walk around the room saying their sentences until they find their match.

d. Then have pairs of students say their matched sentences aloud to the class.

4. Concentration

a. Use the cards from the above activity. Place them face down in four rows of 4 each.

b. Divide the class into two teams. The object of the game is for students to find the matching cards. Both teams should be able to see all the cards, since *concentrating* on their location is an important part of playing the game.

c. A student from Team 1 turns over two cards. If they match, the student picks up the cards, that team gets a point, and the student takes another turn. If the cards don't match, the student turns them face down, and a member of Team 2 takes a turn.

d. The game continues until all the cards have been matched. The team with the most correct matches wins the game.

Variation: This game can also be played in groups and pairs.

5. Compare the Pictures

a. Find magazine pictures that represent two styles or kinds of the same thing. For example, find pictures of two different houses, cars, watches, animals, dresses, suits, appliances.

b. Give these sets of pictures to pairs of students, and have them create conversations in which they compare their pictures, using possessive adjectives and any vocabulary they know. For example:

Student A: Your *(house)* is much larger than mine.

Student B: Yes, but yours is much more beautiful than mine.

Student A: Really? I think yours is much more interesting.

Student B: But yours is more expensive.

READING *Brownsville*

FOCUS

- Comparatives

NEW VOCABULARY

although	hospitable
because of	polite
bus system	real
change (v)	reliable
changes (n)	used to
definitely	

READING THE STORY

Optional: Preview the story by having students talk about the story title and/or illustrations. You may choose to introduce new vocabulary beforehand, or have students encounter the new vocabulary within the context of the reading.

1. Have students read silently, or follow along silently as the story is read aloud by you, by one or more students, or on the audio program.

2. Ask students if they have any questions. Check understanding of vocabulary. Explain that the expression *used to* describes something that happened regularly in the past.

3. Check students' comprehension, using some or all of the following questions:

> Why was Brownsville a very good place to live?
> Describe Brownsville today.
> Where did the Taylor family move? Why?
> Why were the Taylors happier in Brownsville?

✓ READING *CHECK-UP*

Q & A

1. Call on a pair of students to present the model.

2. Check understanding of new vocabulary: *mayor, definitely, Why do you say that?*

   > ### Language Note
   >
   > The expression *they say* means *people in general say.*

3. Have students work in pairs to create new dialogs.

4. Call on pairs to present their dialogs to the class.

READING EXTENSION

1. *Retell the Story!*

   Retell the story with key words on the board.

   a. Write the following on the board:

streets	clean
parks	safe
bus system	reliable
schools	good

   b. Have students look at the key words on the board and tell about Brownsville in the past:

   > The streets were clean.
   > The parks were safe.
   > The bus system was reliable.
   > The schools were good.

   c. Have students look at the key words on the board and tell how Brownsville has changed:

   > The streets aren't as clean as they used to be.
   > The parks aren't as safe as they used to be.
   > The bus system isn't as reliable as it used to be.

The schools aren't as good as they used to be.

d. Have students tell why the Taylors moved to Newport:

> The streets are cleaner.
> The parks are safer.
> The bus system is more reliable.
> The schools are better.

e. Write the following on the board:

> friendly
> nice
> polite
> hospitable

f. Now have students compare the people in Brownsville with the people in Newport:

> The people in Brownsville are friendlier than the people in Newport.
> The people in Brownsville are nicer than the people in Newport.
> The people in Brownsville are more polite than the people in Newport.
> The people in Brownsville are more hospitable than the people in Newport.

g. Next, have students compare the people in Newport with the people in Brownsville:

> The people in Newport aren't as friendly as the people in Brownsville.
> The people in Newport aren't as nice as the people in Brownsville.
> The people in Newport aren't as polite as the people in Brownsville.
> The people in Newport aren't as hospitable as the people in Brownsville.

2. **True or False?**

Have students decide whether the following statements about the story are true or false. You can do this as a class, in pairs or groups, or as a game with competing teams.

> The streets in Brownsville used to be clean. *(True)*

> The parks in Brownsville are safer than they used to be. *(False)*

> The bus system in Brownsville was more reliable in the past. *(True)*

> The bus system in Newport is more reliable than the bus system in Brownsville. *(True)*

> The schools in Brownsville are better than the schools in Newport. *(False)*

> The people in Newport aren't as friendly as the people in Brownsville. *(True)*

> The people in Brownsville are nicer than the people in Newport. *(True)*

> The people in Newport are more polite than the people in Brownsville. *(False)*

> The people in Brownsville aren't as hospitable as the people in Newport. *(False)*

> The Taylor family lives in Newport, but they were happier in Brownsville. *(True)*

How to Say It!

> **Agreeing & Disagreeing:** When disagreeing with someone, it is appropriate to say so *(I disagree. I disagree with you. I don't think so.)* and then offer an opinion *(I think . . . , In my opinion, . . .)*.

1. Set the scene: "People are talking. One person agrees. Another person disagrees."

2. Present the expressions.

3. Full-Class Repetition.

4. Ask students if they have any questions. Check understanding of new vocabulary: *in my opinion, agree, disagree.*

5. Group Choral Repetition.

 INTERACTIONS

1. There are three conversations. Introduce and practice each separately. For each conversation:

   a. Set the scene: "People are talking about places they know."

   b. Model each line, and have students repeat chorally and individually.

   c. Ask students if they have any questions.

   d. Call on one or two pairs of students to present each dialog.

2. Introduce the suggested topics for conversation and check understanding of new vocabulary: *wide, modern, rainy, snowy.*

3. Have pairs of students talk about two cities they know. Encourage them to express their opinions and agree or disagree, using the expressions presented in the lesson.

4. For homework, have students write a short dialog in which people compare two cities. Have students present their dialogs in the next class.

WORKBOOK

Page 50

EXPANSION ACTIVITY

In My Opinion

1. Have each student write a statement that uses a comparative to express an opinion.

2. Collect all the statements, mix them up, and have each student draw one.

3. Next, have students read the statements they've drawn. Call on one or two other students to respond by *agreeing* or *disagreeing* and telling why. For example:

   A. I think our class is smarter than Mrs. Garcia's class.
   B. I agree. Our class is much smarter.
      or
      I disagree. I think her class is smarter than ours.

PRONUNCIATION

> **Yes/No Questions with *or*:** When presenting two alternatives, the pitch rises on the first and falls on the second.

Focus on Listening

Practice the sentences in the left column. Say each sentence or play the audio one or more times. Have students listen carefully and repeat.

Focus on Pronunciation

Practice the sentences in the right column. Have students say each sentence and then listen carefully as you say it or play the audio.

If you wish, have students continue practicing the sentences to improve their pronunciation.

JOURNAL

Have students write their journal entries at home or in class. Encourage students to use a dictionary to look up words they would like to use. Students can share their written work with other students if appropriate. Have students discuss what they have written as a class, in pairs, or in small groups.

CHAPTER SUMMARY

GRAMMAR

1. Divide the class into pairs or small groups.

2. Have students take turns forming sentences from the words in the grammar boxes. Student A says a sentence, and Student B points to the words from each column that are in the sentence. Then have students switch: Student B says a sentence, and Student A points to the words.

KEY VOCABULARY

Have students ask you any questions about the meaning or pronunciation of the vocabulary. If students ask for the pronunciation, repeat after the student until the student is satisfied with his or her own pronunciation.

EXPANSION ACTIVITIES

1. **Do You Remember the Words?**

   Check students' retention of the vocabulary depicted on the opening page of Chapter 5 by doing the following activity:

   a. Have students open their books to page 39 and cover the list of vocabulary words.

   b. Either call out a number and have students tell you the word, or say a word and have students tell you the number.

   Variation: You can also do this activity as a game with competing teams.

2. **Student-Led Dictation**

   a. Tell each student to choose a word or phrase from the Key Vocabulary list on text page 48 and look at it very carefully.

   b. Have students take turns dictating their words to the class. Everybody writes down that student's word.

   c. When the dictation is completed, call on different students to write each word on the board to check the spelling.

3. **Beanbag Toss**

   a. Call out the topic: *Describing People.*

   b. Have students toss a beanbag back and forth. The student to whom the beanbag is tossed must name a word for describing people. For example:

Student 1:	interesting
Student 2:	tall
Student 3:	capable

   (continued)

EXPANSION ACTIVITIES (Continued)

c. Continue until all the words in the category have been named. Then continue with another category. For example:

describing books	describing houses
describing jobs	describing pet animals
describing cars	describing clothes

Variation: You can also do this activity as a game with competing teams.

4. Letter Game

a. Divide the class into two teams.

b. Say: "I'm thinking of an adjective that starts with *a*."

c. The first person to raise his or her hand and guess correctly *[attractive]* wins a point for his or her team.

d. Continue with other letters of the alphabet and adjectives.

The team that gets the most correct answers wins the game.

5. Movable Categories

a. Write out the adjectives from the list on page 48 on separate cards.

b. Give each student one or two cards.

c. Call out one of the following categories:

adjectives for describing food
adjectives for describing a store
adjectives for describing a park
adjectives for describing a person
adjectives for describing a computer
adjectives for describing a movie
adjectives for describing a building
adjectives for describing a baby
adjectives for describing a class

d. All those students whose words are appropriate for the chosen category go to the right side of the room. All the other students go to the left side.

e. Those who are in the right group call out their words for the class to verify.

f. Continue with other categories.

1. Board Game

a. On poster boards or on manila file folders, make up game boards with a pathway consisting of separate spaces. You may use any theme or design you wish.

b. Divide the class into groups of 2 to 4 students and give each group a game board and a die, and each person something to be used as a playing piece.

c. Give each group a pile of cards face-down with sentences written on them. Some sentences should be correct, and others incorrect. For example:

> My old rocking chair was much more comfortable.
> His new sports car is more faster.
> Tokyo is expensive than Rome.
> The people in Brownsville are politer than the people in Newport.
> Your house is much larger than my.
> Hers pronunciation is much better than his.
> The weather in Chicago isn't as good as the weather in San Francisco.
> His son isn't as smarter as mine.
> Yours is much better than theirs.
> I think you should to vote for Linda Lee.
> Do I should buy a computer notebook?
> Fur gloves are warmer then leather gloves.
> In my opinion, the people in Jamesville aren't as hospitable as the people in Gainesville.
> Our new house is larger than our old house.
> This fan is more quieter than that fan.

d. Each student in turn rolls the die, moves the playing piece along the game path, and after landing on a space, picks a card, reads the sentence, and says if it is *correct* or *incorrect*. If the sentence is incorrect and the student is able to give the correct version, that student takes an additional turn.

e. The first student to reach the end of the pathway is the winner.

2. Telephone

a. Divide the class into large groups. Have each group sit in a circle.

b. Whisper a short story to one student. For example:

> "I bought a new car. It's much more powerful than my old car. It's faster and shinier. It's also much more expensive."

c. The first student whispers the story to the second student, and so forth around the circle.

d. When the story gets to the last student, that person says it aloud. Is it the same story you started with? The group with the most accurate story wins.

3. Ask Me a Question!

a. Divide the class into groups of 3 or 4.

b. One student in each group thinks of something you can buy in a store.

c. The other students in the group then try to guess the item by asking questions with adjectives. Comparative questions are useful in this game. For example:

> Student 1: Is it smaller than my backpack?
> Teacher: No, it isn't.
> Student 2: Is it bigger than my car?
> Teacher: No, it isn't.
> Student 3: Is it exciting?
> Teacher: Yes, it is.
> Student 4: Is it light?
> Teacher: No, it isn't.
> Student 1: Is it expensive?
> Teacher: Yes, it is.
> Student 2: Does it use electricity?
> Teacher: Yes, it does.
> Student 3: Is it a desktop computer?
> Teacher: Yes, it is!

d. Have students play the game in pairs, asking each other Yes/No questions.

4. Category Game

a. Divide the class into groups of four students.

b. Write out the following cards and give two to each student in the group.

(continued)

large modern tall beautiful (a building)	rainy snowy hot warm (the weather)
beautiful capable intelligent sympathetic (a woman)	handsome understanding talkative honest (a man)
fancy expensive delicious busy friendly (a restaurant)	healthy cute quiet small smart (a baby)
powerful light expensive fast (a computer)	exciting short interesting good (a book or movie)

c. Have the student read the adjectives to the group. The group members try to guess the what the adjectives describe.

d. The team that guesses all the cards first wins.

Variation: Have students create their own cards that they read aloud to the class.

5. Dialog Builder!

a. Divide the class into pairs.

b. Write a line on the board from a conversation such as the following:

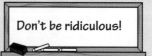

Don't be ridiculous!

Other possible lines:

That's right.
Why do you say that?
You know, it isn't easy being _____.

c. Have each pair create a conversation incorporating that line. Students can begin and end their conversations any way they wish, but they must include that line in their dialogs.

d. Call on students to present their conversations to the class.

WORKBOOK PAGE 40

A. OLD AND NEW

1. softer
2. lighter
3. larger
4. hotter
5. friendlier
6. safer
7. smaller
8. fancier
9. warmer
10. bigger
11. easier
12. nicer
13. cheaper
14. uglier

B. WHAT'S THE WORD?

1. shorter
2. cuter
3. fatter
4. busier

WORKBOOK PAGE 41

C. THEY'RE DIFFERENT

1. more talkative
2. more interesting
3. more attractive
4. more comfortable
5. more intelligent
6. longer
7. colder
8. thinner
9. healthier
10. more powerful
11. more handsome
12. whiter
13. more beautiful

D. WHAT'S THE WORD?

1. more delicious
2. better
3. more expensive
4. more energetic

WORKBOOK PAGE 42

E. PUZZLE

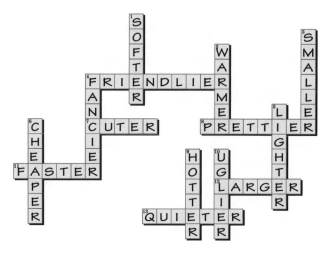

F. LISTENING

Listen and choose the correct words to complete the sentences.

1. A. Yesterday was cool.
   B. I know. But today is . . .

2. A. Ronald is tall.
   B. You're right. But his son Jim is . . .

3. A. This briefcase is very attractive.
   B. Really? I think THAT briefcase is . . .

4. A. Nancy is very nice.
   B. Do you know her sister Sally? She's . . .

5. A. Tom is very fast.
   B. You're right. But his brother John is . . .

6. A. Michael is a very friendly person.
   B. I know. But his wife is . . .

7. A. Your roommate is very interesting.
   B. You're right. But I think YOUR roommate is . . .

8. A. The supermarket on Center Street was very busy today.
   B. Yes, I know. But the supermarket on Main Street was . . .

Answers

1. a
2. b
3. b
4. a
5. b
6. a
7. a
8. b

G. LET'S COMPARE!

1. Jack's tie is fancier than John's tie.
2. The printer is cheaper than the computer.
3. The meatballs are more delicious than the chicken.
4. Rick is more talkative than Dick.
5. Carol's car is smaller than Carla's car.
6. Frank is more talented than Fred.

I. LISTENING

Listen and circle the correct answer.

1. Yesterday was hotter than today.
2. The tomatoes are more expensive than the potatoes.
3. Aunt Betty is younger than cousin Jane.
4. Bob is shorter and heavier than Bill.
5. Barry's chair is more comfortable than Larry's chair.
6. The science test was more difficult than the history test.
7. Irene's office is bigger than Eileen's office.
8. Ronald is more capable than Donald.

Answers

1. Yes
2. No
3. No
4. Yes
5. Yes
6. No
7. No
8. Yes

K. WHAT SHOULD THEY DO?

1. You should plant some flowers.
2. He should call the dentist.
3. You should rent a video.
4. You should call the police.
5. They should hire her.
6. She should fire him.

N. WHAT'S THE WORD?

1. his
2. mine
3. hers
4. theirs
5. yours
6. his
7. ours

O. WHAT'S THE WORD?

1. yours, mine
2. his, hers
3. ours, theirs
4. Yours, mine
5. hers, his

P. DIFFERENT, BUT OKAY

1. isn't as quiet as, more interesting
2. isn't as fashionable as, more comfortable
3. aren't as modern as, larger
4. isn't as powerful as, more reliable
5. isn't as warm as, sunnier
6. aren't as talkative as, more understanding
7. as exciting as, better

Q. YOU'RE RIGHT

1. more attractive than Ken's tie
2. nicer than Donald
3. lazier than Larry
4. more difficult than English
5. bigger than Julie's office
6. more talkative than your son

T. WHO SHOULD WE HIRE?

1. lively
2. smarter
3. more talented
4. talented
5. more honest
6. better
7. friendly
8. more intelligent
9. more talkative
10. more polite
11. more capable
12. better
13. delicious
14. more interesting
15. faster
16. nicer

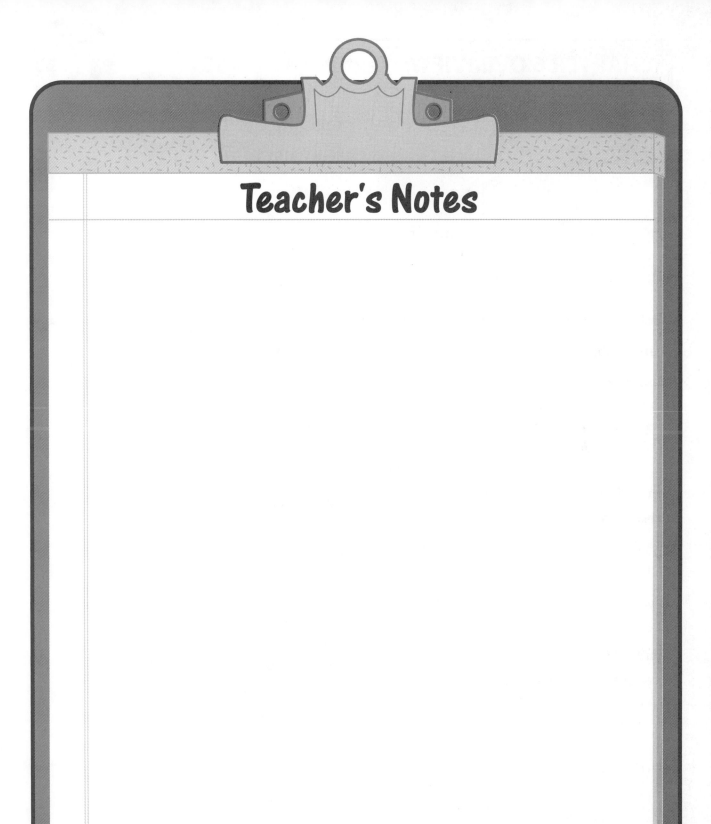

Teacher's Notes

CHAPTER 6 OVERVIEW: Text Pages 49–58

GRAMMAR

SUPERLATIVES

He's	the smartest the nicest the biggest the busiest	person I know.
	the most talented the most interesting	

FUNCTIONS

DESCRIBING

I think your friend is very *kind/friendly/ energetic/generous*.

He's *the kindest/the friendliest/the most energetic/the most generous* person I know.

This is the *smallest* one we have.

EXPRESSING AN OPINION

I think *your friend Margaret is very smart.*

In my opinion, . . .
As far as I'm concerned, . . .
If you ask me, . . .

INITIATING A TOPIC

You know . . .

EXPRESSING AGREEMENT

I agree.
You're right.

EXPRESSING DISAGREEMENT

I disagree.

OFFERING TO HELP

May I help you?

EXPRESSING WANT–DESIRE

I want to buy *a small radio.*

ASKING FOR AND REPORTING INFORMATION

Don't you have *a smaller one?*

Who is *the most popular actress in your country?*
What is *the best city in your country?*

EXPRESSING GRATITUDE

Thank you anyway.

APOLOGIZING

Sorry *we can't help you.*

NEW VOCABULARY

Adjectives

ashamed
best
boring
bright
dependable
elegant
funny
generous
helpful
horrible
kind
lightweight
mean
nice
obnoxious
older
patient
proud
reasonable
rude
sloppy
stubborn
worse
worst
younger

Modal for Giving Advice

should

Miscellaneous

anyway
appliance
bargain
bookcase
certainly
complain
compliment (v)
downstairs
evening gown
girl
history
home entertainment products
location
most
one
products
professor
salespeople
senator
tourist sight
upstairs
vacation place
video camera

EXPRESSIONS

besides that
I'm afraid not.
in addition
Please come again.
Thank you anyway.
you can see why

Text Page 49: Chapter Opening Page

Vocabulary Preview

You may want to present these words before beginning the chapter, or you may choose to wait until they first occur in a specific lesson. If you choose to present them at this point, here are some suggestions:

1. Have students look at the illustrations on text page 49 and identify the words they already know.

2. Present the vocabulary. Say each word and have the class repeat it chorally and individually. Check students' understanding and pronunciation of the words.

3. Practice the vocabulary as a class, in pairs, or in small groups. Have students cover the word list and look at the pictures. Practice the words in the following ways:

   • Say a word and have students tell the number of the illustration.

   • Give the number of an illustration and have students say the word.

FOCUS

- Superlatives with -est

CLOSE UP

SPELLING RULE:	The superlative of one-syllable adjectives is formed by adding -est.
EXAMPLE:	kind – the kind**est**
SPELLING RULE:	For one-syllable adjectives that end in -e, only -st is added.
EXAMPLE:	nice – the nice**st**
SPELLING RULE:	For one-syllable adjectives that end with a single consonant preceded by a single vowel, the final consonant is doubled.
EXAMPLE:	hot – the ho**ttest**
SPELLING RULE:	For two-syllable adjectives that end in -y preceded by a consonant, -y changes to -i.
EXAMPLE:	happy – the happ**iest**

GETTING READY

1. Introduce superlative adjectives.

   a. Put the following on the board:

   Bill   *Ted*   *George*

   b. Tell about these three people:

   Bill is tall.
   Ted is taller than Bill.
   George is *the tallest*.

   Ted is nice.
   George is nicer than Ted.
   Bill is *the nicest*.

c. Say these sentences again, and have students repeat chorally.

2. Read the adjectives in the boxes at the top of text page 50. Have students repeat chorally. Introduce the new word *kind*.

INTRODUCING THE MODEL

1. Have students look at the model illustration.

2. Set the scene: "A mother and daughter are talking."

3. Present the model.

4. Full-Class Repetition.

5. Ask students if they have any questions. Check understanding of the new word *certainly*.

6. Group Choral Repetition.

7. Choral Conversation.

8. Call on one or two pairs of students to present the dialog.

(For additional practice, do Choral Conversation in small groups or by rows.)

SIDE BY SIDE EXERCISES

Examples

1. A. I think your Aunt Emma is very kind.
   B. She certainly is. She's the kindest person I know.

2. A. I think your friend Jim is very bright.
   B. He certainly is. He's the brightest person I know.

Answer Key to Superlative Adjectives 3–9:

3. the nicest (people)
4. the funniest
5. the prettiest
6. the friendliest
7. the laziest
8. the meanest
9. the sloppiest (people)

1. Exercise 1: Check understanding of the word *kind*. Call on two students to present the dialog. Then do Choral Repetition and Choral Conversation practice.

2. Exercise 2: Check understanding of the word *bright*. Same as above.

3. Exercises 3–9: Either Full-Class Practice or Pair Practice.

New Vocabulary

4. funny
8. mean
9. sloppy

WORKBOOK

Page 51

1. Miming

a. Write on cards the adjectives on text page 50.

b. Have students take turns picking a card from the pile and pantomiming the adjective on the card.

c. The class must guess what adjective the person is describing.

Variation: This can be done as a game with competing teams.

2. The People of Centerville

a. Put the following on the board:

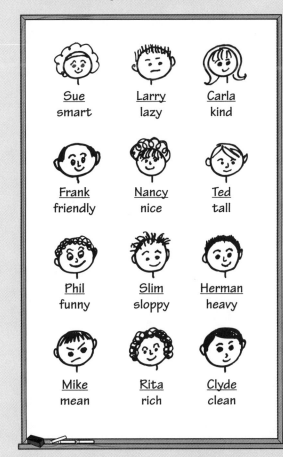

Sue smart	Larry lazy	Carla kind
Frank friendly	Nancy nice	Ted tall
Phil funny	Slim sloppy	Herman heavy
Mike mean	Rita rich	Clyde clean

b. Set the scene:

"Let's talk about the people who live in Centerville. Sue is the smartest person in Centerville."

c. Call on other students to make similar statements about the other people.

d. Call on pairs to ask and answer questions about the people. For example:

A. Who's the nicest person in Centerville?
B. Nancy.

A. Who is Phil?
B. He's the funniest person in Centerville.

Variation: Have students choose one of the characters and pantomime that person. The class must guess who the person is.

3. The People We Know

Have students talk about people they know, using the superlative adjectives on text page 50. For example:

Who is the friendliest person you know?
In what ways is this person friendly?

Who is the sloppiest person you know?
In what ways is this person sloppy?

4. Spelling Game

a. Divide the class into teams.

b. Put the following scrambled words on the board or on a handout. Have students work together in their teams to unscramble the words. The first team to successfully unscramble the words in the fastest time is the winner.

tepapshi	(happiest)
entics	(nicest)
sltatelt	(tallest)
nusteinf	(funniest)
shetnitn	(thinnest)
ziltsea	(laziest)
desktin	(kindest)
rotseths	(shortest)
esritttep	(prettiest)
postlepis	(sloppiest)
silnerifdet	(friendliest)
ttthose	(hottest)
ttsseamr	(smartest)

(continued)

5. Dictate and Discuss

a. Divide the class into pairs or small groups.

b. Dictate sentences such as the following and then have students discuss them:

> Mother Teresa was the kindest person in the world.

> Bill Gates is the richest person in the world.
> President _____ / Prime Minister _____
> is the most honest person in our country.
> Teenagers are the sloppiest people in the world.
> Roberto Begnini is the funniest person in the world.

c. Call on students to share their opinions with the rest of the class.

Text Page 51: The Most Energetic Person I Know

FOCUS

- Superlatives with *most*
- Review of *-est* Superlatives

CLOSE UP

RULE:	The superlative of adjectives that have three or more syllables is formed by placing *the most* before the adjective.
EXAMPLE:	beautiful – **the most** beautiful

RULE:	The superlative of two-syllable adjectives that don't end in *-y* are less predictable. Some are formed with *most*, and some are formed with *-est*.
EXAMPLE:	patient – **the most** patient honest – **the most** honest simple – **the** simpl**est** quiet – **the** quiet**est**

GETTING READY

1. Introduce superlatives formed with *most*.

   a. Put the following on the board:

   Mary   Sue   Jane

   b. Tell about these people:

   Mary is talented.
   Sue is more talented than Mary.
   Jane is *the most talented*.

   Mary is intelligent.
   Sue is more intelligent than Mary.
   Jane is *the most intelligent*.

   c. Say these sentences again, and have students repeat.

2. Read the adjectives in the boxes at the top of text page 51. Have students repeat chorally.

INTRODUCING THE MODEL

1. Have students look at the model illustration.

2. Set the scene: "Two friends are talking."

3. Present the model.

4. Full-Class Repetition.

5. Ask students if they have any questions. Check understanding of vocabulary.

6. Group Choral Repetition.

7. Choral Conversation.

8. Call on one or two pairs of students to present the dialog.

   (For additional practice, do Choral Conversation in small groups or by rows.)

SIDE BY SIDE EXERCISES

Examples

1. A. I think your friend Carlos is very interesting.
   B. He certainly is. He's the most interesting person I know.

2. A. I think your grandfather is very generous.
   B. He certainly is. He's the most generous person I know.

Answer Key to Superlative Adjectives 3–11:

3. the most talented (people)
4. the most patient
5. the most stubborn
6. the most polite
7. the brightest
8. the noisiest
9. the rudest
10. the most honest
11. the most boring

1. **Exercise 1:** Call on two students to present the dialog. Then do Choral Repetition and Choral Conversation practice.

2. **Exercise 2:** Check understanding of the word *generous*. Same as above.

3. **Exercises 3–11:** Either Full-Class Practice or Pair Practice.

New Vocabulary

4. patient
5. stubborn
6. younger brother
7. older sister
8. upstairs
9. downstairs
   rude
10. senator
11. history
    professor
    boring

4. **Exercise 12:** Have students use the model as a guide to create 3 conversations, using vocabulary of their choice. (They may use any adjectives they wish.) Encourage students to use dictionaries to find new words they want to use. This exercise can be done orally in class or for written homework. If you assign it for homework, do one example in class to make sure students understand what's expected. Have students present their conversations in class the next day.

WORKBOOK

Pages 52–54

EXPANSION ACTIVITIES

1. Miming

a. Write on cards the adjectives on text page 51.

b. Have students take turns picking a card from the pile and pantomiming the adjective on the card.

c. The class must guess what adjective the person is describing.

Variation: This can be done as a game with competing teams.

2. Superlative Grammar Chain

a. Have students sit in a circle.

b. Start by saying:

   Andrew is very interesting.

c. Student 1 must respond with the appropriate superlative, and then add another adjective. For example:

   That's right. He's the most interesting person I know. He's also very polite.

Student 2 continues with the superlative and another adjective:

> That's right. He's the most polite person I know. He's also very energetic.

d. Continue until everyone has had at least one turn.

3. The People of Greenville

a. Put the following on the board:

Peter — polite
Timothy — talented
Emily — energetic
George — generous
Bob — boring
Irma — interesting
Steven — stubborn
Inga — intelligent
Ted — tall
Paul — patient
Fran — friendly
Nick — noisy

b. Set the scene:

> "Greenville is a city near Centerville. Let's talk about the people who live there. Peter is the most polite person in Greenville."

c. Call on other students to make similar statements about the other people.

d. Call on pairs to ask and answer questions about the people. For example:

> A. Who's the most talented person in Greenville?
> B. Timothy.

> A. Who is Inga?
> B. She's the most intelligent person in Greenville.

Variation: Have students choose one of the characters and pantomime that person. The class must guess who the person is.

4. The People We Know

As a class, in pairs, or in small groups, have students talk about people they know, using the superlative adjectives on text page 50. For example:

> Who is the most generous person you know? In what ways is this person generous?

> Who is the most stubborn person you know? In what ways is this person stubborn?

> Who is the most interesting person you know? In what ways is this person interesting?

> Who is the most talented person you know? In what ways is this person talented?

> Who is the most energetic person you know? In what ways is this person energetic?

5. Superlative Game

a. Divide the class into teams.

b. Give each team the following list of adjectives:

boring	mean
bright	nice
energetic	noisy
friendly	patient
funny	polite
generous	pretty
hot	rude
intelligent	sloppy
interesting	stubborn
kind	talented
lazy	

c. Have the team members work together to write the superlatives of each of the adjectives. Remind them to check the spelling of the adjectives.

d. The first team to turn in a list of correctly spelled superlatives, is the winner.

(continued)

6. Our City

a. Put a list of adjectives on the board. These adjectives should describe things in a city. For example:

tall	expensive	nice
long	pretty	modern
fast	ugly	old
noisy	interesting	busy
cheap		

b. Set the scene:

"Let's talk about _(name of your city)_ . _(name of street)_ is the busiest street in this city."

c. Call on students to make *superlative* statements about their city, using the list of adjectives on the board or any others they wish.

d. Write the following conversational model on the board:

A. What's the $\left\{ \begin{array}{l} \text{most} \rule{2cm}{0.4pt} \\ \rule{2cm}{0.4pt} \text{est} \end{array} \right\}$ _____ in this city?

B. In my opinion, _____ is the $\left\{ \begin{array}{l} \text{most} \rule{2cm}{0.4pt} \\ \rule{2cm}{0.4pt} \text{est} \end{array} \right\}$ _____.

e. Call on students to talk about their cities. For example:

A. What's the nicest hotel in this city?
B. In my opinion, the Plaza is the nicest hotel.

A. What's the cheapest restaurant in this city?
B. In my opinion, Joe's Diner is the cheapest restaurant.

f. If you wish, you may have students disagree with what others say. For example:

A. What's the nicest hotel in this city?
B. In my opinion, the Plaza is the nicest hotel.
C. I disagree. I think the Mayflower is the nicest hotel.

READING *The Nicest Person / The Most Obnoxious Dog*

FOCUS

- Superlatives

NEW VOCABULARY

Story 1	Story 2	
compliment (v)	ashamed	horrible
girl	complain	obnoxious
proud		

READING THE STORIES

Optional: Preview the stories by having students talk about the story titles and/or illustrations. You may choose to introduce new vocabulary beforehand, or have students encounter the new vocabulary within the context of the readings.

1. Have students read silently, or follow along silently as the stories are read aloud by you, by one or more students, or on the audio program.

2. Ask students if they have any questions. Check understanding of vocabulary.

3. Check students' comprehension, using some or all of the following questions:

   Story 1
   Why are Mr. and Mrs. Jackson proud of their daughter?
   What do the Jackson's friends and neighbors say about Linda?
   According to them, what's she like?

   Story 2
   Why are Mr. and Mrs. Hubbard ashamed of their dog?
   What do the Hubbards' friends and neighbors say about Rex?
   According to them, what's he like?

✓ READING *CHECK-UP*

CHOOSE

1. most polite
2. talented
3. nice
4. stubborn
5. noisiest
6. obnoxious

Q & A

1. Call on a pair of students to present each model.
2. Have students work in pairs to create new dialogs.
3. Call on pairs to present their new dialogs to the class.

How About You?

Have students do the activity in pairs or as a class.

READING EXTENSION

Contrasting Adjectives

1. Put the following on the board:

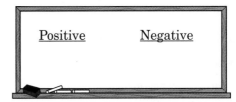

Positive	Negative

2. As a class, have students identify all the positive adjectives in the two stories. Write their suggestions in the <u>Positive</u> column on the board.

3. Have students identify all the negative adjectives in the story. Write their suggestions in the <u>Negative</u> column.

4. Divide the class into pairs or small groups, and have students brainstorm additional adjectives to add to each of these lists.

5. Have students share their ideas with the class.

How to Say It!

> **Expressing an Opinion:** There are many expressions to use when offering an opinion. Three common ones are *In my opinion, As far as I'm concerned, If you ask me.*

1. Set the scene: "Two students are talking about another student."

2. Present the expressions.

3. Full-Class Repetition.

4. Ask students if they have any questions. Check understanding of the new expressions: *As far as I'm concerned, . . , If you ask me, . . .*

5. Group Choral Repetition.

6. Have students work in pairs or small groups to create dialogs using the expressions.

7. Call on several pairs to present their conversations to the class.

 **LISTENING**

Listen to the sentence. Is the person saying something good or something bad about someone else?

1. She's the nicest person I know.

2. He's the laziest student in our class.

3. He's the most boring person I know.

4. She's the most generous person in our family.

5. They're the most honest people I know.

6. He's the rudest person in our apartment building.

7. He's the most dependable person in our office.

8. She's the kindest neighbor on our street.

9. She's the most stubborn person I know.

Answers

1. a

2. b

3. b

4. a

5. a

6. b

7. a

8. a

9. b

 PRONUNCIATION

> **Linking Words with Duplicated Consonants:** When the final consonant of one word is the same as the beginning consonant of the following word, the two sounds blend into one and are pronounced at the beginning of the second word. For example:
>
> nicest teacher—*nices̲ teacher*
>
> stubborn neighbor—*stubbor̲ neighbor*

Focus on Listening

Practice the sentences in the left column. Say each sentence or play the audio one or more times. Have students listen carefully and repeat.

Focus on Pronunciation

Practice the sentences in the right column. Have students say each sentence and then listen carefully as you say it or play the audio.

If you wish, have students continue practicing the sentences to improve their pronunciation.

FOCUS

- Expressions with *one:*

  this one

  the _____ one

- Contrast of Comparative and Superlative Adjectives:

  a small radio

  the smallest one

GETTING READY

Review comparative and superlative adjectives.

1. Read the expressions in the boxes at the top of text page 54.

2. Introduce the irregular superlative *good–(better)–best*.

INTRODUCING THE MODEL

1. Have students look at the model illustration.

2. Set the scene: "A salesperson and a customer are talking in a store."

3. Present the model.

4. Full-Class Repetition.

5. Ask students if they have any questions. Check understanding of new vocabulary: *this one, I'm afraid not, Thank you anyway, Please come again.*

   > **Language Note**
   >
   > The expressions *May I help you? and Please come again.* are commonly used by salespeople when talking with customers in stores.

6. Group Choral Repetition.

7. Choral Conversation.

8. Call on one or two pairs of students to present the dialog. Before they present the dialog, ask the *salesperson* in each conversation the name of his or her store.

Students can either use the name of a real store in their community or *invent* the name of a store where that particular product might be sold.

SIDE BY SIDE EXERCISES

Examples

1. A. May I help you?
   B. Yes, please. I want to buy a large TV.
   A. I think you'll like this one. It's VERY large.
   B. Don't you have a larger one?
   A. No, I'm afraid not. This is the largest one we have.
   B. Thank you anyway.
   A. Sorry we can't help you. Please come again.

2. A. May I help you?
   B. Yes, please. I want to buy a comfortable rocking chair.
   A. I think you'll like this one. It's VERY comfortable.
   B. Don't you have a more comfortable one?
   A. No, I'm afraid not. This is the most comfortable one we have.
   B. Thank you anyway.
   A. Sorry we can't help you. Please come again.

Answer Key to Adjectives 3–9:

3. better
   the best
4. cheaper
   the cheapest
5. faster
   the fastest
6. more elegant
   the most elegant
7. smaller
   the smallest
8. more lightweight
   the most lightweight
9. more powerful
   the most powerful
10. taller
    the tallest
11. shorter
    the shortest

1. **Exercise 1:** Call on two students to present the dialog. Then do Choral Repetition and Choral Conversation practice.

2. **Exercise 2:** Same as above.

3. **Exercises 3–11:** Either Full-Class Practice or Pair Practice.

New Vocabulary

6. elegant
   evening gown
8. lightweight
   video camera
11. bookcase

---

4. **Exercise 12:** Have students use the model as a guide to create their own conversations, using vocabulary of their choice. (They can use any products and adjectives they wish.) Encourage students to use dictionaries to find new words they want to use. This exercise can be done orally in class or for written homework. If you assign it for homework, do one example in class to make sure students understand what's expected. Have students present their conversations in class the next day.

WORKBOOK

Pages 55–57

EXPANSION ACTIVITIES

1. Disappearing Dialog

   a. Write the model conversation on the board.

   b. Ask two student volunteers to read the conversation.

   c. Erase a few of the words from each line of the dialog. Have two different students read the conversation.

   d. Erase more words and call on two more students to read the conversation.

   e. Continue erasing words and calling on pairs of students to say the model until all the words have been erased and the dialog has disappeared.

2. Let's Compare!

   Ask about the items on text page 55:

   What's the largest item on the page?
   What's the smallest?
   What's the most expensive?
   What's the cheapest?
   What's the most useful?

3. Ask Me a Question!

   a. Divide the class into groups of three or four.

   b. One student in each group thinks of something you can buy at a department store.

   c. The other students in the group then try to guess the item by asking Yes/No questions. For example:

   [thinking of a rocking chair]
   Student 1: I'm thinking of something you can buy at a department store.
   Student 2: Do you wear it?
   Student 1: No, you don't.

   Student 3: Do you listen to it?
   Student 1: No, you don't.

   Student 4: Do you sit on it?
   Student 1: Yes, you do.

   Student 2: Is it comfortable?
   Student 1: Yes, it is.

   Student 3: Is it a sofa?
   Student 1: No, it isn't.

   Student 4: Is it a rocking chair?
   Student 1: Yes, it is.

   d. Have the remaining students in each group take their turn thinking of something for the others to guess.

4. Tic Tac Vocabulary

a. Have students draw a tic tac grid and fill it in with 9 of the following words:

bookcase	radio
CD player	rocking chair
cell phone	TV
computer	video camera
evening gown	watch
novel	

b. Say the beginnings of the following sentences, and tell students to cross out the word that finishes each sentence:

I'm listening to CDs on my new . . .
I'm going to watch my favorite program on my new . . .
What time is it? I'll look at my new . . .
I'm going to relax tonight in my comfortable new . . .
Alice is going to a very fancy party tonight. She's going to wear her elegant new . . .
I'm going to call all my friends on my new . . .
I'm going to take movies of my children with my wonderful new lightweight . . .
I'm going to put my books and dictionaries in my new . . .
I don't have time to read, so I'm going to find a very short . . .
I'm listening to my favorite talk program on my new . . .
I can't talk right now. I'm reading my e-mail on my new . . .

c. The first student to cross out three words in a straight line—either horizontally, vertically, or diagonally—wins the game.

d. Have the winner call out the words to check for accuracy.

5. In Your Opinion

a. Divide the class into pairs or small groups.

b. Have the pairs or groups discuss the following:

In your opinion, what's the best place in town to buy a good CD player?
What's the best place to buy a comfortable rocking chair?
What's the best place to buy large TV?
What's the best place to buy a good, cheap watch?
What's the best place to buy an elegant evening gown?

c. Have students report back to the class. Make a list of students' suggestions and, if you wish, *publish* them as a class guide to shopping in the community.

6. Ten-Second Commercials!

a. Divide the class into pairs.

b. Tell students that they're going to write a very short radio or TV commercial for a product.

c. Have students choose one of the following products for their advertisements:

TV	bicycle
novel	earrings
leather gloves	computer
sofa	printer
evening gown	fan
cell phone	car
bookcase	pet food

d. Have students work together to think of the best adjectives to describe their product. For example:

This cell phone is the best! It's the smallest and most lightweight in the world. And it's cheap! In fact, it's the cheapest one you can buy.

e. Call on students to present their *10-second commercials* to the class.

READING *Bob's Bargain Department Store / The Lord and Lady Department Store / The Super Saver Department Store*

FOCUS

- Superlatives
- Comparatives

NEW VOCABULARY

Story 1	Story 3
appliance	in addition
bargain	reasonable
besides that	you can see why
dependable	
helpful	
home entertainment products	
location	
products	
salespeople	
worst	

READING THE STORIES

Optional: *Preview the stories by having students talk about the story titles and/or illustrations. You may choose to introduce new vocabulary beforehand, or have students encounter the new vocabulary within the context of the readings.*

1. Have students read silently, or follow along silently as the stories are read aloud by you, by one or more students, or on the audio program.

2. Ask students if they have any questions. Check understanding of vocabulary.

3. Check students' comprehension, using some or all of the following questions:

Why don't people shop at Bob's Bargain Department Store?
Tell about the furniture, the clothes, the appliances, and the home entertainment products at Bob's Bargain Department Store.
Tell about the location and the salespeople.

What kind of products does the Lord and Lady Department Store sell?
Tell about the furniture, the clothes, the appliances, and the home entertainment products at the Lord and Lady Department Store.
Tell about the location and the salespeople.
Why don't people shop there?

Tell about the furniture at the Super Saver Department Store.
Tell about the clothes.
Tell about the appliances.
Tell about the home entertainment products.
Tell about the location and the salespeople.
Why do people like to shop there?

✓ READING *CHECK-UP*

TRUE OR FALSE?

1. False
2. True
3. False
4. False
5. True
6. False

How About You?

Have students answer the questions, in pairs or as a class.

Commercials

1. Divide the class into at least three groups.

2. Assign each group one of the three stores featured in the readings. Have students work together to develop a short TV advertisement for their store.

3. Have students present their commercials to the class.

Option: Have the class vote on the best commercial.

INTERACTIONS *Sharing Opinions*

1. Introduce the questions. Check understanding of new vocabulary: *tourist sight, vacation place.*

2. For homework, have students write answers to the questions. Have students present their opinions in the next class without referring to their written homework. You can do this as a class, in pairs, or in small groups.

EXPANSION ACTIVITIES

1. Survey

a. Have students conduct a survey by interviewing friends, members of their families, or other students in the school.

b. Have students compile their results and present them to the class.

2. Travel Brochures

Have students create a travel brochure of their country or region.

a. Brainstorm questions students could answer in their brochures. For example:

What are the most interesting tourist sights?
What are the most popular vacation places?
What's the best beach?
Where can you hear the best music?
What are the best restaurants?

b. Divide the class into small groups. Have students use classroom time as well as homework time to develop their brochures.

c. Have students present their brochures to the class.

 JOURNAL

Have students write their journal entries at home or in class. Encourage students to use a dictionary to look up words they would like to use. Students can share their written work with other students if appropriate. Have students discuss what they have written as a class, in pairs, or in small groups

WORKBOOK

Check-Up Test: Pages 58–59

✓ CHAPTER SUMMARY

GRAMMAR

1. Divide the class into pairs or small groups.

2. Have students take turns forming sentences from the words in the grammar box. Student A says a sentence, and Student B points to the words from each column that are in the sentence. Then have students switch: Student B says a sentence, and Student A points to the words.

KEY VOCABULARY

Have students ask you any questions about the meaning or pronunciation of the vocabulary. If students ask for the pronunciation, repeat after the student until the student is satisfied with his or her own pronunciation.

EXPANSION ACTIVITIES

1. Do You Remember the Words?

Check students' retention of the vocabulary depicted on the opening page of Chapter 6 by doing the following activity:

a. Have students open their books to page 49 and cover the list of vocabulary words.

b. Either call out a number and have students tell you the word, or say a word and have students tell you the number.

Variation: You can also do this activity as a game with competing teams.

2. Miming

a. Write on cards the adjectives on text page 58.

b. Have students take turns picking a card from the pile and pantomiming the adjective on the card.

c. The class must guess what adjective the person is describing.

Variation: This can be done as a game with competing teams.

3. Student-Led Dictation

a. Tell each student to choose a word from the Key Vocabulary list on text page 58 and look at it very carefully.

b. Have students take turns dictating their words to the class. Everybody writes down that student's word.

c. When the dictation is completed, call on different students to write each word on the board to check the spelling.

4. Letter Game

a. Divide the class into two teams.

b. Say, "I'm thinking of an adjective that starts with *l*."

c. The first person to raise his or her hand and guess correctly *[lazy]* wins a point for his or her team.

d. Continue with other letters of the alphabet.

The team that gets the most correct answers wins the game.

5. Words That Describe

a. Divide the class into small groups.

b. Write the following topics on the board:

describing books	describing houses
describing jobs	describing people
describing cars	describing clothes
describing pets	

c. Have each group write down as many words as they can think of to describe each category on the board.

d. Have students read their lists to the class. Compare the descriptive words that everybody chose.

Variation: You can do the activity as a game in which each group reads its list of words without naming the category. The class must guess the category based on the descriptive words.

6. Movable Categories

a. Write the adjectives in the list on text page 58 on separate cards.

b. Give each student one or two cards.

c. Call out one of the following categories:

   words for describing a store
   words for describing a salesperson
   words for describing a city
   words for describing a TV
   words for describing a jacket
   words for describing a printer

d. All those students whose words are appropriate for the category go to the right side of the room. All the other students go to the left side.

e. Those who are in the right group call out their adjectives for the class to verify.

f. Continue with other categories.

END-OF-CHAPTER ACTIVITIES

1. Board Game

a. On poster boards or on manila file folders, make up game boards with a pathway consisting of separate spaces. You may use any theme or design you wish.

b. Divide the class into groups of 2 to 4 students and give each group a game board and a die, and each student something to be used as a playing piece.

c. Give each group a pile of cards face-down with sentences written on them. Some sentences should be *correct*, and others *incorrect*. For example:

> This rocking chair is the comfortablest in the store.
> Our sports car is the most fast you can buy.
> This salesperson is the most helpful in town.
> That evening gown is eleganter than this evening gown.
> If you ask me, Jane's pronunciation is the most good in the class.
> My grandmother is the most interesting woman I know.
> Your landlord is the lazy person I know.
> My roommate is friendliest than your roommate.
> Your upstairs neighbor is the quietest person I know.
> That store sells the most worst home entertainment products.
> Their products are the better in town.
> That store is most convenient than this store.
> Our neighbor's dog is the meanest dog in town.
> Our history teacher is brightest teacher in the school.

d. Each student in turn rolls the die, moves the playing piece along the game path, and after landing on a space, picks a card, reads the sentence, and says if it is *correct* or *incorrect*. If the sentence is incorrect and the student is able to give the correct version, that student takes an additional turn.

e. The first student to reach the end of the pathway is the winner.

2. Telephone

a. Divide the class into large groups. Have each group sit in a circle.

b. Whisper a short story to one student. For example:

> "In my opinion, my nephew is the most wonderful boy in the world. He's the brightest and funniest child I know. He's also the most energetic and the most interesting child in our family. And just think, he's only two months old!"

c. The first student whispers the story to the second student, and so forth around the circle.

d. When the story gets to the last student, that person says it aloud. Is it the same story you started with? The group with the most accurate story wins.

3. Dialog Builder!

a. Divide the class into pairs.

b. On the board write a line from a conversation such as the following:

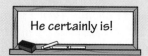

He certainly is!

Other possible lines:

> You're right.
> Thank you anyway.
> No, I'm afraid not.
> Sorry we can't help you.
> Don't you have a more expensive one?

c. Have each pair create a conversation incorporating that line. Students can begin and end their conversations any way they wish, but they must include that line in their dialogs.

d. Call on students to present their conversations to the class.

WORKBOOK ANSWER KEY AND LISTENING SCRIPTS

WORKBOOK PAGE 51

A. WHAT ARE THEY SAYING?

1. the brightest
2. the neatest
3. the nicest
4. the fanciest
5. the friendliest
6. the quietest
7. the cutest
8. the biggest
9. the sloppiest
10. the meanest

WORKBOOK PAGE 52

B. WHAT'S THE WORD?

1. talented, the most talented
2. generous, the most generous
3. energetic, the most energetic
4. polite, the most polite
5. smart, the smartest
6. boring, the most boring
7. patient, the most patient
8. honest, the most honest
9. noisy, the noisiest
10. interesting, the most interesting
11. stubborn, the most stubborn

WORKBOOK PAGE 53

C. WORLDBUY.COM

1. the most attractive
2. the softest
3. the most elegant
4. the most modern
5. the warmest
6. the best
7. the most reliable
8. the most beautiful
9. the most delicious

WORKBOOK PAGE 55

E. THE BEST IN THE WORLD!

1. more powerful, the most powerful
2. more lightweight, the most lightweight
3. more efficient, the most efficient
4. more dependable, the most dependable
5. brighter, the brightest

WORKBOOK PAGE 56

F. LISTENING

Listen and circle the words you hear.

1. My new chair is much more comfortable than my old chair.
2. Is that the worst city in the country?
3. I want a more energetic president.
4. Don't you have a cheaper one?
5. What was the most important day in your life?
6. Roger is the sloppiest teenager I know.
7. This is the best perfume we have.
8. Sally isn't as lazy as Richard is.
9. You know, I think your dog is meaner than mine.
10. Howard is the most honest person I know.

Answers

1. more comfortable
2. the worst
3. more energetic
4. cheaper
5. the most important
6. the sloppiest
7. the best
8. lazy
9. meaner
10. the most honest

G. PUZZLE

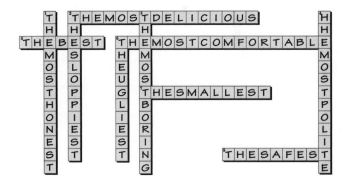

H. LOUD AND CLEAR

1. Andrew, worst actor, terrible, program
2. recommend Carla's recipe, fruitcake, better
3. Robert, friendlier, more energetic, brother
4. Rita reads, newspaper, morning, writes
5. Ronald, sister, perfume, thirtieth birthday
6. car, bigger, more powerful, neighbor's

CHECK-UP TEST: Chapters 4–6

A.

1. it will, It'll
2. they won't
3. I will, I'll
4. she won't
5. we will, We'll

B.

1. might
2. Should
3. might, might
4. should

C.

1. mine
2. his
3. theirs
4. yours

D.

1. taller than
2. more honest than
3. prettier than
4. better, than
5. more dependable than

E.

1. isn't as fast as, more reliable
2. isn't as friendly as, cuter
3. isn't as intelligent as, more interesting
4. isn't as fashionable as, bigger
5. isn't as expensive as, more attractive

F.

1. the quietest
2. the most hospitable
3. the largest
4. the most patient
5. the laziest

G.

Ex. Ronald is younger than Fred.

1. Bob is neater than Bill.
2. The chicken is more expensive than the fish.
3. Moscow is warmer than Miami.
4. Herbert is taller than Steven.
5. Patty is more talented than Pam.

Answers

1. Yes
2. No
3. No
4. Yes
5. No

FEATURE ARTICLE
Did You Know?

PREVIEWING THE ARTICLE

1. Have students talk about the title of the article and the accompanying photographs.

2. You may choose to introduce the following new vocabulary beforehand, or have students encounter it within the context of the article:

> Carnival
> celebration
> costume
> costume party
> foot (feet)
> ice
> igloo
> melt
> pass through
> pool
> rebuild
> subway station
> swimming pool
> waterbed
> wheel
> worker

Language Note

A foot equals .305 meters.

READING THE ARTICLE

1. Have students read silently, or follow along silently as the article is read aloud by you, by one or more students, or on the audio program.

2. Ask students if they have any questions. Check understanding of vocabulary.

3. Check students' comprehension by having students answer the following questions:

> How long is the car in meters?
> *(30.5 meters long)*
>
> Is the car longer than a delivery truck?
> *(Yes. A delivery truck is about 24 feet long.)*

Does everyone in Brazil wear a costume during Carnival?
> *(No.)*

Do people celebrate Carnival indoors?
> *(No. People walk through the streets.)*

How many people walk through Grand Central Terminal very day?
> *(More than 500,000.)*

Is the Ice Hotel a popular summer vacation place?
> *(No. It melts in the spring.)*

Is the winter in Sweden cold?
> *(Yes.)*

FACT FILE
World Geography Facts

1. Introduce the following new vocabulary:

> desert
> geography
> mountain
> ocean
> river
> square mile

2. Tell the students that they're going to take a quick geography test. Have them write their answers to the following questions:

> What's the longest river in the world?
> What's the largest ocean?
> What's the highest mountain?
> What's the biggest desert?

3. Read the text aloud as students follow along, or call on different students to read each section.

Language Note

A *mile* equals 1, 609 meters or 1.6 kilometers.

4. Have students check their answers on the geography test. How many students got all four answers correct?

5. For additional practice, have students identify the longest river, the largest body of water (lake or sea), the highest mountain, or the biggest desert in their own country or region. Have students share their information with the class.

 BUILD YOUR VOCABULARY!
Adjectives with Negative Prefixes

uncomfortable
unfriendly
unhealthy
unsafe
impatient
impolite
inexpensive
dishonest

1. Have students look at the illustrations and identify any words they already know.

2. Present the vocabulary. Say each word and have the class repeat it chorally and individually. Check students' understanding and pronunciation of the words.

EXPANSION ACTIVITIES

1. Vocabulary Chain

a. Start the chain game by saying the positive counterpart of a negative adjective on the *Build Your Vocabulary!* list on text page 59.

b. Student 1 gives the negative of that adjective and then names another positive adjective .

c. Student 2 continues the chain in the way. For example:

Teacher: expensive
Student 1: inexpensive
         polite
Student 2: impolite
         friendly

2. Tic Tac Vocabulary

a. Have students draw a tic tac grid on their papers and then fill in their grids with the following adjectives:

uncomfortable	unfriendly	unhealthy
unsafe	impatient	impolite
inexpensive	dishonest	healthy

b. Say the beginnings of the following sentences, and tell students to cross out the word on their grid that finishes the sentence:

This neighborhood is dangerous at night. It's . . . *(unsafe)*
Maria doesn't like to sit on her old sofa. It's very . . . *(uncomfortable)*
That watch doesn't cost very much! It's really . . . *(inexpensive)*
I don't believe that salesperson. I don't think he's telling the truth. I think he's . . . *(dishonest)*
I said hello to our next-door neighbor this morning, but he didn't say hello to me. I think he's very . . . *(unfriendly)*
Nancy eats wells and exercises every day. She's very . . . *(healthy)*
Nancy's brother doesn't eat well. He eats only cake and cookies. In my opinion, that's very . . . *(unhealthy)*
Carol doesn't like to wait for anybody. She's very . . . *(impatient)*
Those children never say "Thank you" or "Please." I think they're very . . . *(impolite)*

c. The first student to cross out three words in a straight line—either horizontally, vertically, or diagonally—wins the game.

d. Have the winner call out the words to check for accuracy.

3. Match the Conversations

a. Make a set of matching cards based on giving advice. For example:

She's very impolite.	You're right. She should try to be more polite.

He's very unfriendly.	I agree. He should try to be friendlier.
He eats very unhealthy foods.	I know. He should try to eat healthier foods.
We live in an unsafe neighborhood.	That's true. We should move to a safer neighborhood.
Those children are very impatient.	I agree. They should try to be more patient.
Your co-workers are impolite.	I know. They should try to be more polite.
This car is expensive.	You're right. We should look for a more inexpensive one.
I think he's a dishonest salesperson.	I agree. He should definitely be more honest with his customers.

b. Distribute a card to each student.

c. Have students memorize the sentences on their cards, and then have students walk around the room saying their sentences until they find their match.

d. Then have pairs of students say their matched sentences aloud to the class.

4. Concentration

a. Use the cards from the above activity. Place them face down in four rows of 4 each.

b. Divide the class into two teams. The object of the game is for students to find the matching cards. Both teams should be able to see all the cards, since *concentrating* on their location is an important part of playing the game.

c. A student from Team 1 turns over two cards. If they match, the student picks up the cards, that team gets a point, and the student takes another turn. If the cards don't match, the student turns them face down, and a member of Team 2 takes a turn.

d. The game continues until all the cards have been matched. The team with the most correct matches wins the game.

Variation: This game can also be played in groups and pairs.

5. More Negatives!

If you wish, you can introduce students to additional adjectives with negative prefixes. (Note: These are negative forms of adjectives that students have previously learned in the text.)

a. Write on the board:

b. Say the following adjectives and have students give their negative counterparts:

<u>Teacher</u>	<u>Students</u>
dependable	undependable
fashionable	unfashionable
happy	unhappy
intelligent	unintelligent
interesting	uninteresting
kind	unkind
popular	unpopular
reliable	unreliable

c. Write on the board:

d. Say the following adjectives and have students give their negative counterparts:

<u>Teacher</u>	<u>Students</u>
convenient	inconvenient
hospitable	inhospitable

(continued)

EXPANSION ACTIVITIES (Continued)

6. More Concentration

You can do this activity if you introduced students to the adjectives above.

a. Write each of the adjectives in Activity 5 on separate cards. Place the cards face down in five rows of 4 each.

b. Divide the class into two teams. The object of the game is for students to find the matching cards. Both teams should be able to see all the cards, since *concentrating* on their location is an important part of playing the game.

c. A student from Team 1 turns over two cards. If they match, the student picks up the cards, that team gets a point, and the student takes another turn. If the cards don't match, the student turns them face down, and a member of Team 2 takes a turn.

d. The game continues until all the cards have been matched. The team with the most correct matches wins the game.

Variation: This game can also be played in groups and pairs.

 AROUND THE WORLD
Recreation and Entertainment

1. Have students read silently, or follow along silently as the text is read aloud by you, by one or more students, or on the audio program. Check understanding of new vocabulary:

   | camping |
   | entertainment |
   | recreation |

2. Have students first work in pairs or small groups and respond to the question. Then have students tell the class what they talked about. Write any new vocabulary on the board.

EXPANSION ACTIVITIES

1. Ranking

a. Have students brainstorm outdoor recreation activities they enjoy. Write their ideas on the board.

b. Choose five activities, and have students rank them from *expensive* to *inexpensive*. For example:

   1. skiing
   2. scuba diving
   3. sailing
   4. biking
   5. hiking

c. As a class, in pairs, or in small groups, have students compare their lists.

d. Then have students rank the items from *easy* to *difficult*, from *safe* to *unsafe*, and from *fun* to *not so much fun*.

Variation: The same activity may be done using the topic of sports or entertainment.

2. Entertainment Survey

Have students find out about their classmates' preferred types of entertainment.

a. Brainstorm questions students can ask each other about their entertainment preferences. For example:

   What kind of entertainment do you like the most?
   What's your favorite kind of movie?
   What's your favorite kind of music?
   How often do you watch TV?

b. Have each student chose one question to ask. Have students conduct their surveys by circulating around the room, asking each other their question.

c. For homework, have students draw up the survey results in graph form (such as a bar graph or pie chart). In class, have students share their graphs and report their results.

Variation: The same activity may be done using the topic of sports or outdoor recreation.

GLOBAL EXCHANGE

1. Set the scene: "IvanaG is writing to her keypal."

2. Have students read silently, or follow along silently as the message is read aloud by you, by one or more students, or on the audio program.

3. Ask students if they have any questions. Check the understanding of the following new words: *air, amusement park, close, fun, get back.*

4. Suggestions for additional practice:

   • Have students write a response to IvanaG and share their writing in pairs.

   • Have students correspond with a keypal on the Internet and then share their experience with the class.

LISTENING *And Now a Word From Our Sponsors!*

1. Set the scene: "You're watching TV, and you hear these advertisements."

2. Introduce the following new words and expressions: *to be on, I can't believe it!, jewelry, seven days a week, typical, There you have it!*

LISTENING SCRIPT

Listen and match the products.

ANNOUNCER: Are you looking for a special gift for a special person in your life? A birthday gift? An anniversary present? Come to Rings & Things —the best store in town for rings, necklaces, earrings, bracelets, and other fine things. Rings & Things—on Main Street downtown, or at the East Side Mall.

FRIEND 1: That was an excellent dinner!
FRIEND 2: Thank you. I'm glad you liked it.
FRIEND 1: Can I help you wash the dishes?
FRIEND 2: Thanks. But they're already in the dishwasher.

FRIEND 1: Is your dishwasher on?
FRIEND 2: Yes, it is.
FRIEND 1: I can't believe it! Your dishwasher is MUCH quieter than mine.
FRIEND 2: It's new. We got it at the Big Value Store. They sell the quietest dishwashers in town.
ANNOUNCER: That's right. The Big Value Store sells the quietest dishwashers in town. We also have the largest refrigerators, the most powerful washing machines, and the best ovens. And we have the best prices! So come to the Big Value Store, on Airport Road, open seven days a week.

PERSON WHO CAN'T FALL ASLEEP: Oh, I can't believe it! It's three o'clock in the morning, and I can't fall asleep. This bed is so uncomfortable! I need a new bed. I need a new bed NOW!
ANNOUNCER: Do you have this problem? Is your bed uncomfortable? Come to Comfort Kingdom for the most comfortable beds you can buy. We also have the most beautiful sofas and the most attractive tables and chairs in the city. And our salespeople are the friendliest and the most helpful in town. So visit Comfort Kingdom today because life is short, and you should be comfortable!

ANNOUNCER: I'm standing here today in front of Electric City so we can talk to a typical customer. Here's a typical customer now. He's leaving the store with a large box. Let's ask him a question. Excuse me, sir. May I ask you a question?
CUSTOMER: Certainly.
ANNOUNCER: What did you buy today?
CUSTOMER: A VCR.
ANNOUNCER: And why did you buy it at Electric City?
CUSTOMER: Because Electric City has the cheapest and the most dependable products in town.
ANNOUNCER: Is this your first time at Electric City?
CUSTOMER: Oh, no! Last year I bought a radio here, and the year before I bought a TV.
ANNOUNCER: And are you happy with those products?
CUSTOMER : Absolutely! The radio is much better than my old one, and the picture on my new TV is much bigger and brighter.
ANNOUNCER: So are you a happy customer?

CUSTOMER : Definitely! There's no place like Electric City. It's the best store in town.

ANNOUNCER: Well, there you have it! Another happy Electric City customer. Visit an Electric City store near YOU today!

ANNOUNCER: This is it! It's the biggest sale of the year, and it's this weekend at Recreation Station! That's right. Everything is on sale — sneakers, tennis rackets, footballs, basketballs — everything in the store! It's all on sale at Recreation Station. We're the largest! We're the most convenient! We're the best! And this weekend we're the cheapest! It's the biggest sale of the year, and it's this weekend — only at Recreation Station!

Answers

1. b
2. d
3. a
4. e
5. c

WHAT ARE THEY SAYING?

FOCUS

- Superlatives

Have students talk about the people and the situation, and then create role plays based on the scene. Students may refer back to previous lessons as a resource, but they should not simply reuse specific conversations.

Note: You may want to assign this exercise as written homework, having students prepare their role plays, practice them the next day with other students, and then present them to the class.

Teacher's Notes

GRAMMAR

IMPERATIVES

> **Walk up** Main Street.
> **Turn** right.
> **Drive** along Second Avenue to River Street.

FUNCTIONS

ASKING FOR DIRECTIONS

Can you tell me
Could you please tell me
Would you please tell me
   how to get to the *laundromat* from here?

Can you tell me how to get there?

What's the best/easiest/fastest/most
   direct/quickest/shortest way to get to
   Peter's Pet Shop?

GIVING DIRECTIONS

Walk up
Walk down   *Main Street.*
Walk along

You'll see the *laundromat* { on the right / on the left },

across from *the drug store.*
next to *the bakery.*
between *the museum* and *the park.*
at the corner of *Brighton Boulevard* and
  Twelfth Street.

Walk up *Park Street* to *Second Avenue* and
{ turn right.
{ turn left.

Drive along *Second Avenue* to *River Street* and
{ turn right.
{ turn left.

Take *the Main Street bus* and get off at *First
  Avenue.*

ATTRACTING ATTENTION

Excuse me.

EXPRESSING GRATITUDE

Thank you.
Thanks.
Thank you very much.
Thanks very much.
   You're welcome.

ASKING FOR A SUGGESTION

Can you recommend *a good hotel*?

DESCRIBING

The Bellview is a good *hotel*.

I think it's one of the best *hotels* in *town*.

ASKING FOR REPETITION

I'm sorry. Could you please repeat that?
I'm sorry. Could you please say that again?

NEW VOCABULARY

Streets

block (n)
boulevard
road

Giving Directions

along
directions
down
follow
get lost
get off
turn (v)
up
way

Places Around Town

airport
baseball stadium
concert hall
courthouse
flower shop
hardware store
ice cream shop
motel
museum
parking garage
pet shop
playground
shoe store
stadium
toy store
university

Adjectives

direct
lost
stupid
wrong

Miscellaneous

completely
stop (n)
such

EXPRESSIONS

in a hurry
the most direct way
the shortest way

Text Page 61: Chapter Opening Page

VOCABULARY PREVIEW

You may want to present these words before beginning the chapter, or you may choose to wait until they first occur in a specific lesson. If you choose to present them at this point, here are some suggestions:

1. Have students look at the illustrations on text page 61 and identify the words they already know.

2. Present the vocabulary. Say each word and have the class repeat it chorally and individually. Check students' understanding and pronunciation of the words.

3. Practice the vocabulary as a class, in pairs, or in small groups. Have students cover the word list and look at the pictures. Practice the words in the following ways:

   • Say a word and have students tell the number of the illustration.

   • Give the number of an illustration and have students say the word.

Text Page 62: Can You Tell Me How to Get to . . . ?

FOCUS

- Imperatives
- Directions

    walk up
    walk down
    on the right
    on the left

CLOSE UP

RULE:	The imperative is the simple form of the verb with the understood subject *you*. The imperative is used to give directions.
EXAMPLES:	*(You)* **walk** up Main Street. *(You)* **walk** down Main Street.

GETTING READY

1. Review the following locations in the community. Use *Side by Side* Picture Cards or your own visuals. Say each word and have students repeat chorally and individually.

bakery	high school
bank	laundromat
barber shop	library
clinic	police station
drug store	post office

    Check understanding of *shoe store* and *toy store* (depicted on text page 61).

2. Introduce the map of Main Street, using the illustration. Point to each location, say the place, and have students repeat.

3. Introduce the new expressions at the top of text page 62:

walk up	*on the left*
walk down	*on the right*

    a. Point to the map and gesture (↑) as you say: "Walk up Main Street." Have students repeat.

    b. Point to the map and gesture (↓) as you say: "Walk down Main Street." Have students repeat.

    c. Write on the board:

    > Walk _____ Main Street.
    > The _____ is on the right.
    > The _____ is on the left.

    Point to the map as you say these sentences and have students repeat:

    > Walk up Main Street.
    > The shoe store is on the right.
    > The bank is on the left.

    > Walk down Main Street.
    > The bank is on the right.
    > The shoe store is on the left.

    d. Call on students to make similar sentences.

4. Review the expressions *next to, across from,* and *between*. Have students make statements about the map, using these expressions. For example:

    > The bakery is across from the barber shop.

INTRODUCING THE MODELS

There are two model conversations. Introduce and practice each separately. For each model:

1. Have students look at the model illustration.

2. Set the scene:

    1st model: "Two people are standing in front of the post office."

    2nd model: "Two people are standing in front of the drug store."

3. Present the model.

4. Full-Class Repetition.

5. Ask students if they have any questions. Check understanding of vocabulary.

    ### Language Notes

    The expressions *walk up, walk down,* and *walk along* are often used interchangeably when giving directions in a city.

    The expression *Sure* is commonly used in informal conversation in place of *Yes* or *Yes, of course.*

6. Group Choral Repetition.

7. Choral Conversation.

8. Call on one or two pairs of students to present the dialog.

9. Call on another pair of students to present each dialog again. This time have them give alternate directions to the same places by using a different expression at the end. For example, an alternate way to present the 1st model is:

    Walk up Main Street and you'll see the laundromat on the right, *next to the bakery.*

(For additional practice, do Choral Conversation in small groups or by rows.)

SIDE BY SIDE EXERCISES

In these exercises, students can describe the locations of buildings in several possible ways.

Examples

1. A. Excuse me. Can you tell me how get to the clinic from here?
   B. Sure. Walk up Main Street and you'll see the clinic on the right, across from the toy store (*or* next to the bakery/ next to the shoe store/between the bakery and the shoe store).
   A. Thank you.
2. A. Excuse me. Can you tell me how to get to the police station from here?
   B. Sure. Walk down Main Street and you'll see the police station on the right, across from the high school (*or* next to the library/next to the bank/ between the library and the bank).
   A. Thank you.

1. **Exercise 1:** Call on two students to present the dialog. Then do Choral Repetition and Choral Conversation practice. Ask students to tell you alternative directions to the same place.

2. **Exercise 2:** Same as above.

3. **Exercises 3–6:** Either Full-Class Practice or Pair Practice.

WORKBOOK

Page 60

EXPANSION ACTIVITIES

1. True or False?

a. Have students look at the map on text page 62.

b. Make statements about the location of places and have students tell you "True" or "False." If the statement is false, have students correct it. For example:

Teacher: The bakery is next to the clinic.
Student: True.

Teacher: The high school is across from the shoe store.
Student: False. The high school is next to the shoe store.

Variation: Call on students to make true or false statements about the map and have other students respond.

2. Finish the Sentence

Begin a sentence, and have students repeat what you said and add appropriate endings to the sentence. For example:

Teacher	Students
The toy store is . . .	on the left.
	next to the barber shop.
	across from the clinic.
	between the barber shop and the bank.

Variation: This activity may be done as a class, in pairs or small groups, or as a game with competing teams.

3. Do You Remember?

a. Tell students to spend three minutes looking carefully at the map on text page 62.

b. Have students close their books.

c. Ask questions to see how much they remember about the map. For example:

What's across from the bakery?
What's next to the high school?
What's between the bank and the library?
Where's the barber shop?

Variation: Divide the class into teams and do the activity as a game. The team with the most correct answers wins.

4. Mystery Location

Give directions to different *mystery locations* on the map, and have students guess the place. For example:

"You're at the police station. Walk up Main Street and you'll see it on the right, between the laundromat and the clinic. Where are you?" *[the bakery]*

Variation: Have students take turns giving the mystery directions.

5. Name That Place!

a. Have students look at the map on text page 62. Have each student choose a starting place and a destination and write directions. The student should not mention the name of the place. For example:

"You're at the drug store. Go down Main Street. It's on the left. It's across from the bank. It's between the clinic and the high school."

b. Have students take turns reading their directions aloud. The class must look at the map while they listen and then identify the place. *[the shoe store]*

Variation: Do the same activity, but use a drawing of a local street on the board.

6. Act It Out!

a. Write on word cards the names of the buildings from the map on student text page 62.

b. Distribute the cards to 12 students, and have them create that street by standing in the appropriate location in front of the room.

c. Have pairs of students act out the model conversation and the exercises on text page 62, and have Speaker B actually follow the directions that Student A has given. Does Speaker B get to the correct place? Have the class decide.

(continued)

7. **Telephone Directions**

a. Divide the class into large groups. Have each group sit in a circle.

b. Whisper a set of directions to one student. For example:

"Walk up Main Street. The shoe store is on the right, next to the toy store and across from the department store."

c. The first student whispers the directions to the second student, and so forth around the circle. The student listening may ask for clarification by saying, "I'm sorry. What did you say?"

d. When the message gets to the last student, that person says it aloud. Is it the same message you started with? The group with the most accurate message wins.

8. **Picture This!**

Describe a city street, and have students draw and label what you describe. For example:

"This is First Avenue. There's a bank on First Avenue. Next to the bank on the left, there's a supermarket. Across from the supermarket there's a cafeteria."

Variation 1: Do the activity in pairs, where students take turns describing city streets.

Variation 2: One student comes to the board, and the rest of the class gives instructions for that student to draw.

Text Page 63: Could You Please Tell Me How to Get to . . . ?

FOCUS

- Imperatives
- Directions
    walk along

GETTING READY

1. Review the following locations in the community. Use *Side by Side* Picture Cards or your own visuals. Say each word or expression, and have students repeat chorally and individually.

gas station	museum
hospital	park
hotel	zoo

    Check understanding of *playground, university* (depicted on text page 61).

2. Introduce the map of Central Avenue, using the illustration. Point to each location. Say the places and have students repeat.

3. Introduce the new expression *walk along*. Point to the map and gesture (← →) as you say the expression. Have students repeat chorally and individually.

INTRODUCING THE MODEL

1. Have students look at the model illustration.

2. Set the scene: "Two people are talking in front of the parking lot."

3. Present the model.

    ### Language Note

    Could you please tell me . . . ? is a slightly more indirect and polite version of the phrase *Can you tell me. . .?*

4. Full-Class Repetition.

Pronunciation Note

The pronunciation focus of Chapter 7 is **Could you & Would you** (text page 70). You may wish to model this pronunciation at this point *(Could you please tell me how to get to the hospital from here? Could you please tell me how to get to the museum from here?)* and encourage students to incorporate it into their language practice.

5. Ask students if they have any questions.

6. Group Choral Repetition.

7. Choral Conversation.

8. Call on one or two pairs of students to present the dialog. Call on another pair of students to present the dialog again, using alternate locations. For example:

    Walk along Central Avenue and you'll see the hospital on the left, *across from the playground.*

    (For additional practice, do Choral Conversation in small groups or by rows.)

SIDE BY SIDE EXERCISES

As on text page 62, there is more than one correct answer for these exercises.

Examples

1. A. Excuse me. Could you please tell me how to get to the museum from here?
   B. Sure. Walk along Central Avenue and you'll see the museum on the right, across from the university (*or* next to the hospital/next to the gas station/ between the hospital and the gas station).
   A. Thanks.

2. A. Excuse me. Could you please tell me how to get to the university from here?
   B. Sure. Walk along Central Avenue and you'll see the university on the left, across from the gas station and the museum (*or* next to the playground/ next to the parking lot/between the playground and the parking lot).
   A. Thanks.

1. **Exercise 1:** Call on two students to present the dialog. Then do Choral Repetition and Choral Conversation practice. Ask students to tell you alternate directions to the same place.

2. **Exercise 2:** Same as above.

3. **Exercises 3–6:** Either Full-Class Practice or Pair Practice.

WORKBOOK

Page 61

EXPANSION ACTIVITIES

1. **True or False?**

   a. Have students look at the map on text page 63.

   b. Make statements about the location of places, and have students tell you "True" or "False." If the statement is false, have students correct it. For example:

Teacher:	The parking lot is across from the hotel.
Student:	True.
Teacher:	The playground is across from the museum.
Student:	False. The playground is across from the hospital.

   Variation: Call on students to make true or false statements about the map, and have other students respond.

2. **Finish the Sentence**

   Begin a sentence, and have students repeat what you said and add appropriate endings to the sentence. For example:

Teacher	Students
The hospital is . . .	across from the playground.
	next to the park.
	next to the museum.
	between the museum and the park.

   Variation: This activity may be done as a class, in pairs or small groups, or as a game with competing teams.

3. **Do You Remember?**

   a. Tell students to spend three minutes looking carefully at the map on text page 63.

   b. Have students close their books.

   c. Ask questions to see how much they remember about the map. For example:

   > What's next to the park?
   > What's across from the parking lot?
   > What's between the gas station and the hospital?

   Variation: Divide the class into teams and do the activity as a game. The team with the most correct answers wins.

4. **Name That Place!**

   a. Have students look at the map on text page 63. Have each student choose a starting place and a destination and write directions. The student should not mention the name of the place. For example:

   > You're at the zoo. Walk along Central Avenue. It's on the left. It's across from the hotel. It's next to the university.

   b. Have students take turns reading their directions aloud. The class must look at the map while they listen and identify the place. *[the parking lot]*

   Variation: Do the same activity, but use a drawing of a local street on the board.

5. **Act It Out!**

   a. Write on word cards the names of the buildings from the map on student text page 63.

   b. Distribute the cards to 9 students, and have them create that street by standing in the appropriate location in front of the room.

c. Have pairs of students act out the model conversation and the exercises on text page 63, and have Speaker B actually follow the directions that Student A has given. Does Student B get to the correct place? Have the class decide.

6. Memory Game

   a. Divide the class into pairs.

   b. Arrange *Side by Side* Picture Cards of locations or your own visuals to create a map scene, and show it to the class for one minute.

   c. Cover the scene, and have students write a description of the scene.

   d. Have students compare their descriptions with their partner and then look at the map scene to see how much they remembered.

7. True or False Dictation

   a. Arrange *Side by Side* Picture Cards of locations or your own visuals to create a map scene. Show it to the class for one minute.

   b. Have students draw two columns on a sheet of paper—one <u>True</u> and the other <u>False</u>. Hide the scene, and then make several statements about the location of places. Have students write the statements in the appropriate column.

   c. At the end of the dictation, have students check the scene to see if they were correct.

8. Jigsaw Map Contest

   a. Divide the class into groups of four. Give each member of the group one of these cards:

   > The hospital is next to the drug store.
   >
   > The hospital is across from the high school.

   > The library is next to the high school.
   >
   > The library is across from the drug store.

   > The hotel is across from the playground.
   >
   > The hotel is next to the hospital.

   > The high school is across from the hospital.
   >
   > The high school is between the library and the playground.

   b. Have students share their information and draw a map depicting the locations of the buildings.

   c. Students should then show their completed maps to the class. The first group to draw a map with the correct locations wins the map contest.

9. Role Play: Directions in Our City

   a. Make a map of the downtown area of your city—either on the board or on a large piece of paper.

   b. Set the scene: "Student A is a tourist in town. Student B lives there. They're talking in front of the _____ (*any location on the map*)."

   c. Have pairs of students create role plays based on the map of the city and then present them to the class.

Text Pages 64–65: Would You Please Tell Me How to Get to . . . ?

FOCUS

- Imperatives
- Directions

  turn right
  turn left
  drive up/down/along

GETTING READY

1. Using *Side by Side* Picture Cards, your own visuals, or the illustrations on text page 61, introduce or review the following locations in the community: *airport, concert hall, courthouse, flower shop, hardware store, ice cream shop, motel, parking garage, pet shop*. If you are introducing the vocabulary for the first time, refer to the suggestions for presenting it on Teacher's Guide page 180.

2. Introduce the map on text page 62.

   a. Point to each location and street. Say the names of the places and the street names, and have students repeat.

   b. Familiarize students with the map by writing the following model on the board:

   > A. Where's the _____?
   > B. It's on _____ Street/Avenue.

   c. Model the following and have students repeat:

   > A. Where's the hotel?
   > B. It's on Park Street.

   > A. Where's the concert hall?
   > B. It's on River Street.

   d. Call on students to ask and answer similar questions about locations on the map.

INTRODUCING THE MODELS

There are two model conversations. Introduce and practice each separately. For each model:

1. Have students look at the model illustration.

2. Set the scene:

   1st model: "Two people are in front of the park."

   2nd model: "Two people are talking in front of the department store. One of them is driving."

3. Present the model.

   ### Language Note

   Would you please tell me . . . ? is equally as indirect and polite as the phrase *Could you please tell me . . . ?*

4. Full-Class Repetition.

5. Ask students if they have any questions. Check understanding of new vocabulary:

   1st model: *turn right*
   2nd model: *drive along/up, turn left*

6. Group Choral Repetition.

7. Choral Conversation.

8. Call on one or two pairs of students to present the dialog.

   (For additional practice, do Choral Conversation in small groups or by rows.)

SIDE BY SIDE EXERCISES

In these exercises, there are many possible answers for each exercise.

Examples

> 1. A. Excuse me. Would you please tell me how to get to the hospital from here?
>   B. Certainly. Walk along Third Avenue to River Street and turn left. Walk up River Street and you'll see the hospital on the right, across from the parking garage.
>   A. Thanks very much.
> 2. A. Excuse me. Would you please tell me how to get to the zoo from here?
>   B. Certainly. Drive up River Street to Third Avenue and turn left. Drive along Third Avenue and you'll see the zoo on the left, next to the ice cream shop.
>   A. Thanks very much.

1. **Exercise 1:** Call on two students to present the dialog. Then do Choral Repetition and Choral Conversation practice.

2. **Exercise 2:** Same as above.

3. **Exercises 3–8:** Either Full-Class Practice or Pair Practice.

4. **Exercise 9:** Have students use the model as a guide to create their own conversations, using vocabulary of their choice. (They can use any locations they wish.) Encourage students to use dictionaries to find new words they want to use. This exercise can be done orally in class or for written homework. If you assign it for homework, do one example in class to make sure students understand what's expected. Have students present their conversations in class the next day.

WORKBOOK

Pages 62–64

How to Say It!

> **Asking for Repetition:** If someone hasn't understood what has been said, it is polite to ask for repetition.

1. Set the scene: "Two people are talking in front of the flower shop."

2. Present the model.

3. Full-Class Repetition.

4. Ask students if they have any questions.

5. Group Choral Repetition.

6. Choral Conversation.

7. Have students practice conversations from text page 65 in which Speaker A asks for repetition.

8. Call on pairs to present their conversations to the class.

EXPANSION ACTIVITIES

1. Guess the Place!

a. Tell each student to think of a place around town.

b. Have a student come to the front of the room and say: "I'm thinking of a place around town."

c. The other students try to guess the place by asking Yes/No questions. For example:

> Do you buy food there?
> Do you watch the animals there?
> Do you wash your clothes there?
> Do you go there when you're sick?

2. Name That Place!

a. Have students look at the map on student text page 64. Have each student choose a starting place and a destination and write directions. The student should not mention the name of the place. For example:

> You're at the supermarket. Walk along Second Avenue to Park Street and turn left. Walk up Park Street to Third Avenue and turn right. Walk along Third Avenue. It's on the left, across from the flower shop.

b. Have students take turns reading their directions aloud. The class must look at the map while they listen and identify the place. [the shopping mall]

Variation: Do the same activity, but use a drawing of a local street on the board.

3. Do You Remember?

a. Tell students to spend three minutes looking carefully at the map on text page 64

b. Have students close their books.

c. Ask questions to see how much they remember about the map. For example:

> What's across from the hospital?
> What's between the courthouse and the church?
> What's across from the supermarket?
> What's between the pet shop and the laundromat?

What street is the shopping mall on?

Variation: Divide the class into teams and do the activity as a game. The team with the most correct answers wins.

4. Telephone: I'm Sorry. Could You Please Repeat That?

a. Divide the class into large groups. Have each group sit in a circle.

b. Whisper a set of directions to one student. For example:

> "Walk up Elm Street to Park Avenue and turn left. Walk along Park Avenue to Center Street and turn right. Walk up Center Street. You'll see the shoe store on the right, next to the supermarket."

c. The first student whispers the directions to the second student, and so forth around the circle. The student listening may ask for clarification by saying, "I'm sorry. Could you please repeat that?"

d. When the message gets to the last student, that person says it aloud. Is it the same message you started with? The group with the most accurate message wins.

5. Where Did They Go?

Give descriptions of where people went, and have students guess the place. For example:

> George was at the church on River Street. He walked up River Street to Third Avenue and turned left. He walked along Third Avenue to Park Street and turned left again. He walked down Park Street and went to a building on the right, across from the hardware store. Where did he go? [the clinic]

> Carol was at the hotel on Park Street. She walked up Park Street to Second Avenue and turned right. She walked along Second Avenue to River Street and turned left. She walked up River Street and went to a building on the right across from the parking garage. Where did she go? [the hospital]

Mr. and Mrs. Ryan were at the motel on River Street. They drove down River Street to Second Avenue and turned right. They drove along Second Avenue to Park Street and turned left. They drove down Park Street and went to a place across from the hotel. Where did they go? [the park]

Variation: Divide the class into pairs, and have each pair write their own descriptions to read to the class.

6. Match the Directions

a. Make a set of cards such as the following:

> Excuse me. Would you please tell me how to get to the concert hall from here?

> Certainly. Walk up Park Street to Second Avenue and turn right. Walk along Second Avenue to River Street and turn left. It's on the right, between the church and the courthouse.

> Excuse me. Would you please tell me how to get to the clinic from here?

> Certainly. Walk up Park Street. It's on the left, between the book store and the ice cream shop.

> Excuse me. Would you please tell me how to get to the airport from here?

> Certainly. Drive up Park Street to Third Avenue and turn left. Drive along Third Avenue and you'll see it on the right, across from the zoo.

> Excuse me. Would you please tell me how to get to the parking garage from here?

> Certainly. Walk up Park Street to Third Avenue and turn right. Walk along Third Avenue to River Street and turn left. It's on the left, across from the hospital.

> Excuse me. Would you please tell me how to get to the library from here?

> Certainly. Walk up Park Street to Second Avenue and turn right. Walk along Second Avenue to River Street and turn left. It's on the left, between the post office and the bus station.

> Excuse me. Would you please tell me how to get to the flower shop from here?

> Certainly. Drive up Park Street to Third Avenue and turn right. Drive along Third Avenue. It's on the right, between the pet shop and the post office.

b. Divide the class into pairs. Distribute to each pair of students a set of all the cards in random order.

c. Have students match the requests with the directions by reading the map. All directions begin from the hotel.

d. Have pairs of students read their dialogs aloud to the class to check for accuracy.

7. Did They Get to the Right Place?

Describe the way people got to different places on the map on student text page 64, and have the class decide if they got to the correct place. For example:

> Tom wanted to go from the bus station to the shopping mall. He walked along Second Avenue to Park Street and turned right. He walked up Park Street to Third Avenue and turned right. He went to the building on the left. Did he get to the right place?

> Barbara wanted to go from the post office to the department store. She walked along Third Avenue to Park Street and turned left. She walked down Park Street to Second Avenue and turned left again. She went to the first place on the left. Did she get to the right place?

(continued)

Mr. and Mrs. Clark wanted to go from the cafeteria to the zoo. They drove along Second Avenue to Park Street and turned left. They drove down Park Street to First Avenue and turned left again. They went to a place on the right. Did they get to the right place?

Variation: Divide the class into groups, and have each group write their own descriptions to read to the class.

Text Page 66: Take the Main Street Bus

FOCUS

- Directions for Using Public Transportation

  take the bus/subway
  get off at

INTRODUCING THE MODELS

There are two model conversations. Introduce and practice each separately. For each model:

1. Have students look at the model illustration.

2. Set the scene:

   1st model: "A woman wants to take her dog to Peter's Pet Shop."
   2nd model: "A man wants to take his son to Harry's Barber Shop."

3. Present the model.

4. Full-Class Repetition.

5. Ask students if they have any questions. Check understanding of new vocabulary:

   1st model: *the quickest way, get off*
   2nd model: *the easiest way*

6. Group Choral Repetition.

7. Choral Conversation.

8. Call on one or two pairs of students to present the dialog.

   (For additional practice, do Choral Conversation in small groups or by rows.)

SIDE BY SIDE EXERCISES

Answer Key

1. Take the 161st Street bus and get off at Jerome Avenue. Walk up Jerome Avenue, and you'll see the baseball stadium on the left.

2. Take the subway and get off at Center Street. Walk down Center Street, and you'll see the library on the right.

3. Take the subway and get off at Apple Road. Walk up Apple Road, and you'll see the zoo on the left.

4. Take the 10th Avenue bus and get off at Station Street. Walk along Station Street, and you'll see the train station on the right.

1. **Exercise 1:** Check understanding of *baseball stadium*. Call on two students to present the dialog. Then do Choral Repetition and Choral Conversation practice.

2. **Exercise 2:** Same as above.

3. **Exercises 3–4:** Either Full-Class Practice or Pair Practice.

New Vocabulary

3. the most direct way
   road
4. in a hurry
   the shortest way

Spelling Note

The abbreviated form of *Road* is *Rd.*

WORKBOOK

Pages 65–66

1. Telephone Directions

a. Divide the class into large groups. Have each group sit in a circle.

b. Whisper a set of difference to one student. For example:

   "Take the Third Avenue bus and get off at Fourth Avenue. Then take the subway to Fifth Street. Walk up Fifth Street and you'll see the library on the right, across from the concert hall."

c. The first student whispers the directions to the second student, and so forth, around the circle. The student listening may ask for clarifications by saying, "I'm sorry. What did you say?"

d. When the message gets to the last student, that person says it aloud. Is it the same message you started with? The group with the most accurate message wins.

2. Dictation Game

a. Make up a 4 to 5-sentence set of directions. Write the directions in large print on a piece of paper. For example:

   Take the Main Street bus.
   Get off at First Avenue.
   Walk down First Avenue to River Street.
   Turn right.
   You'll see the zoo on the left.

b. Put the paper on the far side of the room or out in the hallway so that the students can't read it from their seats.

c. Divide the class into pairs. One student from each pair runs to read the directions and then returns to dictate the directions to the partner. The runner may go back and forth as many times as necessary. The first pair to finish the set of directions wins.

3. Here's How to Get There!

For homework, have students write directions from their home to a well-known place in the center of their city or town. Encourage students to use a dictionary to find any new words they would like to use. Have students present their directions in class the next day without referring to their written homework.

4. I'm Lost!

a. Put a map of your city or town on the wall, or have a student draw a simple map on the board.

b. Put the following conversational model on the board:

   A. Excuse me, but I'm lost! How do I get to _____?
   B. _____.
   A. Thanks very much.

c. Have students create and present role plays based on the model and real places in the community.

5. Ranking Transportation

a. Dictate the following forms of transportation to the class:

   subway
   bus
   walking
   car
   bicycle

b. Have students rank these forms of transportation from the *most convenient* to the *least convenient*, with the first being the most. For example:

   1. car
   2. bicycle
   3. bus
   4. subway
   5. walking

c. Have students compare their lists in small groups and report to the class.

d. Have students continue ranking these forms of transportation according to the following categories:

> the healthiest
> the most expensive
> the noisiest
> the fastest
> the most comfortable

6. Local Transportation Contest

a. Divide the class into small groups. One group will serve as the judges. Provide each group with a local transportation map.

b. Call out a destination and ask: "What's the best way to get there from here?" Give the groups three minutes to compose a response.

c. Have the groups present their ideas to the judges. Have the judges vote on which is indeed the best way to get there from here.

d. Repeat with other destinations, and have different groups of students serve as the judges.

ROLE PLAY *Can You Tell Me How to Get There?*

FOCUS

- Directions to Locations in the Community
- Introduction of the Expressions:

$$one\ of\ the\ \left\{ \dfrac{\text{_____est}}{most\ \text{_____}} \right\}$$

INTRODUCING THE MODEL

1. Have students look at the illustration.

2. Set the scene: "This family is visiting a new city. They want to find a good hotel."

3. Present the dialog.

4. Full-Class Repetition.

5. Ask students if they have any questions. Check understanding of new vocabulary: *one of the best, boulevard, at the corner of.*

6. Group Choral Repetition.

7. Choral Conversation.

8. Call on one or two pairs of students to present the dialog.

ROLE PLAY ACTIVITY

1. Divide the class into pairs.

2. Have each pair choose one of the first three situations *(restaurant, department store, tourist sight)*, plus the final open-ended one and create role plays based on the model conversation and real places in their city or town. Students should feel free to modify or adapt the model any way they wish.

3. Call on pairs to present their role plays to the class.

4. If you wish, you can have students prepare their role plays for homework and then present them in the next class without referring to anything they might have written.

WORKBOOK

Page 67

EXPANSION ACTIVITY

The Best in Town

Have the class compile and publish their recommendations for *The Best in Town* for local shops, restaurants, and services.

1. Divide the class into small groups.

2. Have each group develop a list of their recommendations for each of the following:

supermarket	shopping mall
restaurant	department store
toy store	movie theater
pet shop	ice cream shop
barber shop	playground

3. Have the groups share their ideas with the class. Determine the top three picks for each category, if necessary through voting.

4. Have students publish their *Best in Town* list and distribute it to others in your school.

READING *Harold Never Got There!*

FOCUS

- Directions

NEW VOCABULARY

block	get lost	stupid
completely	lane	wrong
directions	such	
follow	stop	

READING THE STORY

Optional: Preview the story by having students talk about the story title and/or illustrations. You may choose to introduce new vocabulary beforehand, or have students encounter the new vocabulary within the context of the reading.

1. Have students read silently, or follow along silently as the story is read aloud by you, by one or more students, or on the audio program.

2. Ask students if they have any questions. Check understanding of vocabulary.

3. Check students' comprehension, using some or all of the following questions:

    Where did Harold want to go last night?
    Did he get there?
    Why not? What did he do?

✓ READING *CHECK-UP*

TRUE OR FALSE?

1. True
2. True
3. False
4. True
5. False
6. True
7. False
8. False

WHAT'S THE WORD?

1. to
2. to
3. at
4. of
5. off
6. at
7. on
8. to
9. from

READING EXTENSION

Tic Tac Question Formation

1. Draw a tic tac grid on the board and fill it with question words. For example:

How?	Who?	Where?
What?	Which bus?	Did?
Was?	Why?	When?

2. Divide the class into two teams. Give each team a mark: *X* or *O*.

3. Have each team ask a question about the story that begins with one of the question words, then provide the answer to the question. If the question and answer are correct, the team gets to put its mark in that space. For example:

    X Team: Was Harold very upset?
    Yes, he was.

How?	Who?	Where?
What?	Which bus?	Did?
X	Why?	When?

4. The first team to mark out three boxes in a straight line—vertically, horizontally, or diagonally—wins.

 **LISTENING**

WHAT'S THE WORD?

Listen and choose the word you hear.

1. The clinic is on the right, next to the post office.

2. The library is on the left, across from the park.

3. Walk up Town Road to Main Street.

4. Drive along Fourth Avenue to Station Street.

5. Take the subway to Pond Road.

6. The bus stop is at the corner of Central Avenue and Fifth.

7. Take this bus and get off at Bond Street.

Answers

1. a
2. b
3. b
4. a
5. a
6. b
7. b

WHERE ARE THEY?

Where are these people? Listen and choose the correct place.

1. A. Do you want to buy this shirt?
   B. Yes, please.

2. A. Please give me an order of chicken.
   B. An order of chicken? Certainly.

3. A. Shh! Please be quiet! People are reading.
   B. Sorry.

4. A. Can I visit my wife?
   B. Yes. She and the baby are in Room 407.

5. A. How much does one head cost?
   B. A dollar fifty-nine.

6. A. Hmm. Where's our car?
   B. I think it's on the third floor.

Answers

1. a
2. b
3. b
4. a
5. b
6. b

 IN YOUR OWN WORDS

1. Make sure students understand the instructions.

2. Have students do the activity as written homework, using a dictionary for any new words they wish to use.

3. Have students present their maps and directions, in pairs or as a class.

Text Page 70

th PRONUNCIATION

> ***Could you & Would you:*** In daily English usage, the pronunciation of the final /d/ sound in the words *could* and *would* blends with the beginning /y/ sound in the word *you* to produce a /j/ sound.

Focus on Listening

Practice the sentences in the left column. Say each sentence or play the audio one or more times. Have students listen carefully and repeat.

Focus on Pronunciation

Practice the sentences in the right column. Have students say each sentence and then listen carefully as you say it or play the audio.

If you wish, have students continue practicing the sentences to improve their pronunciation.

JOURNAL

Have students write their journal entries at home or in class. Encourage students to use a dictionary to look up words they would like to use. Students can share their written work with other students if appropriate. Have students discuss what they have written as a class, in pairs, or in small groups

 CHAPTER SUMMARY

GRAMMAR

1. Divide the class into pairs or small groups.
2. Have students take turns reading the sentences in the grammar box. Have them also create several other similar imperative sentences.

KEY VOCABULARY

Have students ask you any questions about the meaning or pronunciation of the vocabulary. If students ask for the pronunciation, repeat after the student until the student is satisfied with his or her own pronunciation.

EXPANSION ACTIVITIES

1. **Do You Remember the Words?**

   Check students' retention of the vocabulary depicted on the opening page of Chapter 7 by doing the following activity:

   a. Have students open their books to page 61 and cover the list of vocabulary words.

   b. Either call out a number and have students tell you the word, or say a word and have students tell you the number.

   Variation: You can also do this activity as a game with competing teams.

2. **Student-Led Dictation**

   a. Tell each student to choose a word or phrase from the Key Vocabulary list on text page 70 and look at it very carefully.

   b. Have students take turns dictating their words to the class. Everybody writes down that student's word.

   c. When the dictation is completed, call on different students to write each word on the board to check the spelling.

3. **Beanbag Toss**

   a. Call out the topic: *Places Around Town.*

   b. Have students toss a beanbag back and forth. The student to whom the beanbag is tossed must name a place around town. For example:

      Student 1:   drug store
      Student 2:   shoe store
      Student 3:   library

   (continued)

EXPANSION ACTIVITIES (Continued)

c. Continue until all the words in the category have been named.

Variation: You can also do this activity as a game with competing teams.

4. Letter Game

a. Divide the class into teams.

b. Say: "I'm thinking of a place around town that starts with *p*."

c. The first person to raise his or her hand and guess correctly *[police station]* wins a point for his or her team.

d. Continue with other letters of the alphabet and clothing items.

The team that gets the most correct answers wins the game.

5. Movable Categories

a. Write the places around town from the list on page 70 on separate cards.

b. Give each student at least one card.

c. Call out one of the following categories:

> places to buy clothes
> places to buy food
> places to go when you're sick
> places for your friends to stay
> places where you can learn
> places for transportation
> places where you can eat
> quiet places
> noisy places
> places for animals
> places to call when you have an emergency
> places to go for sports

d. All those students whose places are appropriate for the chosen category go to the right side of the room. All the other students go to the left side.

e. Those who are in the right group call out their words for the class to verify.

f. Continue with other categories.

END-OF-CHAPTER ACTIVITIES

1. Board Game

a. On poster boards or on manila file folders, make up game boards with a pathway consisting of separate spaces. You may use any theme or design you wish.

b. Divide the class into groups of 2 to 4 students and give each group a game board and a die, and each student something to be used as a playing piece.

c. Give each group a pile of cards face-down with sentences written on them. Some sentences should be correct, and others incorrect. For example:

   Walk up Park Street and turn left.
   Take the Central Avenue bus and get on at Holly Road.
   It's in the corner of Central Avenue and Main Street.
   My house is the last one in the left.
   Walk along Third Avenue three blocks.
   You'll see the library on right.
   You'll see a subway stop in Second Avenue.
   Take the 161st Street bus to the stadium.
   What's the best way to get the train station?
   Thanks you very much.
   Could you please say again?
   You'll see the gas station across to the parking garage.
   Walk down Main Street and you'll see the bakery on the left, next to the high school.
   Take the subway and get off at Central Boulevard.
   Can you tell me how get the post office?

d. Each student in turn rolls the die, moves the playing piece along the game path, and after landing on a space, picks a card, reads the sentence, and says if it is *correct or incorrect*. If the sentence is incorrect and the student is able to give the correct version, that student takes an additional turn.

e. The first student to reach the end of the pathway is the winner.

2. Dictate and Discuss

a. Divide the class into pairs or small groups.

b. Dictate *opinionated* sentences about local transportation in your community such as the following, and have students decide whether they agree or disagree with your opinion. For example:

   The fastest way to get to our school is on a bus.
   The best way to go downtown is in a car.
   The shortest way to the library is along Central Avenue.
   The 10th Avenue bus is faster than the subway.

c. Call on students to share their opinions with the rest of the class.

3. Class Survey

a. Have students brainstorm questions they might want to ask each other about transportation. For example:

   How do you usually get around town?
   Do you like to walk?
   Do you take the bus?
   Do you think the subway is clean?
   In your opinion, which is faster around town—a car or a bus?

b. Have each student choose one question and circulate around the room interviewing classmates.

c. Have students report their findings to the class.

WORKBOOK ANSWER KEY AND LISTENING SCRIPTS

WORKBOOK PAGE 60

A. HOW DO I GET THERE?

1. Walk up, on the right, across from
2. Walk up, on the left, next to
3. Walk up, on the right, across from
4. Walk down, on the left, between
5. Walk down, on the right, next to, across from

WORKBOOK PAGE 61

B. WHICH WAY?

1. Walk along, on the right, across from
2. Walk along, on the left, next to
3. Walk up, on the right, across from
4. Walk down, on the left, next to
5. Walk along, on the right, between

WORKBOOK PAGES 62–63

C. LET'S HELP MR. AND MRS. LEE!

1. Walk along
   turn left
   Walk up
   on the right
   across from
2. Walk up
   turn left
   Walk along
   on the left
   between
3. Walk along
   turn left
   Walk down
   on the right
   next to
4. Walk down
   turn right
   Walk along
   on the left
   across from

D. LISTENING

Look at the map on page 62. Listen and choose the correct answer.

1. Linda was at the hotel on Ninth Avenue. She walked along Ninth Avenue to Elm Street and turned right. She walked up Elm Street to Eighth Avenue and turned right again. She went to a building on the left, between the flower shop and the post office.

2. Roger was at the shoe store on Eighth Avenue. He walked along Eighth Avenue to Oak Street and turned right. He walked down Oak Street and went to a building on the left, across from the parking garage.

3. Mr. and Mrs. Baker were at the book store on Elm Street. They walked up Elm Street to Eighth Avenue and turned right. They walked along Eighth Avenue to a building next to the pet shop and across from the post office.

4. Wanda was at the department store on Ninth Avenue. She walked along Ninth Avenue to Oak Street and turned left. She walked up Oak Street to a building on the right, next to the toy store and across from the library.

5. Alan was at the motel on Oak Street. He walked down Oak Street to Ninth Avenue and turned right. He walked along Ninth Avenue to a place on the left, next to the supermarket and across from the department store.

6. Alice was at the supermarket on Ninth Avenue. She walked along Ninth Avenue to Oak Street and turned left. She walked up Oak Street to Eighth Avenue and turned right. She went to a building on the left, across from the restaurant.

Answers

1. a
2. b
3. a
4. b
5. b
6. a

WORKBOOK PAGE 65

F. IN A HURRY!

1. Take
   get off
   Center Street
   Walk up
   Center
   on the right
2. Take
   get off
   River Street
   Walk down
   River
   on the left

3. Take
get off
State Street
Walk up
State
on the right

WORKBOOK PAGE 67

I. LISTENING: *Where Did They Go?*

Listen and fill in the correct places.

1. David took the Bay Avenue bus and got off at Second Street. He walked up Second Street to Brighton Boulevard and turned right. He walked along Brighton Boulevard to a building on the right, across from the post office. Where did he go?

2. Barbara took the Day Street bus and got off at Second Street. She walked down Second Street to Bay Avenue and turned right. She walked along Bay Avenue to a building between the flower shop and the church. Where did she go?

3. Mr. and Mrs. Jackson took the Bay Avenue bus and got off at First Street. They walked up First Street to Brighton Boulevard and turned left. They walked along Brighton Boulevard to a building on the right, next to the bus station and across from the barber shop. Where did they go?

4. Susan didn't want to take the bus this morning. She was at the library on Bay Avenue. She walked along Bay Avenue to Third Street and turned left. She walked up Third Street to Day Street and turned left again. She walked along Day Street and went to a building on the left, between First Street and Second Street. Where did she go?

5. Mr. and Mrs. Yamamoto wanted to get some exercise this morning. They took the Day Street bus and got off at First Street. They walked down First Street to Brighton Boulevard and turned left. They walked along Brighton Boulevard to Second Street and turned right. They walked down Second Street to Bay Avenue and turned right again. They went to a place on the right, at the corner of First Street and Bay Avenue, next to the

concert hall. Where did they go?

6. George got lost this morning. He took the Bay Avenue bus and got off at First Street. He walked up First Street to Brighton Boulevard and turned right. He walked along Brighton Boulevard to Second Street and turned left. He walked up Second Street to Day Street and turned right. He walked along Day Street to Third Street and turned right again. He walked down Third Street to Brighton Boulevard, and then he was happy. He went to a place at the corner of Third Street and Brighton Boulevard, next to the post office and across from the pet shop. Where did he go?

Answers

1. bank
2. library
3. bakery
4. museum
5. zoo
6. park

J. WHAT'S THE WORD?

1. Excuse
2. Could
3. please
4. how
5. get
6. from
7. Certainly
8. Take
9. subway
10. off
11. up
12. turn
13. Walk
14. left
15. between

GRAMMAR

ADVERBS

He works	slowly. carefully. sloppily. fast. hard. well.

COMPARATIVE OF ADVERBS

He should try to work	quicker. more quickly.
	more carefully. more accurately.
	faster. harder. better.

AGENT NOUNS

actor	singer
dancer	skier
driver	teacher
painter	translator
player	worker
runner	

IF-CLAUSES

If	I we you they	feel	better,	I'll we'll you'll they'll	go to work.
	he she it	feels		he'll she'll it'll	

If	I'm we're you're they're	tired,	I'll we'll you'll they'll	go to sleep early.
	he's she's it's		he'll she'll it'll	

FUNCTIONS

DESCRIBING

He's a *careless driver.*
He drives *very carelessly/slowly/fast/ well/ . . . .*

EXPRESSING AN OPINION

I think *he's a careless driver.*

He should *try to speak slower.*

EXPRESSING AGREEMENT

You're right.
That's right.
That's true.
I know.
I agree.
I agree with you.

You're probably right.

ASKING FOR FEEDBACK

Am I *working fast* enough?
Do I *type fast* enough?

OFFERING FEEDBACK

You *type* too *slowly.*

EXPRESSING INTENTION

I'll try to *type faster* in the future.
If *it rains,* I'll *take the bus.*

INQUIRING ABOUT INTENTION

How are you going to *get to school tomorrow?*
What's *Ken* going to do *tomorrow?*
What are you going to do *tonight* if *you have a lot of homework?*

INITIATING A TOPIC

You know . . .

OFFERING ADVICE

You should *work faster.*
You shouldn't *drive so fast.*

EXPRESSING POSSIBILITY

If you *drive too fast,* you might *have an accident.*

NEW VOCABULARY

Adjectives

accurate
awkward
careful
careless
dishonest
graceful
hard
impolite
scary
slow

Agent Nouns

card player
chess player
director
driver
painter
player
runner
skier
translator
worker

Verbs

dress
evict
itch
oversleep
stay up
translate

Miscellaneous

accident
bad luck
bank account
decision
ear
enough
fork
four-leaf clover
furthermore
good luck
horseshoe
if
in general
knife

ladder
left
luck
mirror
nightmare
rent (n)
shouldn't
somebody
spoon
superstition
under
until

EXPRESSIONS

do well
Hmm.
Oh?
Too bad!
You're probably right.

Text Page 71: Chapter Opening Page

VOCABULARY PREVIEW

You may want to present these words before beginning the chapter, or you may choose to wait until they first occur in a specific lesson. If you choose to present them at this point, here are some suggestions:

1. Have students look at the illustrations on text page 71 and identify the words they already know.

2. Present the vocabulary. Say each word and have the class repeat it chorally and individually. Check students' understanding and pronunciation of the words.

3. Practice the vocabulary as a class, in pairs, or in small groups. Have students cover the word list and look at the pictures. Practice the words in the following ways:

   • Say a word and have students tell the number of the illustration.

   • Give the number of an illustration and have students say the word.

FOCUS

- Adverbs
- Agent Nouns

CLOSE UP

AGENT NOUNS

RULE: Many verbs can be converted into agent nouns by adding *-er* or *-or*.

EXAMPLES: teach–teach**er**
dance–danc**er**
act–act**or**

SPELLING RULE: For one-syllable verbs that end with a single consonant preceded by a single vowel, the final consonant is doubled.

EXAMPLE: run–ru**nner**

ADVERBS OF MANNER

RULE: An adverb of manner is formed by adding *-ly* to the corresponding adjective.

EXAMPLES: slow–slow**ly**
careful–careful**ly**

SPELLING RULE: For adjectives that end in *-y*, the *-y* changes to *-i* and *-ly is* added.

EXAMPLE: lazy–laz**ily**

RULE: There are several irregular adverbs of manner.

EXAMPLES: fast–**fast**
hard–**hard**
loud–**loud/loudly**
good–**well**

GETTING READY

Introduce adverbs of manner.

1. Write on the board.

slow–slowly
careful–carefully

2. Say and demonstrate the following and have students repeat:

I'm slow.

[speaking slowly]
I speak slowly.

[walking slowly]
I walk slowly.

[writing slowly]
I write slowly.

I'm careful.

[speaking carefully]
I speak carefully.

[walking carefully]
I walk carefully.

[writing carefully]
I write carefully.

INTRODUCING THE MODEL

1. Have students look at the model illustration.

2. Set the scene: "Two people are talking about a man who is driving."

3. Present the model

4. Full-Class Repetition.

5. Ask students if they have any questions. Check understanding of new vocabulary: *careless, driver, carelessly*.

6. Group Choral Repetition.

7. Choral Conversation.

8. Call on one or two pairs of students to present the dialog.

(For additional practice, do Choral Conversation in small groups or by rows.)

SIDE BY SIDE EXERCISES

Examples

1. A. I think she's a careful worker.
   B. I agree. She works very carefully.

2. A. I think he's a slow chess player.
   B. I agree. He plays chess very slowly.

1. **Exercise 1:** Introduce the new words *careful, worker*. Call on two students to present the dialog. Then do Choral Repetition and Choral Conversation practice.

2. **Exercise 2:** Introduce the new words *slow, chess player*. Same as above.

3. **Exercises 3–12:** Either Full-Class Practice or Pair Practice.

New Vocabulary

3. graceful
5. skier
6. run
   runner
10. hard
11. accurate
12. dishonest
    card player

WORKBOOK

Pages 68–70

EXPANSION ACTIVITIES

1. Finish the Sentence

Begin the following sentences, then call on individual students to repeat what you said and complete the sentence with the corresponding adverb:

Teacher	Students
A careful driver . . .	drives carefully.
A slow skier . . .	skies slowly.
A hard worker . . .	works hard.
A careless worker . . .	works carelessly.
A fast runner . . .	runs fast.
A beautiful singer . . .	sings beautifully.
A bad actor . . .	acts badly.
A good writer . . .	writes well.
A graceful dancer . . .	dances gracefully.
An accurate translator . . .	translates accurately.
A dishonest card player . . .	plays cards dishonestly.

Variation: You can do this activity as a game with competing teams.

2. Match the Sentences

a. Make the following set of matching cards:

A careless driver . . .	drives carelessly.
A careful driver . . .	drives carefully.
A good painter . . .	paints well.
A bad painter . . .	paints badly.
A fast runner . . .	runs fast.
A slow runner . . .	runs slowly.
An honest card player . . .	plays cards honestly
A dishonest card player . . .	plays cards dishonestly.

b. Distribute a card to each student.

c. Have students memorize the sentence

portion on their cards, then walk around the room trying to find their corresponding match.

d. Then have pairs of students say their completed sentences aloud to the class.

3. Concentration

a. Use the 16 cards you used for Expansion Activity 2 above.

b. Shuffle the cards and place them face down in four rows of 4 each.

c. Divide the class into two teams. The object of the game is for students to find the matching cards. Both teams should be able to see all the cards since *concentrating* on their location is an important part of playing the game.

d. A student from Team 1 turns over two cards. If they match, the student picks up the cards, that team gets a point, and the student takes another turn. If the cards don't match, the student turns them face down, and a member of Team 2 takes a turn.

e. The game continues until all the cards have been matched. The team with the most correct matches wins the game.

Variation: This game can also be played in groups and pairs.

4. Who Are They?

a. Write on cards the following descriptions:

a bad actor/actress	a slow painter
a hard worker	a graceful dancer
a dishonest card player	a fast runner
a careless driver	an accurate translator

(continued)

b. Have students take turns picking a card from the pile and pantomiming the agent noun on the card.

c. The class must guess who the person is (*a fast runner, a hard worker*).

Variation: This can be done as a game with competing teams.

5. Associations

a. Divide the class into pairs or small groups.

b. Call out an adverb, and tell students to write down all the different verbs that adverb can describe. For example:

gracefully: dance, move, walk
slowly: drive, speak, work

c. Have a student from each pair or group come to the board and write their verbs.

Variation: Do the activity as a game in which you divide the class into teams. The team with the most number of associations is the winner.

6. The Good and the Bad

Have students choose an agent noun (for example, *skier, dancer, actor*). Then have them write sentences describing someone who is good at it and sentences describing someone who is bad at it. For example:

A good skier skies carefully.
A good skier skies gracefully.
A good skier doesn't ski carelessly.

A bad skier skies slowly.
A bad skier skies carelessly.
A bad skier doesn't ski gracefully.

7. Memory Chain

a. Divide the class into groups of 5 or 6 students each.

b. Tell each student to think of how he or she does something.

c. One group at a time, have Student 1 begin. For example:

I drive carefully.

d. Student 2 repeats what Student 1 said and adds a statement about himself or herself. For example:

Nancy drives carefully. I run fast.

e. Student 3 continues in the same way. For example:

Nancy drives carefully. Robert runs fast. I don't dance gracefully.

f. Continue until everyone has had a chance to play the *memory chain*.

8. True or False?

Make the following statements with adverbs, and have students tell you whether they are true or false. If a statement is false, have students correct it.

A graceful dancer dances well.
A careful worker works carelessly.
An accurate translator translates badly.
A hard worker is a good worker.
A fast driver doesn't drive slowly.
A careless driver is a good driver.
A dishonest card player doesn't play cards honestly.
A slow chess player doesn't play chess fast.
A good actor acts badly.
A bad teacher doesn't teach well.

Variation: You can do this activity as a game with competing teams.

Text Page 73: You Should Work Faster

FOCUS

- Comparative of Adverbs

CLOSE UP

RULE:	The comparative of one-syllable adverbs or adverbs whose forms are the same as adjectives is formed by adding *-er*.
EXAMPLES:	fast–fast**er** hard–hard**er**
RULE:	For adverbs of manner with three or more syllables, *more* is added.
EXAMPLES:	carefully–**more** carefully gracefully–**more** gracefully accurately–**more** accurately
RULE:	Some adverbs have both comparative forms.
EXAMPLES:	quick**er** **more** quickly loud**er** **more** loudly slow**er** **more** slowly
RULE:	There are some irregular adverbs of manner.
EXAMPLE:	well–**better**

GETTING READY

1. Introduce the comparative of adverbs.

   a. Write on the board:

quickly	carefully
quicker	more carefully

   b. Model and demonstrate the following comparatives and have students repeat:

[walking quickly]
I'm walking quickly.

[walking more quickly]
I'm walking more quickly.

[writing carefully]
I'm writing carefully.

[writing more carefully]
I'm writing more carefully.

2. Present the comparative forms of adverbs at the top of text page 73.

   a. Say each word and have students repeat chorally.

b. Point out that some adverbs have both forms. (Refer students to the footnote at the bottom of text page 73.)

INTRODUCING THE MODELS

There are two model conversations. Introduce and practice each model before going on to the next. For each model:

1. Have students look at the model illustration.

2. Set the scene:

   Model 1: "A worker and a supervisor are talking."
   Model 2: "A little girl and her mother are talking."

3. Present the model.

4. Full-Class Repetition.

5. Ask students if they have any questions. Check understanding of the new word *enough*.

6. Group Choral Repetition.

7. Choral Conversation.

8. Call on one or two pairs of students to present the dialog.

   (For additional practice, do Choral Conversation in small groups or by rows.)

SIDE BY SIDE EXERCISES

Examples

> 1. A. Am I typing quickly enough?
>   B. Actually, you should type quicker (more quickly).
> 2. A. Am I dancing gracefully enough?
>   B. Actually, you should dance more gracefully.

1. **Exercise 1:** Call on two students to present the dialog. Then do Choral Repetition and Choral Conversation practice.

2. **Exercise 2:** Same as above.

3. **Exercises 3–6:** Either Full-Class Practice or Pair Practice.

> **New Vocabulary**
> 5. translate

WORKBOOK

Page 71

EXPANSION ACTIVITIES

1. Guided Conversation Match Game

   a. Make a set of cards with Speaker A's and Speaker B's lines from the dialogs on text page 73:

Am I working fast enough?	Actually, you should work faster.
Am I painting carefully enough?	Actually, you should paint more carefully.
Am I typing quickly enough?	Actually, you should type more quickly.

Am I dancing gracefully enough?	Actually, you should dance more gracefully.
Am I speaking loud enough?	Actually, you should speak louder.
Am I driving slowly enough?	Actually, you should drive slower.
Am I translating accurately enough?	Actually, you should translate more accurately.
Am I playing well enough?	Actually, you should play better.

b. Distribute the cards to students.

c. Have students memorize the sentences on their cards and then walk around the room, saying their sentences until they find their match.

d. Then have pairs of students say their matched sentences aloud to the class.

2. What's the Comparative?

Call out adverbs and have students tell you the comparatives:

fast	loud
slowly	gracefully
carelessly	accurately
well	carefully
hard	quickly

Variation: You can do this activity as a game with competing teams.

3. Concentration

a. Write the following on separate cards:

fast	faster
slowly	more slowly
quickly	more quickly
well	better
accurately	more accurately
gracefully	more gracefully
carefully	more carefully
loud	louder
carelessly	more carelessly
hard	harder

b. Shuffle the cards and place them face down in five rows of 4 each.

c. Divide the class into two teams. The object of the game is for students to find the matching cards. Both teams should be able to see all the cards since *concentrating* on their location is an important part of playing the game.

d. A student from Team 1 turns over two cards. If they match, the student picks up the cards, that team gets a point, and the student takes another turn. If the cards don't match, the student turns them face down, and a member of Team 2 takes a turn.

e. The game continues until all the cards have been matched. The team with the most correct matches wins the game.

Variation: This game can also be played in groups and pairs.

4. Comparative Mime

a. Write the following on the board:

What's the problem?
What should he/she do?

b. Make up the following cards:

You aren't dancing gracefully enough.
You aren't typing fast enough.
You aren't painting carefully enough.
You aren't speaking loud enough.
You aren't playing the violin well enough.
You aren't working fast enough.

c. Call on individual students to pick a card and pantomime the action on the card.

d. Ask the class about what the person is doing. For example:

(continued)

Teacher: What's the problem?
Student: He isn't dancing gracefully enough.
Teacher: What should he do?
Student: He should dance more gracefully.

5. Mystery Conversations

a. Divide the class into pairs.

b. Write the following conversational framework on the board:

A. Am I _____ _____ enough?
B. Actually, you should _____ _____.

c. Write roles such as the following on word cards and give one to each pair of students:

a child and a parent	an employee and a supervisor
a student and a teacher	two friends

two neighbors	a doctor and a patient
a husband and a wife	a sister and a brother

d. Have each pair create a short dialog based on the conversational model on the board. The dialogs should be appropriate for the roles the students have on their cards.

e. Have each pair present their dialog to the class. Then have the other students guess who the people are: Is a child talking to a parent? Is an employee talking to a supervisor?

Text Page 74: He Should Try to Speak Slower

FOCUS

- Comparative of Adverbs

CLOSE UP

RULE: Comparative forms of adverbs of time are formed by adding *-er*.

EXAMPLES: late–lat**er**
early–earli**er**

GETTING READY

Demonstrate and have students repeat some of the comparatives at the top of text page 74. For example:

[speaking softly]
I'm speaking softly.

[speaking softer]
I'm speaking softer.

[writing carefully]
I'm writing carefully.

[writing more carefully]
I'm writing more carefully.

INTRODUCING THE MODEL

1. Have students look at the model illustration.

2. Set the scene: "Two people are talking about Bob."

3. Present the model.

4. Full-Class Repetition.

5. Ask students if they have any questions.

6. Group Choral Repetition.

7. Choral Conversation.

8. Call on one or two pairs of students to present the dialog.

(For additional practice, do Choral Conversation in small groups or by rows.)

SIDE BY SIDE EXERCISES

In the exercises, students use the opposite of the adverb in each statement. All of those words can be found in the grammar boxes at the top of text page 74 if students need them as a reference.

Examples

1. A. Timothy types very slowly.
   B. You're right. He should try to type quicker/more quickly.

2. A. Carol skates very carelessly.
   B. You're right. She should try to skate more carefully.

Answer Key to Comparative Adverbs 3–9:

3. louder/more loudly
4. earlier
5. later
6. neater/more neatly
7. softer/more softly
8. more politely
9. better

1. **Exercise 1:** Call on two students to present the dialog. Then do Choral Repetition and Choral Conversation practice.

2. Exercise 2: Same as above.

3. Exercises 3–9: Either Full-Class Practice or Pair Practice.

> **New Vocabulary**
>
> 6. dress (v)
> 8. impolite

EXPANSION ACTIVITIES

1. Tic Tac Adverbs

a. Have students draw a tic tac grid on their papers and then fill in their grids with 9 of the following adverbs:

loudly	neatly
fast	politely
early	accurately
slowly	softly
better	impolitely
late	sloppily

b. Say the beginnings of the following sentences, and tell students to cross out the word that finishes each sentence:

He likes noisy music. He plays it very . . .

I don't walk quickly enough. I walk . . .

He always wears very clean clothes. He dresses very . . .

It's difficult to hear him when he speaks. He speaks very . . .

He doesn't like to drive slowly. He likes to drive very . . .

They don't speak English very well. They want to speak it . . .

She always says "please" and "thank you." She speaks very . . .

He never says "please" or "thank you." He speaks very . . .

They always arrive before everyone else. They like to arrive . . .

They always arrive after everyone else. They always arrive . . .

She's very careful when she translates. She translates very . . .

He always wears dirty clothes that aren't very nice. He dresses very . . .

c. The first student to cross out three words in a straight line—either horizontally, vertically, or diagonally—wins the game.

d. Have the winner call out the words to check for accuracy.

2. Match the Conversations

a. Make a set of matching cards based on giving advice. For example:

They speak very impolitely.	They should try to speak more politely.
They arrive very late.	They should try to arrive earlier.
They speak very loudly.	They should try to speak softer.
They do their homework carelessly.	The should try to do it more carefully.
They dress sloppily.	They should try to dress more neatly.
They walk very slowly.	They should try to walk faster.
They don't listen very well.	They should try to listen better.
They don't type accurately.	They should try to type more accurately.
They don't work hard.	They should try to work harder.

b. Distribute a card to each student.

c. Have students memorize the sentences on their cards, and then have students walk around the room saying their sentences until they find their match.

d. Then have pairs of students say their matched sentences aloud to the class.

3. Concentration

a. Use the cards from the above activity. Place them face down in three rows of 6 each.

b. Divide the class into two teams. The object of the game is for students to find the matching cards. Both teams should be able to see all the cards since *concentrating* on their location is an important part of playing the game.

c. A student from Team 1 turns over two cards. If they match, the student picks up the cards, that team gets a point, and the student takes another turn. If the cards don't match, the student turns them face down, and a member of Team 2 takes a turn.

d. The game continues until all the cards have been matched. The team with the most correct matches wins the game.

Variation: This game can also be played in groups and pairs.

4. Always and Never!

a. Write each of the following statements about people on word cards:

Brian always speaks very softly.

Susan never goes to bed early.

Bob and Tim always work slowly.

Dave never dresses neatly.

Gloria always plays her music very loudly.

Those people never play cards honestly.

Karen always plays tennis well.

Jack never does his homework carefully.

They always play cards honestly.

Betty never speaks impolitely.

Boris always translates carefully.

b. Pass the cards out to students, and have each student in turn read the statement on the card.

c. Then call on another student to make a similar statement, using *always* or *never* and the opposite adverb. For example:

[card] | Brian always speaks very softly. |
|---|

Student: I know. He never speaks loudly.

[card] | Susan never goes to bed early. |
|---|

Student: I know. She always goes to bed late.

5. Giving Advice

a. Write the statements below on word cards.

b. Give the cards to students, and have each student read the problem to the class.

c. Call on other students to give advice, using the appropriate comparative adverb. For example:

[problem] | Joe never says "Thank you" or "You're welcome." |
|---|

Student's Advice: He should try to speak more politely.

Problems:

Joe never says "Thank you" or "You're welcome."

Mrs. Morgan drives very carelessly.

(continued)

Rick's friends don't want to play cards with him because he sometimes plays dishonestly.

Nancy likes Max. She wants to go out with him, but her parents think he dresses sloppily.

Arthur arrives late at the office every day. His boss always gets angry at him.

Louise is a good student, but she sometimes speaks impolitely.

When Frank washes the dishes, he always breaks something.

Irene is lazy. She's afraid her boss might fire her.

When Roger talks, everybody gets an earache.

Janet wants to get a new job, but she works very slowly.

Steven likes to play his CD player very loudly, but when he plays it, his brothers and sisters can't do their homework.

How to Say It!

Expressing Agreement: In English, there are many ways to express agreement. The expressions on text page 74 are used frequently to agree with the other speaker as well as to provide feedback in a conversation.

1. Set the scene: "These people are agreeing."

2. Present the expressions.

3. Full-Class Repetition.

4. Ask students if they have any questions. Check understanding of the expressions.

5. Group Choral Repetition.

6. Have students practice conversations on text page 74 again, using these different expressions of agreement.

7. Call on pairs to present their conversations to the class.

READING *Trying Harder*

FOCUS

- Adverbs
- Comparatives of Adverbs

NEW VOCABULARY

awkward	furthermore
director	in general
do well	

READING THE STORY

Optional: *Preview the story by having students talk about the story title and/or illustrations. You may choose to introduce new vocabulary beforehand, or have students encounter the new vocabulary within the context of the reading.*

1. Have students read silently, or follow along silently as the story is read aloud by you, by one or more students, or on the audio program.

2. Ask students if they have any questions. Check understanding of vocabulary.

3. Check students' comprehension, using some or all of the following questions:

    What does Michael's boss think about his work?
    According to Michael's boss, how does he type?
    What should he do?
    How does he file?
    What should he do?
    How does he speak on the telephone?
    What should he do?

What does Stella's director think about her work?
According to Stella's director, how does she speak?
What should she do?
How does she walk?
What should she do?
How does she dance?
What should she do?

What does Billy's teacher think about his behavior at school?
According to Billy's teacher, when does he arrive at school?
What should he do?
How does he dress?
What should he do?
How does he speak?
What should he do?

✓ READING *CHECK-UP*

Q & A

1. Call on a pair of students to present the model.

2. Have students work in pairs to create new dialogs.

3. Call on pairs to present their new dialogs to the class.

WHAT'S THE OPPOSITE?

1. slowly
2. carelessly
3. quietly
4. impolitely
5. well
6. neatly
7. gracefully
8. later
9. slower

Job Descriptions

1. Present a job description. For example:

   receptionist

   A good receptionist should answer the
   telephone politely.
   A good receptionist should dress neatly.
   A good receptionist should be friendly.

2. Have students write a job description for a
   job they know well. Encourage them to
   include adverbs in their descriptions. If
   students don't have any job experience, have
   them describe the responsibilities of a good
   student.

3. Have students share their descriptions in
   small groups and then with the class.

Text Page 76: If

FOCUS

* *If*-Clauses to Express Present Real Conditional

CLOSE UP

RULE: *If*-clauses with future meaning are used when speaking about different possibilities in the future. The *if*-clause describes a condition (for example, *If it rains . . ., If the weather is good, . . .*), and the main clause describes the result if that condition is met. The verb in the *if*-clause is in the simple present. The verb in the result (or *main*) clause is often in the future. When the *if*-clause comes first in a sentence, it is followed by a comma.

EXAMPLES: If it**'s** sunny, I**'ll walk**.
If the weather **is** bad, he**'ll go** to the movies.
If they **have** a boy, they**'ll name** him John.

GETTING READY

Review the future with *will*.

1. Put the following conversational model on the board:

> A. Will _____ arrive soon?
> B. Yes. _____ arrive in a few minutes.

2. Ask the following questions, and have students respond chorally and individually, using the appropriate contraction with *will*:

Will the train arrive soon?	(Yes. It'll . . .)
Will Jane arrive soon?	(Yes. She'll . . .)
Will David arrive soon?	(Yes. He'll . . .)
Will your friends arrive soon?	(Yes. They'll . . .)
Will we arrive soon?	(Yes. We'll . . .)
Will you arrive soon?	(Yes. I'll . . .)

INTRODUCING THE MODEL

1. Have students look at the model illustration.

2. Set the scene: "This husband and wife are going to have a baby soon. They might have a boy, or they might have a girl."

3. Present the model.

4. Full-Class Repetition.

5. Ask students if they have any questions. Check understanding of the new word *if*.

Pronunciation Note

The pronunciation focus of Chapter 8 is **Contrastive Stress** (text page 80). You should model this pronunciation at this point and encourage students to incorporate it into their language practice.

If they have a bóy, they'll name him Jóhn.
If they have a gírl, they'll name her Jáne.

6. Group Choral Repetition.

7. Choral Conversation.

8. Call on one or two pairs of students to present the dialog.

(For additional practice, do Choral Conversation in small groups or by rows.)

Answer Key

1. A. How are you going to get to school tomorrow?
   B. If it rains, I'll take the bus. If it's sunny, I'll walk.

2. A. What's Roger going to do this Saturday afternoon?
   B. If the weather is good, he'll go to the beach. If the weather is bad, he'll go to the movies.

3. A. What's Rosa going to have for dinner tonight?
   B. If she's very hungry, she'll have a big dinner. If she isn't very hungry, she'll have a sandwich.

4. A. What's Ken going to do tomorrow?
   B. If he feels better, he'll go to work. If he doesn't feel better, he'll go to the doctor.

1. **Exercise 1:** Call on two students to present the dialog. Then do Choral Repetition and Choral Conversation practice.

2. **Exercise 2:** Same as above.

3. **Exercises 3–4:** Either Full-Class Practice or Pair Practice.

How About You?

1. For homework, have students write answers to the questions.

2. Have students present their answers in the next class without referring to their written homework. Call on pairs of students to ask and answer.

WORKBOOK

Pages 74–76

EXPANSION ACTIVITIES

1. Scrambled Sentences

   a. Divide the class into teams.

   b. Write individual sentences out of order on the board. For example:

   > I'll early. to If sleep tired, I'm go
   >
   > it tomorrow, go rains If movie. a I'll to
   >
   > she go work. feels If to back better, she'll

   c. The first person to raise his or her hand, come to the board, and write the sentence in the correct order earns a point for that team.

   d. The team with the most points wins the scrambled sentence game.

   Variation: Write the words to several sentences on separate cards. Divide the class into small groups, and have students work together to put the sentences into correct order.

2. Match the Sentences

   a. Make the following set of matching cards:

If they have a boy, . . .	they'll name him Carl.
If they have a girl, . . .	they'll name her Carla.
If it rains, . . .	I'll take an umbrella.

If the weather is cold, . . .	I'll wear mittens or gloves.
If I'm very hungry, . . .	I'll have a big dinner.
If I'm not hungry, . . .	I'll have a very small dinner.
If I'm sick, . . .	I'll call the doctor.
If I have a lot of homework, . . .	I'll study all weekend.

b. Distribute the cards to students.

c. Have students memorize the sentence portions on their cards and then walk around the room, saying their phrases until they find their match.

d. Then have pairs of students say their matched sentences aloud to the class.

3. Grammar Chain: What If?

a. Have the class sit in a circle.

b. Begin the grammar chain by saying:

   If it's sunny tomorrow, I'll go to the beach.

c. Student 1 rephrases the result into a condition and then adds a new result. For example:

   If I go to the beach, I'll go swimming

d. Student 2 continues the chain in the same way. For example:

   If I go swimming, I'll see a big fish.

e. Continue until everyone has had a turn.

Text Page 77: If You Drive Too Fast, You Might Have an Accident

FOCUS

* *If*-Clauses with *might*

CLOSE UP

RULE: *If*-clauses with *might* are used when speaking about different possibilities in the future. The *if*-clause describes a condition, and the main clause describes the result if the condition is met. The verb in the *if*-clause is in the simple present. The verb in the result *(main)* clause can be a modal of possibility (such as *might, can, could*). When the *if*-clause comes first in a sentence, it is followed by a comma.

EXAMPLES: If you **drive** too fast, you **might** have an accident.
If you **eat** too quickly, you **might** get a stomachache.

INTRODUCING THE MODEL

1. Have students look at the model illustration.

2. Set the scene: "A mother and son are talking in a car."

3. Present the model.

4. Full-Class Repetition.

5. Ask students if they have any questions. Check understanding of new vocabulary: *shouldn't, Oh?, accident, Hmm., You're probably right.*

   ### Language Note

   The adverb *too* is used to mean *excessively* and has a negative connotation: *If you drive too fast, you might have an accident.* Students sometimes confuse this word with *very*, which does not normally have this negative connotation.

6. Group Choral Repetition.

7. Choral Conversation.

8. Call on one or two pairs of students to present the dialog.

   (For additional practice, do Choral Conversation in small groups or by rows.)

SIDE BY SIDE EXERCISES

Examples

1. A. You know . . . you shouldn't eat so quickly.
   B. Oh?
   A. Yes. If you eat too quickly, you might get a stomachache.
   B. Hmm. You're probably right.

2. A. You know . . . you shouldn't sing so loudly.
   B. Oh?
   A. Yes. If you sing too loudly, you might get a sore throat.
   B. Hmm. You're probably right.

1. **Exercise 1:** Call on two students to present the dialog. Then do Choral Repetition and Choral Conversation practice.

2. **Exercise 2:** Same as above.

3. **Exercises 3–8:** Either Full-Class Practice or Pair Practice.

New Vocabulary

5. ear
6. scary
   nightmare

---

4. **Exercise 9:** Have students use the model as a guide to create their own conversations, using vocabulary of their choice. Encourage students to use dictionaries to find new words they want to use. This exercise can be done orally in class or for written homework. If you assign it for homework, do one example in class to make sure students understand what's expected. Have students present their conversations in class the next day.

WORKBOOK

Page 77

EXPANSION ACTIVITIES

1. Different Emotions

Have students practice reading the model conversation, using any combination of these different emotions:

Speaker A is upset and angry.
Speaker A is worried about Speaker B.
Speaker B is interested in what Speaker A says.
Speaker B isn't interested in what Speaker A says.
Speaker B is angry at what Speaker A says.

2. Match the Sentences

a. Make the following set of matching cards:

If you eat too fast, . . .	you might get a stomachache.
If you touch those wires, . . .	you might get a shock.
If you don't watch your step, . . .	you might fall.
If you drive too fast, . . .	you might have a car accident.
If you go sailing, . . .	you might get seasick.

If you read all night, . . .	you might hurt your eyes.
If you speak impolitely, . . .	people won't listen to you.
If you arrive late for work. . . .	you might lose your job.
If you do your homework carelessly, . . .	you might not do well on the test.
If you dance too fast, . . .	you might step on my feet.

b. Distribute the cards to students.

c. Have students memorize the sentence portions on their cards and then walk around the room, saying their phrases until they find their corresponding match.

d. Then have pairs of students say their completed sentences aloud to the class.

3. Sense or Nonsense?

a. Divide the class into four groups.

b. Make four sets of the cards from Expansion Activity 2 above.

(continued)

c. Mix up the cards and distribute sets of cards to each group, keeping the *if*-clauses and endings cards in different piles.

d. Have students take turns picking up one card from each pile and reading the sentence to the group. For example:

| If you speak impolitely, . . . | you might get seasick. |

e. That group decides if the sentence makes sense or is *nonsense*.

f. After all the cards have been picked, have the groups lay out all the cards and put together all the sentence combinations that make sense.

4. Grammar Chain: Watch Out!

   a. Have the class sit in a circle.

   b. Start the chain game by saying:

   > Watch out! If you drive too fast, you might have an accident.

   c. Student 1 rephrases the result into a condition and then adds a new result. For example:

   > If you have an accident, you might have to go to the hospital.

   d. Student 2 continues the chain in the same way. For example:

   > If you have to go to the hospital, you might be very upset.

   e. Continue until everyone has had a turn.

5. Sentence Game

   a. Divide the class into pairs or small groups.

b. Write the following *might*-clauses on the board:

> You might lose your job.
> The teacher might get mad at you.
> You might get a sore throat.
> You might have nightmares.
> You might break your leg.
> You might catch a cold.
> You might meet a new friend.
> You might have a wonderful time.
> You might get an earache.

c. Have the groups brainstorm possible *if*-clauses to precede each of these *might*-clauses.

d. Have students share their ideas with the class.

6. Dictate and Discuss

   a. Divide the class into pairs or small groups.

   b. Dictate sentences such as the following, and then have students discuss them:

   > If you drive too slowly, you might have an accident.
   > If you don't sleep enough, you'll make more mistakes.
   > If you go to many rock concerts, you'll hurt your ears.
   > If you practice English every day, you'll learn a lot.
   > If you sit next to an open window, you might catch a cold.
   > If you watch too much TV, you'll become a boring person.

   c. Call on students to share their opinions with the rest of the class.

READING *Good Decisions*

FOCUS

- *If*-clauses

NEW VOCABULARY

bank account	oversleep
decision	rent (n)
evict	stay up
left	until

READING THE STORY

Optional: *Preview the story by having students talk about the story title and/or illustrations. You may choose to introduce new vocabulary beforehand, or have students encounter the new vocabulary within the context of the reading.*

1. Have students read silently, or follow along silently as the story is read aloud by you, by one or more students, or on the audio program.

2. Ask students if they have any questions. Check understanding of vocabulary.

3. Check students' comprehension, using some or all of the following questions:

   What does Ronald want to do?
   What will happen if he stays up late to watch a movie?
   What will happen if he doesn't get to bed until after midnight?
   What will happen if he's tired in the morning?
   What will happen if he oversleeps?
   What will happen if he's late for work?

   What does Barbara want to do?
   What will happen if she buys a new car?
   What will happen if she has to take a lot of money out of her bank account?

   What will happen if she doesn't have much left?
   What will happen if she doesn't have enough money to pay the rent?

✓ READING *CHECK-UP*

WHICH WORD IS CORRECT?

1. doesn't, tired
2. he's, fire
3. buys, won't
4. doesn't, evict
5. want, aren't

READING EXTENSION

Sequencing

1. Dictate the following sentences:

   He might oversleep.
   His boss might fire him.
   He won't get to bed until after midnight.
   He'll be late for work.
   He wants to watch a movie on TV.
   He'll be tired in the morning.

2. Have students read the story again and then put the sentences in the logical sequence.

3. In class, have students read their sequences aloud.

4. Repeat with the following sentences from the second story:

   She'll have to take a lot of money out of her back account.
   Her landlord might evict her.
   She won't have enough money to pay the rent.
   She wants to buy a car.
   She won't have much money left.

How About You?

Have students complete the sentences any way they wish and then share their ideas with the class.

LISTENING

Listen and choose the best answer to complete the sentence.

1. If I do my homework carelessly, . . .
2. If Sally doesn't feel better soon, . . .
3. If you sit at your computer for a long time, . . .
4. If I stay up late tonight, . . .
5. If you don't speak loudly, . . .
6. If you don't work hard, . . .

Answers

1. b
2. a
3. b
4. b
5. b
6. a

 ON YOUR OWN: *Superstitions*

FOCUS

- Review of *if* and *will*

ON YOUR OWN ACTIVITY

1. Introduce the three *good luck* superstitions.*

   a. Go over the new vocabulary: *good luck, four-leaf clover, horseshoe.*

   b. Read from the book or play the audio one or more times.

   c. Ask students to tell about any other *good luck* superstitions they know.

2. Introduce the four *bad luck* superstitions.

   a. Go over the new vocabulary: *bad luck, under, ladder.*

   b. Read from the book or play the audio one or more times.

   c. Ask students to tell you about any other *bad luck* superstitions they know.

3. Introduce the other superstitions.

   a. Go over the new vocabulary: *itch, somebody, say good things, say bad things, knife, fork, spoon, mirror.*

   b. Read from the book or play the audio one or more times.

   c. Ask students to tell about any other superstitions they know.

   *In the United States, as in countries all over the world, *superstitions* are part of the folk culture passed on through word of mouth. Students usually enjoy discussing these colorful beliefs.

WORKBOOK

Page 78

PRONUNCIATION

 CHAPTER SUMMARY

Contrastive Stress: In English, stress always falls on the words that bring new information. When contrasting *conditions* and *results*, the pitch rises equally on the key words in the *condition clause* and on the key words in the *result clause*.

GRAMMAR

1. Divide the class into pairs or small groups.

2. Have students take turns forming sentences from the words in the grammar boxes. Student A says a sentence, and Student B points to the words from each column that are in the sentence. Then have students switch: Student B says a sentence, and Student A points to the words.

Focus on Listening

Practice the sentences in the left column. Say each sentence or play the audio one or more times. Have students listen carefully and repeat.

Focus on Pronunciation

Practice the sentences in the right column. Have students say each sentence and then listen carefully as you say it or play the audio.

If you wish, have students continue practicing the sentences to improve their pronunciation.

KEY VOCABULARY

Have students ask you any questions about the meaning or pronunciation of the vocabulary. If students ask for the pronunciation, repeat after the student until the student is satisfied with his or her own pronunciation.

 JOURNAL

Have students write their journal entries at home or in class. Encourage students to use a dictionary to look up words they would like to use. Students can share their written work with other students if appropriate. Have students discuss what they have written as a class, in pairs, or in small groups

WORKBOOK

Check Up Test: Pages 79–80

EXPANSION ACTIVITIES

1. **Do You Remember the Words?**

   Check students' retention of the vocabulary depicted on the opening page of Chapter 8 by doing the following activity:

   a. Have students open their books to page 71 and cover the list of vocabulary words.

   b. Either call out a number and have students tell you the word, or say a word and have students tell you the number.

   Variation: You can also do this activity as a game with competing teams.

2. **Student-Led Dictation**

   a. Tell each student to choose a word from the Key Vocabulary list on text page 80 and look at it very carefully.

(continued)

EXPANSION ACTIVITIES (Continued)

b. Have students take turns dictating their words to the class. Everybody writes down that student's word.

c. When the dictation is completed, call on different students to write each word on the board to check the spelling.

3. Beanbag Toss

a. Call out the topic: *Adverbs.*

b. Have students toss a beanbag back and forth. The student to whom the beanbag is tossed must name an adverb. For example:

> Student 1: accurately
> Student 2: well
> Student 3: sloppily

c. Continue until all the adverbs have been named.

Variation: You can also do this activity as a game with competing teams.

4. Letter Game

a. Divide the class into teams.

b. Say: "I'm thinking of an adjective that starts with *i.*"

c. The first person to raise his or her hand and guess correctly [impolite] wins a point for his or her team.

d. Continue with other letters of the alphabet.

The team that gets the most correct answers wins the game.

5. Movable Categories

a. Write out the adverbs from the list on text page 80 on separate cards.

b. Give each student one or two cards.

c. Call out one of the following categories:

> how someone plays a game
> how someone drives
> how someone translates languages
> how someone types
> how someone dances
> how someone sings
> how someone teaches
> how someone speaks
> how someone dresses

d. All those students whose adverbs are appropriate for the chosen category go to the right side of the room. All the other students go to the left side.

e. Those who are in the right group call out their words for the class to verify.

f. Continue with other categories.

1. Board Game

   a. On poster boards or on manila file folders, make up game boards with a pathway consisting of separate spaces. You may use any theme or design you wish.

   b. Divide the class into groups of 2 to 4 students and give each group a game board and a die, and each student something to be used as a playing piece.

   c. Give each group a pile of cards face-down with sentences written on them. Some sentences should be correct, and others incorrect. For example:

   > If she's tired, she'll go to bed early.
   > If he will speak louder, people will hear him.
   > She should paint more quicker.
   > They should try to run more fast.
   > They should speak to their parents more politely.
   > If it will rain, they go to the movies.
   > If you sit at your computer too long, you get a headache.
   > If I do my homework carefully, I'll learn a lot.
   > If she goes to bed late, she might oversleep.
   > If he should work harder, he'll get a better job.
   > If they have a girl, they'll name him Sam.
   > He drives very faster.
   > You translate very accurately.

   d. Each student in turn rolls the die, moves the playing piece along the game path, and after landing on a space, picks a card, reads the sentence, and says if it is *correct* or *incorrect*. If the sentence is incorrect and the student is able to give the correct version, that student takes an additional turn.

   e. The first student to reach the end of the pathway is the winner.

2. Telephone

   a. Divide the class into large groups. Have each group sit in a circle.

   b. Whisper a short story to one student. For example:

   "Lisa wants to watch a scary movie tonight. If she watches a scary movie tonight, she won't sleep well. If she doesn't sleep well, she'll be tired in the morning. So she might watch a comedy instead."

   c. The first student whispers the story to the second student, and so forth around the circle.

   d. When the story gets to the last student, that person says it aloud. Is it the same story you started with? The group with the most accurate story wins.

3. Dialog Builder!

   a. Divide the class into pairs.

   b. Write a line on the board from a conversation such as the following:

   > Hmm. You're probably right.

   Other possible lines:

   > That's right.
   > Actually, you should try to . . .
   > I know.
   > Oh?

   c. Have each pair create a conversation incorporating that line. Students can begin and end their conversations any way they wish, but they must include that line in their dialogs.

   d. Call on students to present their conversations to the class.

4. Tic Tac Vocabulary

   a. Have students draw a tic tac grid on their papers and then fill in their grids with the following adverbs:

awkwardly	badly	carefully
fast	impolitely	softly
neatly	slowly	early

(continued)

b. Tell students that you're going to say the *opposites* of the words in their grids. So when they hear a word, they should look for the opposite of that word and cross it out.

c. The first person to cross out three opposites in a straight line—either vertically horizontally, or diagonally—wins the game.

d. Have the winner call out the words to check the accuracy.

WORKBOOK ANSWER KEY AND LISTENING SCRIPTS

12. Everybody in the store likes Jane. She works hard, and when she talks to customers she's very . . .

WORKBOOK PAGE 68

A. WHAT DO YOU THINK?

1. terribly
2. accurately
3. gracefully
4. badly
5. carefully
6. dishonestly
7. carelessly
8. slowly
9. fast
10. beautiful
11. hard
12. good

Answers

1. slow
2. beautifully
3. dishonest
4. sloppily
5. accurate
6. rudely
7. safely
8. reliable
9. softly
10. cheaply
11. carefully
12. patient

WORKBOOK PAGE 69

B. ANSWER

CAREFUL
(CAREFULLY)

1. careful, carefully
2. terribly, good
3. beautifully, graceful
4. good, fast
5. safely, careless
6. badly, politely
7. cheaply, expensive
8. reliable, energetically

C. LISTENING

Listen and circle the correct word to complete the sentence.

1. He's a good worker, but he's . . .
2. She's an excellent violinist. She plays the violin . . .
3. I don't think he's an honest card player. To tell the truth, everybody says he's . . .
4. I can't read their homework because they write very . . .
5. Maria never makes mistakes. She's very . . .
6. Their son Marvin is very polite. He never speaks . . .
7. When you leave the party, please drive home . . .
8. Their car is very old. I don't think it's . . .
9. People can't hear you very well when you speak . . .
10. We never buy expensive clothes. We live very . . .
11. You rode your motorcycle carelessly yesterday. That's strange. You usually ride it very . . .

WORKBOOK PAGE 71

E. WHAT'S THE WORD?

1. faster
2. louder/more loudly
3. more carefully
4. more accurately
5. quicker/more quickly
6. more gracefully
7. better
8. harder
9. slower/more slowly

WORKBOOK PAGE 72

F. RALPH SHOULD TRY HARDER!

1. earlier
2. neater/more neatly
3. slower/more slowly
4. more politely
5. faster/quicker/more quickly
6. more carefully
7. softer/more softly

WORKBOOK PAGE 73

H. GrammarSong

1. careful
2. carefully
3. careful
4. carefully
5. beautiful
6. beautifully
7. beautiful
8. beautifully

(continued)

9. graceful
10. gracefully
11. graceful
12. gracefully
13. stronger
14. longer
15. better
16. better

WORKBOOK PAGE 74

I. WHAT'S THE ANSWER?

1. a
2. b
3. a
4. b
5. b
6. a
7. a
8. b
9. a
10. a
11. b
12. b

J. MATCHING

1. d
2. f
3. a
4. c
5. b
6. e

WORKBOOK PAGE 75

K. IF

1. arrive, we'll
2. it rains
3. is, will go
4. plays, he'll have
5. make, will be
6. touches, he'll get
7. it's, will go
8. eats, she'll get
9. do, I'll be
10. have, we'll name
11. there's, will
12. go, they'll eat/they'll have

L. SCRAMBLED SENTENCES

1. If he goes to the party, he'll wear his new suit.
2. If she misses the bus, she'll be late for work.
3. If I practice, I'll play chess better.
4. If I go to the bakery, I'll buy an apple pie.
5. If you don't finish school, you'll be sorry.
6. If Sam works hard in school, he'll get a good job.

WORKBOOK PAGE 78

P. PLEASE DON'T!

1. I have to read
2. I'll
3. I'm
4. I fall asleep
5. won't
6. he'll/she'll
7. they're
8. they tell
9. he'll/she'll
10. he'll
11. he's
12. he'll
13. he has
14. won't
15. he doesn't
16. he'll be
17. he's
18. he'll

WORKBOOK PAGES 79–80

Check-Up Test: Chapters 7-8

A.

1. terribly
2. carefully
3. badly
4. hard

B.

1. honest, dishonestly
2. quick, quiet
3. good, well
4. safely, careless

C.

1. later
2. more politely
3. more gracefully
4. louder/more loudly

D.

1. eat/have, you'll
2. is, will be
3. have, they'll name
4. I'm not

E.

1. we take, we'll go
2. feel, might go
3. might get
4. doesn't, I'll go

F.

Listen and fill in the correct places.

1. Mrs. Mendoza was at the hotel at the corner of First Avenue and Grove Street. She walked up Grove Street to Second Avenue and turned left. She walked along Second Avenue to a building on the left, between the pet shop and the cafeteria. Where did she go?

2. Edward was at the football stadium on First Avenue. He walked along First Avenue to Elm Street and turned left. He walked up Elm Street to Second Avenue and turned right. He walked along Second Avenue to a building on the right, at the corner of Grove Street and Second Avenue, across from the bank. Where did he go?

3. Mr. and Mrs. Wong were at the post office on Second Avenue. They walked along Second Avenue to Grove Street and turned left. They walked down Grove Street to First Avenue and turned right. They went to a building on the left, across from the museum and the parking garage. Where did they go?

4. Thomas was at the hospital on Second Avenue. He walked along Second Avenue to Elm Street and turned right. He walked down Elm Street to First Avenue and turned left. He walked along First Avenue to a building on the left, at the corner of Grove Street and First Avenue, across from the supermarket. Where did he go?

5. Maria was at the shoe store on First Avenue. She walked along First Avenue to Grove Street and turned left. She walked up Grove Street to Second Avenue and turned left again. She walked along Second Avenue to a building on the right, between the toy store and the barber shop, across from the ice cream shop. Where did she go?

Answers

1. ice cream shop
2. concert hall
3. shopping mall
4. hotel
5. book store

FEATURE ARTICLE
You're Hired!

PREVIEWING THE ARTICLE

1. Have students talk about the title of the article and the accompanying photograph.

2. You may choose to introduce the following new vocabulary beforehand, or have students encounter it within the context of the article:

answer
confident
confidently
correct
describe
directly
enthusiastically
experience
express
eye contact
firm
firmly
handshake
honestly
interest
interview
interviewer
job applicant
job interview
learn
personnel officer
promptly
shake hands
skills
successful
thank-you note
tip
truth

READING THE ARTICLE

1. Have students read silently, or follow along silently as the article is read aloud by you, by one or more students, or on the audio program.

2. Ask students if they have any questions. Check understanding of vocabulary.

3. Check students' comprehension by having students answer the following questions:

When you have a job interview, . . .

How should you dress?
When should you arrive?
How should you shake hands? Why?
How should you look at the interviewer?
How should you listen to the interviewer's questions?
What should you say about yourself?
How should you speak?
How should you answer questions?
What should you do after the interview?

4. Have students discuss the questions at the end of the article in small groups or as a class.

EXPANSION ACTIVITY

Role Play: What's Wrong?

1. Divide the class into pairs.

2. Have each pair develop a role play of a job interview based on the advice in the article. The job applicant should follow all but *one piece of the advice* given in the article. For example:

The job applicant dresses neatly, shakes hands firmly, and smiles, but doesn't speak enthusiastically.
   or
The job applicants speaks politely and enthusiastically and listens carefully, but doesn't tell the truth.

3. Have students perform their role plays for the class. The class tries to identify what's wrong in each interview.

BUILD YOUR VOCABULARY!
Occupations

assembler	photographer
designer	programmer
director	supervisor
gardener	welder
inspector	writer

1. Have students look at the illustrations and identify any words they already know.

2. Present the vocabulary. Say each word and have the class repeat it chorally and individually. Check students' understanding and pronunciation of the words.

EXPANSION ACTIVITIES

1. Beanbag Toss

a. Call out the category: *Occupations*.

b. Have students toss a beanbag back and forth. The student to whom the beanbag is tossed must name an occupation from the *Build Your Vocabulary!* section. For example:

Student 1: assembler
Student 2: supervisor
Student 3: writer

c. Continue until all the occupations have been named.

2. Miming

a. Write on cards the occupations from text page 81.

b. Have students take turns picking a card from the pile and pantomiming the occupation on the card.

c. The class must guess what the occupation is.

Variation: This can be done as a game with competing teams.

3. Associations

a. Divide the class into pairs or small groups.

b. Call out the name of an occupation, and tell students to write down all the words they associate with that occupation. For example:

assembler: machines, factory, parts
programmer: computers, numbers
gardener: outdoors, sun, plants, flowers

c. Have a student from each pair or group come to the board and write their words.

Variation: Do the activity as a game in which you divide the class into teams. The team with the most number of associations is the winner.

4. Match the Conversations

a. Make a set of matching cards based on occupations. For example:

Can you design beautiful clothes?	Of course I can. I'm a very good designer.
Can you direct science fiction movies?	Of course I can. I'm a very good director.
Can you inspect buildings?	Of course I can. I'm a very good inspector.
Can you write novels and short stories?	Of course I can. I'm a very good writer.
Can you supervise people well?	Of course I can. I'm a very good supervisor.
Can you weld things?	Of course I can. I'm a very good welder.
Can you program computers?	Of course I can. I'm a very good programmer.
Can you assemble machines?	Of course I can. I'm a very good assembler.

b. Distribute a card to each student.

c. Have students memorize the sentences on their cards, and then have students walk around the room saying their sentences until they find their match.

d. Then have pairs of students say their matched sentences aloud to the class.

(continued)

EXPANSION ACTIVITIES (Continued)

5. Concentration

   a. Make sentence cards from the above activity, writing the description on one card and the occupation on another.

   b. Shuffle the cards and place them face down in four rows of 4 each.

   c. Divide the class into two teams. The object of the game is for students to find the matching cards. Both teams should be able to see all the cards, since *concentrating* on their location is an important part of playing the game.

   d. A student from Team 1 turns over two cards. If they match, the student picks up the cards, that team gets a point, and the student takes another turn. If the cards don't match, the student turns them face down, and a member of Team 2 takes a turn.

   e. The game continues until all the cards have been matched. The team with the most correct matches wins the game.

   Variation: This game can also be played in groups and pairs.

AROUND THE WORLD
Men and Women at Work

1. Have students read silently or follow along silently as the text is read aloud by you, by one or more students, or on the audio program. Check understanding of new vocabulary:

   | airline pilot |
   | homemaker |
   | nurse |

2. Bring a map to class and point out the location of the countries mentioned: *Vietnam, Costa Rica, Bandgladesh, France, England, United States.*

3. Have students first work in pairs or small groups and respond to the questions. Then have students tell the class what they talked about. Write any new vocabulary on the board.

EXPANSION ACTIVITY

Dictate and Discuss

1. Divide the class into pairs or small groups.

2. Dictate sentences such as the following, and then have students discuss them:

   Women are better nurses than men.
   Men are better supervisors.
   Women are better teachers than men.
   Homemakers do important work.

3. Call on students to share their opinions with the rest of the class.

GLOBAL EXCHANGE

1. Set the scene: "Glen25 is writing to his keypal."

2. Have students read silently, or follow along silently as the message is read aloud by you, by one or more students, or on the audio program.

3. Ask students if they have any questions. Introduce the expression *pretty well*.

4. Suggestions for additional practice:

   • Have students write a response to Glen25 and share their writing in pairs.

   • Have students correspond with a keypal on the Internet and then share their experience with the class.

LISTENING *Attention, All Employees!*

1. Set the scene: "You're at different workplaces, and you hear these announcements."

2. Introduce new vocabulary: *exit, repeat, Cut!, as you know, safely.*

LISTENING SCRIPT

Listen to these announcements at different workplaces. Match the workplace and the word you hear.

Attention, all employees! This is Ms. Barnum, the factory supervisor. There were three accidents in our factory last week. Nobody was hurt badly, but I worry about these accidents. Please try to work more carefully. Thank you for your attention.

Attention, all employees! There is a small fire in the building. Please walk quickly to the nearest exit! Don't run! I repeat: There is a small fire in the building. Please walk quickly to the nearest exit!

May I have your attention, please? The president of our company will visit our office tomorrow. Please dress neatly for her visit. Thank you.

Cut! Okay, everybody! That was good, but you're still singing too softly. Please try to sing more loudly. Okay? Let's try it again.

Attention, please! As you know, the weather is very bad this afternoon, and according to the weather forecast, the storm is going to get worse. Therefore, we are going to close the office early today. All employees can leave at three-thirty. Get home safely! See you tomorrow.

Answers
1. d
2. c
3. a
4. e
5. b

 WHAT ARE THEY SAYING?

FOCUS

• Giving Feedback

Have students talk about the people and the situation, and then create role plays based on the scene. Students may refer back to previous lessons as a resource, but they should not simply reuse specific conversations.

Note: You may want to assign this exercise as written homework, having students prepare their role plays, practice them the next day with other students, and then present them to the class.

GRAMMAR

IMPERATIVES

What	was	I he she it	doing?
	were	we you they	

I He She It	was	eating.
We You They	were	

REFLEXIVE PRONOUNS

I You He She It We You They	took a walk by	myself. yourself. himself. herself. itself. ourselves. yourselves. themselves.

WHILE-CLAUSES

I lost my wallet **while I was jogging through the park.**
He cut himself **while he was shaving.**

FUNCTIONS

ASKING FOR AND REPORTING INFORMATION

What were you doing *last night at 8:00*?
What was Doris doing *last night* when *the
   lights went out*?

I saw *you yesterday*.
   When?
At about *2:30*.

Yesterday at 2:30 I was *cooking dinner*.

Which *apartment* do you live in?
   Apartment 1.

Were you *home at the time of the robbery*?

   No, I wasn't. I was *washing my clothes at
      the laundromat*.

What did *the burglars take*?
   They took some money.
How much?
   About *three hundred dollars*.

What did you do yesterday?

Who did you *go bowling* with?

I had a bad day today.
   Why? What happened?

I lost my wallet while I was *jogging through
   the park*.

SYMPATHIZING

I'm sorry to hear that.
That's too bad.
That's terrible!
That's a shame!
What a shame!
What a pity!
How awful!

INITIATING A TOPIC

You look upset.

ADMITTING AN ERROR

I guess I made a mistake.

NEW VOCABULARY

Verbs

attend
bite
break into
burn
crash (into)
cut
drop
faint
fall–fell
get off
get on
get out of
go fishing
go out
hurt
practice
roller-blade
spill
stop
take care of
trip

Driving on the Road

bridge
flat tire
intersection
pick-up truck
stop sign

Adjectives

away
elderly
gone
superstitious
unfortunate
unlucky

Reflexive Pronouns

myself
yourself
himself
herself
itself
ourselves
yourselves
themselves

Miscellaneous

about *2:30*
all over town
barbecue
blackout
burglar
circus
college student
drawer
football game

fortunately
lady
lights
merry-go-round
Ohio
out of town
package
robbery
through
which
while

EXPRESSIONS

at the same time
do yourself a favor
have no idea
poke *himself* in the eye
take a test
take care of
walk down *the stairs*
walk into
walk out of

Text Page 83: Chapter Opening Page

VOCABULARY PREVIEW

You may want to present these words before beginning the chapter, or you may choose to wait until they first occur in a specific lesson. If you choose to present them at this point, here are some suggestions:

1. Have students look at the illustrations on text page 83 and identify the words they already know.

2. Present the vocabulary. Say each word and have the class repeat it chorally and individually. Check students' understanding and pronunciation of the words.

3. Practice the vocabulary as a class, in pairs, or in small groups. Have students cover the word list and look at the pictures. Practice the words in the following ways:

   • Say a word and have students tell the number of the illustration.

   • Give the number of an illustration and have students say the word.

FOCUS

- Past Continuous Tense

CLOSE UP

RULE:	The past continuous tense describes an activity that was in progress at a specific time in the past. In this lesson, the action that was in progress was interrupted by a blackout. The interruption is expressed by the simple past.
EXAMPLES:	Doris **was taking** a bath when the lights **went** out. David **was cooking** when the lights **went** out.
RULE:	The past continuous tense is formed with the simple past of *to be* + verb + *-ing*.
EXAMPLES:	I **was reading** the newspaper. She **was taking** a bath. He **was cooking**. We **were studying**. They **were watching** TV.

GETTING READY

Introduce the past continuous tense.

1. Put the following on the board:

Bob   Betty
was working
were working

2. Tell about the people on the board: "At 9:00 yesterday morning, everybody was busy."

    A. What was Bob doing at 9:00?
    B. He was working.

    A. What was Betty doing at 9:00?
    B. She was working.

A. What were Bob and Betty doing at 9:00?
B. They were working.

3. Ask the following questions, and call on students to answer:

    What was Bob doing?
    What was Betty doing?
    What were Bob and Betty doing?

4. Ask a male student:

    Teacher: Bob, what were you doing yesterday morning at 9:00?
    Student: I was working.

    Ask a female student:

    Teacher: Betty, what were you doing yesterday morning at 9:00?
    Student: I was working.

    Ask both students:

    Teacher: What were you doing yesterday morning at 9:00?
    Students: We were working.

INTRODUCING THE MODELS

There are two model conversations. Introduce and practice each separately. For each model:

1. Have students look at the model illustration.

2. Introduce the new vocabulary: *blackout, lights go out, all over town.*

3. Set the scene: "Last night at 8:00 there was a blackout in Centerville. The lights went out all over town."

4. Present the model.

5. Full-Class Repetition.

   ### Pronunciation Note

   The pronunciation focus of Chapter 9 is **Did & Was** (text page 92). You may wish to model this pronunciation at this point (*What was David doing when the lights went out?*) and encourage students to incorporate it into their language practice.

6. Ask students if they have any questions. Check understanding of vocabulary.

7. Group Choral Repetition.

8. Choral Conversation.

9. Call on one or two pairs of students to present the dialog.

   (For additional practice, do Choral Conversation in small groups or by rows.)

SIDE BY SIDE EXERCISES

Examples

1. A. What was David doing last night when the lights went out?
   B. He was cooking.

2. A. What were Mr. and Mrs. Park doing last night when the lights went out?
   B. They were watching TV.

1. **Exercise 1:** Call on two students to present the dialog. Then do Choral Repetition and Choral Conversation practice.

2. **Exercise 2:** Same as above.

3. **Exercises 3–9:** Either Full-Class Practice or Pair Practice.

   ### Answer Key to Exercises 3–9:

   3. She was washing her hair.
   4. We were studying.
   5. I was reading the newspaper.
   6. He was cleaning his apartment.
   7. She was eating dinner.
   8. They were shopping.
   9. He was feeding his dog.

4. **What were YOU doing last night at 8:00?**

   Have students tell about themselves.

WORKBOOK

Pages 81–83

1. Who Is It?

Make statements about the people in the exercises. Have students respond by telling who you're talking about. For example:

She was eating dinner.	Alice *(Exercise 7)*
She was taking a bath.	Doris *(Model 1)*
He was cooking.	David *(Exercise 1)*
He was feeding his dog.	Sam *(Exercise 9)*
She was washing her hair.	Helen *(Exercise 3)*
He was cleaning his apartment.	Larry *(Exercise 6)*
They were riding in the elevator.	Mr. and Mrs. Green *(Model 2)*
They were watching TV.	Mr. and Mrs. Park *(Exercise 2)*

2. Memory Game: True or False?

a. Find a picture from a magazine and show it to the class for one minute. The picture should depict a scene with a lot of activity.

b. Put the picture away, and then make several statements about the picture, using the past continuous tense. The statements may be true or false.

c. Students have to decide if each statement is true or false.

d. Then have students look at the picture to see if they were right.

Variation: This can be done as a dictation with a *True* column and a *False* column. Tell students to write each statement in the appropriate column. At the end of the dictation, have students check the picture to see if they were correct.

3. Role Play: What Were You Doing?

Have students create role plays based on the situation on text page 84.

a. For conversation cues, select visuals from *Side by Side* Picture Cards (36–67, 88–90) or make your own appropriate visuals.

b. Hold up a visual, and call on students to create a conversation. For example:

[*visual:* listen to the radio]
A. What were you doing last night when the lights went out?
B. I was listening to the radio.

[*visual:* feed __ cat]
A. What were you doing last night when the lights went out?
B. I was feeding my cat.

4. Can You Hear the Difference?

a. Write on the board:

Right Now	Yesterday
He's reading.	He was reading.
She's studying.	She was studying.
It's working.	It was working.
We're reading.	We were reading.
You're typing.	You were typing.
They're eating.	They were eating.

b. Choose a sentence randomly from one of the two columns and say it to the class. Have the class listen and identify whether the sentence is about *right now* or about *yesterday.*

c. Have students continue the activity in pairs. One student says a sentence, and the other identifies whether it is about *right now* or *yesterday.* Then have them reverse roles.

d. Write other similar sentences on the board and continue the practice.

5. What Were You Doing Yesterday at 4:00 P.M.?

a. Collect information about what students were doing yesterday afternoon at 4:00 P.M.

b. Put this information on a handout in the following form:

Find someone who . . .

1. was studying English. _____
2. was working. _____
3. was watching TV. _____
4. was playing soccer. _____
5. was sleeping. _____

(continued)

c. Have students circulate around the room asking each other questions to identify the above people.

d. The first student to identify all the people wins.

6. Picture Story: A Blackout at the Presto Office

a. Put the following on the board:

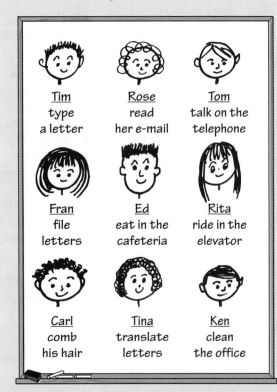

Tim type a letter	**Rose** read her e-mail	**Tom** talk on the telephone
Fran file letters	**Ed** eat in the cafeteria	**Rita** ride in the elevator
Carl comb his hair	**Tina** translate letters	**Ken** clean the office

b. Point to the cues on the board as you begin the story, "A Blackout at the Presto Office."

"Last week there was a blackout at the Presto office in New York. Everybody was working late. They were tired, and they wanted to go home. When the lights went out, everybody was very upset."

c. Call on pairs of students to ask and answer about the people in the story. For example:

A. What was Tim doing when the lights went out?
B. He was typing a letter.

A. What was Rose doing?
B. She was reading her e-mail.

Variation: After students have talked about what people were doing, divide the class into pairs. One member of the pair is an employee of the Presto Company, and the other is a reporter who is doing an interview about the blackout. Encourage students to be imaginative and to add additional details to the story. Call on pairs to present their *interviews* to the class.

7. Information Gap Handouts

a. Tell students *that John, Alice, Mary, Nancy, David,* and *Jane* had a busy day yesterday. Yesterday afternoon they were getting ready for something special. Write out their activities, but divide the information between two different charts. For example:

Chart A:

	Place	Activity
John		buying a cake
Alice and Mary	at the department store	
Nancy		cooking a big dinner
David	at home	
Jane		driving to Nancy and David's house

Chart B:

	Place	Activity
John	at the bakery	
Alice and Mary		buying a birthday present
Nancy	at home	
David		cleaning the house
Jane	in her car	

b. Divide the class into pairs. Give each member of the pair a different chart. Have students share their information and fill in their charts. For example:

Student A: Where was John yesterday afternoon?
Student B: He was at the bakery.
Student A: I see. [writes the information in Chart A]
Student B: What was he doing at the bakery?
Student A: He was buying a cake.
Student B: Okay. [writes the information in Chart B]

c. The pairs continue until each has a complete chart.

d. Have students compare their charts to make sure that they have written the information correctly.

e. Ask the class: Where did John, Alice, Mary, Nancy, David, and Jane meet yesterday evening? Why? What was happening?

Text Page 85: I Saw You Yesterday, but You Didn't See Me

FOCUS

- Past Continuous Tense

CLOSE UP

RULE: The past continuous focuses on the duration of an action, not its completion. The simple past focuses on the completion of an action.

EXAMPLES: I **saw** you yesterday, but you **didn't see** me. *(action completed)*
You **were getting** out of a taxi. *(action in progress)*

INTRODUCING THE MODEL

1. Have students look at the model illustration.
2. Set the scene: "Two friends are talking."
3. Present the model.
4. Full-Class Repetition.
5. Ask students if they have any questions. Check understanding of the expression *at about 2:30.*
6. Group Choral Repetition.
7. Choral Conversation.
8. Call on one or two pairs of students to present the dialog.

   (For additional practice, do Choral Conversation in small groups or by rows.)

SIDE BY SIDE EXERCISES

Examples

1. A. I saw you yesterday, but you didn't see me.
   B. Really? When?
   A. At about 2:30. You were walking into the laundromat.
   B. That wasn't me. Yesterday at 2:30 I was working at my office.
   A. Hmm. I guess I made a mistake.

2. A. I saw you yesterday, but you didn't see me.
   B. Really? When?
   A. At about 2:30. You were walking out of the library.
   B. That wasn't me. Yesterday at 2:30 I was taking a history test.
   A. Hmm. I guess I made a mistake.

1. **Exercise 1:** Introduce the new expression *walk into*. Call on two students to present the dialog. Then do Choral Repetition and Choral Conversation practice.

2. **Exercise 2:** Introduce the new expressions *walk out of, take a test*. Same as above.

3. **Exercises 3–5:** Either Full-Class Practice or Pair Practice.

> **New Vocabulary**
>
> 3. get on
> 4. merry-go-round
>   practice
> 5. through

4. **Exercise 6:** Have students use the model as a guide to create their own conversations, using vocabulary of their choice. Encourage students to use dictionaries to find new words they want to use. This exercise can be done orally in class or for written homework. If you assign it for homework, do one example in class to make sure students understand what's expected. Have students present their conversations in class the next day.

WORKBOOK

Pages 84–85

EXPANSION ACTIVITIES

1. Match the Conversations

a. Make the following set of matching cards:

I saw you yesterday at about 1:30. You were walking into the bank.	That wasn't me. Yesterday at 1:30 I was working at my office.
I saw you yesterday at about 2:30. You were walking out of the post office.	That wasn't me. Yesterday at 2:30 I was washing my clothes at the laundromat.
I saw you yesterday at about 5:30. You were getting on a bus.	That wasn't me. Yesterday at 5:30 I was fixing my car.
I saw you yesterday at about 9:30. You were getting on a merry-go-round.	That wasn't me. Yesterday at 9:30 I was taking a math test.
I saw you yesterday at about 11:30. You were getting out of a taxi.	That wasn't me. Yesterday at 11:30 I was practicing the violin.

I saw you yesterday at about 12:30. You were walking through the park.	That wasn't me. Yesterday at 12:30 I was visiting my grandmother.

b. Distribute a card to each student.

c. Have students memorize the sentences on their cards, and then have students walk around the room saying their sentences until they find their match.

d. Then have pairs of students say their matched sentences aloud to the class.

2. Past Continuous Mime

a. Write on cards the following activities:

cooking	swimming	eating
listening to the radio	taking a photograph	riding a bicycle
planting flowers	playing the guitar	washing dishes
doing homework	doing exercises	cleaning the yard

(continued)

painting	studying	sleeping
vacuuming	watching TV	writing
reading	dancing	singing
laughing	crying	roller-blading
skateboarding	acting	teaching
baking a cake	feeding the dog	fixing the car

b. Have students take turns picking a card from the pile and pantomiming the action on the card.

c. When the person finishes miming, the class must guess what the person *was doing*.

Variation: This can be done as a game with competing teams.

3. Memory Chain

a. Divide the class into groups of 5 or 6 students each.

b. Have each student tell what he or she was doing at 8:00 last night.

c. One group at a time, have Student 1 begin. For example:

   I was studying in the library.

d. Student 2 repeats what Student 1 said and adds a statement about himself or herself. For example:

Victor was studying in the library, and I was washing my clothes at the laundromat.

e. Student 3 continues in the same way. For example:

   Victor was studying in the library, Sandra was washing her clothes at the laundromat, and I was watching a game show on TV.

f. Continue until everyone has had a chance to play the *memory chain*.

4. Alibi

a. Set a robbery scene: "Someone stole some money and some jewelry from the home of Mr. and Mrs. Van Patten."

b. Have a pair of students volunteer to be the suspected robbers. Have them leave the room and develop an alibi for each other: *Where were they? What were they doing? Who saw them?*

c. Have the rest of the class develop past tense questions they will ask the suspects.

d. Have one suspect come into the classroom for interrogation. The class should ask specific questions.

e. Have the second suspect come into the classroom for interrogation. The class should look for inconsistencies between the two stories.

If, after questioning, the two stories are consistent, the suspects are found *innocent*. If inconsistencies arose, the suspects are found *guilty*.

READING *A Robbery*

FOCUS

- Past Continuous Tense

NEW VOCABULARY

attend	gone
away	have no idea
broke (break) into	lady
burglar	Ohio
college student	out of town
elderly	robbery
football game	unfortunate

READING THE STORY

Optional: *Preview the story by having students talk about the story title and/or illustration. You may choose to introduce new vocabulary beforehand, or have students encounter the new vocabulary within the context of the reading.*

1. Have students read silently, or follow along silently as the story is read aloud by you, by one or more students, or on the audio program.

2. Ask students if they have any questions. Check understanding of vocabulary.

3. Check students' comprehension, using some or all of the following questions:

    Were the tenants home yesterday when burglars broke into the building?
    What was the man in Apartment 1 doing?
    What was the woman in Apartment 2 doing?
    What were the people in Apartment 3 doing?
    What was the man in Apartment 4 doing?
    What were the college students in Apartment 5 doing?
    What was the elderly lady in Apartment 6 doing?

✓READING *CHECK-UP*

Q & A

1. Call on a pair of students to present the model. Check understanding of *which, drawer.*

2. Have students work in pairs to create new dialogs. Students should use their imaginations to think of objects that were stolen from the different apartments.

3. Call on pairs to present their new dialogs to the class.

READING EXTENSION

Tic Tac Question the Answer

1. Draw a tic tac grid on the board and fill it with the following short answers to questions:

Yes, they did.	No, they didn't.	Yes, she was.
No, she wasn't.	Yes, he was.	No, he wasn't.
Yes, it certainly was.	No, they weren't.	Yes, they were.

2. Divide the class into teams. Give each team a mark: *X* or *O.*

3. Have each team ask a question about the story with an answer in the grid. For example:

    X Team: Was the woman in Apartment 2 home?
    No, she wasn't.

4. If an answer is appropriate and is stated correctly, that team may replace the answer with its team mark. For example:

CHAPTER 9   251 ●

Yes, they did.	No, they didn't.	Yes, she was.
X	Yes, he was.	No, he wasn't.
Yes, it certainly was.	No, they weren't.	Yes, they were.

5. The first team to mark out three boxes in a straight line—vertically, horizontally, or diagonally—wins.

Text Page 87: He Went to the Movies by Himself

FOCUS

- Reflexive Pronouns

CLOSE UP

RULE: Reflexive pronouns are used when the subject and an object in the sentence are the same person. Reflexive pronouns end in -*self* or -*selves*. The expression *by* + reflexive pronoun means *alone*.

EXAMPLES: **I** went bowling by **myself**.
He went to the movies by **himself**.
She drove to the mountains by **herself**.
We had a picnic by **ourselves**.
They went sailing by **themselves**.

INTRODUCING THE MODEL

1. Have students look at the model illustration.

2. Set the scene: "Two people are talking about John."

3. Present the model.

4. Full-Class Repetition

   ### Pronunciation Note

   The pronunciation focus of Chapter 9 is **Did & Was** (text page 92). You may wish to model this pronunciation at this point *(What did John do yesterday? Who did he go to the movies with?)* and encourage students to incorporate it into their language practice.

5. Ask students if they have any questions. Check understanding of the expression *by himself.*

   ### Language Note

   Who did he go to the movies with? The pronoun *who* rather than *whom* is widely used in informal conversation. The pronoun *whom* as the object of a preposition is used in more formal speech.

6. Group Choral Repetition.

7. Choral Conversation.

8. Call on one or two pairs of students to present the dialog.

   (For additional practice, do Choral Conversation in small groups or by rows.)

9. Have students practice the last line of the model conversation using the other reflexive pronouns.

   a. Have students look at the grammar box at the top of text page 87.

   b. Model the following and have students repeat:

      I went to the movies by myself.

   c. Cue replacements for the other reflexives:

      Teacher: you *[pointing to one student]*
      Students: You went to the movies by yourself.

      Teacher: she *[pointing to a female student]*
      Students: She went to the movies by herself.

Teacher: we [pointing to all the students and himself/herself]

Students: We went to the movies by ourselves.

Teacher: you [pointing to all the students]

Students: You went to the movies by yourselves.

Teacher: they [pointing to two students]

Students: They went to the movies by themselves.

SIDE BY SIDE EXERCISES

Examples

1. A. What did Aunt Ethel do yesterday?
   B. She went to the circus.
   A. Oh. Who did she go to the circus with?
   B. Nobody. She went to the circus by herself.

2. A. What did your parents do yesterday?
   B. They went sailing.
   A. Oh. Who did they go sailing with?
   B. Nobody. They went sailing by themselves.

1. **Exercise 1:** Introduce the new word *circus*. Call on two students to present the dialog. Then do Choral Repetition and Choral Conversation practice.

2. **Exercise 2:** Same as above.

3. **Exercises 3–8:** Either Full-Class Practice or Pair Practice.

> **New Vocabulary**
>
> 7. go fishing

4. **Exercise 9:** Have students use the model as a guide to create their own conversations, using vocabulary of their choice. Encourage students to use dictionaries to find new words they want to use. This exercise can be done orally in class or for written homework. If you assign it for homework, do one example in class to make sure students understand what's expected. Have students present their conversations in class the next day.

WORKBOOK

Page 86

EXPANSION ACTIVITIES

1. Finish the Sentence

Begin a sentence and have individual students repeat what you said and complete it with the appropriate reflexive. For example:

Teacher	Students
My mother fixed her car . . .	by herself.
We went bowling . . .	by ourselves.
My brother drove to the beach . . .	by himself.
I went sailing . . .	by myself.
Did you go to the circus . . .	by yourself?
Bob and Carol played volleyball . . .	by themselves.
Our car started . . .	by itself.
Did you and your friends go fishing . . .	by yourselves?

2. Match the Sentences

a. Make a set of split sentence cards such as the following:

I went to the movies . . .	by myself.
My brother had a picnic . . .	by himself.
My sister went to the ballgame . . .	by herself.
My friend and I took a long walk . . .	by ourselves.

Our neighbors painted their house . . .	by themselves.
The car started . . .	by itself.
You can't fix that . . .	by yourself.
You and your friends can't go there . . .	by yourselves.

b. Distribute a card to each student.

c. Have students memorize the sentence portion on their cards, then walk around the room trying to find their corresponding match.

d. Then have pairs of students say their completed sentences aloud to the class.

3. Concentration

a. Use the cards from the above activity. Place them face down in two rows of 8 each.

b. Divide the class into two teams. The object of the game is for students to find the matching cards. Both teams should be able to see all the cards since *concentrating* on their location is an important part of playing the game.

c. A student from Team 1 turns over two cards. If they match, the student picks up the cards, that team gets a point, and the student takes another turn. If the cards don't match, the student turns them face down, and a member of Team 2 takes a turn.

d. The game continues until all the cards have been matched. The team with the most correct matches wins the game.

Variation: This game can also be played in groups and pairs.

4. Class Discussion

a. Write the following questions on the board or on a handout for students:

> Do you ever go to the movies by yourself?
> Do you go to the circus by yourself?
> Where are other places you might go by yourself?
> Do you like to go places by yourself? Why or why not?

b. Divide the class into small groups and have students discuss the questions. Then have students share their ideas with the class.

Text Pages 88–89: I Had a Bad Day Today

FOCUS

- *While*-Clauses with the Past Continuous Tense

CLOSE UP

RULE: *While* is commonly used to introduce a clause in the past continuous tense. Although *when* can be substituted in its place, *while* emphasizes the duration of an activity.

EXAMPLES: I lost my wallet **while** I was jogging.
(During the time I was jogging, I lost my wallet.)

He cut himself **while** he was shaving.
(During the time he was shaving, he cut himself.)

INTRODUCING THE MODELS

There are two model conversations. Introduce and practice each separately. For each model:

1. Have students look at the model illustration.

2. Set the scene:

    1st model: "A man is talking with a neighbor about what happened this morning."
    2nd model: "Two people at work are talking about why Harry is upset."

3. Present the model.

4. Full-Class Repetition.

5. Ask students if they have any questions. Check understanding of the *while*-clause.

6. Group Choral Repetition.

7. Choral Conversation

8. Call on one or two pairs of students to present the dialog.

    (For additional practice, do Choral Conversation in small groups or by rows.)

SIDE BY SIDE EXERCISES

Examples

1. A. You look upset.
   B. I had a bad day today.
   A. Why? What happened?
   B. I hurt myself while I was fixing my fence.
   A. I'm sorry to hear that.

2. A. Emma looks upset.
   B. She had a bad day today.
   A. Why? What happened?
   B. She dropped her packages while she was walking out of the supermarket.
   A. I'm sorry to hear that.

1. **Exercise 1:** Call on two students to present the dialog. Then do Choral Repetition and Choral Conversation practice.

2. **Exercise 2:** Introduce the new words *drop, package*. Same as above.

3. **Exercises 3–9:** Either Full-Class Practice or Pair Practice.

New Vocabulary

3. flat tire
   bridge
4. trip
   fell
   walk down the stairs
5. burn
   barbecue
6. faint

EXPANSION ACTIVITIES

1. Picture Story

a. Put the following cues on the board:

Mr. Larson
cut himself
(swim)

Mrs. Larson
got seasick
(ride/boat)

Elizabeth
lost her glasses
(play football/
beach)

Larry
hurt himself
(jog)

Bobby
got a bad sunburn
(sleep/beach)

b. Point to the cues as you tell the following story:

"Last month the Larson family had a terrible vacation in Hawaii. Mr. Larson cut himself while he was swimming. Mrs. Larson got seasick while she was riding on a boat. Their daughter Elizabeth lost her glasses while she was playing football on the beach. Their son Larry hurt himself while he was jogging. And their son Bobby got a bad sunburn while he was sleeping on the beach. The Larson family certainly had a terrible vacation!"

c. Call on pairs of students to ask and answer questions about the people in the story. For example:

  A. Where did the Larsons go for their vacation?
  B. They went to Hawaii.

  A. What happened to Mr. Larson?
  B. He cut himself while he was swimming.

d. Have students role play characters in the story and tell what happened. Encourage students to expand the story, using any vocabulary they wish. For example:

  Mrs. Larson: While I was riding on a boat, I got seasick. Then I fainted!

2. Telephone Story

a. Divide the class into large groups. Have each group sit in a circle.

b. Whisper the following story to one student:

  "Henry had a bad day today. He cut himself while he was shaving, he burned himself while he was cooking, he fainted while he was waiting for the bus, and he tripped and fell while he was walking down the stairs."

c. The first student whispers the story to the second student, and so forth around the circle. The student listening may ask for clarification by saying, "I'm sorry. What did you say?"

(continued)

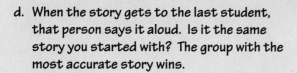

d. When the story gets to the last student, that person says it aloud. Is it the same story you started with? The group with the most accurate story wins.

3. Class Story

a. Have students look at one of the illustrations on page 88 or 89 of the text.

b. Ask questions about one of the situations to help them imagine a storyline. For example (using Exercise 3 on page 88):

> What are these people's names?
> What happened to them?
> How did they feel?
> What did they do next?
> Then what happened?

c. Have students dictate the story to you as you write it on the board. Ask them how to spell various words as they're dictating the story to you. Also, ask the class to point out any grammar errors they find in the story.

4. Miming Game

a. Write different injuries on separate cards. For example:

> You cut yourself while you were slicing bread.

> You burned yourself while you were cooking.

> You tripped and fell while you were carrying a bag of groceries.

> You fainted while you were waiting in line at a store.

> You fell off a ladder while you were cleaning windows.

> You dropped a box on your foot while you were walking down the stairs.

> A dog bit you while you were waiting for the bus.

> A can of paint fell on you while you were walking under a ladder.

b. Have students take turns picking a card from the pile and pantomiming the injuries.

c. The class must then guess the injury and what the person was doing when the accident occurred.

Variation: This can be done as a game with competing teams.

5. Busy People!

a. Explain that busy people try to do more by doing at least two things at the same time. For example:

> Last night I helped my son with his homework while I was cooking dinner.

b. Write the following model on the board:

> I _____ while I _____ing.

c. As a class, in pairs, or in small groups, have students tell about something they did while they were doing something else.

6. Find the Right Person!

a. Have students write on a piece of paper something true about themselves, using the past continuous tense and *while*. For example:

> I studied English while I was eating breakfast today.
> I ate candy while I was watching TV last night.

b. Collect the pieces of paper and copy all the sentences on the board or on a handout for students.

c. Have students interview others in the class to find out *who did what*. For example:

> Student A: Did you study English while you were eating breakfast today?
> Student B: No, I didn't.

d. The first student to identify everybody is the winner.

7. Dialog Builder!

a. Divide the class into pairs.

b. Write the following line on the board:

That's terrible! How did it happen?

c. Have each pair create a conversation incorporating that line. Students can begin and end their conversations any way they wish, but they must include that line in their dialogs.

d. Call on students to present their conversations to the class.

8. Chain Story

a. Begin by saying, "I had a very bad day yesterday. I burned myself while I was taking a shower."

b. Student 1 repeats what you said and adds another item. For example: "I had a very bad day yesterday. I burned myself while I was taking a shower. Then I cut myself while I was making breakfast."

c. Continue around the room in this fashion, with each student repeating what the previous one said and adding another sentence.

d. You can do the activity again, beginning and ending with different students.

If the class is large, you may want to divide students into groups to give students more practice.

How to Say It!

> **Reacting to Bad News:** There are many ways to express sympathy in reaction to bad news. The use of *what (What a shame! What a pity!)* conveys deep emotion.

1. Present the expressions.

2. Full-Class Repetition.

3. Ask students if they have any questions. Check understanding of the expressions.

4. Group Choral Repetition.

5. Have students practice the conversations on text pages 88 and 89 again, using these expressions for reacting to the bad news.

6. Call on pairs to present their conversations.

How About You?

Have students do the activity in pairs or as a class.

READING *Friday the 13th*

FOCUS

- Reflexive Pronouns
- Past Continuous Tense
- *While*-Clauses

NEW VOCABULARY

do yourself a favor	superstitious
poke *himself* in the eye	take care of
roller-blade	unlucky

READING THE STORY

Optional: *Preview the story by having students talk about the story title and/or illustrations. You may choose to introduce new vocabulary beforehand, or have students encounter the new vocabulary within the context of the reading.*

1. Have students read silently, or follow along silently as the story is read aloud by you, by one or more students, or on the audio program.

2. Ask students if they have any questions. Check understanding of vocabulary.

   ### Culture Note

   In the United States, if the thirteenth day of the month falls on a Friday, it is considered an unlucky day.

3. Check students' comprehension, using some or all of the following questions:

What day was yesterday?
What do many people believe?
What happened to the writer of the story yesterday?
What happened to his wife?
What happened to his son?
What happened to his daughter?
What happened to both his children?
What happened to his entire family?
According to the writer, what should you do the next time it's Friday the 13th?

✓ READING *CHECK-UP*

Q & A

1. Call on a pair of students to present the model.

2. Have students work in pairs to create new dialogs.

3. Call on pairs to present their new dialogs to the class.

WHICH WORD IS CORRECT?

1. a
2. b
3. a
4. b
5. a

READING EXTENSION

Have the class discuss the following questions:

Are you superstitious?
Do you believe that certain days are lucky or unlucky?
Is Friday the 13th unlucky in your country?
Are there any days that are unlucky in your country?
What are they?
Are you careful on those unlucky days?

LISTENING

Listen to the conversations. What happened to these people? Listen and choose the correct answer.

1. A. How did you do that?
   B. I did it while I was shaving.

2. A. When did it happen?
   B. While I was getting off a bus.

3. A. Why do you think it happened?
   B. It was a very hot day.

4. A. The park isn't as safe as it used to be.
   B. You're right.

5. A. What were they doing?
   B. They were playing outside.

6. A. How did it happen?
   B. He dropped the glass.

Answers

1. a   4. a

2. a   5. a

3. b   6. b

READING *An Accident*

FOCUS

- Past Continuous Tense
- *While*-Clauses

NEW VOCABULARY

at the same time	pickup truck
crash (into)	stop (v)
fortunately	stop sign
intersection	

READING THE STORY

Optional: *Preview the story by having students talk about the story title and/or illustration. You may choose to introduce new vocabulary beforehand, or have students encounter the new vocabulary within the context of the reading.*

1. Have students read silently, or follow along silently as the story is read aloud by you, by one or more students, or on the audio program.

2. Ask students if they have any questions. Check understanding of vocabulary.

3. Check students' comprehension, using some or all of these questions:

   Where was the accident?
   What kind of car was the man driving?
   How was he driving?
   What was he doing while he was driving?
   What was the woman driving?
   How was she driving?
   What was she doing while she was driving?
   How did the accident happen?
   Who came while they were shouting at each other?
   Was anyone badly hurt?

✓ READING *CHECK-UP*

TRUE, FALSE, OR MAYBE?

1. True   5. True

2. False   6. Maybe

3. False   7. True

4. Maybe

How About You?

Have students answer the questions, in pairs or as a class.

PRONUNCIATION

> **Did & Was:** In daily English usage, the pronunciation of *did* and *was* is often reduced.

Focus on Listening

Practice the sentences in the left column. Say each sentence or play the audio one or more times. Have students listen carefully and repeat.

Focus on Pronunciation

Practice the sentences in the right column. Have students say each sentence and then listen carefully as you say it or play the audio.

If you wish, have students continue practicing the sentences to improve their pronunciation.

JOURNAL

Have students write their journal entries at home or in class. Encourage students to use a dictionary to look up words they would like to use. Students can share their written work with other students if appropriate. Have students discuss what they have written as a class, in pairs, or in small groups.

CHAPTER SUMMARY

GRAMMAR

1. Divide the class into pairs or small groups.
2. Have students take turns forming sentences from the words in the grammar boxes. Student A says a sentence, and Student B points to the words from each column that are in the sentence. Then have students switch: Student B says a sentence, and Student A points to the words.

KEY VOCABULARY

Have students ask you any questions about the meaning or pronunciation of the vocabulary. If students ask for the pronunciation, repeat after the student until the student is satisfied with his or her own pronunciation.

EXPANSION ACTIVITIES

1. **Do You Remember the Words?**

   Check students' retention of the vocabulary depicted on the opening page of Chapter 9 by doing the following activity:

   a. Have students open their books to page 83 and cover the list of vocabulary words.

   b. Either call out a number and have students tell you the word, or say a word and have students tell you the number.

   Variation: You can also do this activity as a game with competing teams.

2. **Student-Led Dictation**

   a. Tell each student to choose a word or phrase from the Key Vocabulary list on text page 92 and look at it very carefully.

   b. Have students take turns dictating their words to the class. Everybody writes down that student's word.

   c. When the dictation is completed, call on different students to write each word on the board to check the spelling.

3. **Beanbag Toss**

   a. Call out the topic: *Bad Luck Verbs.*

   b. Have students toss a beanbag back and forth. The student to whom the beanbag is tossed must name a *bad luck* verb. For example:

Student 1:	fall
Student 2:	trip
Student 3:	spill

   c. Continue until all the words in the category have been named.

Variation: You can also do this activity as a game with competing teams.

4. Letter Game

   a. Divide the class into teams.

   b. Say: "I'm thinking of a verb that starts with *p*."

   c. The first person to raise his or her hand and guess correctly *[poke]* wins a point for his or her team.

   d. Continue with other letters of the alphabet and verbs.

   The team that gets the most correct answers wins the game.

5. Miming

   a. Write on cards the verbs from text page 92.

   b. Have students take turns picking a card from the pile and pantomiming the action on the card.

   c. The class must guess what the verb is.

   Variation: This can be done as a game with competing teams.

END-OF-CHAPTER ACTIVITIES

1. Board Game

a. On poster boards or on manila file folders, make up game boards with a pathway consisting of separate spaces. You may use any theme or design you wish.

b. Divide the class into groups of 2 to 4 students and give each group a game board and a die, and each player something to be used as a playing piece.

c. Give each group a pile of cards face-down with sentences written on them. Some sentences should be correct, and others incorrect. For example:

> How did he hurt herself?
> We took a walk by ourself.
> Larry was cooking dinner when the lights went out.
> Yesterday at 2:30 they were fixed the bathroom sink.
> I drove in the mountains by myself.
> He went fishing by themselves.
> She got a flat tire while she was driving home.
> They shopped when someone stole their car.
> A dog bit him while he was riding his bike.
> He spilled the milk while he were drinking.
> She herself poked in the eye.
> They went to the movies by theirselves.

d. Each student in turn rolls the die, moves the playing piece along the game path, and after landing on a space, picks a card, reads the sentence, and says if it is *correct or incorrect*. If the sentence is incorrect and the student is able to give the *correct* version, that student takes an additional turn.

e. The first student to reach the end of the pathway is the winner.

2. Chain Story: What a Bad Day!

a. Begin by saying, "Yesterday was a very unlucky day. I fell on the floor while I was getting up."

b. Student 1 repeats what you said and adds another item. For example: "Yesterday was a very unlucky day. I fell on the floor while I was getting up. Then I burned myself while I was taking a shower."

c. Continue around the room in this fashion, with each student repeating what the previous one said and adding another sentence.

d. You can do the activity again, beginning and ending with different students.

If the class is large, you may want to divide students into groups to give students more practice.

3. Scrambled Sentences

a. Divide the class into teams.

b. Write individual sentences out of order on the board. For example:

> she   her   dropped   while   the
> walking   was   out   of   packages
> she   department store
>
> tire   he   he   a   driving   got
> bridge   a   was   flat   over
> while
>
> library   while   bicycle   reading   my
> the   somebody   was   stole   I
> in

c. The first person to raise his or her hand, come to the board, and write the sentence in the correct order earns a point for that team.

d. The team with the most points wins the scrambled sentence game.

Variation: Write the words to several sentences on separate cards. Divide the class into small groups, and have students work together to put the sentences into correct order.

4. Question Game

a. Write the following sentence on the board:

> Doris hurt herself while she was getting out of her car.

b. Underline different elements of the sentence, and have students create a question based on that portion of the sentence. For example:

> <u>Doris</u> hurt herself while she was getting out of her car.

Who hurt herself while she was getting out of her car?

> Doris hurt herself while <u>she was getting out of her car</u>.

What was Doris doing when she hurt herself?

> Doris <u>hurt herself</u> while she was getting out of her car.

What did Doris do while she was getting out of her car?

c. Continue with other sentences.

WORKBOOK ANSWER KEY AND LISTENING SCRIPTS

A. WHAT WERE THEY DOING?

1. He was driving to the beach.
2. She was walking down Main Street.
3. They were jogging.
4. We were playing basketball.
5. He was riding his motorcycle.
6. She was fixing her fence.
7. They were painting their house.
8. We were skateboarding.

WORKBOOK PAGE 82

B. WHAT WERE THEY DOING?

1. were baking
2. was wearing
3. were playing
4. was riding
5. were watching
6. was sleeping
7. were having
8. was chatting
9. was talking

WORKBOOK PAGE 83

D. THE WRONG DAY!

1. He was cleaning
2. She was vacuuming
3. He was sweeping
4. She was washing
5. They were making
6. They were baking

E. LISTENING

Listen and choose the correct answer.

1. A. What was he doing yesterday when the lights went out?
   B. He was shaving.
2. A. What was she doing yesterday when you saw her?
   B. She was skating.
3. A. What were they doing when it started to rain?
   B. They were swimming at the beach.
4. A What was he doing yesterday when you called?
   B. He was studying math.

5. A What were you doing when your friends arrived?
   B. We were eating.
6. A. What was she doing when you saw her?
   B. She was talking with her mother.
7. A. What was he doing when you called?
   B. He was taking a shower.
8. A. What were you doing when the guests arrived?
   B. I was sweeping the living room.

Answers

1. a		**5.** b
2. b		**6.** a
3. b		**7.** a
4. a		**8.** b

WORKBOOK PAGE 84

F. WHAT'S THE WORD?

1. into		**5.** on
2. out of		**6.** along
3. off		**7.** out of
4. into		**8.** off

G. LISTENING

Listen and put the number under the correct picture.

1. I saw you yesterday at about 3:00.
   You were walking into the bank.
2. I saw you yesterday at about 1:30.
   You were jogging through the park.
3. I saw you yesterday at about 2:00.
   You were getting off the D Train.
4. I saw you yesterday at about 5:00.
   You were getting on the B Train.
5. I saw you yesterday at about 4:45.
   You were getting out of a taxi on Fifth Street.
6. I saw you yesterday at about noon.
   You were getting into a taxi on Sixth Street.
7. I saw you yesterday at about 11:45.
   You were getting on a bus.
8. I saw you yesterday at about 9:00.
   You were getting off a bus.

Answers

5	2	6	3
8	4	1	7

WORKBOOK PAGE 86

I. NOBODY WANTS TO

1. myself
2. herself
3. ourselves
4. yourself
5. themselves
6. himself
7. yourselves

J. WHAT'S THE WORD?

1. a		**4.** a	
2. b		**5.** a	
3. b		**6.** b	

WORKBOOK PAGE 87

K. WHAT HAPPENED?

1. tripped, she was walking
2. bit, he was riding
3. fainted, he was watching
4. stole, we were having
5. dropped, she was getting on
6. cut, I was shaving
7. burned, they were cooking
8. lost, he was roller-blading
9. hurt, we were skiing
10. fell, they were painting

WORKBOOK PAGE 88

L. WHAT'S THE WORD?

1. up	**5.** at
2. over	**6.** through
3. on	**7.** under
4. out of	

M. LISTENING

Listen and choose the correct answer.

1. A. Why does Sally look so upset?
   B. She lost her new boot.

2. A. What happened to Howard?
   B. He burned himself while he was cooking.

3. A. When did you see them?
   B. While they were walking out of the park.

4. A. You look upset. What happened?
   B. Someone stole our new fan.

5. A. I had a bad day today.
   B. Why? What happened?
   A. I dropped my new CD player.

6. A. What happened to Charlie?
   B. A dog bit him while he was walking.

7. A. What were you doing when the accident happened?
   B. We were driving over a bridge.

8. A. What happened to Helen?
   B. She tripped and fell on the kitchen floor.

9. A. When did they drop their packages?
   B. While they were walking up the stairs.

10. A. What was Jane doing when she hurt herself?
    B. She was cooking on the barbecue.

11. A. You look upset. What's the matter?
    B. I cut myself while I was chopping.

12. A. What happened to Fred?
    B. He fainted at the bus stop.

Answers

1. a		**7.** b	
2. b		**8.** a	
3. b		**9.** b	
4. a		**10.** a	
5. a		**11.** a	
6. b		**12.** b	

WORKBOOK PAGE 90

O. LOUD AND CLEAR

1. niece, reading, e-mail, keypal, Greece
2. William tripped, himself, his office building
3. Steve, asleep, three fifteen, cookies, meat
4. Hill, busy, clinic, children, city, sick
5. Lee, beach, Tahiti, sleeping, she's, CDs
6. little sister, isn't, sandwich, spilled, milk.

GRAMMAR

COULD

Could	I he she it we you they	go?

Yes,	I he she it we you they	could.

No,	I he she it we you they	couldn't.

BE ABLE TO

Was	I he she it	able to go?
Were	we you they	

No,	I he she it	wasn't	able to.
	we you they	weren't	

HAVE GOT TO

(I have)	I've	got to work.
(We have)	We've	
(You have)	You've	
(They have)	They've	
(He has)	He's	
(She has)	She's	
(It has)	It's	

TOO + ADJECTIVE

He was **too short**.
She was **too busy**.

I'll He'll She'll It'll We'll You'll They'll	be able to help you.

I He She It We You They	won't be able to help you.

FUNCTIONS

INQUIRING ABOUT ABILITY

Could you *walk the day after your operation*?
Were you able to *solve the math problem last
  night*?

EXPRESSING ABILITY

I'm sure I'll be able to *move by myself*.

EXPRESSING INABILITY

No, I couldn't.
No, I wasn't able to.

I couldn't do it.

He can't *get into his apartment*.
He couldn't *dance in the school play*.
She wasn't be able to *go to the concert*.
She won't be able to *get to the airport on time*.

EXPRESSING REGRET

I'm afraid *I won't be able to help you move
  tomorrow*.

EXPRESSING CERTAINTY

I'm sure *I'll be able to move by myself*.

DESCRIBING

I was too short/sick/young/ . . . .

Did you enjoy yourself *at the picnic?*

EXPRESSING OBLIGATION

I had to *fix a flat tire.*

I've got to *take my son to the doctor.*
I have to *drive my parents to the airport.*
I need to *fly to Denver.*

Martha is upset/frustrated/ disappointed.

NEW VOCABULARY

Adjectives

clumsy
weak
windy

Verbs

assemble
crash
enjoy *herself*
fly
hand in
hook up
lift
perform
promise
set up
solve
understand

Work

assistant
co-worker
overtime

School

lesson
math problem
prom
school dance
school play
science project
term paper

Expressions of Ability

could
couldn't
be able to

Expressions of Obligation

have got to
have to
need to

Miscellaneous

a while
amusement park
ballet lesson

eye doctor
football practice
key
ocean
operation
pipe
ponytail
repair truck
side
someone
symphony
team
tennis match
tuxedo
vet (veterinarian)

EXPRESSIONS

Don't worry about it!
for quite a while
go to lunch with
get into the movie
go camping

Text Page 93: Chapter Opening Page

VOCABULARY PREVIEW

You may want to present these words before beginning the chapter, or you may choose to wait until they first occur in a specific lesson. If you choose to present them at this point, here are some suggestions:

1. Have students look at the illustrations on text page 93 and identify the words they already know.

2. Present the vocabulary. Say each word and have the class repeat it chorally and individually. Check students' understanding and pronunciation of the words.

3. Practice the vocabulary as a class, in pairs, or in small groups. Have students cover the word list and look at the pictures. Practice the words in the following ways:

   • Say a word and have students tell the number of the illustration.

   • Give the number of an illustration and have students say the word.

FOCUS

- Could/Couldn't
- Too + Adjective

CLOSE UP

RULE:	The modal *could* is the past tense of *can*. It has the meaning of past ability.
EXAMPLES:	**Could** Peter play on the basketball team? 　　　No, he **couldn't**. **Could** Max and Ruth finish their dinner yesterday? 　　　No, they **couldn't**.
RULE:	*Too* + adjective is used to give a reason for being unable to do something. *Too* has a negative meaning.
EXAMPLES:	Lisa was **too** busy. She couldn't go to lunch with her co-workers. Sasha was **too** tired. He couldn't finish his homework last night.

GETTING READY

Introduce *could* and *couldn't*.

1. Write on the board:

> *Jimmy*
> 2 years old — walk
> 4 years old — write his name
> 7 years old — read
> 8 years old — ride a bicycle

2. Say: "When Jimmy was two years old, he could walk." Then have students repeat chorally.

3. Ask and have students answer:

> What could Jimmy do when he was two years old?
> What could he do when he was four years old?
> What could he do when he was seven years old?
> What could he do when he was eight years old?

4. Ask Yes/No questions about Jimmy, and have students answer "Yes, he could" or "No, he couldn't." For example:

> Teacher: Could Jimmy walk when he was two years old?
> Student: Yes, he could.
>
> Teacher: Could he ride a bicycle when he was two years old?
> Student: No, he couldn't.

INTRODUCING THE MODEL

1. Have students look at the model illustration.

2. Set the scene: "Two people are talking about Peter."

3. Present the model.

4. Full-Class Repetition.

5. Ask students if they have any questions. Check understanding of the word *team*.

6. Group Choral Repetition.

7. Choral Conversation.

8. Call on one or two pairs of students to present the dialog.

   (For additional practice, do Choral Conversation in small groups or by rows.)

SIDE BY SIDE EXERCISES

Examples

1. A. Could Lisa go to lunch with her co-workers today?
   B. No, she couldn't. She was too busy.

2. A. Could Sasha finish his homework last night?
   B. No, he couldn't. He was too tired.

1. **Exercise 1:** Introduce the new expressions *go to lunch with, co-worker*. Call on two students to present the dialog. Then do Choral Repetition and Choral Conversation practice.

2. **Exercise 2:** Same as above.

3. **Exercises 3–9:** Either Full-Class Practice or Pair Practice.

> **New Vocabulary**
> 5. operation
>   weak
> 6. get into
> 8. perform
>   school play

Language Note

The expression *get into* (Exercise 6) means to gain admission. Whoever cannot meet the minimum age requirement for a movie cannot *get into the movie*.

Culture Note

School play (Exercise 8). In many schools in the United States, students participate in theatrical productions as an extracurricular activity.

WORKBOOK

Pages 91–92

1. Who Is It?

Make statements about the people in the exercises. Have students respond by telling who you're talking about. For example:

She was too shy to perform in school plays.	Rita *(Exercise 8)*
He was too young to get into the movie.	Timmy *(Exercise 6)*
She was too busy to go to lunch.	Lisa *(Exercise 1)*
He was too short to play on the basketball team.	Peter *(model)*
He was too upset to tell about the accident.	Ben *(Exercise 7)*
He was too tired to finish his homework.	Sasha *(Exercise 2)*
They were too full to finish dinner.	Max and Ruth *(Exercise 3)*
They were too nervous to eat.	Stuart and Gloria *(Exercise 9)*

2. Find the Right Person: When We Were Young

a. Collect information about what students could do when they were five years old.

b. Put this information on a handout in the following form:

> Find someone who . . .
>
> 1. could play the piano. _____
> 2. could ride a bike. _____
> 3. could swim across a lake. _____
> 4. could count to 100. _____
> 5. could read. _____

c. Have students circulate around the room asking each other questions to identify the above people.

d. The first student to identify all the people wins.

3. Harvey, the Genius!

a. Bring a magazine picture of a man to class or draw a face on the board. Point to the man and say, "This is Harvey. Harvey is *(45)* years old, and he works in a bank. What's so special about Harvey? When he was a little boy, everybody said he was a genius."

b. Write these models for questions on the board:

> When could Harvey _____?
> What could Harvey do when he was _____?

c. Call on pairs of students to create conversations about Harvey, using any vocabulary they wish. Encourage students to exaggerate and be playful in describing the abilities of *Harvey, the Genius.* For example:

A. When could Harvey read?
B. He could read when he was one year old.

A. What could Harvey do when he was three years old?
B. He could play the guitar.

4. Match the Sentences

a. Make a set of matching sentences such as the following:

He couldn't get into the movie.	He was too young.
He couldn't eat dessert.	He was too full.
He couldn't walk after his operation.	He was too weak.
He couldn't put the notebook on the bookshelf.	He was too short.
He couldn't get into the sports car.	He was too tall.
He couldn't stop crying.	He was too upset.
He couldn't perform the role play for the class.	He was too shy.

(continued)

b. Distribute a card to each student.

c. Have students memorize the sentences on their cards, then walk around the room trying to find their corresponding match.

d. Then have pairs of students say their matched sentences aloud to the class.

5. Concentration

a. Use the cards from the above activity. Place them face down in two rows of 7 each.

b. Divide the class into two teams. The object of the game is for students to find the matching cards. Both teams should be able to see all the cards since *concentrating* on their location is an important part of playing the game.

c. A student from Team 1 turns over two cards. If they match, the student picks up the cards, that team gets a point, and the student takes another turn. If the cards don't match, the student turns them face down, and a member of Team 2 takes a turn.

d. The game continues until all the cards have been matched. The team with the most correct matches wins the game.

Variation: This game can also be played in groups and pairs.

6. They Couldn't!

a. Divide the class into pairs or small groups.

b. Dictate the following sentences, and have students write a response to each using *couldn't*. For example:

Teacher	Students
She was too short.	She couldn't play basketball.
They were too tired.	They couldn't stay awake.
He was too young.	He couldn't get into the concert.

c. Have students from each pair or group come to the board and write their sentences.

Text Page 95: They Weren't Able to

FOCUS

- Be Able to

  Was / Were Able to
  Wasn't / Weren't Able to

CLOSE UP

RULE: *To be able* to do something is another way of expressing ability.

EXAMPLES: Was Jimmy able to lift his grandmother's suitcase? =
Could Jimmy lift his grandmother's suitcase?

Were Nancy and Mark able to go camping last weekend? =
Could Nancy and Mark go camping last weekend?

GETTING READY

Introduce the forms of *was able to*.

1. Have students practice Exercise 8 on text page 94 again.

2. Then change *could* to *was able to* and have students repeat.

   A. Was Rita able to perform in school plays when she was young?
   B. No, she wasn't able to. She was too shy.

3. Do the same for Exercise 9 on text page 94. Have students practice the exercise. Then change *could* to *were able to* and have students repeat:

   A. Were Stuart and Gloria abie to eat at their wedding?
   B. No, they weren't able to. They were too nervous.

4. Practice all the forms of *was able to*. Have students repeat:

I was able to.	I wasn't able to.
He was able to.	He wasn't able to.
She was able to.	She wasn't able to.
We were able to.	We weren't able to.
You were able to.	You weren't able to.
They were able to.	They weren't able to.

INTRODUCING THE MODEL

1. Have students look at the model illustration.

2. Set the scene: "Jimmy's grandmother arrived by plane this morning. Jimmy met her at the airport."

3. Present the model.

4. Full-Class Repetition.

5. Ask students if they have any questions. Check understanding of the word *lift*.

6. Group Choral Repetition.

7. Choral Conversation.

8. Call on one or two pairs of students to present the dialog.

   (For additional practice, do Choral Conversation in small groups or by rows.)

Examples

> 1. A. Was Diane able to sit down on the subway this morning?
>   B. No, she wasn't able to. It was too crowded.
>
> 2. A. Was Charlie able to eat the food at the restaurant last night?
>   B. No, he wasn't able to. It was too spicy.

1. Exercise 1: Call on two students to present the dialog. Then do Choral Repetition and Choral Conversation practice.

2. Exercise 2: Check understanding of the word *spicy*. Same as above.

3. Exercises 3–8: Either Full-Class Practice or Pair Practice.

New Vocabulary

3. go camping
4. solve
   math problem
6. ocean
7. ponytail
8. tuxedo
   prom

WORKBOOK

Page 93

EXPANSION ACTIVITIES

1. Side by Side Again

Do *Side by Side* Exercises 1–9 on text page 94 again, using *able to* in place of *could*.

2. What Was It?

The pronoun *it* may refer to many different nouns. Ask questions about the exercises. Have students name the noun *it* refers to. For example:

What was too crowded?	the subway *(Exercise 1)*
What was too heavy?	the suitcase *(Model)*
What was too dark?	the night *(Exercise 5)*
What was too small?	the tuxedo *(Exercise 8)*
What was too cold?	the ocean *(Exercise 6)*
What was too difficult?	the math problem *(Exercise 4)*
What was too short?	Tracy's hair *(Exercise 7)*
What was too windy?	the weather *(Exercise 3)*
What was too spicy?	the food at the restaurant *(Exercise 2)*

3. Finish the Sentence!

Begin the following sentences, and have students add an appropriate conclusion:

> We weren't able to find our friends at the movie theater because . . .
> Jim couldn't eat his dinner last night because . . .
> Helen wasn't able to lift her suitcase because . . .
> Roger and Dan couldn't do their homework last night because . . .
> Carol couldn't finish her sandwich yesterday because . . .
> William wasn't able to play soccer yesterday because . . .
> Peggy couldn't sing in the concert last night because . . .
> Ruth couldn't wear her sister's dress to the job interview because . . .
> Tom and his brother weren't able to go skiing yesterday because . . .

4. Telephone

a. Divide the class into large groups. Have each group sit in a circle.

b. Whisper a short story to one student. For example:

"I had a terrible vacation. I wasn't able to go swimming because it was too cold. I wasn't able to go camping because it was too windy. And I wasn't able to go to my favorite restaurant because it was too crowded."

c. The first student whispers the story to the second student, and so forth around the circle.

d. When the story gets to the last student, that person says it aloud. Is it the same story you started with? The group with the most accurate story wins.

5. Chain Game: Let's Go Out!

a. Write the following conversational model on the board:

> A. Let's _____ !
> B. No, it's too _____. Let's _____.

b. Have the class sit in a circle.

c. Begin the grammar chain by saying:

Let's go to a concert!

d. Student 1 gives a reason why they can't and offers another suggestion. For example:

No, it's too noisy. Let's go to a restaurant!

e. Student 2 continues the chain in the same way. For example:

No, it's too expensive. Let's see a play!

f. Continue until everyone has had a turn.

6. Larry's Terrible Night Out

a. Put the following on the board:

Larry

go to his favorite restaurant (busy)
order his favorite dish (expensive)
sit near the window (crowded)
drink his coffee (cold)
get a taxi home (late)
find his house key (dark)
go to sleep (upset)

b. Set the scene: "Larry went to a restaurant last weekend because it was his birthday. But he didn't have a very good evening. First, he wasn't able to go to his favorite restaurant because it was too busy."

c. Have students use the cues on the board to tell more about what Larry wasn't able to do and why.

d. You can also have students ask each other questions about Larry. For example:

A. Was Larry able to go to his favorite restaurant?
B. No, he wasn't able to.
A. Why not?
B. Because it was too busy.

e. Have someone pretend to be Larry, and have other students ask him questions. For example:

A. Were you able to order your favorite dish?
B. No, I wasn't able to.
A. Why not?
B. Because it was too expensive.

FOCUS

- Had to
- Review: *Wasn't Able to / Weren't Able to Couldn't*
- Review: Reflexive Pronouns

CLOSE UP

RULE:	*Had to* + verb expresses past obligation.
EXAMPLES:	She **had to study** for an examination.
	He **had to visit** his boss in the hospital.

RULE:	Some verbs, such as *enjoy*, are commonly followed by reflexive pronouns.
EXAMPLES:	Did Paul **enjoy himself**?
	Did Mr. and Mrs. Lee **enjoy themselves**?

GETTING READY

Review reflexive pronouns, using the new expression *enjoy _____ self/selves*.

1. Say: "Mary had a party last weekend, and everybody had a wonderful time. I really enjoyed myself."

2. Ask: "Did David have a good time?" Then have students repeat:

    Yes, he enjoyed himself.

3. Ask the questions below, and have students respond according to the pattern:

    Yes, _____ enjoyed _____ self/selves.

    a. Did Susan have a good time?

    b. Did Sam have a good time?

    c. Did Mr. and Mrs. Garcia have a good time?

    d. Did we have a good time?

4. Then ask individual students: "Did you have a good time at Mary's party?"

INTRODUCING THE MODEL

1. Have students look at the model illustration.

2. Set the scene: "Two people are talking about what Barbara did last night."

3. Present the model using *wasn't able to*. Then present the model using *couldn't*.

4. Full-Class Repetition.

5. Ask students if they have any questions. Check understanding of new vocabulary: *enjoy herself, study for an examination*.

6. Group Choral Repetition.

7. Choral Conversation.

8. Call on one pair of students to present the dialog using *wasn't able to*. Then have another pair present the dialog using *couldn't*.

(For additional practice, do Choral Conversation in small groups or by rows.)

SIDE BY SIDE EXERCISES

Examples

> 1. A. Did Paul enjoy himself at the tennis match last week?
>   B. Unfortunately, he wasn't able to/couldn't go to the tennis match last week. He had to visit his boss in the hospital.
> 2. A. Did Amanda enjoy herself at the soccer game yesterday afternoon?
>   B. Unfortunately, she wasn't able to/couldn't go to the soccer game yesterday afternoon. She had to go to the eye doctor.

1. **Exercise 1:** Introduce the new expression *tennis match*. Call on two students to present the dialog. Then do Choral Repetition and Choral Conversation practice.

2. **Exercise 2:** Introduce the new expression *eye doctor*. Same as above.

3. **Exercises 3–7:** Either Full-Class Practice or Pair Practice.

New Vocabulary

3. overtime
4. symphony
5. science project
6. amusement park
7. school dance

Language Note

Exercise 3: Overtime is time spent working after completing a full schedule of work.

4. **Exercise 8:** Have students use the model as a guide to create their own conversations, using vocabulary of their choice. Encourage students to use dictionaries to find new words they want to use. This exercise can be done orally in class or for written homework. If you assign it for homework, do one example in class to make sure students understand what's expected. Have students present their conversations in class the next day.

WORKBOOK

Pages 94–95

EXPANSION ACTIVITIES

1. **Memory Chain**

    a. Tell the class: "Last night we had a class party, and nobody came! What happened?" Tell each student to think of a reason why he or she wasn't able to come to the class party.

    b. Divide the class into groups of 5 or 6 students each.

    c. One group at a time, have Student 1 begin. For example:

    > I had to work overtime.

    d. Student 2 repeats what Student 1 said and adds a statement about himself or herself. For example:

    > Rita had to work overtime, and I had to baby-sit for my neighbors.

    e. Student 3 continues in the same way.

    f. Continue until everyone has had a chance to play the *memory chain*.

2. **Information Gap Handouts**

    a. Tell students that your friend Paul had a very busy weekend. He had to do a lot of things. Make up a schedule for Paul's weekend, but divide the information between two different schedules. For example:

(continued)

Chart A:

	Friday	Saturday	Sunday
morning		wash his car	
afternoon	get a haircut		go to the laundromat
evening		go to a dance	

Chart B:

	Friday	Saturday	Sunday
morning	go to work		visit his grandparents
afternoon		pick up flowers	
evening	pick up his tuxedo		clean his house

b. Divide the class into pairs. Give each member of the pair a different schedule. Have students share their information and fill in their schedules. For example:

Student A: What did Paul have to do Friday morning?
Student B: He had to go to work.
Student A: Okay [writes the information in Schedule A].
Student B: What did he have to do Friday afternoon?

c. The pairs continue until each has a filled calendar.

d. Have students look at their partner's schedule to make sure that they have written the information correctly.

3. Our Obligations

a. Have students write down two things they had to do yesterday, last weekend, and last year.

b. Have students compare their lists in pairs or in small groups.

4. The Secretary's Day

a. Write the following schedule on the board:

9:00-10:00	type letters/read e-mails
10:00-11:00	answer the telephone/make appointments
11:00-12:00	go to the post office/mail some packages
(Lunch)	
1:00–2:30	translate a few letters
2:30–3:30	go shopping/buy paper and pens for the office
3:30–5:00	meet some visitors at the airport/recommend hotels and restaurants

b. Set the scene: "Bob Stevens is a secretary for a large company. He has to work hard every day. Here's what he had to do last Friday."

c. Point to the cues on the board as you begin the story:

From 9 o'clock to 10 o'clock he had to type letters and read e-mails.

d. Call on students to tell each additional part of the story as you point to the cues.

e. Practice question-asking by calling on pairs of students to create conversations. For example:

A. What did Bob have to do from 10 o'clock to 11 o'clock?
B. He had to answer the telephone and make appointments.

f. Call on a few individuals to role play the secretary. Have other students ask questions about last Friday.

5. Find the Right Person!

a. Collect information about what students had to do last weekend.

b. Put this information on a handout in the following form:

> Find someone who . . .
> 1. had to finish an English project. _____
> 2. had to attend a wedding. _____
> 3. had to visit a friend in the hospital. _____
> 4. had to plan a birthday party. _____
> 5. had to write a report for work. _____

c. Have students circulate around the room, asking each other questions to identify the above people.

d. The first student to identify all the people wins.

6. Scrambled Sentences

a. Divide the class into two teams.

b. Write individual sentences or questions out of order on the board. For example:

> the   go   had   because   to   to
> eye   to   to   wasn't   movies   go
> able   doctor   he   the   he
>
> to   projects   game   we   go
> science   to   our   weren't   had
> the   on   soccer   we   work   to
> able   because
>
> match   go   had   she   boss   the
> the   wasn't   to   because   to
> she   her   in   to   able   tennis
> hospital   visit

c. The first person to raise his or her hand, come to the board, and write the sentence in the correct order earns a point for that team.

d. The team with the most points wins the scrambled sentences game.

Variation: Write the words to several sentences on separate cards. Divide the class into small groups, and have students work together to put the sentences into correct order.

7. I'm Glad I Couldn't Go!

a. Write this conversational framework on the board:

> A. Hi, _____. This is _____.
> B. Hi, _____.
> A. I'm really sorry I (couldn't/wasn't able to) go to the _____ with you last _____.
> B. Don't worry about it! The _____ was terrible, and I didn't enjoy myself at all.
> A. Oh, really? Then I'm glad I couldn't go!

b. Have pairs of students role play this conversation, using the following cues. Either write them on the board or on cards.

> concert/music
> theater/play
> restaurant/food
> beach/weather
> lecture/professor

Example:

A. Hi, Susan. This is Richard.
B. Hi, Richard.
A. I'm really sorry I couldn't go to the concert with you last Saturday.
B. Don't worry about it! The music was terrible, and I didn't enjoy myself at all.
A. Oh, really? Then I'm glad I couldn't go!

READING Mrs. Murphy's Students Couldn't Do Their Homework

FOCUS

- Could

NEW VOCABULARY

lesson
promise (v)

READING THE STORY

Optional: Preview the story by having students talk about the story title and/or illustration. You may choose to introduce new vocabulary beforehand, or have students encounter the new vocabulary within the context of the reading.

1. Have students read silently, or follow along silently as the story is read aloud by you, by one or more students, or on the audio program.

2. Ask students if they have any questions. Check understanding of vocabulary.

3. Check students' comprehension, using some or all of the following questions:

> Why didn't Mrs. Murphy know what to do with her students today?
> Why couldn't Bob do his homework?
> Why couldn't Sally do her homework?
> Why couldn't John do his homework?
> Why couldn't Donna do her homework?
> Why couldn't all the other students do their homework?
> What do the students promise Mrs. Murphy?

✓ READING *CHECK-UP*

Q & A

1. Call on a pair of students to present the model.

2. Have students work in pairs to create new dialogs.

3. Call on pairs to present their new dialogs to the class.

READING EXTENSION

Have students discuss the following questions:

> What's another title for the reading?
> Did the students have good excuses for not doing their homework? Why or why not?

 ## LISTENING

Listen and choose the correct answer.

1. I couldn't sit down on the bus.
2. Tony wasn't able to paint his house.
3. Jennifer couldn't find her purse last night.
4. They didn't enjoy the food at the restaurant.
5. Why weren't the plumbers able to fix it?
6. Why couldn't you go to work yesterday?

Answers

1. b
2. a
3. b
4. b
5. a
6. a

FOCUS

- Will/Won't Be Able to
- Have Got to

CLOSE UP

RULE: *To be able to* is the only expression of ability in English that can be used in the future tense. (*Can* and *could* are present and past forms.)

EXAMPLE: **I'll be able to move** to my new apartment tomorrow.

RULE: The affirmative form of *have got to + verb* expresses obligation. The auxiliary verb *have* often contracts with the subject pronouns.

EXAMPLES:
I **have got to** drive.   ⟶   **I've got to** drive.
You **have got to** study.   ⟶   **You've got to** study.
She **has got to** go.   ⟶   **She's got to** go.
We **have got to** fly.   ⟶   **We've got to** fly.
They **have got to** work.   ⟶   **They've got to** work.

GETTING READY

1. Introduce *have got to*, using the box at the top of the text page 98.

   a. Write on the board:

   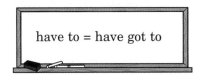

   have to = have got to

   b. Have students listen and repeat:

   I've got to work.
   We've got to work.
   You've got to work.
   They've got to work.
   He's got to work.
   She's got to work.
   It's got to work.

2. Introduce *will / won't be able to*.

a. Say: "I can't go shopping today, but I'll be able to go shopping tomorrow." Then, read the sentence fragments below, and have students finish them, using *will be able to*.

   He can't study today, . . .
   She can't come to class today, . . .
   We can't work late today, . . .
   They can't go swimming today, . . .
   I can't call him today, . . .
   You can't visit her today, . . .

b. Say: "I can go jogging today, but I won't be able to go jogging tomorrow." Then do the same as above, using *won't be able to*.

   He can help you today, . . .
   She can visit them today, . . .
   We can go shopping today, . . .
   They can work today, . . .
   I can come to class early today, . . .
   You can go today, . . .

INTRODUCING THE MODEL

1. Have students look at the model illustration.

2. Set the scene: "Two friends are talking. One of them has some bad news."

3. Present the model.

4. Full-Class Repetition.

   ### Pronunciation Note

   The pronunciation focus of Chapter 10 is **Have to & Have Got to** (text page 102). You may wish to model this pronunciation at this point (*I've got to take my son to the doctor*) and encourage students to incorporate it into their language practice.

5. Ask students if they have any questions. Check understanding of the new expression *Don't worry about it!*

6. Group Choral Repetition.

7. Choral Conversation.

8. Call on one or two pairs of students to present the dialog.

   (For additional practice, do Choral Conversation in small groups or by rows.)

SIDE BY SIDE EXERCISES

Examples

1. A. I'm afraid I won't be able to help you paint your apartment tomorrow.
   B. You won't? Why not?
   A. I've got to drive my parents to the airport.
   B. Don't worry about it! I'm sure I'll be able to paint my apartment by myself.

2. A. I'm afraid I won't be able to help you repair your fence tomorrow.
   B. You won't? Why not?
   A. I've got to take care of my niece and nephew.
   B. Don't worry about it! I'm sure I'll be able to repair my fence by myself.

1. **Exercise 1:** Call on two students to present the dialog. Then do Choral Repetition and Choral Conversation practice.

2. **Exercise 2:** Same as above.

3. **Exercises 3–7:** Either Full-Class Practice or Pair Practice.

> **New Vocabulary**
> 3. football practice
> 4. set up fly
> 5. hook up ballet
> 6. assemble
> 7. vet

Language Note

Vet (Exercise 7) is the commonly used abbreviation of *veterinarian*, a doctor who treats animals.

4. **Exercise 8:** Have students use the model as a guide to create their own conversations, using vocabulary of their choice. Encourage students to use dictionaries to find new words they want to use. This exercise can be done orally in class or for written homework. If you assign it for homework, do one example in class to make sure students understand what's expected. Have students present their conversations in class the next day.

WORKBOOK

Pages 96–97

1. Different Emotions

Have students practice reading the model conversation, using any combination of these different emotions:

Speaker A is upset that she can't help her friend.
Speaker A isn't upset that she can't help her friend.
Speaker B is disappointed.
Speaker B isn't disappointed.

2. Finish the Sentence!

Begin a sentence, and have students repeat what you said and add appropriate endings to the sentence. For example:

Teacher	Students
He's got to paint . . .	the apartment.
	the room.
She's got to repair . . .	the car.
	the fence.
	the fan.
We've got to assemble . . .	the bike.
	the toy.
	the table.
They've got to hook up . . .	the TV.
	the fax machine.
	the VCR.

Variation: This activity may be done as a class, in pairs or small groups, or as a game with competing teams.

3. Obligations! Obligations!

a. Have students write down two things they have got to do today, tomorrow, and next week.

b. Have students compare their lists in pairs or small groups.

4. Memory Chain

a. Divide the class into groups of 5 or 6 students each.

b. Tell each student to think of something that he or she has got to do this week.

c. One group at a time, have Student 1 begin. For example:

I've got to go to the dentist on Tuesday.

d. Student 2 repeats what Student 1 said and adds a statement about himself or herself. For example:

Sally has got to go to the dentist on Tuesday, and I've got to get a haircut on Friday.

e. Student 3 continues in the same way. For example:

Sally has got to go to the dentist on Tuesday, Miguel has got to get a haircut on Friday, and I've got to work late on Wednesday.

f. Continue until everyone has had a chance to play the *memory chain*.

5. What Have They Got to Do?

a. Write the following conversational model on the board:

> A. _____ want(s) to be the best _____ in _____.
> B. Then ____ got to practice.
> A. You're right. ____ got to _____ every day.

b. Make up word cards with the following cues:

Paula piano player practice the piano	Tom typist type
Julia actress act	Peter baseball player play baseball
Helen English teacher study English grammar	Hector violinist play the violin
Patty plumber fix sinks	Mike mechanic repair cars

(continued)

Jane and Tom singers sing	Donna dancer dance
Dave swimmer swim	Frank chef cook

c. Give the word cards to pairs of students, and have them create conversations based on the model. For example:

   A. Paula wants to be the best piano player in (*New York*).

   B. Then she's got to practice the piano.

   A. You're right. She's got to practice the piano every day.

   A. Tom wants to be the best typist in (*our office*).

   B. Then he's got to type.

   A. You're right. He's got to type every day.

6. **Role Play: I Won't Be Able to Help You**

a. Divide the class into pairs.

b. Give the cue cards below to the pairs, and have them create role plays based on the situations.

> Your friend is here to see you. You're excited because he or she is going to help you carry your new refrigerator into the house. You've got to do it this morning because you're having a party tonight, and you have to buy food and put it in the refrigerator.

> You're really sorry. You can't help your friend today. Your back hurts, and you've got to go to the doctor.

> Your friend is here to see you. You're pleased because he or she is going to help you fix your car. You have to fix it today because tomorrow you've got to drive to your cousin's wedding.

> You're very sorry. You can't help your friend. You weren't able to finish your homework last night, and you have to do it today. Tell your friend you can help tomorrow.

> Your friend is here to see you. You're happy that he or she is going to help you set up your new computer. You've got to do it soon because you've got to finish an important English project this weekend, and you need your computer to do it.

> You're sorry. You can't help your friend today. You weren't able to take your dog to the vet yesterday, and you've got to do it today. Also, you'll be busy tomorrow because you've got to wait for the plumber. Tell your friend you can help on Monday.

7. **Class Discussion: Helping Friends**

The situations in this lesson are about friends helping each other. Have students write and talk about how they help their friends.

a. Brainstorm with the class ways to help friends.

b. Individually, have students write a list of the ways they help their friends.

c. Have students share their lists in small groups. Then call on students to tell about their discussions.

How to Say It!

Expressing Obligation: There are many phrases to express obligation. *I've got to* and *I have to* express an equally urgent sense of obligation. *I need to* conveys a slightly less urgent sense of obligation.

1. Set the scene: "The two friends from the model conversation on text page 98 are talking."

2. Present the expressions.

3. Full-Class Repetition.

4. Ask students if they have any questions.

5. Group Choral Repetition.

6. Have students practice the conversations on text pages 98 and 99 again, using different ways of expressing obligation.

7. Call on pairs to present their conversations to the class.

READING The Bathroom Pipe Is Broken / The Television Is Broken

FOCUS

- Be Able to

NEW VOCABULARY

Story 1	Story 2
broke (break)	repair truck
for quite a while	side
pipe	

READING THE STORIES

Optional: Preview the stories by having students talk about the story titles and/or illustrations. You may choose to introduce new vocabulary beforehand, or have students encounter the new vocabulary within the context of the readings.

1. Have students read silently, or follow along silently as the stories are read aloud by you, by one or more students, or on the audio program.

2. Ask students if they have any questions. Check understanding of vocabulary.

✓ READING *CHECK-UP*

ANSWER THESE QUESTIONS

1. No, she couldn't. She was sick.

2. No, she can't. She's too busy.

3. No, she won't be able to. Tomorrow is Sunday.

4. No, he couldn't. He was fixing televisions on the other side of town.

5. No, he can't. His repair truck is broken.

6. No, he won't be able to. He'll be out of town.

CHOOSE

Before doing the exercise, introduce the words *someone, understand.*

1. have to

2. got to

3. got to

4. aren't

5. have

6. has

7. be able to

READING EXTENSION

Tic Tac Question the Answer

1. Draw a tic tac grid on the board and fill it with short answers to questions. For example:

Yes, she was.	No, she won't.	No, she wasn't.
No, she couldn't.	No, she can't.	Yes, they are.
Yes, she is.	No, they won't.	No, she doesn't.

2. Divide the class into teams. Give each team a mark: *X* or *O*.

3. Have each team ask a question about the first story, *The Bathroom Pipe Is Broken*, with an answer in the grid. For example:

> X Team: Was the plumber able to fix their pipe yesterday?
> No, she wasn't.

4. If an answer is appropriate and is stated correctly, that team may replace the answer with its team mark. For example:

Yes, she was.	No, she won't.	**X**
No, she couldn't.	No, she can't.	Yes, they are.
Yes, she is.	No, they won't.	No, she doesn't.

5. The first team to mark out three boxes in a straight line—vertically, horizontally, or diagonally—wins.

6. Repeat the game with the second story, *The Television Is Broken.*

ON YOUR OWN *Frustrated, Disappointed, and Upset*

FOCUS

Review of Expressions of Ability:

- Present Ability   *Can / Can't*
- Past Ability   *Could / Couldn't*
    Was / Wasn't Able to
- Future Ability: *Will / Won't Be Able to*

NEW VOCABULARY

clumsy
crash
hand in
key
term paper

ON YOUR OWN ACTIVITY

For each situation:

1. Have students follow along in the text as you read or play the audio one or more times.

2. Ask students if they have any questions. Check understanding of new vocabulary.

3. Ask questions about each situation. For example:

    How does Martha feel?
    Why is she upset?
    Where does she need to go?
    Why can't she get to the airport on time?

Is Frank happy?
Why is he frustrated?
Can he get into his apartment?
Why not?

What's the matter with Emily?
Why did she lose all her work?
Will she be able to hand in her term paper tomorrow?

Could Ted dance in the school play last year?
Was he disappointed?
What did his teacher say?

4. Have students in pairs or in small groups talk about situations in which they were frustrated, disappointed, or upset. If you wish, you can then call on students to tell the class about the people they spoke to.

WORKBOOK

Pages 98–100

JOURNAL

Have students write their journal entries at home or in class. Encourage students to use a dictionary to look up words they would like to use. Students can share their written work with other students if appropriate. Have students discuss what they have written as a class, in pairs, or in small groups.

Text Page 102

PRONUNCIATION

> ***Have to & Have Got to***: In daily English usage, the pronunciation of *to* at the end of each of these phrases is reduced to a /*ta*/ sound. The /*v*/ sound in the verb phrase *have to* is pronounced /*f*/. Thus, *have to* is pronounced "hafta" and *got to* is pronounced "gotta."

Focus on Listening

Practice the sentences in the left column. Say each sentence or play the audio one or more times. Have students listen carefully and repeat.

Focus on Pronunciation

Practice the sentences in the right column. Have students say each sentence and then listen carefully as you say it or play the audio.

If you wish, have students continue practicing the sentences to improve their pronunciation.

WORKBOOK

Check-Up Test: Pages 101–102

CHAPTER SUMMARY

GRAMMAR

1. Divide the class into pairs or small groups.
2. Have students take turns forming sentences from the words in the grammar boxes. Student A says a sentence, and Student B points to the words from each column that are in the sentence. Then have students switch: Student B says a sentence, and Student A points to the words.

KEY VOCABULARY

Have students ask you any questions about the meaning or pronunciation of the vocabulary. If students ask for the pronunciation, repeat after the student until the student is satisfied with his or her own pronunciation.

EXPANSION ACTIVITIES

1. **Do You Remember the Words?**

   Check students' retention of the vocabulary depicted on the opening page of Chapter 10 by doing the following activity:

   a. Have students open their books to page 93 and cover the list of vocabulary words.

   b. Either call out a number and have students tell you the word, or say a word and have students tell you the number.

   Variation: You can also do this activity as a game with competing teams.

2. **Student-Led Dictation**

   a. Tell each student to choose a word from the Key Vocabulary list on text page 102 and look at it very carefully.

   b. Have students take turns dictating their words to the class. Everybody writes down that student's word.

   c. When the dictation is completed, call on different students to write each word on the board to check the spelling.

3. **Beanbag Toss**

   a. Call out the topic: *Adjectives.*

   b. Have students toss a beanbag back and forth. The student to whom the beanbag is tossed must name an adjective from the Key Vocabulary list. For example:

Student 1:	busy
Student 2:	dark
Student 3:	crowded

   (continued)

EXPANSION ACTIVITIES (Continued)

   c. Continue until all the adjectives have been named.

Variation: You can also do this activity as a game with competing teams.

4. Letter Game

   a. Divide the class into teams.

   b. Say: "I'm thinking of an adjective that starts with s."

   c. The first person to raise his or her hand and guess correctly [spicy] wins a point for his or her team.

   d. Continue with other letters of the alphabet and verbs.

The team that gets the most correct answers wins the game.

5. Miming

   a. Write on cards the adjectives from text page 102.

   b. Have students take turns picking a card from the pile and pantomiming the adjective on the card.

   c. The class must guess what adjective the person is describing.

Variation: This can be done as a game with competing teams.

6. Movable Categories

   a. Write the adjectives from the list on text page 102 on separate cards.

   b. Give each student one or two cards.

   c. Call out one of the following categories:

      adjectives for describing a person
      adjectives for describing food
      adjectives for describing a restaurant
      adjectives for describing a test
      adjectives for describing a beach
      adjectives for describing a pet

   d. All those students whose adjectives are appropriate for the chosen category go to the right side of the room. All the other students go to the left side.

   e. Those who are in the right group call out their words for the class to verify.

   f. Continue with other categories.

1. Board Game

a. On poster boards or on manila file folders, make up game boards with a pathway consisting of separate spaces. You may use any theme or design you wish.

b. Divide the class into groups of 2 to 4 students and give each group a game board and a die, and each person something to be used as a playing piece.

c. Give each group a pile of cards face-down with sentences written on them. Some sentences should be correct, and others incorrect. For example:

> I've to work today.
> She's got to take her niece to school.
> They got to study for the examination.
> Will she can help me move tomorrow?
> We weren't able to swim the ocean.
> He couldn't perform in the school play.
> Was you able to solve the science problem last night?
> No, he wasn't able.
> Unfortunately, they couldn't to go to the symphony.
> Were you able walk after the operation?
> She had to work overtime last night.
> Did Carla enjoy themselves at the amusement park?
> They've to drive their parents to the airport.
> She has to help you hook up the VCR.
> I got to practice harder.

d. Each student in turn rolls the die, moves the playing piece along the game path, and after landing on a space, picks a card, reads the sentence, and says if it is *correct* or *incorrect*. If the sentence is incorrect and the student is able to give the correct version, that student takes an additional turn.

e. The first student to reach the end of the pathway is the winner.

2. Scrambled Sentences

a. Divide the class into teams.

b. Write individual sentences out of order on the board. For example:

afraid	take	nephew	won't	I
able	to	help	be	you
care of	niece	your	and	
tomorrow	I'm			

assemble	able	sure	by	be
bicycle	I'll	I'm	my	myself
to	son's			

help	afraid	VCR	won't	hook
able	new	I'm	I	you	your
up	to	be		

c. The first person to raise his or her hand, come to the board, and write the sentence in the correct order earns a point for that team.

d. The team with the most points wins the scrambled sentence game.

Variation: Write the words to several sentences on separate cards. Divide the class into small groups, and have students work together to put the sentences into correct order.

3. Question Game

a. Write the following sentence on the board:

> Sally won't be able to go to the symphony tonight because she's got to finish her term paper.

b. Underline different elements of the sentence, and have students create a question for that portion of the sentence. For example:

> <u>Sally</u> won't be able to go to the symphony tonight because she's got to finish her term paper.

Who won't be able to go to the symphony tonight?

(continued)

Sally won't be able to go <u>to the symphony</u> tonight because she's got to finish her term paper.

Where won't Sally be able to go tonight?

Sally won't be able to go to the symphony <u>tonight</u> because she's got to finish her term paper.

When won't Sally be able to go to the symphony?

Sally won't be able to go to the symphony tonight <u>because she's got to finish her term paper.</u>

Why won't Sally be able to go to the symphony tonight?

c. Continue with other sentences.

4. Dialog Builder!

a. Divide the class into pairs.

b. Write the following phrases on the board:

Why are you so upset?
Unfortunately, ...
I'm afraid . . .
You couldn't?
You won't be able to?

c. Have each pair create a conversation incorporating all of these lines. Students can begin and end their conversations any way they wish, but they must include these lines in their dialogs.

d. Call on pairs to present their conversations to the class.

WORKBOOK ANSWER KEY AND LISTENING SCRIPTS

WORKBOOK PAGE 91

A. WHAT'S THE WORD?

1. couldn't, can
2. couldn't, can
3. couldn't, can
4. couldn't
5. can't
6. could, could
7. couldn't
8. couldn't, can
9. couldn't
10. couldn't, could
11. can't
12. couldn't

WORKBOOK PAGE 94

D. WHAT'S THE WORD?

1. couldn't/wasn't able to, had to
2. couldn't/wasn't able to, had to
3. could/was able to
4. couldn't/wasn't able to
5. could/were able to, couldn't/wasn't able to, had to
6. couldn't/weren't able to, had to
7. could/was able to, could/was able to, couldn't/wasn't able to, couldn't/wasn't able to
8. couldn't/weren't able to, had to
9. couldn't/wasn't able to, had to

WORKBOOK PAGE 95

F. WHAT'S THE WORD?

1. b
2. b
3. a
4. b
5. b
6. a

WORKBOOK PAGE 96

G. WHY NOT?

1. He's got to
2. She's got to
3. I've got to
4. We've got to
5. He's got to
6. They've got to
7. you've got to

WORKBOOK PAGE 97

H. MY FRIEND LISA

1. She won't be able to go jogging every morning.
2. She won't be able to ride her bicycle to school every day.
3. She won't be able to play tennis on the school team.
4. She won't be able to swim every afternoon.
5. She won't be able to do exercises every evening.
6. She'll be able to play the violin.
7. She'll be able to bake delicious cakes and cookies.
8. She'll be able to make her own clothes.
9. She'll be able to fix her computer when it's broken.

I. THEY'LL BE ABLE TO

1. couldn't, she'll be able to
2. couldn't, we'll be able to
3. couldn't, he'll be able to
4. couldn't, I'll be able to

WORKBOOK PAGE 98

J. THEY WON'T BE ABLE TO

1. won't be able to, I've got to
2. won't be able to, She's got to
3. won't be able to, they've got to
4. won't be able to, he's got to
5. won't be able to, We've got to

K. LISTENING

Listen to each story, and then choose the correct answers to the questions you hear.

William's New Apartment

William is having problems with his new apartment. Yesterday he was very frustrated. It was a hot day, and he wasn't able to open his living room windows. And today he's upset because all the lights in his apartment went out. William is very disappointed. Now he won't be able to cook dinner or watch his favorite programs on TV.

1. Why was William frustrated yesterday?
2. Why is he upset today?
3. Why is he disappointed?

Mr. and Mrs. Clark's New Computer

Mr. and Mrs. Clark are having problems with their new computer. Yesterday they were frustrated because they couldn't assemble the computer easily. And today they're upset because the computer crashed. Mr. and Mrs. Clark are very disappointed. Now they won't be able to send any e-mail to their grandchildren.

4. Why were Mr. and Mrs. Clark frustrated yesterday?
5. Why are they upset today?
6. Why are they disappointed?

Answers

1.	b	4.	b
2.	a	5.	a
3.	a	6.	b

WORKBOOK PAGE 100

N. GrammarSong

1.	day	9.	day
2.	today	10.	today
3.	go	11.	go
4.	no	12.	no
5.	to	13.	to
6.	do	14.	do
7.	play		
8.	day		

WORKBOOK PAGES 101–102

Check-Up Test: Chapters 9-10

A.

1. were playing
2. was driving
3. were jogging
4. was shaving
5. were reading
6. was riding
7. was sitting

B.

1. ourselves
2. himself
3. yourselves
4. yourself
5. themselves
6. herself

C.

1. off
2. on
3. out of
4. through
5. into
6. couldn't
7. won't be able to
8. couldn't, had to

D.

1. wasn't
2. will be
3. weren't
4. I'll be
5. wasn't, had to
6. you've
7. won't be, she's

E.

Listen to the story, and then choose the correct answers to the questions you hear.

Poor Janet!

Last year Janet's teacher said she couldn't dance in the school play because she was too clumsy. Janet was very upset. This year Janet practiced every day, and now she dances much better. Unfortunately, last week she fell down while she was dancing and she hurt herself. Janet is very disappointed. She won't be able to dance in the play this year.

1. Why was Janet upset last year?
2. What did Janet do this year?
3. What happened while Janet was dancing last week?
4. Why is Janet disappointed?

Answers

1. b
2. a
3. b
4. b

FEATURE ARTICLE
Families and Time

PREVIEWING THE ARTICLE

1. Have students talk about the title of the article and the accompanying photographs.

2. You may choose to introduce the following new vocabulary beforehand, or have students encounter it within the context of the article:

> family members
> free-time
> individual
> member
> nowadays
> separate
> single-parent family
> technology

READING THE ARTICLE

1. Have students read silently, or follow along silently as the article is read aloud by you, by one or more students, or on the audio program.

2. Ask students if they have any questions. Check understanding of vocabulary.

3. Check students' comprehension by having students read the text again and take notes on the differences between families in the past and today. For example:

In the Past	Today
The father worked, and the mother stayed home.	Both parents work.
The mother did the food shopping, cooking, and cleaning.	Both parents do the food shopping, cooking, and cleaning.
Parents used to have more time with their children.	Parents don't have as much time with their children.
Children came home to a parent in the house.	Children often come home to an empty house.
Families spent time together.	Family members do things by themselves.

4. Have students discuss the questions at the end of the reading in small groups or as a class.

EXPANSION ACTIVITY

Survey on Family Life

Have students find out about each others' family lives.

1. Brainstorm with the class questions students can ask each other about family life. For example:

   > What things does your family do together?
   > What's your favorite family activity?
   > When does your family spend time together?
   > How many televisions does your family have?
   > Do you do Internet activities with a family member?
   > Who does the housework in your home?

2. Have each student chose one question to ask, and then the students conduct their surveys by circulating around the room, asking each other their questions.

3. For homework, have students write a summary of their surveys. In the next class, have students report their results.

 FACT FILE *Countries Where People Spend the Most Time at Work*

1. Before reading the Fact File, ask students: "What do you think? How many hours does a person work in a year? In what country do you think people spend the most time at work?" Write students' ideas on the board. After reading the table, have students check their predictions.

2. Introduce the new word *Thailand*.

3. Read the information aloud as the class follows along.

4. To check comprehension, ask students:

> In which country do people spend the most time at work? *(Thailand)*
>
> How many more hours a year do people in the United States work compared with people in Japan? *(77 hours)*
>
> How many more hours a year do people in France work compared with people in Germany? *(96 hours)*
>
> How many hours a week do people work in Thailand? *(If they don't take a vacation, they work an average of 42.3 hours a week.)*

 BUILD YOUR VOCABULARY!
Home Appliances

> coffee maker
> dishwasher
> dryer
> garbage disposal
> iron
> microwave
> toaster
> vacuum cleaner
> washing machine/washer

1. Have students look at the illustrations and identify any words they already know.

2. Present the vocabulary. Say each word and have the class repeat it chorally and individually. Check students' understanding and pronunciation of the words.

EXPANSION ACTIVITIES

1. Clap in Rhythm

Object: Once a clapping rhythm is established, students must continue naming different appliances.

a. Have students sit in a circle.

b. Establish a steady even beat—one-two-three-four, one-two-three-four—by having students clap their hands to their laps twice

and then clap their hands together twice. Repeat throughout the game, maintaining the same rhythm.

c. The object is for each student in turn to name an appliance word each time the hands are clapped together twice. Nothing is said when students clap their hands on their laps.

Note: The beat never stops! If a student misses a beat, he or she can either wait for the next beat or else pass to the next student.

2. Associations

a. Divide the class into pairs or small groups.

b. Call out the name of an appliance and tell students to write down all the things they associate with that appliance. For example:

dishwasher:	detergent/dishes/washing
vacuum cleaner:	rugs/carpet/bags
iron:	laundry/shirts/dresses

c. Have a student from each pair or group come to the board and write their words.

Variation: Do the activity as a game in which you divide the class into teams. The team with the most number of associations is the winner.

3. Ranking

a. Have students rank the appliances listed on text page 103 from the *most convenient* to the *least convenient.*

b. As a class, in pairs, or in small groups, have students compare their lists.

c. Then rank the items according to these additional criteria:

> helps working parents the most to helps working parents the least
> most expensive to least expensive

 AROUND THE WORLD
Child Care

1. Have students read silently or follow along silently as the text is read aloud by you, by one or more students, or on the audio program. Check understanding of new vocabulary:

> child care
> community
> day-care center
> during
> pre-school

2. Have students first work in pairs or small groups to respond to the question. Then have students tell the class what they talked about. Write any new vocabulary on the board.

EXPANSION ACTIVITIES

1. Advantages and Disadvantages

a. Have students draw two columns on a piece of paper. At the top of one column, have students write <u>Advantages</u>. At the top of the other column, have them write <u>Disadvantages</u>.

b. Say one of the forms of child care, and have students brainstorm its advantages and disadvantages. Write students' ideas in the columns on the board and discuss them as a class. For example:

Day-Care at a Factory

<u>Advantages</u>	<u>Disadvantages</u>
It's convenient.	It's noisy for children.
The parent can see the child on a break and at lunch.	Children miss their homes.

2. Dictate and Discuss

a. Divide the class into pairs or small groups.

b. Dictate sentences such as the following, and then have students discuss them:

> A family member can take better care of a child than a teacher.
> All businesses should provide child care for their employees.
> Children who go to pre-school do better in school, than children who don't go to pre-school.
> Children spend too much time away from their families.

c. Call on students to share their opinions with the rest of the class.

GLOBAL EXCHANGE

1. Set the scene: "KoolKid 2 is writing to his keypal."

2. Have students read silently or follow along silently as the message is read aloud by you, by one or more students, or on the audio program.

3. Ask students if they have any questions. Check understanding of new vocabulary: *exam, files, over, schoolwork, study notes.*

4. Suggestions for additional practice:

   • Have students write a response to KoolKid2 and share their writing in pairs.

   • Have students correspond with a keypal on the Internet and then share their experience with the class.

LISTENING *You Have Five Messages!*

Set the scene: "Jim is moving to a new apartment. He left messages asking five friends to help him move. Now there are five messages on Jim's answering machine."

LISTENING SCRIPT

Listen to the messages on Jim's machine. Match the people and their messages.

You have five messages.

Message One, Friday 2:15 P.M.: Hi, Jim. This is Pete. I just got your message. I'm sorry I won't be able to help you move to your new apartment tomorrow, but I've got to work overtone. 'Bye. *[beep]*

Message Two, Friday 3:10 P.M.: Hi, Jim. It's Susie. Sorry I won't be able to help you move tomorrow. I've got to visit my grandparents out of town. Good luck! Talk to you soon. *[beep]*

Message Three, Friday 3:55 P.M.: Jim? Hi. It's Marty! How are you? I'm not so good. I'm having problems with my car. I have to take it to a mechanic, so I'm afraid I won't be able to help you move. Sorry. Give me a call sometime. Okay? Take care. *[beep]*

Message Four, Friday 5:48 P.M.: Hello, Jim? It's Judy. You know, I really want to help you move, but I've got to stay home all day tomorrow and wait for the plumber. My kitchen sink is broken, and there's water everywhere! Hope your move goes okay. Sorry I can't help. Let's talk soon. *[beep]*

Message Five, Sunday 9:29 P.M.: Jim? It's Tom. Gee, I'm really sorry I wasn't able to help you move yesterday. I wasn't feeling well, and I had to stay in bed all day. I'm feeling much better now. Call me. Maybe we can get together soon. *[beep]*

Answers

1. d

2. e

3. a

4. c

5. b

EXPANSION ACTIVITY

Ask the class the following questions:

What day of the week did Jim move?
Did Jim's friends help him?
In your opinion, which of his friends' excuses were good excuses? Which were bad excuses?
How do you think Jim felt on moving day?

 WHAT ARE THEY SAYING?

FOCUS

- Giving Excuses

Have students talk about the people and the situation and then create role plays based on the scene. Students may refer back to previous lessons as a resource, but they should not simply reuse specific conversations.

Note: You may want to assign this exercise as written homework, having students prepare their role plays, practice them the next day with other students, and then present them to the class.

Teacher's Notes

GRAMMAR

MUST

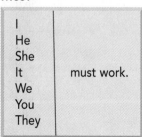

I He She It We You They	must work.

I He She It We You They	mustn't eat candy.

MUSTN'T VS. DON'T HAVE TO

I **don't have to** stop eating cookies.
But I **mustn't** eat as many cookies as I did before.

MUST VS. SHOULD

Should I stop eating rich desserts?
You **must** stop eating rich desserts.

COUNT/NON-COUNT NOUNS: NON-COUNT

He must eat	more less	bread. fish. meat.

COUNT

He must eat	more fewer	cookies. potatoes. eggs.

FUNCTIONS

ASKING FOR ADVICE

Should I *stop eating rich desserts?*

What should I do?

Do you have any advice?
Do you have any suggestions?

OFFERING ADVICE

You should *go to my doctor.*
I think you should *drink some hot tea.*

INQUIRING ABOUT OBLIGATION

Do you have to *stop eating ice cream?*

EXPRESSING OBLIGATION

You must *eat less bread.*
You must *stop eating rich desserts.*

I mustn't *eat as much ice cream as I did before.*

ASKING FOR AND REPORTING INFORMATION

The doctor told *him he's a little too heavy.*

What did *the doctor* say?

EXPRESSING WORRY

I'm really worried about *your heart.*

EXPRESSING WANT–DESIRE

I want to *get a medical checkup.*

NEW VOCABULARY

Medical Checkup

blood pressure
blood test
cardiogram
checkup
chest X-ray
examination room
height
lab technician
measure
medical checkup
nurse
physical examination
pulse
scale
stethoscope
weight
X-ray
X-ray technician

Medical Problems

bloody nose
hiccups

The Body

back
blood
chest
finger
heart
knee
nose

Foods

apple cake
beef stew
dog biscuits
fruit
grapefruit
margarine
potato chips

Construction

blueprints
bricks
cement
construction materials
electrical wiring
wiring
wood

Verbs

build-built
come in
examine
fall down
last
lead
lose weight
measure
require
rub

Expressions of Obligation

must
must not
supposed to

Adjectives

annual
awful
complete
fatty
lean
overweight
own
rich (fatty)
serious
worried
yearly

Determiners

fewer
less

Miscellaneous

cookbook
diet
exactly
hearing (n)
ice
ingredients
instructions

EXPRESSIONS

as a matter of fact
take life a little easier

Text Page 105: Chapter Opening Page

Vocabulary Preview

You may want to present these words before beginning the chapter, or you may choose to wait until they first occur in a specific lesson. If you choose to present them at this point, here are some suggestions:

1. Have students look at the illustrations on text page 105 and identify the words they already know.

2. Present the vocabulary. Say each word and have the class repeat it chorally and individually. Check students' understanding and pronunciation of the words.

3. Practice the vocabulary as a class, in pairs, or in small groups. Have students cover the word list and look at the pictures. Practice the words in the following ways:

   • Say a word and have students tell the number of the illustration.

   • Give the number of an illustration and have students say the word.

FOCUS

- Steps in a Medical Checkup
- Review of Future: *Will* and the Past Tense

CLOSE UP

RULE:	Many common verbs have irregular past tense forms.

EXAMPLES:	**Present**	**Past**
	come	came
	lead	led
	say	said
	shake	shook
	stand	stood
	take	took

NTRODUCING THE MODEL

1. Have students look at the model illustration.
2. Set the scene: "Two friends are talking."
3. Present the model.
4. Full-Class Repetition.
5. Ask students if they have any questions. Check understanding of new vocabulary: *medical checkup, complete.*
6. Group Choral Repetition.
7. Choral Conversation.
8. Call on one or two pairs of students to present the dialog.

INTRODUCING THE CHECKUP

1. Set the scene: "One friend is telling the other what will happen when she goes to the doctor for a medical checkup."
2. For each step of the checkup:

   a. Have students look at the illustration.
   b. Have students listen as you read or play the audio one or more times.
   c. Have students repeat chorally.
   d. Ask students if they have any questions. Check understanding of new vocabulary.

> **New Vocabulary**
>
> 1. scale
>   measure
>   height
>   weight
> 2. nurse
>   blood pressure
> 3. lab technician
>   blood tests
> 4. X-ray technician
>   chest X-ray
> 5. lead
>   examination
>   room
> 6. come in
> 8. examine
>   nose
> 9. heart
>   stethoscope
> 10. pulse
> 11. cardiogram

Vocabulary Note

A cardiogram is a procedure used to detect and diagnose heart problems. It is sometimes referred to as an E.K.G.

e. Call on a few students to present each step of the checkup.

3. Review the checkup, using these key words on the board:

> 1. stand/scale/nurse/measure/ height/weight
> 2. nurse/take/blood pressure
> 3. lab technician/do/blood tests
> 4. X-ray technician/take/ chest X-ray
> 5. nurse/lead/examination room
> 6. doctor/come in/shake hands/say "hello"
> 7. ask/questions/health
> 8. examine/eyes/ears/nose/throat
> 9. listen/heart/stethoscope
> 10. take/pulse
> 11. do/cardiogram
> 12. doctor/talk/health

a. With books closed, point to each step and have students listen and repeat chorally as you read the steps to the examination again or play the audio.

b. Next, call on individual students to retell the steps.

c. Review the checkup by asking the following questions:

> Why do you have to stand on a scale?
> Who will take your blood pressure?
> What will the lab technician do?
> What will the X-ray technician do?
> Where will the nurse lead you?
> What will the doctor say when she sees you?
> What will the doctor ask you about?
> What will the doctor examine?
> How will the doctor listen to your heart?
> Will the doctor take your pulse?
> Then what will the doctor do?
> Finally, what will the doctor talk with you about?

YOUR CHECKUP (Text Page 107)

1. Write the following irregular past tense forms on the board:

> come–came   shake–shook
> lead–led   stand–stood
> say–said   take–took

Have students repeat them after you.

2. Students pretend they had a checkup yesterday and tell what happened.

a. Have students look at the illustrations.

b. Call on individual students to present each checkup step.

c. Do Choral Repetition.

d. Call on one or two students to tell about the whole checkup.

Answer Key

> 1. I stood on a scale, and the nurse measured my height and my weight.
> 2. The nurse took my blood pressure.
> 3. The lab technician did some blood tests.
> 4. The X-ray technician took a chest X-ray.
> 5. Then the nurse led me into an examination room.
> 6. The doctor came in, shook my hand, and said "hello."
> 7. He asked me some questions about my health.
> 8. Then, he examined my eyes, ears, nose, and throat.
> 9. Next, he listened to my heart with a stethoscope.
> 10. After that, he took my pulse.
> 11. Then, he did a cardiogram.
> 12. Finally, the doctor talked with me about my health.

WORKBOOK

Page 103

EXPANSION ACTIVITIES

1. Match the Sentences

a. Make the following set of split sentence cards:

The nurse will measure	your height and your weight.
The nurse will take	your blood pressure.
The lab technician will do	some blood tests.
The X-ray technician will take	a chest X-ray.
The nurse will lead you into	an examination room.
The doctor will shake	your hand.
The doctor will ask you some	questions about your health.
The doctor will examine	your eyes, nose, ears, and throat.
The doctor will listen to your heart	with a stethoscope.
The doctor will take	your pulse.

b. Distribute a card to each student.

c. Have students memorize the sentence portion on their cards, then walk around the room trying to find their corresponding match.

d. Then have pairs of students say their completed sentences aloud to the class.

2. Concentration

a. Use the cards from the above activity. Place them face down in four rows of 5 each.

b. Divide the class into two teams. The object of the game is for students to find the matching cards. Both teams should be able to see all the cards, since *concentrating* on their location is an important part of playing the game.

c. A student from Team 1 turns over two cards. If they match, the student picks up the cards, that team gets a point, and the student takes another turn. If the cards don't match, the student turns them face down, and a member of Team 2 takes a turn.

d. The game continues until all the cards have been matched. The team with the most correct matches wins the game.

Variation: This game can also be played in groups or pairs.

3. Tic Tac Vocabulary

a. Write the following words on the board:

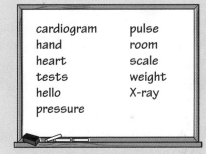

cardiogram	pulse
hand	room
heart	scale
tests	weight
hello	X-ray
pressure	

b. Have students draw a tic tac grid on a piece of paper and fill it in with any nine of the words on the board.

c. Say the beginnings of the following sentences and tell students to cross out the word that finishes each sentence:

I stood on a . . .
The nurse measured my height and my . . .
The nurse took my blood . . .
The lab technician did some blood . . .
The X-ray technician took a chest . . .
The nurse led me into an examination . . .
The doctor shook my . . .
The doctor said . . .
The doctor listened to my . . .
The doctor did a . . .
The doctor took my . . .

(continued)

d. The first student to cross out three words in a straight line—either horizontally, vertically, or diagonally—wins the game.

e. Have the winner call out the words to check for accuracy.

4. Miming

a. Write the following actions on cards:

take someone's blood pressure	measure someone's weight and height
take a chest X-ray	examine the eyes, nose, throat, and ears
listen to the heart with a stethoscope	take someone's pulse
do a cardiogram	lead someone into an examination room

b. Have pairs of students take turns picking a card from the pile and pantomiming the action on the card.

c. The class must guess what the person is doing.

Variation: This can be done as a game with competing teams.

5. Put in Order

a. Dictate the following sentences:

> The nurse led me into an examination room.
> The doctor examined me.
> The doctor talked with me about my health.
> The nurse took my blood pressure.
> The doctor said, "hello."
> The nurse measured my height and my weight.
> The doctor asked me some questions.

b. Have students put the sentences in the order of the medical checkup on text pages 106–107.

6. Calling for a Doctor's Appointment

a. Write the following conversational model on the board or on a large poster:

> A. Dr. Lee's office. May I help you?
> B. Yes. I'd like to make an appointment for a checkup with Dr. Lee.
> A. Will this be your first visit to Dr. Lee?
> B. Yes, it will. A friend recommended her to me.
> A. What's your name?
> B. _____.
> A. Okay, (Mr./Miss/Mrs./Ms.) _____. Would you be able to come to the office on _____ at _____?
> B. On _____ at _____? Yes. That will be fine.
> A. What's your telephone number, please?
> B. _____.
> A. Thank you very much, (Mr./Miss/Mrs./Ms.) _____. We'll see you on _____ at _____.
> B. Thank you. Good-bye.
> A. Good-bye.

b. Present the conversation with one of your students, using any date, time, and telephone number you wish.

c. Ask students if they have any questions. Check understanding of *I'd like to = I want to.*

d. Divide the class into pairs and have students practice the conversation.

e. Call on pairs to present their conversations to the class. For added realism, have students hold telephone receivers as they present their conversations.

7. Dictate and Discuss

a. Divide the class into pairs or small groups.

b. Dictate sentences such as the following and then have students discuss them:

> You should have a checkup every three years.
> A good doctor asks a lot of questions.
> A good doctor gives complete examinations.
> A good doctor is always friendly and polite.
> Technicians and nurses aren't important in your checkup.

c. Call on students to share their opinions with the rest of the class.

FOCUS

- Must
- *Less* with Non-Count Nouns
- *Fewer* with Count Nouns

CLOSE UP

RULE: The modal *must* expresses obligation or necessity. The modal *must* is an auxiliary verb that combines with the base form of the verb. It doesn't contract with subject pronouns.

EXAMPLES: I **must** eat fewer cookies.
You **must** eat less bread.
She **must** eat more lean meat.
He **must** eat fewer eggs.

Count and non-count nouns take different determiners.

RULE: The determiner *less* is used with non-count nouns.

EXAMPLES: You must eat **less** candy.
You must eat **less** fatty meat.

RULE: The determiner *fewer* is used with count nouns.

EXAMPLES: You must eat **fewer** cookies.
You must eat **fewer** rich desserts.

RULE: The determiner *more* is used with both count and non-count nouns.

EXAMPLES: You must eat **more** green vegetables. *(count noun)*
You must eat **more** margarine. *(non-count noun)*

GETTING READY

1. Introduce *must*.

   a. Write on the board:

   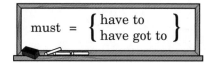

   $$must = \begin{Bmatrix} \text{have to} \\ \text{have got to} \end{Bmatrix}$$

b. Give a few examples of strong obligations or rules. For example:

   The school says we must study hard, and we must always do our homework.

   Our supervisor says we must arrive at work on time, and we must work very hard.

2. Introduce *less* and *fewer*.

a. Write on the board: less Say:

> Yesterday Fred ate too much candy and he felt terrible. Today he's going to eat *less candy*.

> Last week Judy bought too much milk. She didn't need all of it. This week she's going to buy *less milk*.

b. Write on the board: fewer Say:

> In 2000 Susan had 4 accidents while she was driving. In 2001 she had *fewer accidents*—she had only 2!

> Last night Antonio made vegetable stew, but he put in too many onions. Next time he's going to put in *fewer onions*.

INTRODUCING THE MODEL

1. Have students look at the illustration.

2. Set the scene: "The doctor is talking to Henry."

3. Present the model.

4. Ask students if they have any questions. Check understanding of new vocabulary: *yearly checkup, diet, potato chips, fruit.*

5. Talk about Henry's diet. Write the diet on the board.

a. Point to *bread* and say: "He must eat less bread." Have students repeat chorally.

b. Point to *cookies* and say: "He must eat fewer cookies." Have students repeat chorally.

c. Point to each of the other foods in the left column and have students respond chorally and individually:

He must eat $\begin{Bmatrix} \text{less} \\ \text{fewer} \end{Bmatrix}$ _____.

d. Point to each of the foods in the right column and have students respond chorally and individually:

He must eat more _____.

SIDE BY SIDE EXERCISES

Answer Key

1. (−) She must eat less fatty meat, fewer potatoes, less rice, and fewer rich desserts.
   (+) Also, she must eat more lean meat, more grapefruit, and more green vegetables.
2. (−) He must eat less butter, fewer eggs, less cheese, and less ice cream.
   (+) Also, he must eat more margarine and more yogurt, and he must drink more skim milk.
3. (−) He must eat less fatty meat and fewer dog biscuits.
   (+) Also, he must eat more lean meat, and he must drink more water.

Exercises 1–3:

For each exercise:

1. Have students look at the illustration in the book.

2. Read the introduction.

3. Ask students if they have any questions. Introduce new vocabulary.

> **New Vocabulary**
>
> 1. annual
>   fatty meat
>   rich
>   lean meat
>   grapefruit
> 2. worried
>   margarine
> 3. dog biscuits

Language Note

Rich desserts: When referring to desserts, the adjective *rich* usually means that the dessert is made with a lot of butter or cream.

4. Call on individual students to tell about each food item. For example:

fatty meat: "She must eat less fatty meat."

(For additional practice, do Choral Repetition.)

5. After telling about each individual food, call on one or two students to tell the whole diet.

Exercise 4: Read the introduction. Ask students if they have any questions. Check understanding of new vocabulary: *physical examination, overweight.* Call on individual students to tell about their *diets.*

WORKBOOK

Pages 104–106

EXPANSION ACTIVITIES

1. Food Confessions

a. Set the scene: "I always eat too many cookies. My doctor says I must eat fewer cookies and more fruit."

b. Write the following on the board:

> I always (eat/drink) too (much/many)
> _____.
> My doctor says I must (eat/drink)
> (less/fewer) _____ and more _____.

c. Give each student a word card with two food items. For example:

candy fruit	potatoes vegetables	soda milk
french fries carrots	fatty meat fish	salt pepper
rich desserts apples and oranges	chocolate cake pears and grapes	butter margarine
salt pepper	chocolate cake oranges	cookies yogurt

d. Have each student make a *food confession,* using the model on the board. For example:

> I always eat too much candy.
> My doctor says I must eat less candy and more fruit.

e. Have students continue the activity, using any other food items they wish.

2. Drawing Game

a. Write on two sets of cards as many of the following food vocabulary items as you wish:

bread	fish	vegetables	fruit
candy	potato chips	lean meat	fatty meat
grapefruit	rich desserts	butter	eggs
cheese	dog biscuits	rice	potatoes

b. Divide the class into two teams. Have each team sit together in a different part of the room.

c. Place each set of cards on a table or desk in front of the room. Also place a pad of paper and pencil next to each team's set of cards.

d. When you say, "Go!", a person from each team comes to the table, picks a card from that team's pile, draws the item on the card, and shows the drawing to the rest of the team. The team then guesses what the word is.

e. When a team correctly guesses a word, another team member picks a card and draws the word written on that card.

(continued)

f. Continue until each team has guessed all the words in their pile.

g. The team that guesses the words in the shortest time wins the game.

3. Category Dictation

a. Have students draw two columns on a piece of paper. At the top of one column, have students write Healthy Foods. At the top of the other column, have them write Unhealthy Foods.

b. Dictate various food items from the text, and have students write them in the appropriate column. For example:

Healthy Foods	Unhealthy Foods
lean meat	fatty meat
fruit	rich desserts
vegetables	potato chips

Variation: Repeat with the column headings Less and Fewer.

4. Ranking

a. Dictate the following food items to the class:

potato chips	butter
fish	rice
vegetables	eggs
meat	cheese
fruit	chocolate cake

b. Have students rank these food items from the *healthiest* to the *least healthy*, with the first being the *healthiest*.

c. As a class, in pairs, or in small groups, have students compare their lists.

5. Grammar Chain

a. Write the following *conversational model* on the board:

A. I like to eat _____.
B. You must eat (fewer/less) _____
   and more _____.
   I like to eat _____.

b. Start the chain game.

Teacher: I like to eat cookies.

c. Student A responds with advice, based on the model on the board, and then continues the chain by speaking to Student B. For example:

Student A: You must eat fewer cookies and more fruit. *[to Student B]* I like to eat potato chips.

Student B: You must eat fewer potato chips and more fresh vegetables. *[to Student C]* I like to eat ice cream.

6. Telephone

a. Divide the class into large groups. Have each group sit in a circle.

b. Whisper the following advice to one student:

"If you want to lose weight, you must eat less bread, fewer potatoes, less candy, and fewer rich desserts. Also, you must eat more fish, more green vegetables, and more fruit."

c. The first student whispers the advice to the second student, and so forth around the circle. The student listening may ask for clarification by saying, "I'm sorry. Could you repeat that?"

d. When the message gets to the last student, that person says it aloud. Is it the same message you started with? The group with the most accurate message wins.

7. Good Advice or Bad Advice?

Say sentences such as the following, and have students decide if you're giving them *good advice* or *bad advice*:

If you want to lose weight, you must eat more cookies.
If you want to lose weight, you must eat less bread.
If you want to lost weight, you must eat fewer green vegetables and more candy.

If you want to lose weight, you must eat less
    lean meat and more fatty meat.
If you want to lose weight, you must drink more
    water.
If you want to lose weight, you must eat less
    candy and more fruit.
If you want to lose weight, you must eat more
    potatoes and less fish.

Variation: Call on students to make similar
statements using any food vocabulary they wish.
Have others decide if their advice is *good* or *bad*
for someone who wants to lose weight.

8. Find the Right Person

a. Collect information about students' favorite
    unhealthy foods and how often they eat
    them.

b. Put this information on a handout in the
    following form:

Find someone who . . .

1. eats potato chips every day.   _____
2. goes to an ice-cream shop   _____
    twice a week.
3. likes to put a lot of butter   _____
    on bread.
4. makes french fries with a   _____
    lot of oil.
5. drinks 3 cans of soda   _____
    every day.

---

c. Have students circulate around the room,
    asking each other questions to identify the
    above people.

d. The first student to identify all the people
    wins.

 LISTENING

**Listen and choose the correct word to
complete the sentence.**

1. A. I had my yearly checkup today.
    B. What did the doctor say?
    A. She said I must eat fewer . . .

2. A. I had my annual checkup today.
    B. What did the doctor say?
    A. He said I must eat less . . .

3. A. How was your medical checkup?
    B. Okay. The doctor said I must drink
    less . . .

4. A. Did the doctor put you on a diet?
    B. Yes. She said I must eat fewer . . .

5. A. I went to my doctor for an examination
    today.
    B. Oh. What did the doctor say?
    A. He said I must eat less . . .

6. A. My doctor put me on a diet today.
    B. Really?
    A. Yes. I must eat fewer . . .

Answers

1. b

2. a

3. a

4. b

5. a

6. b

 Make a List!

Assign this as homework. Encourage students
to use dictionaries to find new words they want
to use. In class, have students compare their
lists.

READING *Carol's Apple Cake / Paul's Beef Stew*

FOCUS

• Fewer/Less

NEW VOCABULARY

Story 1	Story 2
apple cake	awful
as a matter of fact	beef stew
cookbook	
ingredients	
instructions	
require	
supposed to	

READING THE STORIES

Optional: Preview the stories by having students talk about the story titles and/or illustrations. You may choose to introduce new vocabulary beforehand, or have students encounter the new vocabulary within the context of the reading.

1. Have students read silently, or follow along silently as the stories are read aloud by you, by one or more students, or on the audio program.

2. Ask students if they have any questions. Check understanding of vocabulary.

3. Check students' comprehension, using some or all of the following questions:

   Story 1
   What did Carol bake yesterday?
   Why couldn't she follow all the instructions in her cookbook?
   What did she use?
   What was the result?

Story 2
What did Paul cook yesterday?
Why couldn't he follow all the instructions in his cookbook?
What did he use?
What was the result?

✓ READING *CHECK-UP*

WHAT'S THE WORD?

1. Have students look at the illustration in the book.

2. Introduce the following new vocabulary:

blueprints	exactly
bricks	fall down
build–built	last (v)
cement	own
construction materials	require
electrical wiring	wood

3. Have students complete the exercise on their own and then share their responses with the class.

Answers

1. less
2. fewer
3. less
4. fewer
5. less
6. fewer

READING EXTENSION

Have students discuss the following questions:

When you cook, do you follow recipes?
Do you ever use or put in less of an ingredient than the recipe says?
Why or why not?
When was the last time you made something that tasted terrible?
What was it?
What happened?

FOCUS

- Mustn't
- Mustn't vs. Don't Have to

CLOSE UP

RULE:	The affirmative forms of *have to* and *must* both express a strong obligation to do something. The negative form of *have to* expresses no obligation to do something.
EXAMPLES:	I **don't have to stop** eating ice cream. *(I can still eat ice cream.)*
	He **doesn't have to stop** eating cookies. *(He can still eat cookies.)*
RULE:	The negative form of *must* expresses the strong obligation *not* to do something. *Must* contracts with *not*.
EXAMPLES:	I **mustn't eat** as much ice cream as I did before. *(I can't eat as much ice cream as I did before.)*
	He **mustn't** eat as many cookies as he did before. *(He can't eat as many as he did before.)*
RULE:	Some verbs, such as *stop*, are commonly followed by gerunds.
EXAMPLES:	Do you have to **stop eating** candy? She doesn't have to **stop eating** butter.

INTRODUCING THE MODELS

There are two model conversations. Introduce and practice each separately. For each model:

1. Have students look at the model illustration.

2. Set the scene:

   Model 1: "A wife and husband are talking."
   Model 2: "A mother and son are talking."

3. Present the model.

4. Full Class Repetition.

Pronunciation Note

The pronunciation focus of Chapter 11 is ***Must & Mustn't*** (text page 114). Model this pronunciation at this point (I must lose some weight. I mustn't eat as much ice cream.) and encourage students to incorporate it into their language practice.

5. Ask students if they have any questions. Check understanding of new vocabulary: *lose weight, as much / many _____ as.*

6. Group Choral Repetition.

7. Choral Conversation.

8. Call on one or two pairs of students to present the dialog.

(For additional practice, do Choral Conversation in small groups or by rows.)

SIDE BY SIDE EXERCISES

Examples

1. A. I had my yearly checkup today.
    B. What did the doctor say?
    A. He said I'm a little too heavy and I must lose some weight.
    B. Do you have to stop eating candy?
    A. No. I don't have to stop eating candy. But I mustn't eat as much candy as I did before.

2. A. Billy had his yearly checkup today.
    B. What did the doctor say?
    A. She said he's a little too heavy and he must lose some weight.
    B. Does he have to stop eating french fries?
    A. No. He doesn't have to stop eating french fries. But he mustn't eat as many french fries as he did before.

1. **Exercise 1:** Call on two students to present the dialog. Then do Choral Repetition and Choral Conversation practice.

2. **Exercise 2:** Same as above.

3. **Exercises 3–4:** Either Full Class Practice or Pair Practice.

WORKBOOK

Pages 107–108

EXPANSION ACTIVITIES

1. Beanbag Toss: Diet Advice

Have students toss a beanbag back and forth. The student to whom the beanbag is tossed says one food forbidden on a diet. For example:

Student 1: You must stop eating french fries.
Student 2: You must stop eating candy.
Student 3: You must stop eating fast food.

2. Survey

a. Have students interview each other for advice on how to lose weight.

b. Have students report back to the class about their interviews.

Variation: Have students also interview friends and family members and report to the class.

3. Rules of the School

a. Have students make up a set of rules for an imaginary school. (Have students give the school a name.) Write the rules on the board as students say them. For example:

Students mustn't talk during class.
Students mustn't wear jeans.

b. Write on the board:

A. Can students _____?
B. { Yes, they can.
     No. They mustn't _____.

c. Call on pairs of students to create conversations about the school. For example:

A. Can students eat during class?
B. Yes, they can. They can eat whenever they want.

A. Can students have long hair?
B. No. They mustn't have long hair. They must have short hair.

4. Students' Rules

a. Have students work in small groups to brainstorm what they think the rules for the class should be.

b. Have each group share their ideas with the rest of the students.

c. Have the class vote on the ten best rules. Post them on the wall.

5. More Rules and Regulations

a. Write on the board:

You must _____.
You mustn't _____.

b. Brainstorm with students rules and regulations in different settings, such as at home, on the bus, on the subway, at work, in the library, in a store. For example:

<u>In the Library</u>
You mustn't eat or drink.
You must be quiet.
You must show your bag when you leave.

Text Page 112: Really, Doctor?

FOCUS

• Must vs. Should

INTRODUCING THE MODEL

1. Have students look at the model illustration.

2. Set the scene: "Mr. Jones is in the doctor's office. He had a checkup a few minutes ago, and now the doctor is talking to him."

3. Present the model.

4. Full-Class Repetition.

5. Ask students if they have any questions. Check understanding of new vocabulary: *stop, serious.*

6. Group Choral Repetition.

7. Choral Conversation.

8. Call on one or two pairs of students to present the dialog.

   (For additional practice, do Choral Conversation in small groups or by rows.)

SIDE BY SIDE EXERCISES

Examples

1. A. I'm really worried about your knees.
   B. Really, Doctor? Should I stop jogging?
   A. (Mr./Miss/Mrs./Ms.) _____! You MUST stop jogging! If you don't, you're going to have serious problems with your knees some day.

2. A. I'm really worried about your back.
   B. Really, Doctor? Should I start doing exercises?
   A. (Mr./Miss/Mrs./Ms.) _____! You MUST start doing exercises! If you don't, you're going to have serious problems with your back some day.

1. **Exercise 1:** Check understanding of the word *knee*. Call on two students to present the dialog. Then do Choral Repetition and Choral Conversation practice.

2. **Exercise 2:** Check understanding of the word *back*. Same as above.

3. **Exercises 3–5:** Either Full-Class Practice or Pair Practice.

> ### New Vocabulary
> 4. take life a little easier
> 5. hearing (n)

4. **Exercise 6:** Have students use the model as a guide to create their own conversations, using vocabulary of their choice. Encourage students to be *playful* as well as realistic. Possible cues include:

   blood pressure
   stop eating so much salt

   teeth
   stop eating so much candy

   weight
   go on a diet

   eyes
   stop reading by candlelight

   back
   stop lifting heavy things

This exercise can be done orally in class or for written homework. If you assign it for homework, do one example in class to make sure students understand what's expected. Have students present their conversations in class the next day.

WORKBOOK

Page 109

1. Different Emotions

Have students practice reading the model conversation, using any combination of these different emotions:

Speaker A is just a little worried about his patient.
Speaker A is very upset with his patient.
Speaker B can't believe the problem is serious.
Speaker B believes the problem is serious.

Encourage students to expand the conversation any way they wish.

Variation: Call on pairs of students to present their conversations, and have the class guess what emotions the speakers are conveying.

2. Just Do It!

a. Write the following conversational model on the board:

> A. I know I should _____, but I can't.
> B. I don't believe that. If you really want to _____, you can! As my _____ always says, you have to stop talking about it and just do it!

b. Divide the class into pairs and have students create conversations based on the model on the board. For example:

A. I know I should go on a diet, but I can't.
B. I don't believe that. If you really want to go on a diet, you can! As my Uncle Charlie always says, you have to stop talking about it and just do it!

A. I know I should study harder, but I can't.
B. I don't believe that. If you really want to study harder, you can! As my grandmother always says, you have to stop talking about it and just do it!

3. What Do They Tell Everybody?

Have students listen as you read the first situation below. Then read each of the others and call on a student to complete the answer according to the model.

1. Jane stopped jogging because she had problems with her knees. Now she tells everyone:

    "You must stop jogging! If you don't stop jogging, I'm sure you'll have problems with your knees!"

2. Fred stopped eating rich foods because he had problems with his heart. Now he tells everyone:

    "_____!"

3. Carol stopped eating candy because she had problems with her teeth. Now she tells everyone:

    "_____!"

4. Sam stopped eating salt because he had problems with his blood pressure. Now he tells everyone:

    "_____!"

5. Sally stopped eating spicy foods because she had problems with her stomach. Now she tells everyone:

    "_____!"

6. Edward started doing exercises because he had problems with his back. Now he tells everyone:

    "_____!"

7. Sandra started swimming because she had problems with her weight. Now she tells everyone:

    "_____!"

(continued)

EXPANSION ACTIVITIES (Continued)

4. Class Discussion: Healthy Habits

The situations in this lesson are about developing a healthy lifestyle. Have students write and talk about healthy habits.

a. Have groups of students brainstorm healthy habits.

b. Have students share their ideas with the class.

5. Find the Right Person

a. Collect information about students' healthy habits.

b. Put this information on a handout in the following form:

Find someone who . . .
1. jogs every day. _____
2. likes to eat fruit. _____
3. takes life easy. _____
4. does exercises every day. _____
5. drinks a lot of water every day. _____

c. Have students circulate around the room, asking each other questions to identify the above people.

d. The first student to identify all the people wins.

How to Say It!

> **Asking for Advice:** In U.S. culture, it is not considered polite to offer advice without being asked first. Three ways to ask for advice are presented here.

1. Set the scene: "A grandson is talking to his grandmother."

2. Present the expressions.

3. Full-Class Repetition.

4. Ask students if they have any questions. Check understanding of the expressions.

5. Group Choral Repetition.

 INTERACTIONS

1. Have students listen to the introduction to home remedies as you read from the text. Or you may wish to call on students to read the introduction.

2. Ask students if they have any questions. Check understanding of new vocabulary: *finger, rub, ice, bloody nose, hiccups.*

3. Divide the class into pairs.

4. Have the pairs practice conversations in which Speaker A asks for advice, and Speaker B offers a home remedy solution to Speaker A's medical problem. Speaker A should use any of the three expressions for asking for advice introduced in the *How to Say It!* section. For example:

   A. I have a cold. Do you have any advice?
   B. I think you should go home and go to sleep.

   A. I have a cold. Do you have any suggestions?
   B. I think you should wear a heavy sweater.

5. Have the pairs present their conversations to the class, and have students discuss whether or not they agree with other people's home remedy solutions.

EXPANSION ACTIVITIES

1. **What's the Medical Problem?**

   a. Have students write a remedy for a common medical problem, such as:

a bloody nose	a toothache
the hiccups	a headache
a cold	a stomachache
a backache	stress

   b. Have students read their remedies aloud without naming the medical problem. The class must listen and try to identify the medical problem.

2. **Class Publication**

   Have students compile their home remedies and publish them in a booklet.

WORKBOOK

Page 110

PRONUNCIATION

> **Must & Mustn't:** The /t/ in the middle of *mustn't* is not pronounced.

Focus on Listening

Practice the sentences in the left column. Say each sentence or play the audio one or more times. Have students listen carefully and repeat.

Focus on Pronunciation

Practice the sentences in the right column. Have students say each sentence and then listen carefully as you say it or play the audio.

If you wish, have students continue practicing the sentences to improve their pronunciation.

 JOURNAL

Have students write their journal entries at home or in class. Encourage students to use a dictionary to look up words they would like to use. Students can share their written work with other students if appropriate. Have students discuss what they have written as a class, in pairs, or in small groups.

 CHAPTER SUMMARY

GRAMMAR

1. Divide the class into pairs or small groups.
2. Have students take turns forming sentences from the words in the grammar boxes. Student A says a sentence, and Student B points to the words from each column that are in the sentence. Then have students switch: Student B says a sentence, and Student A points to the words.

KEY VOCABULARY

Have students ask you any questions about the meaning or pronunciation of the vocabulary. If students ask for the pronunciation, repeat after the student until the student is satisfied with his or her own pronunciation.

EXPANSION ACTIVITIES

1. **Do You Remember the Words?**

   Check students' retention of the vocabulary depicted on the opening page of Chapter 11 by doing the following activity:

   a. Have students open their books to page 105 and cover the list of vocabulary words.

   b. Either call out a number and have students tell you the word, or say a word and have students tell you the number.

   Variation: You can also do this activity as a game with competing teams.

2. **Student-Led Dictation**

   a. Tell each student to choose a word or phrase from the Key Vocabulary list on text page 114 and look at it very carefully.

   b. Have students take turns dictating their words to the class. Everybody writes down that student's word.

   c. When the dictation is completed, call on different students to write each word on the board to check the spelling.

3. **Beanbag Toss**

   a. Call out the topic: *Medical Checkup Words.*

   b. Have students toss a beanbag back and forth. The student to whom the beanbag is tossed must name a word in that category. For example:

      Student 1: doctor
      Student 2: X-ray
      Student 3: heart

   c. Continue until all the words in the category have been named.

Variation: You can also do this activity as a game with competing teams.

4. **Letter Game**

   a. Divide the class into teams.

   b. Say: "I'm thinking of a food that starts with g."

   c. The first person to raise his or her hand and guess correctly [grapefruit] wins a point for his or her team.

   d. Continue with other letters of the alphabet and food items.

   The team that gets the most correct answers wins the game.

5. **Movable Categories**

   a. Write the foods from the list on text page 114 on separate cards.

   b. Give each student one or two cards.

   c. Call out one of the following categories:

      healthy foods
      things we drink
      fatty foods
      unhealthy foods
      sweet foods
      fresh foods

   d. All those students whose food words are appropriate for the category go to the right side of the room. All the other students go to the left side.

   e. Those who are in the right group call out their words for the class to verify.

   f. Continue with other categories.

1. Board Game: Health Information

a. On poster boards or on manila file folders, make up game boards with a pathway consisting of separate spaces. You may use any theme or design you wish.

b. Divide the class into groups of 2 to 4 students and give each group a game board and a die, and each student something to be used as a playing piece.

c. Give each group a pile of cards face-down with statements written on them. Some sentences should be true, and others false. For example:

> Cheese is a fatty food.
> Jogging can be bad for your knees.
> Skim milk is a fatty food.
> A lab technician does blood tests.
> A cardiogram measures your blood pressure.
> A scale measures your weight.
> A doctor listens to your heart with a
>   stethoscope.
> A doctor takes your pulse on your foot.
> Green vegetables are not healthy.
> Yogurt is a healthy food.
> Fatty meat is healthier than lean meat.
> People shouldn't drink water. They should
>   drink soda.
> Candy is healthier than fruit.
> A checkup is a physical examination.

d. Each student in turn rolls the die, moves the playing piece along the game path, and after landing on a space, picks a card, reads the sentence, and says if it is *true or false*. If the response is correct, the student takes an additional turn.

e. The first student to reach the end of the pathway is the winner.

2. What's Wrong?

a. Divide the class into pairs or small groups.

b. Write several sentences such as the following on the board or on a handout. Some of the sentences should be correct, and others incorrect. For example:

> You must eat less fish.
> She should eat fewer rice.
> They must eat more vegetables.
> You should eat more potatoes.
> We must eat fewer potato chips.
> I should eat less cookies.
> You must eat fewer fatty meat.
> He should to stop jogging.
> She must to start doing exercises.
> You mustn't eat rich desserts.
> He doesn't have stop eating bread.
> Do I should stop eating desserts?

c. The object of the activity is for students to identify which sentences are incorrect and then correct them.

d. Have students compare their answers.

Variation: Do the activity as a game with competing teams. The team that successfully completes the task in the shortest time is the winner.

3. Key Word Role Play

a. Write the following on the board:

> I'm really worried about . . .
> Should I stop . . . ?
> You must . . .
> You mustn't . . .
> You don't have to . . .

b. Divide the class into pairs.

c. Tell each pair to create a role play between a doctor and patient, using the expressions on the board.

d. Call on pairs to present their role plays to the class.

WORKBOOK ANSWER KEY AND LISTENING SCRIPTS

A. MATCHING

1. d
2. g
3. e
4. h
5. a
6. b
7. f
8. c

B. HOW WAS YOUR MEDICAL CHECKUP?

1. b
2. b
3. a
4. b
5. a
6. a
7. b
8. b
9. a
10. b

C. WENDY IS WORRIED ABOUT HER HEALTH

1. fewer
2. less
3. more
4. more
5. fewer
6. less
7. more
8. more
9. less
10. fewer
11. more
12. more
13. fewer
14. less
15. more
16. more

E. FIRST DAY AT A NEW JOB

1. must dress, must type
2. must answer, must repair
3. must arrive, must work
4. must sort, must file
5. must dance, must sing
6. must cook, must speak

F. WHAT'S THE WORD?

1. mustn't
2. mustn't
3. don't have to, mustn't
4. don't have to
5. don't have to, mustn't
6. mustn't
7. doesn't have to

G. THE BUTLER SCHOOL

1. must
2. must
3. must
4. don't have to
5. must
6. don't have to
7. must
8. mustn't
9. must
10. mustn't
11. mustn't
12. must
13. don't have to
14. must

J. LISTENING

Listen and choose the correct answer.

1. Mr. Lopez, I'm really worried about your eyes.
2. Mrs. Parker, I'm concerned about your heart.
3. I saw my doctor today, and she's concerned about my stomach.
4. Ms. Smith, I'm worried about your blood pressure.
5. Ricky, I'm concerned about your hearing.
6. I saw my doctor today, and he's concerned about my knees.

Answers

1. b
2. a
3. a
4. b
5. b
6. a

M. LOUD AND CLEAR

1. Hi, happy, here, hotel, Honolulu Hawaii
2. Howard, have, hand, history homework, half
3. Harry, hurt his head, have, helmet
4. Henry, heavy, height, has, having hot dogs
5. Hilda's husband, healthy, He has, hearing
6. Hillary, happy, has, hiccups, horrible headache

Teacher's Notes

CHAPTER 12 OVERVIEW: Text Pages 115–124

GRAMMAR

FUTURE CONTINUOUS TENSE

(I will)	I'll	
(He will)	He'll	
(She will)	She'll	
(It will)	It'll	be working.
(We will)	We'll	
(You will)	You'll	
(They will)	They'll	

TIME EXPRESSIONS

I'll be staying	for	a few months. a few more hours. a few more minutes.
	until	Friday. 10 o'clock. we reach Milwaukee.

We'll be arriving	at 7 A.M. in a few days.

FUNCTIONS

ASKING FOR AND REPORTING INFORMATION

Will you *be home this evening*?
    Yes, I will. I'll be *reading*.

I won't *be home this evening*.

How long will *your Aunt Gertrude be staying with us*?
How much longer will *you be working on my car*?
How late will *your son be studying this evening*?
When will *we be arriving in Sydney*?
How far will *we be driving today*?
How soon will *Santa Claus be coming*?

INQUIRING ABOUT INTENTION

How long will you *be staying with us?*

EXPRESSING INTENTION

I won't *come over at five.*

INQUIRING ABOUT ABILITY

When can you *come over?*

EXPRESSING ABILITY

I can *come over at* _____ *o'clock.*

OFFERING A SUGGESTION

How about _____ *o'clock?*

ASKING FOR PERMISSION

Can I *come over and visit this evening?*

INQUIRING ABOUT AGREEMENT

Is that okay?
Will that be okay?

EXPRESSING AGREEMENT

Fine.
That'll be fine.

GREETING PEOPLE

Hello.

Hi, *Gloria*. This is *Arthur*.

Hi, *Uncle Frank*! How are you?
    Fine!

LEAVE-TAKING

Good-bye.
I'll see you then.
See you at *five*.

OFFERING TO HELP

I'll be glad to help you.

EXPRESSING WANT–DESIRE

I want to *return the tennis racket I borrowed from you.*

INDICATING UNDERSTANDING

I see.

INITIATING A TOPIC

By the way, . . .

IDENTIFYING

This is *David*.

REQUESTS

May I please speak to *Carol*?

Please tell *Kate* that *Maria* called.

EXPRESSING REGRET

I'm sorry.

GRATITUDE

Thank you.

NEW VOCABULARY

Growing Up

adult
age
get older
middle-aged
senior citizen
young adult

Family

Grandma
Grandpa
relative

Furniture

convertible sofa
cot
couch

Holidays

holiday weekend
Santa Claus
Thanksgiving

Calling on the Telephone

beep
brief message
call back
hold on
moment

Verbs

bathe
borrow
clean out
come over
disturb
exercise
have children
iron
knit
mop
pay bills
reach
rearrange
repaint
retire
sew
stay
work on

Determiners

a couple of
plenty (of)
several

Questions

How far
How late
How long
How much longer
How soon

Miscellaneous

actually
answering machine
bill
career
guest room
hammer
master bedroom
Milwaukee
sometime
trombone
videotape

EXPRESSIONS

a couple of days
by the way
for a few months
from top to bottom
Good-bye.
"Happy Thanksgiving!"
how quickly time flies
I see
I'll see you then.
Is that okay?
look forward to
No, that's okay.
See you at *five*.
take a message
take it easy
That's great!
What's up?

VOCABULARY PREVIEW

You may want to present these words before beginning the chapter, or you may choose to wait until they first occur in a specific lesson. If you choose to present them at this point, here are some suggestions:

1. Have students look at the illustrations on text page 115 and identify the words they already know.

2. Present the vocabulary. Say each word and have the class repeat it chorally and individually. Check students' understanding and pronunciation of the words.

3. Practice the vocabulary as a class, in pairs, or in small groups. Have students cover the word list and look at the pictures. Practice the words in the following ways:

   - Say a word and have students tell the number of the illustration.
   - Give the number of an illustration and have students say the word.

Text Page 116: Will They Be Home This Evening?

- Future Continuous Tense

CLOSE UP

RULE: The future continuous tense is formed with *will* + *be* + verb + *ing*.

EXAMPLES: I'll (I **will**) **be** read**ing**.
He'll (He **will**) **be** sew**ing**.
She'll (She **will**) **be** iron**ing**.
We'll (We **will**) **be** bath**ing** the dog.

RULE: The future continuous tense emphasizes the ongoing nature or duration of activity in the future.

EXAMPLES: Will you be home this evening?
    Yes, I will. I'll be reading *(this evening)*.
Will Harriet be home this evening?
    Yes, she will. She'll be mopping the floor *(this evening)*.

GETTING READY

Introduce the future continuous tense.

1. Put the following on the board:

Alice
practice the piano

Tom
do his homework

Mr. and Mrs. Williams
fix their sink

2. Tell about the Williams family:

The Williams family will be home this evening.
Alice will be practicing the piano.
Tom will be doing his homework.
And Mr. and Mrs. Williams will be fixing their sink.

3. Model the following and have students repeat:

  A. What will Alice be doing this evening?
  B. She'll be practicing the piano.

4. Ask about *Tom* and *Mr. and Mrs. Williams*.

INTRODUCING THE MODEL

1. Have students look at the model illustration.

2. Set the scene: "Two people are talking about this evening."

3. Present the model.

4. Full-Class Repetition.

Pronunciation Note

The pronunciation focus of Chapter 12 is **Contractions with *Will*** (text page 124). Model this pronunciation at this point (*I'll be reading. She'll be ironing.*) and encourage students to incorporate it into their language practice.

5. Ask students if they have any questions.

6. Group Choral Repetition

7. Choral Conversation.

8. Call on one or two pairs of students to present the dialog.

   (For additional practice, do Choral Conversation in small groups or by rows.)

9. Use the words in the box at the top of text page 116 to form sentences with the future continuous tense. Have students repeat chorally. For example:

   I'll be working.
   He'll be working.

SIDE BY SIDE EXERCISES

Examples

1. A. Will Amanda be home this evening?
   B. Yes, she will. She'll be ironing.

2. A. Will Jack be home this evening?
   B. Yes, he will. He'll be sewing.

1. **Exercise 1:** Check understanding of the word *iron*. Call on two students to present the dialog. Then do Choral Repetition and Choral Conversation practice.

2. **Exercise 2:** Check understanding of the word *sew*. Same as above.

3. **Exercises 3–8:** Either Full-Class Practice or Pair Practice.

> **New Vocabulary**
> 3. exercise
> 4. pay bills
> 5. knit
> 6. mop
> 7. bathe
> 8. rearrange

4. **Exercise 9:** Have students use the model as a guide to create their own conversations, using vocabulary of their choice. Encourage students to use dictionaries to find new words they want to use. This exercise can be done orally in class or for written homework. If you assign it for homework, do one example in class to make sure students understand what's expected. Have students present their conversations in class the next day.

WORKBOOK

Page 111

1. Miming Game

a. Write on cards the activities from text page 116 as well as other verbs that describe household work. For example:

iron	sew	exercise
pay bills	mop the floor	knit
bathe the dog	rearrange furniture	wash the windows
clean the refrigerator	plant flowers	fix the car

b. Have students take turns picking a card from the pile and pantomiming the action on the card.

c. The class must guess what the person *will be doing* this evening.

Variation: This can be done as a game with competing teams.

2. Make a Sentence

a. Make a set of split sentence cards such as the following:

She'll be knitting	a sweater.
He'll be bathing	the baby.
They'll be mopping	the floor.
I'll be paying	bills.
We'll be rearranging	furniture.
She'll be sewing	a dress.

I'll be reading	a book.
They'll be painting	the walls.

b. Distribute a card to each student.

c. Have students memorize the sentence portion on their cards, then walk around the room trying to find their corresponding match.

d. Then have pairs of students say their completed sentences aloud to the class.

3. Concentration

a. Use the cards from the above activity. Place them face down in four rows of 4 each.

b. Divide the class into two teams. The object of the game is for students to find the matching cards. Both teams should be able to see all the cards, since *concentrating* on their location is an important part of playing the game.

c. A student from Team 1 turns over two cards. If they match, the student picks up the cards, that team gets a point, and the student takes another turn. If the cards don't match, the student turns them face down, and a member of Team 2 takes a turn.

d. The game continues until all the cards have been matched. The team with the most correct matches wins the game.

Variation: This game can also be played in groups and pairs.

4. Sense or Nonsense?

a. Divide the class into four groups.

b. Using the cards from Activity 2, mix up the cards and distribute sets of cards to each group, keeping the beginning and ending cards in different piles.

(continued)

c. Have students take turns picking up one card from each pile and reading the sentence to the group. For example:

They'll be mopping	a dress.

d. That group decides if the sentence makes *sense* or is *nonsense*.

e. After all the cards have been picked, have the groups lay out all the cards and put together all the sentence combinations that make sense.

5. Telephone

a. Divide the class into large groups. Have each group sit in a circle.

b. Whisper the following story to one student:

"Everybody will be home this evening. Jim will be reading, Tim will be writing, and Kim will be ironing. Don will be cooking, Ron will be baking, and John will be cleaning."

c. The first student whispers the story to the second student, and so forth around the circle. The student listening may ask for clarification by saying "I'm sorry. Could you repeat that?"

d. When the story gets to the last student, that person says it aloud. Is it the same story you started with? The group with the most accurate story wins.

6. Memory Chain

a. Divide the class into groups of 5 or 6 students each.

b. Tell each student to make a statement about what he or she will be doing this weekend.

c. One group at a time, have Student 1 begin. For example:

I'll be studying in the library.

d. Student 2 repeats what Student 1 said and adds a statement about himself or herself. For example:

George will be studying in the library. I'll be visiting my grandparents.

e. Student 3 continues in the same way. For example:

George will be studying in the library. Susan will be visiting her grandparents. I'll be cleaning my apartment.

f. Continue until everyone has had a chance to play the *memory chain*.

7. Will You Be Home?

Use *Side by Side* Picture Cards 36–65, your own visuals of everyday activities, or word cards to review the future continuous tense.

a. Write on the board:

> A. Will _____ be home tomorrow morning?
> B. I think so. ____ probably be _____ all morning.

b. Give visuals to pairs of students and have them create conversations about themselves, using the visuals as cues. For example:

A. Will you be home tomorrow morning?
B. I think so. I'll probably be washing my clothes all morning.

c. Have pairs of students create conversations about other students who are holding visuals. For example:

A. Will (Yoko) be home tomorrow morning?
B. I think so. She'll probably be writing letters all morning.

A. Will (Bill) and (Richard) be home tomorrow morning?
B. I think so. They'll probably be studying all morning.

8. Next Year

a. Write the following cues on the board and tell this story:

Maria Lopez

This year . . .	Next year . . .
live in Mexico City	live in London
speak Spanish	speak English
eat Mexican food	eat English food/ drink tea
study in high school	study at a university

"Maria Lopez is from Mexico City. Next year she's going to go to school in London. A lot of things are going to change in Maria's life. This year she lives in Mexico City. Next year she'll be living in London."

b. Call on students to continue the story about Maria Lopez, using the cues on the board.

c. Have students think of other things Maria Lopez will be doing in London next year.

9. **Class Survey**

a. Have students circulate around the room interviewing each other about their evening plans. Have them ask each other:

Where will you be this evening?
What will you be doing?

b. Have students report their findings to the class. Where will most of your classmates be tonight? What will they be doing?

Text Pages 117–118: Hi, Gloria. This is Arthur./ When Can You Come Over?

FOCUS

- Future Continuous Tense

INTRODUCING THE CONVERSATION (Text Page 117)

1. Have students look at the illustration.

2. Set the scene: "Arthur wants to go out on a date with Gloria, but Gloria doesn't want to go out with him."

3. Present the model.

4. Full-Class Repetition.

5. Ask students if they have any questions. Check understanding of the expressions *come over, sometime, Good-bye, I see.*

6. Call on different pairs of students to present portions of the dialog.

7. Call on one or two pairs of students to present the entire dialog.

WHEN CAN YOU COME OVER? (Text Page 118)

In this exercise, students complete the conversation, using any vocabulary they wish.

1. Role play the conversation with one of your stronger students.

2. Ask students if they have any questions. Check understanding of the expressions *What's up?, Is that okay?, I'll see you then.*

3. Divide the class into pairs and have students complete the conversation.

4. Call on pairs to present their conversations to the class.

Language Note

What's Up? is an informal way of asking someone you know well what the purpose of their call is.

WORKBOOK

Pages 112–113

EXPANSION ACTIVITIES

1. **Different Emotions**

   Have students practice reading the conversation, using the following emotions:

   Gloria is very nice to Arthur.
   Gloria isn't very nice to Arthur.

2. **Do You Remember?**

   a. Have students spend three minutes looking carefully at the conversation between Arthur and Gloria.

   b. Tell students to close their books.

   c. Ask the following questions to see how much they remember about Gloria's excuses:

   What will Gloria be doing this evening?
   What will she be doing tomorrow evening?
   What will she be doing this weekend?
   What will she be doing next Wednesday?
   What will she be doing next spring?

   Variation: Divide the class into teams and do the activity as a game. The team with the most correct answers wins.

3. Would You Like to Come?

a. Write on the board:

> A. I'm _____ ing this Saturday { morning.
> afternoon.
>
> Would you like to come?
> B. I'd really like to, but I can't. I'll be
> _____ ing all day.
> A. That's too bad. Maybe we can
> _____ together sometime soon.

b. Call on pairs of students to extend invitations to each other, using the conversational model and any vocabulary they wish.

Examples:

> A. I'm going jogging this Saturday morning. Would you like to come?
> B. I'd really like to, but I can't. I'll be taking care of my younger sister all day.
> A. That's too bad. Maybe we can go jogging together sometime soon.

> A. I'm going to the movies this Saturday afternoon. Would you like to come?
> B. I'd really like to, but I can't. I'll be painting my apartment all day.
> A. That's too bad. Maybe we can go to the movies together sometime soon.

4. Making an Appointment

a. Write the following on the board:

9:00	read her mail
10:00	talk to a client
11:00	write letters
12:00	have lunch
1:00	have lunch
2:00	go to a meeting
3:00	see a client
4:00	play golf
5:00	_____

b. Set the scene: "You're trying to find a time to meet with your lawyer to talk about something important, but your lawyer is VERY busy."

c. Model the following conversation:

> A. Can I see you at 9 o'clock tomorrow?
> B. I'm sorry. I'll be reading my mail at 9 o'clock.
> A. Hmm. How about 10 o'clock?
> B. I'm sorry. I'll be talking to a client at 10 o'clock.

d. Have pairs of students continue the conversation, using the cues on the board and any others they wish, until they have *finally* arranged a time to meet.

5. Information Gap: Arthur and Amanda's Plans

a. Tell students: "Arthur stopped calling Gloria. He has a new girlfriend, Amanda. This Saturday Arthur and Amanda have big plans. Write out their plans, but divide the information between two different charts. For example:

Chart A:

	Place	Activity
1:00		drink tea and talk
2:00	in the park	
4:00		look at the paintings
7:00	in a restaurant	
9:00		see a play
11:00	at a party	

(continued)

Chart B:

	Place	Activity
1:00	at a cafe	
2:00		take a walk
4:00	at a museum	
7:00		eat dinner
9:00	at a theater	
11:00		dance

b. Divide the class into pairs. Give each member of the pair a different chart. Have students share their information and fill in their charts. For example:

Student A: Where will Arthur and Amanda be at 1:00?

Student B: They'll be at a cafe. [Student A writes the information in Chart A.] What will they be doing?

Student A: They'll be drinking tea and talking.

c. The pairs continue until each has a complete chart.

d. Have students look at their partner's chart to make sure that they have written the information correctly.

Text Page 119: Will You Be Home Today at About Five O'Clock?

FOCUS

* Future Continuous Tense

INTRODUCING THE MODEL

1. Have students look at the illustration.

2. Set the scene: "Julie is calling Richard on the telephone. She has Richard's tennis racket, and she wants to return it to him."

3. Present the model.

4. Full-Class Repetition

5. Ask students if they have any questions. Check understanding of the word *disturb*.

   ### Language Note

   At five: This is a shorter way of saying *at five o'clock*.

6. Group Choral Repetition.

7. Choral Conversation.

8. Call on one or two pairs of students to present the dialog.

SIDE BY SIDE EXERCISES

Examples

In the exercises, students can use any names and times they wish.

---

1. A. Hello *(Tom)*. This is *(Sally)*. I want to return the videotape I borrowed from you last week. Will you be home today at about *(two)* o'clock?
   B. Yes, I will. I'll be repainting the kitchen.
   A. Oh. Then I won't come over at *(two)*.
   B. Why not?
   A. I don't want to disturb you. You'll be repainting the kitchen!
   B. Don't worry. You won't disturb me.
   A. Okay. See you at *(two)*.

---

2. A. Hello *(Nancy)*. This is *(Linda)*. I want to return the hammer I borrowed from you last week. Will you be home today at about *(three)* o'clock?
   B. Yes, I will. I'll be cleaning out the garage.
   A. Oh. Then I won't come over at *(three)*.
   B. Why not?
   A. I don't want to disturb you. You'll be cleaning out the garage!
   B. Don't worry. You won't disturb me.
   A. Okay. See you at *(three)*.

---

1. **Exercise 1:** Introduce the words *videotape, repaint*. Call on two students to present the dialog. Then do Choral Repetition and Choral Conversation practice.

2. **Exercise 2:** Introduce the words *hammer, clean out*. Same as above.

3. **Exercise 3:** Either Full-Class Practice or Pair Practice.

4. **Exercise 4:** Have students use the model as a guide to create their own conversations, using vocabulary of their choice. Encourage students to use dictionaries to find new words they want to use. This exercise can be done orally in class or for written homework. If you assign it for homework, do one example in class to make sure students understand what's expected. Have students present their conversations in class the next day.

WORKBOOK

Pages 114–115

1. Disappearing Dialog

a. Write the model conversation on the board.

b. Ask for two student volunteers to read the conversation.

c. Erase a few of the words from each line of the dialog. Have two different students read the conversation.

d. Erase more words, and call on two more students to read the conversation.

e. Continue erasing words and calling on pairs of students to say the model until all the words have been erased and the dialog has disappeared.

2. Information Gap Handouts

a. Tell students: "Lucy wants to return a book she borrowed from Harriet. She calls her. They both have very busy schedules. What time can she bring the book to Harriet's house?" Write out their schedules on two different charts. For example:

Chart A: Lucy's Schedule

	Place	Activity
10:00	(no plans)	(no plans)
11:00–1:00	library	studying
1:00	school	taking an English class
2:00	(no plans)	(no plans)
3:00–5:00	(no plans)	(no plans)
6:00	health club	exercising
7:00	home	cooking dinner
8:00	(no plans)	(no plans)

Chart B: Harriet's Schedule

	Place	Activity
10:00	health club	exercising
11:00–1:00	home	cleaning the house
1:00	(no plans)	(no plans)
2:00	doctor's office	getting a check-up
3:00–5:00	school	taking a test
6:00	home	getting ready to go out
7:00	restaurant	meeting a friend for dinner
8:00	home	watching TV

b. Divide the class into pairs. Give each member of the pair a different chart. Have students ask and answer questions until they find a time they can meet. For example:

Student A: Harriet, will you be home at ten o'clock?

Student B: No, I won't. I'll be exercising at the health club. How about eleven o'clock? Can you come over then?

Student A: No, I can't. I'll be studying at the library. How about two o'clock?

c. The pairs continue until they find a time to meet.

3. Which One Isn't True?

a. Tell students to write three true statements and one false statement about what they will be doing this weekend. For example:

I'll be studying in the library.
I'll be seeing a movie.
I'll be eating in the most expensive restaurant in town.
I'll be visiting my grandmother.

b. Have students take turns reading their statements to the class, and have the class guess which statement isn't true.

How to Say It!

> **Calling People on the Telephone:** In spoken English, *please* is used frequently when making requests. For example:
>
> May I *please* speak to . . .
> *Please* tell Kate . . .
> *Please* leave your name . . .
>
> On the telephone, it is polite for the caller to identify himself or herself by saying *This is* . . .

There are three model conversations. Introduce each conversation before going on to the next.

1. Set the scene: "Two people are talking on the telephone."

2. Introduce new vocabulary:

   Conversation 1: *hold on, moment*
   Conversation 2: *take a message*
   Conversation 3: *answering machine, brief message, beep, call back*

3. Full-Class Repetition.

4. Ask students if they have any questions.

5. Group Choral Repetition.

6. Have students practice different types of telephone conversations.

7. Call on students to present their *telephone calls* to the class.

 LISTENING

Listen to the messages on Bob's machine. Match the messages.

You have eight messages.

Message Number One: "Hello, Robert. This is Aunt Betty. I'm calling to say hello. Call me back. I'll be home all evening. I'll be ironing my clothes. Talk to you soon. 'Bye." *[beep]*

Message Number Two: "Hi, Bob. This is Melanie. I'm making plans for the weekend. Do you want to do something? Call me when you have a chance. I'll be home all day. I'll

be studying for a big test. Talk to you later." *[beep]*

Message Number Three: "Bob? This is Alan. What's up? I'm calling to tell you I won't be able to play tennis with you this Saturday. I'll be attending my cousin's wedding in Dallas. See you soon." *[beep]*

Message Number Four: "Hello, Mr. Kendall. This is Ms. Wong from the State Street Bank. I'm calling about your application for a loan. We need some more information. Please call me at 472-9138. You can call this evening. I'll be working until 8 P.M. Thank you." *[beep]*

Message Number Five: "Hi, Bob. This is Rick. Nancy and I want to invite you over to dinner at our new apartment. Call us back. We'll be home all weekend. We'll be repainting the living room. 'Bye." *[beep]*

Message Number Six: "Hello, Bob. This is Denise. I got your message last week. Sorry I missed you. Call me back. I'll be home this evening. I'll be paying bills. Take care." *[beep]*

Message Number Seven: "Hello. This is a message for Robert Kendall. I'm calling from Dr. Garcia's office. Dr. Garcia won't be able to see you next month. He'll be visiting hospitals in Russia. Please call so we can change your appointment. Thank you, and have a nice day." *[beep]*

Message Number Eight: "Hello, Bobby? This is Mom. Bobby, are you there? Pick up the phone. I guess you aren't there. Dad and I are thinking of you. How are you? Call us, okay? But don't call this afternoon. We'll be exercising at the health club. Well, talk to you soon, Bobby. 'Bye." *[beep]*

Answers

1.	d	**5.**	a
2.	f	**6.**	c
3.	h	**7.**	e
4.	g	**8.**	b

WORKBOOK

Page 116

📖 READING *Growing Up*

FOCUS

- Future Continuous Tense

NEW VOCABULARY

adult	middle-aged
age	reach
career	retire
get older	senior citizen
have children	take it easy
how quickly time flies	young adult

READING THE STORY

Optional: *Preview the story by having students talk about the story title and/or illustrations. You may choose to introduce new vocabulary beforehand, or have students encounter the new vocabulary within the context of the reading.*

1. Have students read silently, or follow along silently as the story is read aloud by you, by one or more students, or on the audio program.

2. Ask students if they have any questions. Check understanding of vocabulary.

3. Check students' comprehension, using some or all of the following questions:

   What will Jessica be doing soon?
   Will she be a baby very much longer?
   What will Tommy be doing soon?
   Will he be a little boy very much longer?
   What will Kathy be doing soon?
   Will she be a teenager very much longer?
   What will Peter and Sally be doing soon?
   Will they be young adults very much longer?
   What will Walter be doing soon?
   Will he be middle-aged very much longer?

✓ READING *CHECK-UP*

TRUE OR FALSE?

1. True   4. True
2. True   5. False
3. False   6. True

READING EXTENSION

1. Dictate the following stages of life, and have students put them in the correct order:

   a little girl or a little boy
   middle-aged
   baby
   young adult
   senior citizen
   teenager

2. Dictate the following activities, and have students write them next to the appropriate stage of life:

   learning to walk
   learning to read
   shaving for the first time
   going out on dates
   living away from home
   starting a career
   going to college
   getting married
   having children
   buying a house
   retiring
   having grandchildren

3. Have students work in pairs to estimate the ages of each stage of life: *baby, child, teenager, young adult, middle-aged, senior citizen.* Have students share their ideas with the class. Are there different perspectives according to the age of the students?

FOCUS

- Future Continuous Tense
- Time Expressions with *for* and *until*

CLOSE UP

RULE:	The preposition *for* is used in time expressions with a period of time.
EXAMPLES:	**for** a few months **for** a few more hours **for** ten more minutes
RULE:	The preposition *until* is used in time expressions with a point in time.
EXAMPLES:	**until** Friday **until** 8 o'clock

INTRODUCING THE MODEL

1. Have students look at the illustration.
2. Set the scene: "A husband and wife are talking. The husband is upset because his wife's Aunt Gertrude just arrived for a visit."
3. Present the model.
4. Full-Class Repetition.
5. Ask students if they have any questions. Check understanding of new vocabulary: *how long, stay, for a few months*.
6. Group Choral Repetition.
7. Choral Conversation.
8. Call on one or two pairs of students to present the dialog.

   (For additional practice, do Choral Conversation in small groups or by rows.)

SIDE BY SIDE EXERCISES

Examples

1. A. How long will they be staying in Vancouver?
   B. They'll be staying in Vancouver until Friday.
2. A. How much longer will you be working on my car?
   B. I'll be working on your car for a few more hours.

1. **Exercise 1:** Check understanding of the word *until*. Call on two students to present the dialog. Then do Choral Repetition and Choral Conversation practice.
2. **Exercise 2:** Introduce the new expressions *how much longer, work on*. Same as above.

3. Exercises 3–8: Either Full Class Practice or Pair Practice.

WORKBOOK

Pages 117–119

> **New Vocabulary**
>
> 3. how late
> 4. trombone
> 6. how far
>   reach
>   Milwaukee
> 8. how soon

EXPANSION ACTIVITIES

1. Different Emotions

Have students practice reading the model conversation, using these different emotions:

> Speaker A is upset.
> Speaker B is trying to calm Speaker A.
>
> Speaker A isn't upset.
> Speaker B is very upset.

2. Student Predictions

a. Have students think of answers to the following questions:

> Where will you be in (*four*) hours?
> What will you be doing?
> Who will you be with?
> What will you be feeling?
> What will you be thinking?

b. Have students share their answers in small groups.

3. Find the Right Person

a. Collect information from the above activity about students' plans for later in the day.

b. Put this information on a handout in the following form:

> Find someone who . . .
>
> 1. will be working.   _____
> 2. will be exercising.   _____
> 3. will be studying.   _____
> 4. will be riding on a bus.   _____
> 5. will be sleeping.   _____

c. Have students circulate around the room, asking each other questions to identify the above people. For example:

> Student A: Will you be studying in four hours?
> Student B: No, I'll be exercising.

d. The first student to identify all the people wins.

4. Class Vacation

Have students brainstorm a perfect vacation for the whole class!

a. Divide the class into pairs or small groups. Have each group answer the following questions:

> Where will we be going?
> What will we be doing?
> How long will we be staying?
> Where else will we be going?
> What sights will we be seeing?
> What kind of food will we be eating?

b. Have each group present their *dream vacation* to the class.

c. Have the class vote. Which vacation is the best?

5. At the Airport

a. Write the following on the board:

> A. Are you taking a trip?
> B. Yes. I'll be leaving for _____ in a few minutes.
> A. How long _____ staying?
> B. _____ $\begin{Bmatrix} \text{for} \\ \text{until} \end{Bmatrix}$ _____.
> A. That's great! What _____ doing while you're there?
> B. _____.
> A. Well, I hope you have a wonderful time!

b. Set the scene: "You're at the airport, and you're going on a trip. You see a friend and begin talking."

c. Divide the class into pairs and give each pair one of the following cards:

Tokyo 7 days _____	Mexico City Saturday _____	Cairo 12 days _____
Honolulu 2 weeks _____	Rome next Tuesday _____	Seoul a week _____
Rio de Janeiro Thursday _____	Moscow 5 days _____	Vancouver next Monday _____
Paris 3 months _____	New York Sunday _____	Sydney a month _____

d. Have students create conversations using the model on the board and the place and time on their cue cards. Students can use their imaginations to tell what they'll be doing in these places.

e. Call on pairs to present their conversations to the class.

Example:

> A. Are you taking a trip?
> B. Yes. I'll be leaving for Paris in a few minutes.
> A. How long will you be staying?
> B. I'll be staying for 3 months.
> A. That's great! What will you be doing while you're there?
> B. I'll be studying French.
> A. Well, I hope you have a wonderful time!

6. Public Opinion Survey: What Do You Think?

a. Brainstorm with the class interesting events in the news. For example:

> issues in education and schools
> issues in world politics
> a famous person coming to town
> a popular fashion

b. Have each student choose a topic to ask another student about and think of questions about that topic, beginning with the following:

> What do you think?
> How much longer will . . . ?
> How soon will . . . ?
> When will . . . ?

c. Have students interview each other. For example:

> What do you think?
> How much longer will *(Nicki Wilson)* be popular?
> How soon will she be making a new album?
> When will she be popular with middle-aged people?

d. Have students share their findings with the class.

Variation: Have students also interview friends and family members and report to the class.

READING *Happy Thanksgiving!*

FOCUS

- Future Continuous Tense

NEW VOCABULARY

a couple of days	guest room
actually	holiday weekend
convertible sofa	master bedroom
cot	relative
couch	several
from top to bottom	Thanksgiving
Grandma	"Happy Thanksgiving!"
Grandpa	

READING THE STORY

***Optional:** Preview the story by having students talk about the story title and/or illustration. You may choose to introduce new vocabulary beforehand, or have students encounter the new vocabulary within the context of the reading.*

1. Have students read silently, or follow along silently as the story is read aloud by you, by one or more students, or on the audio program.

2. Ask students if they have any questions. Check understanding of vocabulary.

   ### Culture Note

   Thanksgiving is a holiday that is celebrated in the United States on the third Thursday in November. This holiday dates back to the seventeenth century, when the Pilgrim settlers in the original colonies that became the United States celebrated the harvest season. Thanksgiving is a time when families traditionally gather to share a festive holiday meal.

3. Check students' comprehension, using some or all of the following questions:

   What holiday is this week?
   Who will be staying with the writer of the story and his wife during the long holiday weekend?
   How long will Uncle Frank be staying?
   Where will he be sleeping?
   How long will his wife's parents be staying?
   Where will they be sleeping?
   How long will cousin Ben be staying?
   Where will he be sleeping?
   How long will cousin Bertha be staying?
   Where will she be sleeping?
   Where will the writer of the story and his wife be sleeping?
   What will he and his wife be doing for the next few days?
   What will their children be doing for the next few days?

✓ READING *CHECK-UP*

Q & A

1. Call on a pair of students to present the model. Check understanding of the expressions *look foward to, actually, plenty of, by the way, That's great!*

2. Have students work in pairs to create new dialogs.

3. Call on pairs to present their new dialogs to the class.

READING EXTENSION

Have students discuss the following questions in small groups and then share their responses with the class.

What holiday is very special in your family?
How do you celebrate it?
Do many people in your family come to stay?
How do you prepare for the holiday?

PRONUNCIATION

> **Contractions with *Will*:** *Will* commonly contracts with subject pronouns. Students often have difficulty with the pronunciation of these contracted forms.

Focus on Listening

Practice the sentences in the left column. Say each sentence or play the audio one or more times. Have students listen carefully and repeat.

Focus on Pronunciation

Practice the sentences in the right column. Have students say each sentence and then listen carefully as you say it or play the audio.

If you wish, have students continue practicing the sentences to improve their pronunciation.

 JOURNAL

Have students write their journal entries at home or in class. Encourage students to use a dictionary to look up words they would like to use. Students can share their written work with other students if appropriate. Have students discuss what they have written as a class, in pairs, or in small groups

 CHAPTER SUMMARY

GRAMMAR

1. Divide the class into pairs or small groups.
2. Have students take turns forming sentences from the words in the grammar boxes. Student A says a sentence, and Student B points to the words from each column that are in the sentence. Then have students switch: Student B says a sentence, and Student A points to the words.

KEY VOCABULARY

Have students ask you any questions about the meaning or pronunciation of the vocabulary. If students ask for the pronunciation, repeat after the student until the student is satisfied with his or her own pronunciation.

EXPANSION ACTIVITIES

1. Do You Remember the Words?

   Check students' retention of the vocabulary depicted on the opening page of Chapter 12 by doing the following activity:

   a. Have students open their books to page 115 and cover the list of vocabulary words and phrases.

   b. Either call out a number and have students tell you the word or phrase, or say a word or phrase and have students tell you the number.

   Variation: You can also do this activity as a game with competing teams.

2. Student-Led Dictation

   a. Tell each student to choose a word from the Key Vocabulary list on text page 124 look at it very carefully.

   b. Have students take turns dictating their words to the class. Everybody writes down that student's word.

   c. When the dictation is completed, call on different students to write each word on the board to check the spelling.

3. Beanbag Toss

   a. Call out the topic: *Verbs.*

   (continued)

EXPANSION ACTIVITIES (Continued)

b. Have students toss a beanbag back and forth. The student to whom the beanbag is tossed must name a verb from Chapter 12. For example:

Student 1: bathe
Student 2: exercise
Student 3: iron

c. Continue until all the verbs have been named.

Variation: You can also do this activity as a game with competing teams.

4. Letter Game

a. Divide the class into two teams.

b. Say, "I'm thinking of a verb that starts with *g*."

c. The first person to raise his or her hand and guess correctly *[grow up]* wins a point for his or her team.

d. Continue with other letters of the alphabet and verbs.

The team that gets the most correct answers wins the game.

1. **Board Game**

   a. On poster boards or on manila file folders, make up game boards with a pathway consisting of separate spaces. You may use any theme or design you wish.

   b. Divide the class into groups of 2 to 4 students and give each group a game board and a die, and each student something to be used as a playing piece.

   c. Give each group a pile of cards face-down with statements written on them. Some sentences should be correct, and others incorrect. For example:

   > I'll be exercising at home tonight.
   > She'll be staying with us until a few months.
   > They'll be studying for 12:00.
   > We'll driving until tomorrow morning.
   > I can't believe how quickly time flies!
   > He'll be study in the library this Saturday.
   > Don't worry. You won't disturb me.
   > Will you be home tonight at 11:00?
   > I'll be pay bills tonight.
   > She won't be able to come over until 5:00.
   > May please I speak to Kate?
   > Please leave your name, telephone number, and a brief message before the beep.
   > They won't be visiting the doctor again soon.

   d. Each student in turn rolls the die, moves the playing piece along the game path, and after landing on a space, picks a card, reads the sentence, and says if it is *correct* or *incorrect*. If the statement is incorrect, the student must correct it. If the response is correct, the student takes an additional turn.

   e. The first student to reach the end of the pathway is the winner.

2. **Dialog Builder**

   a. Divide the class into pairs.

   b. Write three lines on the board, such as the following:

   > Don't worry.
   > Is that okay?
   > Hold on a moment.

   Other possible lines:

   > How quickly time flies.
   > I don't want to disturb you.
   > Why not?

   > I'll see you then.
   > Then I won't come over at 5:00.
   > I'm sorry. She isn't here right now.

   c. Have each pair create a conversation incorporating those lines. Students can begin and end their conversations any way they wish, but they must include those lines in their dialogs.

   d. Call on students to present their conversations to the class.

WORKBOOK ANSWER KEY AND LISTENING SCRIPTS

WORKBOOK PAGE 111

A. THEY'LL ALL BE BUSY

1. Yes, he will. He'll be mopping
2. Yes, they will. They'll be bathing
3. Yes, we will. We'll be exercising
4. Yes, they will. They'll be paying
5. Yes, she will. She'll be knitting
6. Yes, I will. I'll be sewing
7. Yes, he will. He'll be ironing
8. Yes, we will. We'll be rearranging

WORKBOOK PAGES 114–115

D. WHY DON'T YOU?

1. she'll be practicing the violin
   practices the violin
2. he'll be studying
   studies
3. they'll be doing their laundry
   do their laundry
4. she'll be exercising
   exercises
5. he'll be cleaning his apartment
   cleans his apartment
6. they'll be watching TV
   watch TV
7. she'll be washing her car
   washes her car
8. they'll be baking
   bake
9. he'll be taking a bath
   takes a bath
10. they'll be bathing their dog
    bathe their dog

E. LISTENING

Listen and choose the correct answer.

1. A. What will Betty be doing this afternoon?
   B. She'll be ironing dresses.

2. A. What will Sally and Tom be doing this morning?
   B. They'll be working downtown.

3. A. What will your husband be doing today?
   B. He'll be knitting on the front porch.

4. A. Will you be busy tonight?
   B. Yes, I will. I'll be watching sports.

5. A. Will you and Frank be busy in a half hour?
   B. Yes, we will. We'll be feeding the baby.

6. A. What will Charles be doing later tonight?
   B. He'll be taking a bath.

7. A. Will you and your husband be home this morning?
   B. Yes, we will. We'll be home all morning. We'll be baking cakes.

8. A. Will your daughter be busy this afternoon?
   B. Yes, she will. She'll be doing her homework.

9. A. What will Teddy and Timmy be doing this Sunday morning?
   B. I'm sure they'll be sleeping all morning.

10. A. Will your daughter be home this afternoon?
    B. No, she won't. She'll be skateboarding in the park.

11. A. Will you and your wife be busy this afternoon?
    B. Yes, we will. I think we'll be walking the dog.

12. A. I'm sad that you're leaving.
    B. I know. But don't worry. I'll be thinking about you all the time.

Answers

1. b
2. a
3. b
4. a
5. a
6. b
7. b
8. a
9. b
10. a
11. b
12. b

WORKBOOK PAGE 116

F. WHAT'S THE WORD?

1. Hello
2. This
3. May
4. speak
5. isn't
6. right
7. take
8. message
9. tell
10. that
11. called
12. Okay

1.	b	**7.**	b
2.	a	**8.**	b
3.	b	**9.**	b
4.	a	**10.**	a
5.	b	**11.**	b
6.	a	**12.**	a

WORKBOOK PAGE 117

H. UNTIL WHEN?

1. I'll be practicing, for
2. He'll be reading, until
3. She'll be working, until
4. We'll be arriving, at
5. I'll be having, in
6. She'll be studying, until
7. He'll be staying, until
8. I'll be cooking, for

WORKBOOK PAGE 118

I. WHAT'S THE QUESTION?

1. will you be talking on the telephone
2. will they be arriving
3. will she be working on his car
4. will he be leaving
5. will we be driving
6. will you be mopping the floors
7. will she be feeding the dog
8. will they be living away from home
9. will he be playing loud music
10. will we be riding on the roller-coaster

GRAMMAR

PRONOUN REVIEW

Subject Pronouns	Object Pronouns	Possessive Adjectives	Possessive Pronouns	Reflexive Pronouns
I	me	my	mine	myself
you	you	your	yours	yourself
he	him	his	his	himself
she	her	her	hers	herself
it	it	its	—	itself
we	us	our	ours	ourselves
you	you	your	yours	yourselves
they	them	their	theirs	themselves

SOME/ANY

There's **something** wrong with my washing machine.
I'm sure you'll find **somebody/someone** who can fix it.

I don't know **anything** about washing machines.
Do you know **anybody/anyone** who can help me?

POSSESSIVE OF SINGULAR & PLURAL NOUNS

neighbor – neighbor's dog
neighbors – neighbors' son

FUNCTIONS

ASKING FOR AND REPORTING INFORMATION

There's something wrong with *my washing machine.*

Do you know *anybody who can help me?*

I won't *be home tomorrow morning.*
I'll be *taking my son to the dentist.*

Where do you live?
156 Grove Street in Centerville.

What's the name?
Helen Bradley.
And what's the address again?
156 Grove Street in Centerville.
And the phone number?
237-9180.

OFFERING TO HELP

Do you need any help?
Can I help you?
I'll be glad to help you.

EXPRESSING ABILITY

I can *do my homework by myself.*

EXPRESSING INABILITY

I can't *help you.*
I couldn't *fall asleep last night.*

INQUIRING ABOUT AGREEMENT

Is that okay?

EXPRESSING AGREEMENT

That's fine.

EXPRESSING DISAGREEMENT

Not really.

INITIATING A TOPIC

You look tired today.

EXPRESSING HOPE

I hope *you sleep better tonight.*

EXPRESSING REGRET

I'm afraid *I won't be home tomorrow morning.*

OFFERING ADVICE

You should *look in the phone book.*

IDENTIFYING

Armstrong Plumbing Company.

NEW VOCABULARY

Home

faucet
front light
garbage
hall
kitchen sink
lock

Home Repairs

electrician
electronics
heating
locksmith
plumbing

Car

brakes
steering wheel

Verbs

argue
charge
flood
lift weights
rake
rely on
turn

Everyday Objects

address book
camera
headphones
phone book
video/camcorder

Pronouns

anybody
anyone
everything
somebody
someone

Giving Advice

ought to

Miscellaneous

canary
grateful
leaves
moving company
next-door neighbor
since
up
weights

EXPRESSIONS

as soon as possible
for example
go up and down
No, that's okay.
Not really.
That's fine.
there's something wrong with

VOCABULARY PREVIEW

You may want to present these words before beginning the chapter, or you may choose to wait until they first occur in a specific lesson. If you choose to present them at this point, here are some suggestions:

1. Have students look at the illustrations on text page 125 and identify the words they already know.

2. Present the vocabulary. Say each word and have the class repeat it chorally and individually. Check students' understanding and pronunciation of the words.

3. Practice the vocabulary as a class, in pairs, or in small groups. Have students cover the word list and look at the pictures. Practice the words in the following ways:

   • Say a word and have students tell the number of the illustration.

   • Give the number of an illustration and have students say the word.

Text Page 126: I'll Be Glad to Help

FOCUS

- Review of Subject, Object, and Reflexive Pronouns

CLOSE UP

RULE:	The simple future tense is often used to offer help.
EXAMPLE:	**I'll be** glad to help.

RULE:	Verbs that describe states of being (stative verbs) take only simple tenses. *Need* is a stative verb.
EXAMPLE:	He's getting dressed. *(right now)* **Does** he **need** any help? *(right now)*

INTRODUCING THE MODEL

1. Have students look at the illustration.
2. Set the scene: "Johnny's grandmother and mother are talking about him."
3. Present the model.
4. Full-Class Repetition.

   ### Pronunciation Note

   The pronunciation focus of Chapter 13 is **Deleted *h*** (text page 136). You may wish to model this pronunciation at this point and encourage students to incorporate it into their language practice.

   I'll be glad to help him.

   He can get dressed by himself.

5. Ask students if they have any questions. Check understanding of the expression. *No, that's okay.*
6. Group Choral Repetition.
7. Choral Conversation.
8. Call on one or two pairs of students to present the dialog.

   (For additional practice, do Choral Conversation in small groups or by rows.)

SIDE BY SIDE EXERCISES

Examples

1. A. What's your daughter doing?
   B. She's feeding the canary.
   A. Does she need any help? I'll be glad to help her.
   B. No, that's okay. She can feed the canary by herself.

2. A. What's your husband doing?
   B. He's cleaning the garage.
   A. Does he need any help? I'll be glad to help him.
   B. No, that's okay. He can clean the garage by himself.

1. **Exercise 1:** Introduce the new word *canary*. Call on two students to present the dialog. Then do Choral Repetition and Choral Conversation practice.

2. **Exercise 2:** Same as above.

3. **Exercises 3–8:** Either Full Class Practice or Pair Practice.

New Vocabulary

6. rake
   leaves

4. **Exercise 9:** Have students use the model as a guide to create their own conversations, using vocabulary of their choice. Encourage students to use dictionaries to find new words they want to use. This exercise can be done orally in class or for written homework. If you assign it for homework, do one example in class to make sure students understand what's expected. Have students present their conversations in class the next day.

EXPANSION ACTIVITIES

1. Telephone

a. Divide the class into large groups. Have each group sit in a circle.

b. Whisper a set of directions to one student. For example:

   "I told her, and she told him, and he told them, and they told us, and now I'm telling you."

c. The first student whispers the message to the second student, and so forth around the circle.

d. When the message gets to the last student, that person says it aloud. Is it the same message you started with? The group with the most accurate message wins.

2. Match Sentences

a. Write 16 sentences on cards. Use full nouns in the first sentence and their equals with subject and object pronouns in the second. For example:

Your sister is visiting her boyfriend.	She's visiting him.

My mother is visiting my grandparents.	She's visiting them.
My uncle is visiting his daughter.	He's visiting her.
My brother is visiting his cousins.	He's visiting them.
My uncle is visiting his son.	He's visiting him.
Your sister is washing the dishes.	She's washing them.
My husband and I are washing the clothes.	We're washing them.
My niece and nephew are washing the floor.	They're washing it.

b. Distribute a card to each student.

c. Have students memorize the sentences on their cards, then walk around the room trying to find their corresponding match.

d. Then have pairs of students say their matching sentences aloud to the class.

3. Concentration

a. Use the cards from the above activity. Place them face down in four rows of 4 each.

b. Divide the class into two teams. The object of the game is for students to find the matching cards. Both teams should be able to see all the cards, since *concentrating* on their location is an important part of playing the game.

c. A student from Team 1 turns over two cards. If they match, the student picks up the cards, that team gets a point, and the student takes another turn. If the cards don't match, the student turns them face down, and a member of Team 2 takes a turn.

d. The game continues until all the cards have been matched. The team with the most correct matches wins the game.

Variation: This game can also be played in groups or pairs.

4. Grammar Chain

a. Start the chain game by saying:

She can make lunch by . . .

b. Student A must finish the sentence, make a new one using the same structure, and then pass the turn to Student B, who continues the chain. For example:

Student A: . . . herself. He can get dressed by . . .

Student B: . . . himself. They can wash the car by . . .

Etc.

5. Conversation Mime

a. Write the following cues on the board:

A. What's _____ doing?
B. I think (he's/she's) _____.
A. _____ need any help? I'll be glad to help _____.
B. No, that's okay. I'm sure (he/she) can _____ by _____.

b. Make up a set of "action cards" such as the following:

feed the cat	clean the house
rake the leaves	make dinner
iron shirts	assemble a bicycle
bake a cake	rearrange furniture
vacuum the carpet	bathe the dog

c. Have three students at a time come to the front of the class. One student picks a card and pantomimes the action on the card. The other two students comment on what the person is doing by creating a conversation based on the cues on the board. For example:

A. What's Miguel doing?
B. I think he's ironing shirts.
A. Does he need any help? I'll be glad to help him.
B. No, that's okay. I'm sure he can iron shirts by himself.

Text Page 127: I Just Found This Watch

FOCUS

- Review of Possessive Nouns and Possessive Pronouns

CLOSE UP

RULE: When forming the possessive of a noun ending in a sibilant [s, z, š, ž, č, j], the ending is pronounced [ɪz], which forms an additional syllable.

EXAMPLE: Grace's [ɪz]
Mr. and Mrs. Price's [ɪz]

INTRODUCING THE MODEL

1. Have students look at the illustration.
2. Set the scene: "Two friends are talking. One of them just found a watch."
3. Present the model.
4. Full-Class Repetition.
5. Ask students if they have any questions.
6. Group Choral Repetition.
7. Choral Conversation.
8. Call on one or two pairs of students to present the dialog.

   (For additional practice, do Choral Conversation in small groups or by rows.)

SIDE BY SIDE EXERCISES

Examples

1. A. I just found this umbrella. Is it yours?
   B. No, it isn't mine. But it might be Kate's. She lost hers a few days ago.
   A. Really? I'll call her right away.
   B. When you talk to her, tell her I said "Hello."

2. A. I just found this wallet. Is it yours?
   B. No, it isn't mine. But it might be Alan's. He lost his a few days ago.
   A. Really? I'll call him right away.
   B. When you talk to him, tell him I said "Hello."

1. **Exercise 1:** Call on two students to present the dialog. Then do Choral Repetition and Choral Conversation practice.

2. **Exercise 2:** Same as above.

3. **Exercises 3–11:** Either Full Class Practice or Pair Practice.

New Vocabulary

4. camera
6. headphones
10. address book

---

4. **Exercise 12:** Have students use the model as a guide to create their own conversations, using vocabulary of their choice. Encourage students to use dictionaries to find new words they want to use. This exercise can be done orally in class or for written homework. If you assign it for homework, do one example in class to make sure students understand what's expected. Have students present their conversations in class the next day.

WORKBOOK

Page 121

EXPANSION ACTIVITIES

1. Clap and Listen

a. Have students close their books.

b. Present the model, and every time you come to a pronoun, clap your hands or tap on the desk instead of saying the word. For example:

"I just found this watch. Is it *[clap]*?" (Students respond "yours.")
"No, it isn't *[clap]*." (Students respond "mine.")

c. Continue for the rest of the conversation.

d. Do the same with Exercise 1 and Exercise 4 to practice the other pronoun forms.

2. Listen for Pronouns!

a. Put the following on the board:

b. Say sentences with pronouns, and have students call out "One" if they hear a masculine pronoun, "Two" if they hear a feminine pronoun, and "Three" if they hear a plural pronoun. For example:

I'll call her right away.	*(Two)*
Tell him I said "Hello."	*(One)*
I think this is theirs.	*(Three)*
Give this to them.	*(Three)*
This is hers.	*(Two)*
This isn't theirs. It's his.	*(Three, One)*

3. Listen for Possessives

a. Put the following on the board:

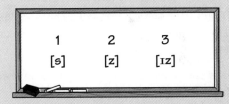

b. Say possessive phrases, and have students call out "One" if they hear the possessive sound [s], "Two" if they hear the sound [z], and "three" if they hear the sound [ɪz]. For example:

Bob's car	*(Two)*
Kate's house	*(One)*
Grace's watch	*(Three)*
George's camera	*(Three)*
Jenny's glasses	*(Two)*
Janet's ring	*(One)*
Mr. Price's cell phone	*(Three)*

(continued)

4. Tic Tac Finish the Sentence

a. Have students draw a tic tac grid on their papers and fill in the grid with any nine of the nouns from the exercises on page 127.

b. Say the beginnings of the following sentences, and tell students to cross out any word on their grid that completes the sentences.

> Where does George live? I need to look in my . . .
> I have ten dollars in my . . .
> I'm going to take their photograph with my new . . .
> What time is it? I can't find my . . .
> It's raining. Where's your . . . ?
> I'm listening to music with my new . . .
> How much is thirty-nine plus forty-seven? I need to use a . . .
> I'll call them on my . . .
> When I go to the beach, I always wear my . . .
> When I go to work, I always carry important papers in my . . .
> When I'm in English class, I always write new words in my . . .
> Sally got married last week. Did you see her new . . . ?

c. The first person to cross out three words in a straight line—either vertically, horizontally, or diagonally—wins the game.

d. Have the winner call out the words to check the accuracy.

5. Drawing Game

a. Make duplicate sets of the following cards:

sunglasses	wallet	camera
watch	headphones	cell phone
umbrella	briefcase	address book
ring	calculator	notebook

b. Divide the class into two teams. Have each team sit together in a different part of the room.

c. Place each set of cards on a table or desk in front of the room. Also, place a pad of paper and pencil next to each team's set of cards.

d. When you say "Go!," a person from each team comes to the table, picks a card from that team's pile, draws the item on the card, and shows the drawing to the rest of the team. The team then guesses what the word is.

e. When a team correctly guesses a word, another team member picks a card and draws the word written on that card.

f. Continue until each team has guessed all the words in their pile.

g. The team that guesses the words in the shortest time wins the game.

6. Do You Remember?

a. Have students spend three minutes looking carefully at text page 127. Tell them to concentrate on the people and the objects they lost.

b. Have students close their books, and ask the following questions:

Who lost a calculator?	(Ruth)
Who lost a briefcase?	(Janet)
Who lost a wallet?	(Alan)
Who lost a ring?	(Robert)
Who lost a notebook?	(Grace)
Who lost an umbrella?	(Kate)
Who lost an address book?	(Henry)
Who lost a watch?	(Fred)
Who lost a cell phone?	(Mr. and Mrs. Price)
Who lost a camera?	(Mr. and Mrs. Ryan)
Who lost a pair of sunglasses?	(Jessica)
Who lost a pair of headphones?	(George)

Variation: You can do the activity as a game with competing teams. The team with the most correct answers is the winner.

7. Conversation Chain: Is This Yours?

a. Collect a personal item such as a notebook, a pen, a glove, or a watch from every student in the class.

b. Starting with the first student, hold the item and model the following:

> Teacher: Is this yours?
> Student A: No. It isn't mine. But it might be (his/hers).
> Teacher: Ask (him/her).

(Student A takes the item from the teacher and shows it to Student B.)

> Student A: Is this yours?
> Student B: No. It isn't mine. But it might be (his/hers).
> Student A: Ask (him/her).

c. Continue the *chain* until a student actually *does* get his or her own item. Have that student respond: "Yes. It's mine. Thank you."

d. Continue the practice with other items.

FOCUS

- Review of Verb Tenses: Past Continuous, Simple Past, Simple Present

CLOSE UP

RULE:	The *past continuous* focuses on the duration of an action, not its completion. The *simple past* focuses on the completion of an action.
EXAMPLE:	My neighbors **were arguing** last night. *(action in progress)*
	How late **did** they **argue**?
	They **argued** until 3 A.M. *(action completed)*
RULE:	The *simple present* tense describes habitual activities.
EXAMPLE:	My neighbors **don't argue** very often.
SPELLING RULE:	To indicate possession of a singular noun, an apostrophe (') is added before the possessive -*s* ending. To indicate possession of a plural noun already ending in *s*, only an apostrophe is added.
EXAMPLES:	my neighbor – my neighbor**'s** dog
	my neighbors – my neighbors**'** son

INTRODUCING THE MODEL

1. Have students look at the model illustration.
2. Set the scene: "Two friends are talking. One of them is very upset about what happened last night."
3. Present the model.
4. Full-Class Repetition.
5. Ask students if they have any questions. Check understanding of the word *argue*.
6. Group Choral Repetition.
7. Choral Conversation. Call on one or two pairs of students to present the dialog.

   (For additional practice, do Choral Conversation in small groups or by rows.)

SIDE BY SIDE EXERCISES

Examples

1. A. You look tired today.
   B. Yes, I know. I couldn't fall asleep last night.
   A. Why not?
   B. My downstairs neighbor was singing.
   A. How late did he sing?
   B. Believe it or not, he sang until 2 A.M.
   A. That's terrible! Did you call and complain?
   B. No, I didn't. I don't like to complain.
   A. Well, I hope you sleep better tonight.
   B. I'm sure I will. My downstairs neighbor doesn't sing very often.

2. A. You look tired today.
   B. Yes, I know. I couldn't fall asleep last night.
   A. Why not?
   B. My neighbor's dog was barking.
   A. How late did it bark?
   B. Believe it or not, it barked until 4 A.M.
   A. That's terrible! Did you call and complain?
   B. No, I didn't. I don't like to complain.
   A. Well, I hope you sleep better tonight.
   B. I'm sure I will. My neighbor's dog doesn't bark very often.

1. **Exercise 1:** Call on two students to present the dialog. Then do Choral Repetition and Choral Conversation practice.

2. **Exercise 2:** Same as above.

3. **Exercises 3–9:** Either Full Class Practice or Pair Practice.

New Vocabulary

5. hall
7. next-door neighbors
9. lift weights

4. **Exercise 10:** Have students use the model as a guide to create their own conversations, using vocabulary of their choice. Encourage students to use dictionaries to find new words they want to use. This exercise can be done orally in class or for written homework. If you assign it for homework, do one example in class to make sure students understand what's expected. Have students present their conversations in class the next day.

WORKBOOK

Pages 122–124

EXPANSION ACTIVITIES

1. **Scrambled Conversation**

   a. Write each line of the model conversation on text page 128 or any of the exercises on text pages 128–129 on a separate card. Scramble the cards.

   b. Give the cards to 10 students. Have them unscramble the lines and put together the conversation.

   c. Have students line up in front of the class and say their lines. The rest of the class decides if the conversation is in the correct order.

2. **Miming: What Was I Doing?**

   a. Write down on cards the activities from text pages 128 and 129.

   b. Have students take turns picking a card from the pile and pantomiming the action on the card for 10 seconds.

   c. After the person stops, the class must guess what the person was doing.

   Variation: This can be done as a game with competing teams.

   (continued)

3. Chain Story

a. Begin by saying "I couldn't fall asleep last night because all my neighbors were making noise."

b. Student 1 repeats what you said and adds another item. For example: "I couldn't fall asleep last night because all my neighbors were making noise. My downstairs neighbors were listening to loud music."

c. Continue around the room in this fashion, with each student repeating what the previous one said and adding another sentence.

d. You can do the activity again, beginning and ending with different students.

If the class is large, you may want to divide students into groups to give students more practice.

4. Expand the Sentence

Tell students that the object of the activity is to build a long sentence on the board, one word at a time.

a. Write the following on the board:

> I was very upset last night because

b. Have a student come to the board and add a word. For example:

> I was very upset last night because my

c. Have a second student add another word. For example:

> I was very upset last night because my neighbors

d. Continue until each student in the class has had one or more turns to add a word to expand the sentence into the longest one they can think of. For example:

> I was very upset last night because my neighbors across the hall were vacuuming their apartment until 3 A.M. and I wasn't able to fall asleep, so I decided to call the landlord and complain about them.

5. Role Play: They Called and Complained

a. Divide the class into pairs or small groups.

b. Have each pair or group choose one of the conversations in the lesson— either the model or any of the exercises—and create a role play in which the person who can't fall asleep decides to call the landlord and complain about the noise.

c. Have students present their role plays to the class and compare how each of the situations gets resolved.

6. Tell a Story: The Worst Day

a. Write on the board:

> Yesterday was one of the worst days _____ can remember!

b. Divide the class into small groups of 3 to 5 students. Have each group create a story of at least ten sentences about a character who had a very bad yesterday. Encourage students to use any vocabulary they wish and to draw from their own experiences in describing the unlucky events.

c. Have one person from each group present the story to the class.

d. Have the class decide which character had the worst day.

7. Information Gap Handouts

a. Tell students: "Fred couldn't fall asleep last night." Write out what happened in Fred's apartment building, but divide the information between two different charts. For example:

Chart A:

```
                  ┌──────────────────────┐
                  │ His upstairs         │
                  │ neighbors _____   │
                  │ all night.           │
        ┌─────────┴──────────┬───────────┴──────────┐
        │          ( Fred )  │  The next-door       │
practiced the piano│        │  neighbors' baby     │
until 1 A.M.       │  Fred  │  cried until 5 A.M.   │
        └─────────┬──────────┴───────────┬──────────┘
                  │ His downstairs       │
                  │ neighbors listened   │
                  │ to loud music until  │
                  │ midnight.            │
                  └──────────────────────┘
```

Chart B:

```
                  ┌──────────────────────┐
                  │ His upstairs         │
                  │ neighbors danced     │
                  │ all night.           │
        ┌─────────┴──────────┬───────────┴──────────┐
His neighbor across│        │                      │
the hall practiced │  Fred  │  cried until 5 A.M.  │
the piano until 1 A.M.      │                      │
        └─────────┬──────────┴───────────┬──────────┘
                  │ His downstairs       │
                  │ neighbors _____   │
                  │ until midnight.      │
                  └──────────────────────┘
```

b. Divide the class into pairs. Give each member of the pair a different chart. Have students share their information and fill in their charts. For example:

Student A: What did his upstairs neighbors do all night?

Student B: They danced.

c. The pairs continue taking turns to ask each other a question until each has a complete chart.

d. Have students look at their partner's chart to make sure that they have written the information correctly.

 ON YOUR OWN *Neighbors*

1. For homework, have students write answers to the questions.

2. In the next class, have students share their answers as a class, in pairs, or in small groups. Encourage students to tell about their neighbors without referring to their written homework.

If you chose to do the activity as pair practice, have students report to the class about the other member of the pair.

FOCUS

- Something, Somebody/Someone
- Anything, Anybody/Anyone

CLOSE UP

RULE:	The determiner *some* can combine with *-thing, -body, and -one*. These pronouns are used in affirmative statements. *Somebody* and *someone* are synonyms.
EXAMPLES:	There's **something** wrong with my washing machine. I'm sure you'll find **somebody** who can fix it. I'm sure you'll find **someone** who can fix it.

RULE:	The word *any* can combine with *-thing, -body, and -one*. These pronouns are used in questions and negative statements. *Anybody* and *anyone* are synonyms.
EXAMPLES:	I don't know **anything** about washing machines. Do you know **anybody** who can help me? Do you know **anyone** who can help me?

GETTING READY

Introduce words with *some-* and *any-*.

1. Put the following on the board:

2. Form sentences with all the pronouns in each group. Have students repeat the sentences chorally. For example:

Do you see anything?
Do you see anybody?
Do you see anyone?

3. Call on pairs of students to practice the sentences conversationally.

    A. Do you see anything?
    B. No. I don't see anything.
    A. I'm sure you'll see something soon.

    A. Do you see anybody?
    B. No. I don't see anybody.
    A. I'm sure you'll see somebody soon.

    A. Do you see anyone?
    B. No. I don't see anyone.
    A. I'm sure you'll see someone soon.

4. Create other conversations with your students, using similar patterns. For example:

    Do you hear anything/anybody/anyone?
    Did you find anything/anybody/anyone?

INTRODUCING THE MODEL

1. Have students look at the model illustration.

2. Set the scene: "Two friends are talking. One of them is having a problem with his washing machine."

3. Present the model.

4. Full-Class Repetition.

5. Ask students if they have any questions. Check understanding of new vocabulary: *there's something wrong with, phone book.*

6. Group Choral Repetition.

7. Choral Conversation.

8. Call on one or two pairs of students to present the dialog.

9. Substitute *anyone* and *someone* in place of *anybody* and *somebody*. Call on one or two pairs of students to present the dialog, using these words.

    (For additional practice, do Choral Conversation in small groups or by rows.)

SIDE BY SIDE EXERCISES

In these exercises, students can use *somebody/someone* and *anybody/anyone* interchangeably.

Examples

1. A. There's something wrong with my refrigerator.
   B. I'm sorry. I can't help you. I don't know anything about refrigerators.
   A. Do you know anybody/anyone who can help me?
   B. Not really. You should look in the phone book. I'm sure you'll find somebody/someone who can fix it.

2. A. There's something wrong with my dishwasher.
   B. I'm sorry. I can't help you. I don't know anything about dishwashers.
   A. Do you know anybody/anyone who can help me?
   B. Not really. You should look in the phone book. I'm sure you'll find somebody/someone who can fix it.

1. Exercise 1: Call on two students to present the dialog. Then do Choral Repetition and Choral Conversation practice.

2. Exercise 2: Introduce the word *dishwasher*. Same as above.

3. Exercises 3–7: Either Full Class Practice or Pair Practice.

New Vocabulary

3. faucet

---

4. Exercise 8: Have students use the model as a guide to create their own conversations, using vocabulary of their choice. Encourage students to use dictionaries to find new words they want to use. This exercise can be done orally in class or for written homework. If you assign it for homework, do one example in class to make sure students understand what's expected. Have students present their conversations in class the next day.

WORKBOOK

Pages 125–126

EXPANSION ACTIVITIES

1. Miming: They're Having Trouble!

a. Write the following on the board:

> He's having trouble with his _____.
> She's having trouble with her _____.

b. Write on cards the items from text page 130.

c. Have students take turns picking a card from the pile and pantomiming someone having trouble with that particular item.

d. The class must guess what the person is having trouble with. For example:

> He's having trouble with his dishwasher.
> She's having trouble with her video camera.

Variation: This can be done as a game with competing teams.

2 Clue!

a. Have one student leave the classroom for several minutes. Choose one of the items from text pages 127 or 130. For example:

briefcase	refrigerator
sunglasses	garbage disposal
notebook	video camera
address book	headphones
kitchen faucet	calculator
bathtub	umbrella
cell phone	dishwasher
ring	computer
wallet	

b. Have the class talk about all the ways they use this item. Then have each student think of or write one sentence beginning with "It's something . . ." that tells about the item. For example:

> It's something I carry in my bag.
> It's something I keep for many years.
> It's something that helps me remember my friend's telephone numbers.
> It's something I don't want to lose.

[answer: address book]

c. Have the student outside the class return and listen to the clues of the class. Then the student tries to guess the object.

Variation: This activity can be done as a game with competing teams.

3. Ranking

a. Dictate the following to the class:

cell phone	refrigerator
washing machine	dishwasher
computer	television
calculator	answering machine
garbage disposal	

b. Have students rank these items from the *easiest to fix* to the *most difficult to fix*, with the first being the easiest.

c. As a class, in pairs, or in small groups, have students compare their lists.

d. Then rank the items according to these additional criteria:

> *most expensive to least expensive*
> *most important in my daily life to least important*

4. Look in the Phone Book

a. Have each student choose one of the items on text page 130 and look in the phone book to find someone who can fix that particular item.

b. Make a list on the board of students' findings.

Option: If you wish, compile students' findings and publish a *Class Guide to Home Repair*.

5. Class Survey

a. Have students interview each other to find out which of the items on text page 130 students can fix by themselves.

b. Have students report back to the class about their interviews.

Option: Have students decide who the *handiest* student in the class is.

6. Class Discussion: Taking Care of Things

Situations in this chapter present problems with commonly used items. Have students write and talk about how to take care of these items to keep them working well.

a. Divide the class into small groups.

b. Have each group decide on an item and brainstorm ways to take care of that item so it doesn't break. Encourage students to use dictionaries to look up words they would like to use to express their ideas.

c. Have the groups write down their suggestions and then present them to the class. For example:

a refrigerator

You should close the door quickly.
You shouldn't put too much food in the refrigerator.
You should clean under the refrigerator once a year.

a car

You should change the oil every three months.
You should put air in the tires every few months.
You should check the water in the radiator.

FOCUS

- Review of Verb Tenses: Future Continuous, Future Tense with *Will*

INTRODUCING THE MODEL

1. Have students look at the illustration.

2. Set the scene: "Someone is calling the plumber."

3. Present the model.

4. Full-Class Repetition.

5. Ask students if they have any questions. Check understanding of new vocabulary: *kitchen sink, as soon as possible, Not really, That's fine.*

6. Group Choral Repetition.

7. Choral Conversation.

8. Call on one or two pairs of students to present the dialog.

   (For additional practice, do Choral Conversation in small groups or by rows.)

SIDE BY SIDE EXERCISES

In these exercises, students use their own names and addresses. Also, students should make up times and excuses.

Example

> 1. A. Ajax Home Electronics Service. Can I help you?
>   B. Yes. There's something wrong with my TV. Can you send a repairperson to fix it as soon as possible?
>   A. Where do you live?
>   B. *(209 Main Street)* in *(Littleton)*.
>   A. I can send a repairperson tomorrow morning. Is that okay?

> B. Not really. I'm afraid I won't be home tomorrow morning. I'll be *(working)*.
> A. How about tomorrow afternoon?
> B. Tomorrow afternoon? What time?
> A. Between *(two)* and *(five)*.
> B. That's fine. Somebody will be here then.
> A. What's the name?
> B. *(Roger Watson)*.
> A. And what's the address again?
> B. *(209 Main Street)* in *(Littleton)*.
> A. And the phone number?
> B. *(398-7630)*.
> A. Okay. We'll have someone there tomorrow afternoon.
> B. Thank you.

1. **Exercise 1:** Introduce the new word *electronics*. Call on two students to present the dialog. Then do Choral Repetition and Choral Conversation practice.

2. **Exercise 2:** Introduce the new word *electrician*. Same as above.

3. **Exercises 3–4:** Either Full-Class Practice or Pair Practice.

> **New Vocabulary**
> 3. plumbing
>   heating
> 4. locksmith

WORKBOOK

Pages 127–131

1. Match and Sequence

a. Make the following set of matching cards:

Can I help you?	Yes. I'm having a problem with my doorbell.
Where do you live?	19 Blake Road in Westville.
I can send an electrician tomorrow morning. Is that okay?	Not really. I'll be working tomorrow morning.
How about tomorrow afternoon?	Tomorrow afternoon? Sure. What time?
Between two and five. Is that okay?	Between two and five? Yes. Someone will be home then.
What's the name?	Alex Green.
And the phone number?	976-1277.
We'll see you tomorrow. Good-bye.	Thank you. Good-bye.

b. Distribute a card to 16 students.

c. Have students memorize the sentences on their cards, and then have them walk around the room saying their sentences until they find their match.

d. Then have students sequence the sentences in logical order and present the conversation to the class.

2. Sense or Nonsense?

Read the following to the class, and have students decide if they *make sense* or are *nonsense*:

If you're having problems with your car, you should call a mechanic.

If you're having problems with your doorbell, you should call a plumber.

If you're having problems with your kitchen sink, you should call an electrician.

If you're having problems with your bathtub, you should call a locksmith.

If you're having problems with your TV, you should call a repairperson.

If you're having problems with your kitchen sink, you should call a plumber.

3. Associations

a. Divide the class into pairs or small groups.

b. Write the following on the board:

> Which appliances use electricity?
> Which appliances use plumbing?
> Which appliances use electronics?
> Which appliances have locks?

c. Have students in each pair or group make a list of appliances that belong in each group.

d. Have students present their lists to the class.

Variation: Do the activity as a game in which you divide the class into teams. The team with the most number of appliances is the winner.

(continued)

4. Role Play: It's Broken Again

a. Write on the board:

> A. I can't believe it. Our _____ is broken again.
> B. Are you SURE?! The _____ just fixed it last week.
> A. I guess (he/she) isn't a very good _____. Maybe we should call (somebody/someone) else next time.

b. Have pairs of students role-play the conversation. Begin by giving each pair one of the cues below, either on the board or on a word card. Then have one or two pairs do the role play, using any vocabulary they wish.

Cues:

sink plumber	doorbell electrician
car mechanic	lock locksmith
TV repairperson	front light electrician
shower plumber	washing machine repairperson

5. Movable Categories

a. Write the following items on separate cards:

a cell phone	headphones	a shower
a car lock	a faucet	a car
a computer	a dishwasher	a calculator
a doorbell	a television	a gas stove
an answering machine	a video camera	a garbage disposal

b. Give each student one card.

c. Call out the following phrase:

> A mechanic can fix . . .

d. All those students whose words are appropriate for the category go to the right side of the room. All the other students go to the left side.

e. Those who are in the right group call out their words for the class verify.

f. Continue with the following categories:

> An electronic repairperson can fix . . .
> A plumber can fix . . .
> A locksmith can fix . . .

READING *Trouble with Cars*

FOCUS

- Pronoun Review

NEW VOCABULARY

brakes
charge
go up and down
since
steering wheel
turn (v)

READING THE STORY

Optional: *Preview the story by having students talk about the story title and/or illustrations. You may choose to introduce new vocabulary beforehand, or have students encounter the new vocabulary within the context of the reading.*

1. Have students read silently, or follow along silently as the story is read aloud by you, by one or more students, or on the audio program.

2. Ask students if they have any questions. Check understanding of vocabulary.

3. Check students' comprehension, using some or all of the following questions:

   What's wrong with Charlie's car?
   What did he try to do?
   Was he able to?
   Why not?
   What did he finally do?
   What did the mechanic do?
   Why is Charlie annoyed?

   What's wrong with Betty's car?
   What did she try to do?
   Was she able to?
   Why not?

   What did she finally do?
   What did the mechanic do?
   Why is Betty annoyed?

   What's wrong with Mark and Nancy's car?
   What did they try to do?
   Were they able to?
   Why not?
   What did they finally do?
   What did the mechanic do?
   Why are Mark and Nancy annoyed?

✓ READING *CHECK-UP*

WHAT'S THE WORD?

1. his/himself
2. them/their
3. her/her
4. my/mine (It)
5. them/myself
6. our/ourselves/our

READING EXTENSION

Have students discuss the following questions:

   Do you or your family have a car?
   Do you ever have problems with it?
   When was the last time you had a problem with the car? What happened?
   Can you recommend a good mechanic?

 LISTENING

WHAT'S THE WORD?

Listen and choose the word you hear.

1. Do you know him well?
2. I'll be glad to help them.
3. Did you see him today?
4. Yours will be ready at five o'clock.
5. Careful! You might hurt yourselves!
6. We're having trouble with her car.

Answers

1. a
2. b
3. b
4. a
5. b
6. b

WHAT ARE THEY TALKING ABOUT?

Listen and choose what the people are talking about.

1. I'm going to have to call the plumber.
2. It's broken. We won't be able to wash the dishes.
3. I'm upset. I can't watch my favorite program.
4. It doesn't work. I can't call anybody!
5. My mechanic fixed the brakes.

Answers

1. b
2. a
3. a
4. b
5. b

How About You?

Have students answer the questions, in pairs or as a class.

How to Say It!

> **Giving Advice:** In giving advice, the modal *ought* to has the same meaning as the modal *should*. To soften the advice, the speaker may preface it with "I think . . ."

1. Set the scene: "Two friends are talking."
2. Introduce *ought to*. Present the expressions.
3. Full-Class Repetition.
4. Ask students if they have any questions.
5. Group Choral Repetition.
6. Have students practice conversations in which they talk about problems and give advice.
7. Call on pairs to present their conversations to the class.

EXPANSION ACTIVITY

What's the Problem?

1. For homework, have students write a description of a problem with one of the following products:

cell phone	kitchen faucet	calculator
car lock	dishwasher	garbage disposal
computer	television	answering machine
telephone	shower	car
headphones	video camera	gas stove

2. In the next class, have pairs of students describe their problems to each other, and have their partners give advice.

 **IN YOUR OWN WORDS**
That's What Friends Are For

FOCUS

- Tense Review
- Review of Pronouns

1. Have students read silently, or follow along silently as the situations are read aloud by you, by one or more students, or on the audio program.

2. Ask students if they have any questions. Check understanding of new vocabulary: *everything, flood (v), for example, grateful, moving company.*

3. Make sure students understand the instructions. Check understanding of the expression *rely on*.

4. Have students do the activity as written homework, using a dictionary for any new words they wish to use.

5. Have students present and discuss what they have written, in pairs or as a class.

PRONUNCIATION

> **Deleted *h*:** The initial /*h*/ sound of the pronouns *him, her, his, himself,* and *herself* is often deleted.

Focus on Listening

Practice the sentences in the left column. Say each sentence or play the audio one or more times. Have students listen carefully and repeat.

Focus on Pronunciation

Practice the sentences in the right column. Have students say each sentence and then listen carefully as you say it or play the audio.

If you wish, have students continue practicing the sentences to improve their pronunciation.

JOURNAL

Have students write their journal entries at home or in class. Encourage students to use a dictionary to look up words they would like to use. Students can share their written work with other students if appropriate. Have students discuss what they have written as a class, in pairs, or in small groups.

WORKBOOK

Check-Up Test: Pages 132–133

CHAPTER SUMMARY

GRAMMAR

1. Divide the class into pairs or small groups.

2. Have students take turns forming sentences with pronouns. For *Some/Any* and *Possessives,* have students take turns reading the sentences and phrases in the grammar boxes.

KEY VOCABULARY

Have students ask you any questions about the meaning or pronunciation of the vocabulary. If students ask for the pronunciation, repeat after the student until the student is satisfied with his or her own pronunciation.

EXPANSION ACTIVITIES

1. **Do You Remember the Words?**

   Check students' retention of the vocabulary depicted on the opening page of Chapter 13 by doing the following activity:

   a. Have students open their books to page 125 and cover the list of vocabulary words.

   b. Either call out a number and have students tell you the word, or say a word and have students tell you the number.

   Variation: You can also do this activity as a game with competing teams.

2. **Student-Led Dictation**

   a. Tell each student to choose a word or phrase from the Key Vocabulary list on text page 136 and look at it very carefully.

   b. Have students take turns dictating their words to the class. Everybody writes down that student's word.

   c. When the dictation is completed, call on different students to write each word on the board to check the spelling.

3. **Beanbag Toss**

   a. Call out the topic: *Occupations.*

b. Have students toss a beanbag back and forth. The student to whom the beanbag is tossed must name an *occupation* from the Key Vocabulary list. For example:

Student 1:   electrician
Student 2:   mechanic
Student 3:   plumber

c. Continue until all the words in the category have been named.

d. Do the same with the *Objects* in the Key Vocabulary list.

Variation: You can also do this activity as a game with competing teams.

4. Letter Game

a. Divide the class into two teams.

b. Say: "I'm thinking of an appliance that begins with *d.*"

c. The first person to raise his or her hand and guess correctly [*dishwasher*] wins a point for his or her team.

d. Continue with other letters of the alphabet.

The team that gets the most correct answers wins the game.

END-OF-CHAPTER ACTIVITIES

1. Board Game

a. On poster boards or on manila file folders, make up game boards with a pathway consisting of separate spaces. You may use any theme or design you wish.

b. Divide the class into groups of 2 to 4 students, and give each group a game board and a die, and each player something to be used as a playing piece.

c. Give each group a pile of cards face-down with sentences written on them. Some sentences should be correct, and others incorrect. For example:

He can make lunch by herself.
They can fix the kitchen faucet by theirselves.
That umbrella isn't mine. It's her.
We need to get ours television fixed.
You can do your homework by yourself.
You and your brother can do the dishes by yourself.
Is this your?
I'll be glad to help her.
We can rake the leaves by ourselves.
I don't know something about cars.
Do you know anybody who can fix this TV?
She can't find somebody to fix her car.
I know anything about computers.
I can't find anything wrong with the phone.

My neighbors are singing very often.
You ought call a mechanic.

d. Each student in turn rolls the die, moves the playing piece along the game path, and after landing on a space, picks a card, reads the sentence, and says if it is *correct* or *incorrect*. If the statement is incorrect, the student must correct it. If the response is correct, the student takes an additional turn.

e. The first student to reach the end of the pathway is the winner.

2. Finish the Sentence!

Begin a sentence, and have students add appropriate endings to the sentence. For example:

Teacher	Students
A mechanic fixes . . .	cars.
	motorcycles.
	trucks.
An electrician fixes . . .	electric stoves.
	lights.
	doorbells.
A plumber fixes . . .	showers.
	faucets.
	sinks.

(continued)

Variation: This activity may be done as a class, in pairs or small groups, or as a game with competing teams.

3. **Dialog Builder**

   a. Divide the class into pairs.

   b. Write a line from a conversation on the board. For example:

   > I'm sorry. I can't help you.

   Other possible lines:

   > Is that okay?
   > That's terrible!
   > I'm sure you'll find somebody who can fix it.
   > Believe it or not, . . .
   > Tell him I said "Hello."
   > I'll be glad to help them.
   > I'm sure I will.

   c. Have each pair create a conversation incorporating that line. Students can begin and end their conversations any way they wish, but they must include that line in their dialogs.

   d. Call on students to present their conversations to the class.

4. **Question Game**

   a. Write the following sentence on the board:

   > Charlie tried to fix the brakes by himself, but he wasn't able to since he doesn't know anything about cars.

   b. Underline different elements of the sentence, and have students create a question based on that portion of the sentence. For example:

   > <u>Charlie</u> tried to fix the brakes by himself, but he wasn't able to since he doesn't know anything about cars.

   Who tried to fix the brakes by himself?

   > Charlie tried to fix <u>the brakes</u> by himself, but he wasn't able to since he doesn't know anything about cars.

   What did Charlie try to fix?

   > Charlie tried to fix the brakes by himself, but he wasn't able to <u>since he doesn't know anything about cars.</u>

   Why wasn't Charlie able to fix the brakes?

   c. Continue with other sentences.

WORKBOOK ANSWER KEY AND LISTENING SCRIPTS

WORKBOOK PAGE 120

A. BY THEMSELVES

1. His, him, himself
2. Their, them, themselves
3. Her, her, herself
4. you, You, yourself
5. him, himself
6. myself, me
7. Our, us, ourselves
8. yourselves, you

WORKBOOK PAGE 121

B. THE LOST ROLLERBLADES

1. yours
2. mine
3. his
4. hers
5. theirs
6. ours

C. SCRAMBLED SENTENCES

1. Did he fix his car by himself?
2. Is this address book yours?
3. She can feed the cats by herself.
4. Did you give him her telephone number?
5. When you call Bob, tell him I have his new sunglasses.
6. I need to use your cell phone because I lost mine.

WORKBOOK PAGE 122

D. WHAT'S THE WORD?

1. a
2. b
3. b
4. b
5. a
6. b
7. a
8. b

E. LISTENING

Listen to each conversation, and then choose the correct answers to the questions you hear.

Conversation 1

A. I just found this brown wallet on my desk. Is it yours?
B. No. It isn't mine. But it might be John's. He lost his last Tuesday.

A. Thanks. I'll call him right away.
B. I hope it's his. He was very upset when he lost it.
    1. What color is John's wallet?
    2. What did Mary lose at work?
    3. Is the wallet Mary's?

Conversation 2

A. Hello, John? This is Jane. I just found a brown wallet on my desk at work. Is it yours?
B. No. Unfortunately, it isn't mine. Mine is black. But it might be Mary's. She lost hers, too.
A. Okay. I'll call her right away.
B. I hope it's hers. She was very upset when she lost it.
    4. Where was the wallet?
    5. Is the wallet John's?
    6. When did John lose it?

Answers

1. b	4. a
2. b	5. c
3. a	6. c

WORKBOOK PAGES 123–124

F. NOISY NEIGHBORS

1. neighbors'
2. are listening
3. listened
4. for
5. wasn't
6. fall
7. hard
8. at
9. he'll call
10. his

11. next-door
12. their
13. noisy
14. to complain
15. move
16. to
17. myself

18. her
19. are barking
20. loudly
21. barked
22. until
23. might
24. to argue
25. nice

(continued)

26. to be tired
27. I'm practicing
28. during
29. until
30. I eat
31. a few
32. tells
33. have to
34. don't
35. won't
36. well

WORKBOOK PAGES 125–126

G. WHAT'S THE WORD?

1. anything
   nobody
   anything
   anybody
2. anything
   nobody
   yourself
3. Somebody
   Nobody
4. someone
   any
5. anybody
   someone

6. anyone
   nobody
7. somebody
   anything
   Nobody
   something
   Nobody

H. LISTENING: *The Prom*

Listen and choose the correct response.

1. How was the prom last Saturday?
2. How was your new tuxedo?
3. Was there any good music?
4. How late did you stay?
5. Why did you leave so early?
6. Do you think next year's prom will be better?

Answers

1. b
2. a
3. b
4. a
5. b
6. b

WORKBOOK PAGE 129

L. LISTENING

Listen and choose the person you should call.

1. A. I'm having trouble with my new car!
   B. You should call . . .
2. A. There's water on my bathroom floor!
   B. You should call . . .
3. A. My keys won't open the door lock!
   B. You should call . . .
4. A. My upstairs neighbor lifts weights at two
      o'clock in the morning.
   B. You should call . . .
5. A. The lights in my kitchen won't go on!
   B. You should call . . .
6. A. Someone stole my bicycle!
   B. You should call . . .
7. A. I can't turn off my kitchen faucet!
   B. You should call . . .
8. A. My computer crashes every day!
   B. You should call . . .

Answers

1. b
2. c
3. b
4. c
5. a
6. b
7. c
8. b

WORKBOOK PAGE 130

M. WHAT'S THE WORD?

1. Two, too
2. week, weak
3. They're, their
4. right, write
5. Where, wear
6. hour, our
7. know, No
8. buy, by
9. hole, whole
10. You're, Your
11. eight, ate

CHECK-UP TEST: Chapters 11–13

A.

1. They'll be paying
2. I'll be going
3. He'll be reading
4. She'll be working
5. We'll be getting married

B.

1. will you be practicing the piano
2. will he be ironing
3. will she be leaving
4. will they be driving
5. will you be chatting online

C.

1. less, fewer, less
2. don't have to
3. mustn't, much
4. don't have to
5. for
6. until
7. at
8. at
9. someone, anything
10. somebody
11. Someone
12. mine
13. their, hers
14. her
15. ours

D.

Listen and choose the correct answers to complete the sentences.

1. Good morning. I'm Doctor Johnson. Today I'll be giving you. . . . .
2. First, you'll stand on a scale and the nurse will measure . . . . .
3. Next, the nurse will take your . . . .
4. Then you'll go to the lab for some blood tests and . . . .
5. Next, we'll go into the examination room and I'll look at your . . . .

Answers

1. a
2. b
3. a
4. b
5. a

FEATURE ARTICLE
Communities

NEW VOCABULARY

> keep to themselves
> megacity
> public transportation
> Time will tell.

PREVIEWING THE ARTICLE

Have students look at the photograph and identify the community depicted as urban, suburban, or rural. Introduce the new vocabulary.

READING THE ARTICLE

1. Have students read silently, or follow along silently as the article is read aloud by you, by one or more students, or on the audio program.

2. Ask students if they have any questions. Check understanding of new vocabulary.

3. Check students' comprehension by having students decide whether these statements are true or false:

    People in urban communities live far apart. *(False)*
    In urban communities, businesses are close to where people live. *(True)*
    People in urban communities often walk or take public transportation. *(True)*
    Some people in suburban communities use public transportation. *(True.)*
    In a suburban community, businesses and stores are close to where people live. *(False)*
    In rural communities, people live far from each other. *(True.)*
    In rural communities, people can walk to stores. *(False.)*

4. Have students discuss the questions at the end of the reading, in small groups or as a class.

EXPANSION ACTIVITIES

1. Advantages and Disadvantages

    a. Have students draw two columns on a piece of paper. At the top of one column, have students write <u>Advantages</u>. At the top of the other column, have them write <u>Disadvantages</u>.

    b. Say one of the types of communities, and have students brainstorm its advantages and disadvantages. Write students' ideas in the columns, and have students copy on their papers. For example:

    Urban

<u>Advantages</u>	<u>Disadvantages</u>
Work is nearby.	It can be expensive.
Stores are nearby.	Some neighborhoods are dangerous.

2. Dictate and Discuss

    a. Divide the class into pairs or small groups.

    b. Dictate sentences such as the following and then have students discuss them:

    > Cities are more dangerous than suburbs.
    > It's easier to raise a family in a rural community than in a city.
    > Megacities are the best cities.
    > Suburbs are better than urban and rural communities.
    > It's more expensive to live in the city than in the suburbs.

    c. Call on students to share their opinions with the rest of the class.

1. Before reading the Fact File, ask students: "What do you think? What are the ten largest cities in the world? What were the ten largest cities in the world fifty years ago?" Write students' ideas on the board. After reading the table, have students check their predictions.

2. Bring a map to class and point out the locations of the cities: *Calcutta (India), Chicago (US), Buenos Aires (Argentina), Rhein-Ruhr (Germany), Shanghai (China), Moscow (Russia), Paris (France), Tokyo (Japan), London (England), New York (US), Jakarta (Indonesia), Dhaka (Bangladesh), Beijing (China), Lagos (Nigeria), Mumbai (India), Sao Paolo (Brazil).*

3. Read the information aloud as the class follows along.

4. To check comprehension, ask students:

   In 1950, where were many of the world's largest cities? *(Europe and North America)*

   What cities are still very large? *(New York, Shanghai, and Tokyo)*

   In 2010, where will many of the world's largest cities be? *(Asia)*

   How many people lived in Tokyo in 1950? *(6 million)*

   How many people will live in Tokyo in 2010? *(28 million)*

   How many people lived in New York in 1950? *(11 million)*

   How many people will live in New York in 2010? *(16 million)*

5. For further discussion, ask students:

   Why do you think cities are growing so fast in some nations?

   Why do you think cities are growing more slowly in rich nations?

   Do you want to live in a megacity in the future? Why or why not?

> appliance repairperson
> cable TV installer
> chimneysweep
> exterminator
> house painter
> TV repairperson

1. Have students look at the illustrations and identify any words they already know.

2. Present the vocabulary. Say each word and have the class repeat it chorally and individually. Check students' understanding and pronunciation of the words.

EXPANSION ACTIVITIES

1. Clap in Rhythm

   Object: Once a clapping rhythm is established, students must continue naming different household repair people.

   a. Have students sit in a circle.

   b. Establish a steady even beat—one-two-three-four, one-two-three-four—by having students clap their hands to their laps twice and then clap their hands together twice. Repeat throughout the game, maintaining the same rhythm.

   c. The object is for each student in turn to name a repairperson each time the hands are clapped together twice. Nothing is said when students clap their hands on their laps.

   Note: The beat never stops! If a student misses a beat, he or she can either wait for the next beat or else pass to the next student.

2. Match the Conversations

   a. Make a set of matching conversation cards. For example:

I lost the keys to the house.	I'll call the locksmith right away.

   (continued)

EXPANSION ACTIVITIES (Continued)

Our kitchen sink is broken.	I'll call the plumber right away.
The lights don't work in the living room.	I'll call the electrician right away.
There's a bird in our chimney!	I'll call the chimneysweep right away.
Let's watch that special news program on cable.	I'll call the cable TV installer right away.
We have mice in the kitchen!	I'll call the exterminator right away.
Let's change the color of the walls.	I'll call the house painter right away.
The TV is broken!	I'll call the TV repairperson right away.
Our clothes dryer doesn't work.	I'll call the appliance repairperson right away.

b. Distribute a card to each student.

c. Have students memorize the sentences on their cards, and then have students walk around the room saying their sentences until they find their match.

d. Then have pairs of students say their matched sentences aloud to the class.

3. Concentration

a. Use the cards from the above activity. Place them face down in three rows of 6 each.

b. Divide the class into two teams. The object of the game is for students to find the matching cards. Both teams should be able to see all the cards since *concentrating on their location* is an important part of playing the game.

c. A student from Team 1 turns over two cards. If they match, the student picks up the cards, that team gets a point, and the student takes another turn. If the cards don't match, the student turns them face down, and a member of Team 2 takes a turn.

d. The game continues until all the cards have been matched. The team with the most correct matches wins the game.

Variation: This game can also be played in groups and pairs.

4. Recommendations

a. Have students interview each other for suggestions of a good house painter, appliance repairperson, TV repairperson, and chimneysweep.

b. Have students report back to the class.

c. Have the class *publish* its recommendations.

 AROUND THE WORLD
Where Friends Get Together

1. Have students read silently, or follow along silently as the text is read aloud by you, by one or more students, or on the audio program. Check understanding of new vocabulary: *plaza, coffee shop*.

2. Have students first work in pairs or small groups to respond to the questions. Then have students tell the class what they talked about. Write any new vocabulary on the board.

EXPANSION ACTIVITY

Survey on Places to Get Together

Have students find out where their classmates meet with friends.

1. Brainstorm questions that students can ask each other. For example:

   Where do you get together with friends?
   Where is your favorite place to walk?
   Where is your favorite place to have a picnic?
   What do you talk about when you get together with friends?

2. Have each student chose one question to ask and then conduct their surveys by circulating around the room asking each other their questions.

3. For homework, have students draw up the survey results in graph form (such as a bar graph or pie chart). In class, have students share their graphs and report their results.

 GLOBAL EXCHANGE

1. Set the scene: "JuanR is writing to his keypal."

2. Introduce new vocabulary: *present (v), whole, through the years*. Note the irregular plural: *life–lives*.

3. Have students read silently or follow along silently as the message is read aloud by you, by one or more students, or on the audio program.

4. Ask students if they have any questions. Check understanding of vocabulary.

5. Suggestions for additional practice:

   • Have students write a response to JuanR and share their writing in pairs.

   • Have students correspond with a keypal on the Internet and then share their experience with the class.

 **LISTENING**

1. Set the scene: "Many people are having problems today, and they're calling for help."

2. Introduce the following new words and expressions: *drain, get back to you, turn off, call back, answering service.*

LISTENING SCRIPT

Listen to the messages and conversations. Match the caller with the repairperson.

1. A. Hello. This is Dan, the Drain Man. I'm not here to take your call. Please leave your name, number, and the time you called. Also, please describe the problem. I'll get back to you as soon as possible. Have a great day!
   B. Hello. This is Amy Francis. My number is 355-3729. It's three o'clock Friday afternoon. My kitchen faucet is broken. I can't turn off the water! Please call back as soon as possible. Thank you.

2. A. Hello. This is Helen's Home Repair. If you break it, we can fix it! Nobody is here right now. Leave a message after the beep, and we'll call you back. Thank you.
   B. Hi. This is Paul Mendoza. My front steps are broken, and I need somebody who can fix them. My phone number is 266-0381. Please call back soon. I'm having a party this weekend, and nobody will be able to get into my house! Thank you.

3. A. Hi. This is Kevin's Key Service. Leave a message and I'll call you back. Thanks.
   B. Good morning. My name is Jim Carney. I'm really embarrassed. I just lost my keys while I was jogging, and I can't get into my apartment. I'm calling from my neighbor's apartment across the hall. I live at 44 Wilson Road, Apartment 3B. My neighbor's number is 276-9184. Please call back soon. Thank you.

(continued)

4. A. Gary's Garage. May I help you?
   B. Yes. I think there's something wrong with my steering wheel.
   A. What's the problem?
   B. It's difficult to turn right, and it's VERY difficult to turn left!
   A. Hmm. That's not good. What's your name?
   B. Jennifer Park.
   A. Phone number?
   B. 836-7275.
   A. Can you be here tomorrow morning at eight?
   B. Yes. That's fine. Thank you.

5. A. Hello. Rita's Repair Company.
   B. Hi. Is this Rita?
   A. No. This is the answering service. May I help you?
   B. Yes. My doorbell is broken. It won't stop ringing!
   A. I can hear that. Your name, please?
   B. Ed Green.
   A. Address?
   B. 2219 High Street.
   A. And your phone number?
   B. 923-4187.
   A. Will someone be home all day?
   B. Yes. I'll be here.
   A. Okay. Rita will be there before 5 P.M.
   B. Thank you.

Answers

1. c

2. e

3. b

4. a

5. d

 WHAT ARE THEY SAYING?

FOCUS

- Home Repair Problems

Have students talk about the people and the situation, and then create role plays based on the scene. Students may refer back to previous lessons as a resource, but they should not simply reuse specific conversations.

Note: You may want to assign this exercise as written homework, having students prepare their role plays, practice them the next day with other students, and then present them to the class.

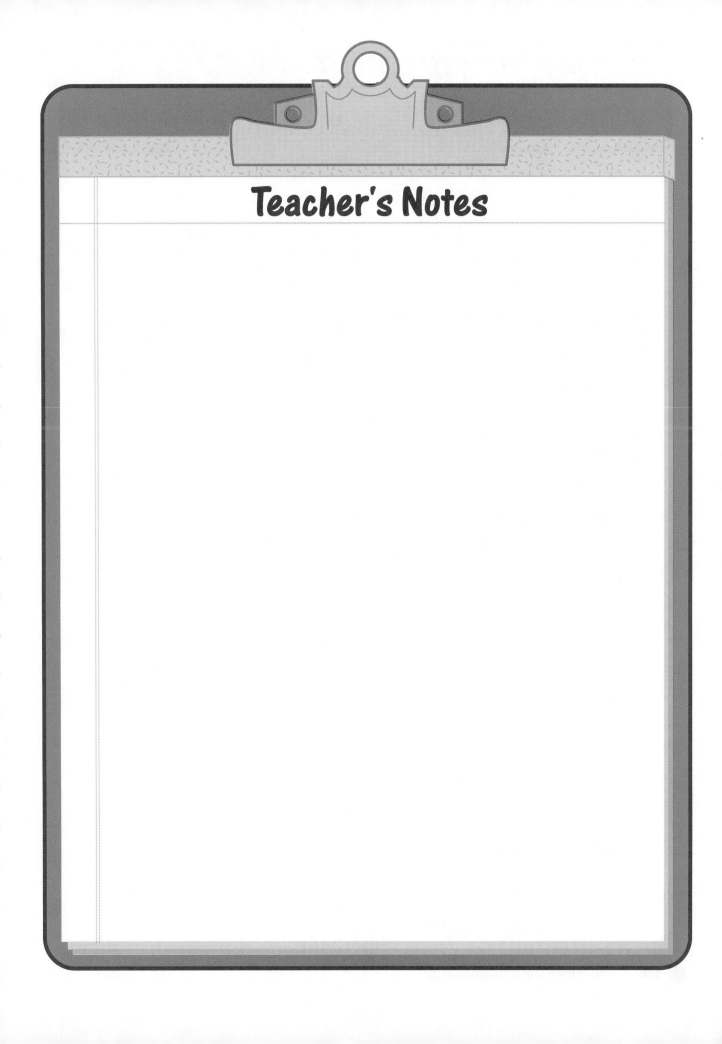

Teacher's Notes

SIDE BY SIDE PICTURE CARDS

Numerical List

1. pen
2. book
3. pencil
4. notebook
5. bookshelf
6. globe
7. map
8. board
9. wall
10. clock
11. bulletin board
12. computer
13. table
14. chair
15. ruler
16. desk
17. dictionary
18. living room
19. dining room
20. kitchen
21. bedroom
22. bathroom
23. attic
24. yard
25. garage
26. basement
27. restaurant
28. bank
29. supermarket
30. library
31. park
32. movie theater
33. post office
34. zoo
35. hospital
36. read
37. cook
38. study
39. eat
40. watch TV
41. sleep
42. play the piano
43. play the guitar
44. play cards
45. play baseball
46. drink
47. teach
48. sing
49. listen to music
50. plant
51. listen to the radio
52. swim
53. fix ___ sink
54. fix ___ car
55. fix ___ TV

56. fix ___ bicycle
57. clean ___ apartment
58. clean ___ yard
59. feed ___ cat
60. feed ___ dog
61. paint
62. do ___ exercises
63. wash ___ clothes
64. wash ___ windows
65. wash ___ car
66. brush ___ teeth
67. wash ___ hair
68. tall – short
69. young – old
70. heavy/fat – thin
71. new – old
72. married – single
73. handsome – ugly
74. beautiful/pretty – ugly
75. large/big – small/little
76. noisy – quiet
77. expensive – cheap
78. easy – difficult
79. rich – poor
80. sunny
81. cloudy
82. raining
83. snowing
84. hot
85. warm
86. cool
87. cold
88. ride ___ bicycle
89. bake
90. dance
91. school
92. hotel
93. gas station
94. bus station
95. clinic
96. fire station
97. bakery
98. video store
99. barber shop
100. laundromat
101. drug store
102. church
103. department store
104. police station
105. hair salon
106. book store
107. health club
108. cafeteria

109. train station
110. sad
111. happy
112. angry
113. nervous
114. thirsty
115. hungry
116. hot
117. cold
118. sick
119. embarrassed
120. tired
121. scared
122. cry
123. smile
124. shout
125. bite ___ nails
126. perspire
127. shiver
128. blush
129. yawn
130. cover ___ eyes
131. mechanic
132. secretary
133. teacher
134. baker
135. truck driver
136. chef
137. singer
138. dancer
139. actor
140. actress
141. have lunch
142. have dinner
143. go swimming
144. go shopping
145. go dancing
146. go skating
147. go skiing
148. go bowling
149. headache
150. stomachache
151. toothache
152. backache
153. earache
154. cold
155. fever
156. cough
157. sore throat
158. work
159. type
160. shave
161. wait for the bus
162. sit
163. apples

164. bananas
165. bread
166. cake
167. carrots
168. cheese
169. chicken
170. eggs
171. fish
172. grapes
173. ketchup
174. lemons
175. lettuce
176. mayonnaise
177. meat
178. mustard
179. onions
180. oranges
181. pears
182. pepper
183. potatoes
184. salt
185. soy sauce
186. tomatoes
187. butter
188. coffee
189. cookies
190. flour
191. ice cream
192. milk
193. orange juice
194. rice
195. soda
196. sugar
197. tea
198. yogurt
199. airport
200. baseball stadium
201. concert hall
202. courthouse
203. flower shop
204. hardware store
205. ice cream shop
206. motel
207. museum
208. parking garage
209. pet shop
210. playground
211. shoe store
212. toy store
213. university
214. high school

Alphabetical List

actor **139**
actress **140**
airport **199**
angry **112**
apples **163**
attic **23**

backache **152**
bake **89**
baker **134**
bakery **97**
bananas **164**
bank **28**
barber shop **99**
baseball stadium **200**
basement **26**
bathroom **22**
beautiful **74**
bedroom **21**
big **75**
bite ___ nails **125**
blush **128**
board **8**
book **2**
book store **106**
bookshelf **5**
bread **165**
brush ___ teeth **66**
bulletin board **11**
bus station **94**
butter **187**

cafeteria **108**
cake **166**
carrots **167**
chair **14**
cheap **77**
cheese **168**
chef **136**
chicken **169**
church **102**
clean ___ apartment **57**
clean ___ yard **58**
clinic **95**
clock **10**
cloudy **81**
coffee **188**
cold **117**
cold **154**
cold **87**
computer **12**
concert hall **201**
cook **37**
cookies **189**
cool **86**
cough **156**
courthouse **202**
cover ___ eyes **130**
cry **122**

dance **90**
dancer **138**

department store **103**
desk **16**
dictionary **17**
difficult **78**
dining room **19**
do ___ exercises **62**
drink **46**
drug store **101**

earache **153**
easy **78**
eat **39**
eggs **170**
embarrassed **119**
expensive **77**

fat **70**
feed ___ cat **59**
feed ___ dog **60**
fever **155**
fire station **96**
fish **171**
fix ___ bicycle **56**
fix ___ car **54**
fix ___ sink **53**
fix ___ TV **55**
flour **190**
flower shop **203**

garage **25**
gas station **93**
globe **6**
go bowling **148**
go dancing **145**
go shopping **144**
go skating **146**
go skiing **147**
go swimming **143**
grapes **172**

hair salon **105**
handsome **73**
happy **111**
hardware store **204**
have dinner **142**
have lunch **141**
headache **149**
health club **107**
heavy **70**
high school **214**
hospital **35**
hot **116**
hot **84**
hotel **92**
hungry **115**

ice cream **191**
ice cream shop **205**

ketchup **173**
kitchen **20**

large **75**

laundromat **100**
lemons **174**
lettuce **175**
library **30**
listen to music **49**
listen to the radio **51**
little **75**
living room **18**

map **7**
married **72**
mayonnaise **176**
meat **177**
mechanic **131**
milk **192**
motel **206**
movie theater **32**
museum **207**
mustard **178**

nervous **113**
new **71**
noisy **76**
notebook **4**

old **69, 71**
onions **179**
orange juice **193**
oranges **180**

paint **61**
park **31**
parking garage **208**
pears **181**
pen **1**
pencil **3**
pepper **182**
perspire **126**
pet shop **209**
plant **50**
play baseball **45**
play cards **44**
play the guitar **43**
play the piano **42**
playground **210**
police station **104**
poor **79**
post office **33**
potatoes **183**
pretty **74**

quiet **76**

raining **82**
read **36**
restaurant **27**
rice **194**
rich **79**
ride ___ bicycle **88**
ruler **15**

sad **110**
salt **184**

scared **121**
school **91**
secretary **132**
shave **160**
shiver **127**
shoe store **211**
short **68**
shout **124**
sick **118**
sing **48**
singer **137**
single **72**
sit **162**
sleep **41**
small **75**
smile **123**
snowing **83**
soda **195**
sore throat **157**
soy sauce **185**
stomachache **150**
study **38**
sugar **196**
sunny **80**
supermarket **29**
swim **52**

table **13**
tall **68**
tea **197**
teach **47**
teacher **133**
thin **70**
thirsty **114**
tired **120**
tomatoes **186**
toothache **151**
toy store **212**
train station **109**
truck driver **135**
type **159**

ugly **73, 74**
university **213**

video store **98**

wait for the bus **161**
wall **9**
warm **85**
wash ___ car **65**
wash ___ clothes **63**
wash ___ hair **67**
wash ___ windows **64**
watch TV **40**
work **158**

yard **24**
yawn **129**
yogurt **198**
young **69**

zoo **34**

Categories

Adjectives

angry **112**
beautiful **74**
big **75**
cheap **77**
cold **117**
difficult **78**
easy **78**
embarrassed **119**
expensive **77**
fat **70**
handsome **73**
happy **111**
heavy **70**
hot **116**
hungry **115**
large **75**
little **75**
married **72**
nervous **113**
new **71**
noisy **76**
old **69, 71**
poor **79**
pretty **74**
quiet **76**
rich **79**
sad **110**
scared **121**
short **68**
sick **118**
single **72**
small **75**
tall **68**
thin **70**
thirsty **114**
tired **120**
ugly **73, 74**
young **69**

Ailments

backache **152**
cold **154**
cough **156**
earache **153**
fever **155**
headache **149**
sore throat **157**
stomachache **150**
toothache **151**

Classroom

board **8**
book **2**
bookshelf **5**
bulletin board **11**
chair **14**
clock **10**
computer **12**
desk **16**
dictionary **17**
globe **6**

map **7**
notebook **4**
pen **1**
pencil **3**
ruler **15**
table **13**
wall **9**

Community

airport **199**
bakery **97**
bank **28**
barber shop **99**
baseball stadium **200**
book store **106**
bus station **94**
cafeteria **108**
church **102**
clinic **95**
concert hall **201**
courthouse **202**
department store **103**
drug store **101**
fire station **96**
flower shop **203**
gas station **93**
hair salon **105**
hardware store **204**
health club **107**
high school **214**
hospital **35**
hotel **92**
ice cream shop **205**
laundromat **100**
library **30**
motel **206**
movie theater **32**
museum **207**
park **31**
parking garage **208**
pet shop **209**
playground **210**
police station **104**
post office **33**
restaurant **27**
school **91**
shoe store **211**
supermarket **29**
toy store **212**
train station **109**
university **213**
video store **98**
zoo **34**

Foods

apples **163**
bananas **164**
bread **165**
butter **187**
cake **166**
carrots **167**
cheese **168**

chicken **169**
coffee **188**
cookies **189**
eggs **170**
fish **171**
flour **190**
grapes **172**
ice cream **191**
ketchup **173**
lemons **174**
lettuce **175**
mayonnaise **176**
meat **177**
milk **192**
mustard **178**
onions **179**
orange juice **193**
oranges **180**
pears **181**
pepper **182**
potatoes **183**
rice **194**
salt **184**
soda **195**
soy sauce **185**
sugar **196**
tea **197**
tomatoes **186**
yogurt **198**

Home

attic **23**
basement **26**
bathroom **22**
bedroom **21**
dining room **19**
garage **25**
kitchen **20**
living room **18**
yard **24**

Occupations

actor **139**
actress **140**
baker **134**
chef **136**
dancer **138**
mechanic **131**
secretary **132**
singer **137**
teacher **133**
truck driver **135**

Verbs

bake **89**
bite ___ nails **125**
blush **128**
brush ___ teeth **66**
clean ___ apartment **57**
clean ___ yard **58**
cook **37**
cover ___ eyes **130**

cry **122**
dance **90**
do ___ exercises **62**
drink **46**
eat **39**
feed ___ cat **59**
feed ___ dog **60**
fix ___ bicycle **56**
fix ___ car **54**
fix ___ sink **53**
fix ___ TV **55**
go bowling **148**
go dancing **145**
go shopping **144**
go skating **146**
go skiing **147**
go swimming **143**
have dinner **142**
have lunch **141**
listen to music **49**
listen to the radio **51**
paint **61**
perspire **126**
plant **50**
play baseball **45**
play cards **44**
play the guitar **43**
play the piano **42**
read **36**
ride ___ bicycle **88**
shave **160**
shiver **127**
shout **124**
sing **48**
sit **162**
sleep **41**
smile **123**
study **38**
swim **52**
teach **47**
type **159**
wait for the bus **161**
wash ___ car **65**
wash ___ clothes **63**
wash ___ hair **67**
wash ___ windows **64**
watch TV **40**
work **158**
yawn **129**

Weather

cloudy **81**
cold **87**
cool **86**
hot **84**
raining **82**
snowing **83**
sunny **80**
warm **85**

GLOSSARY

The number after each word indicates the page where the word first appears in the text.
(adj) = adjective, (adv) = adverb, (n) = noun, (v) = verb.

a few **14**
a little **14**
a while **100**
able to **95**
about **85**
absolutely **36**
accident **77**
account **78**
accurate **72**
accurately **73**
actor **71**
actually **123**
add **24**
address book **104**
adult **121**
advice **8**
age **121**
ago **6**
agree **47**
air **60**
airline **82**
airline pilot **82**
airport **61**
all over **36**
along **63**
although **46**
amount **27**
amusement park **60**
anniversary **7**
annual **108**
answer **81**
answering machine **120**
any more **32**
anybody **130**
anyone **130**
anyway **54**
apart **8**
appetite **22**
appetizer **25**
apple **11**
apple cake **110**
apple pie **13**
appliance **56**
argue **128**
arm **36**
arrive **29**
ashamed **52**
assemble **99**
assembler **81**
assistant **100**
attend **86**

attractive **41**
away **86**
awful **110**
awkward **75**
awkwardly **75**

back **112**
bad luck **79**
badly **74**
bag **16**
bagel **27**
baked (adj) **25**
baking soda **24**
ballet **99**
banana **11**
Bangladesh **32**
bank account **78**
barbecue **89**
bargain **56**
baseball stadium **61**
bathe **115**
be back **30**
beautifully **72**
because of **46**
beef **110**
beef stew **110**
beep **120**
begin **29**
besides **56**
best **54**
better **44**
bill **115**
billion **27**
bite **83**
blackout **84**
block (n) **68**
blood pressure **105**
blood test **105**
bloody nose **113**
bloom (v) **32**
blueprints **110**
bookcase **55**
boring **51**
borrow **115**
bottle **19**
boulevard **67**
bowl **23**
box (n) **19**
brakes (n) **133**
bread **11**
break (v) **35**

break into **83**
brick **110**
bridge **88**
brief **120**
bright **50**
broiled (adj) **25**
build **110**
bunch **19**
burglar **86**
burn (v) **83**
bus system **46**
butter **12**

cabinet **12**
cable TV **137**
cake **11**
California **8**
camera **127**
camcorder **125**
camping **60**
can (n) **19**
canary **126**
capable **43**
card player **72**
cardiogram **105**
care **17**
career **121**
careful **34**
carefully **72**
careless **72**
carelessly **72**
carrot **11**
CD **8**
CD player **7**
celebration **59**
cement **110**
cent **21**
cereal **19**
certainly **50**
change (v) **46**
changes (n) **46**
charge (v) **133**
chat online **2**
checkup **106**
cheese **8**
chess player **72**
chest **105**
chest X-ray **105**
chicken **11**
chicken soup **23**
child care **104**

chili **27**
chimneysweep **137**
chocolate (adj) **15**
chocolate bar **27**
chocolate cake **15**
chocolate ice cream **23**
chop up **24**
circus **87**
clean out **115**
close **60**
clumsy **101**
coast **8**
cocoa beans **27**
coffee **12**
coffee maker **103**
coffee shop **138**
college student **86**
come **32**
come home **44**
come in **106**
come over **117**
communicate **8**
community **104**
company picnic **35**
company president **82**
complain **52**
complete (adj) **106**
completely **68**
compliment (v) **52**
concert hall **61**
condominium **8**
confident **81**
confidently **81**
construction **110**
convertible sofa **123**
cookbook **110**
cookie **12**
corner **67**
correct **81**
cost (v) **21**
Costa Rica **82**
costume **59**
costume party **59**
cot **123**
couch **123**
could **94**
couldn't **94**
counter **12**
course **43**
courthouse **61**
co-worker **94**

Teacher's Notes

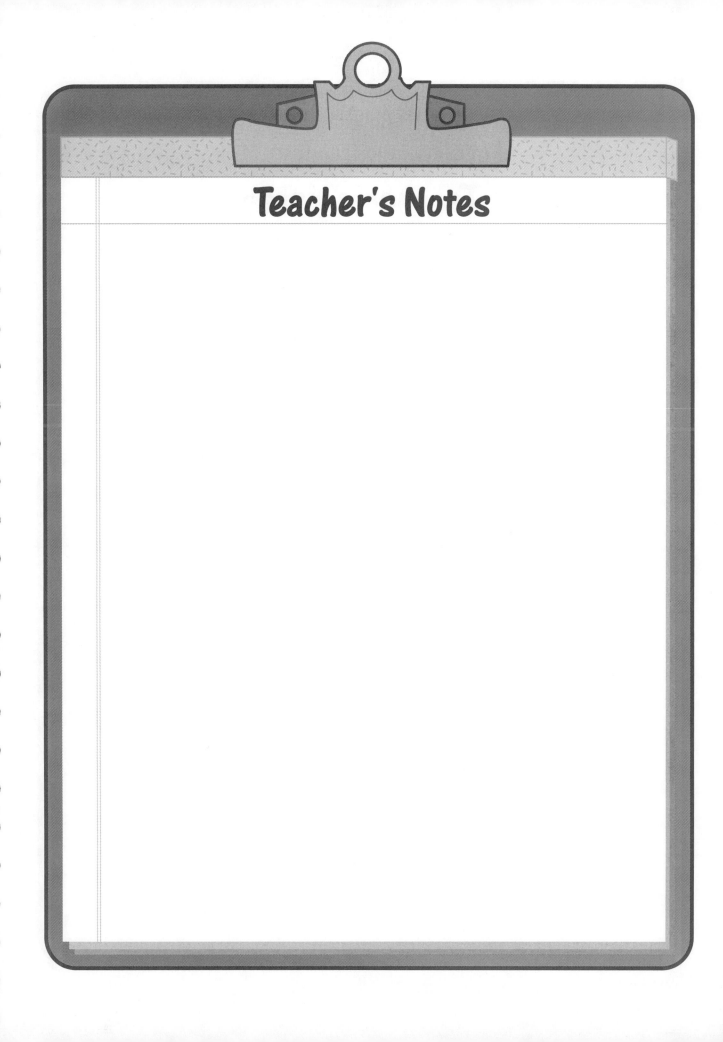

Teacher's Notes

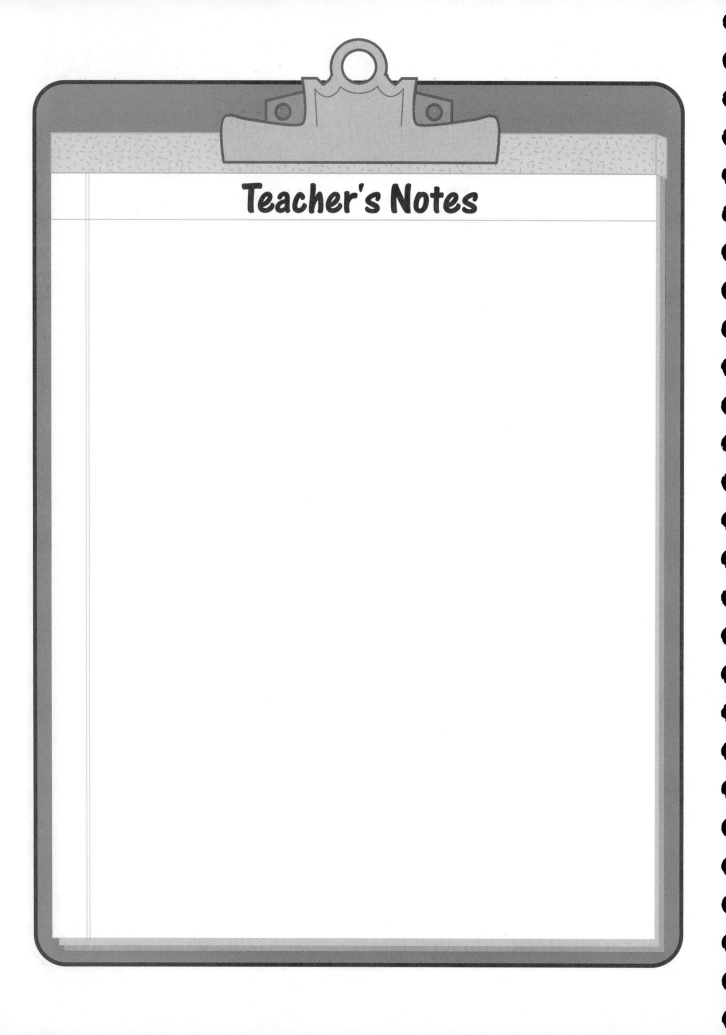

Teacher's Notes

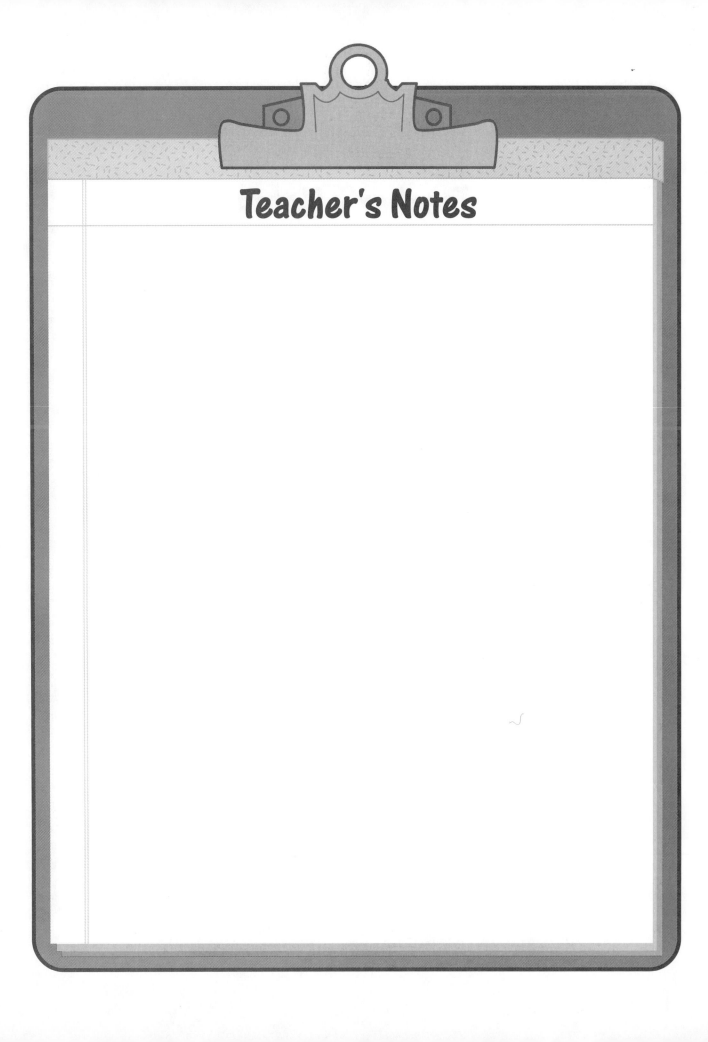

Teacher's Notes

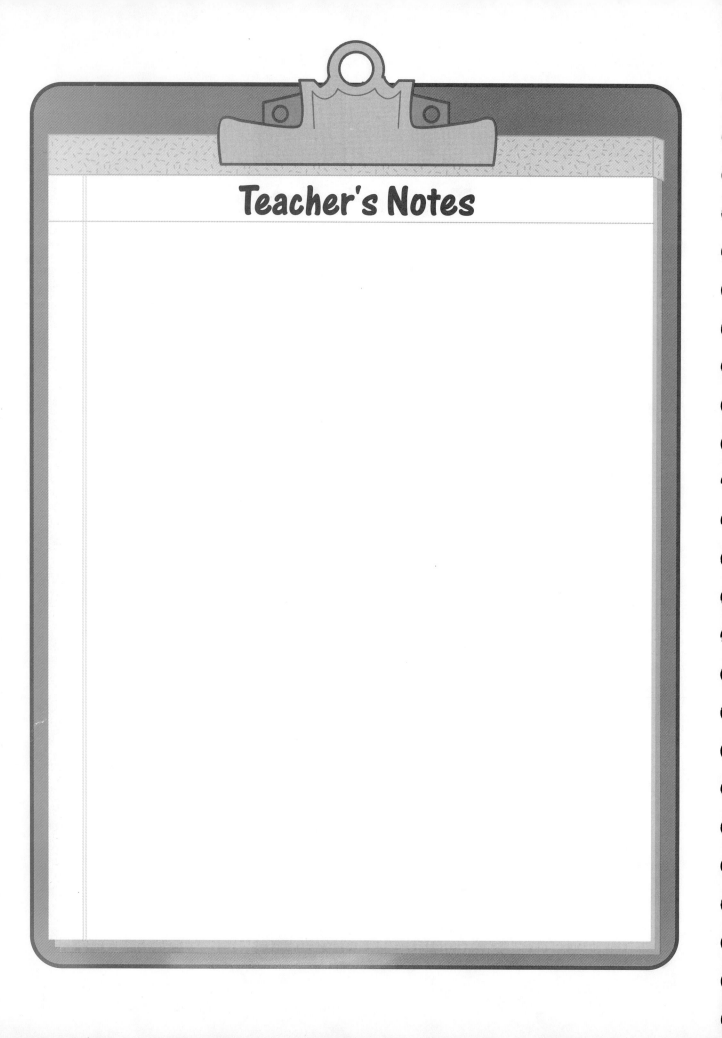

Teacher's Notes

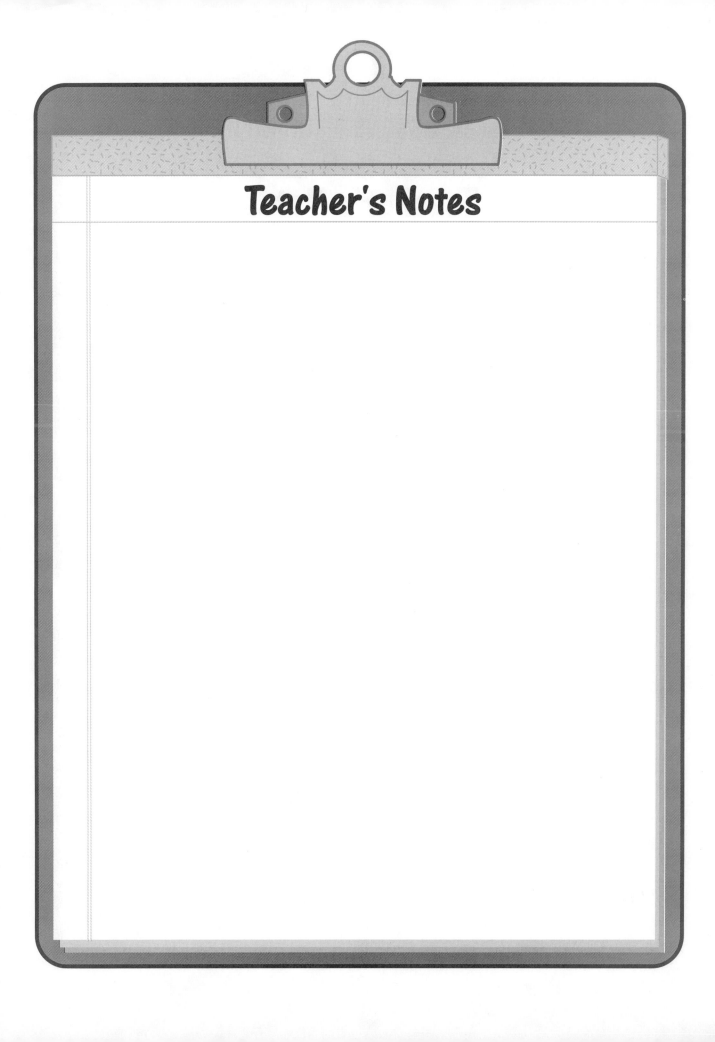

Teacher's Notes

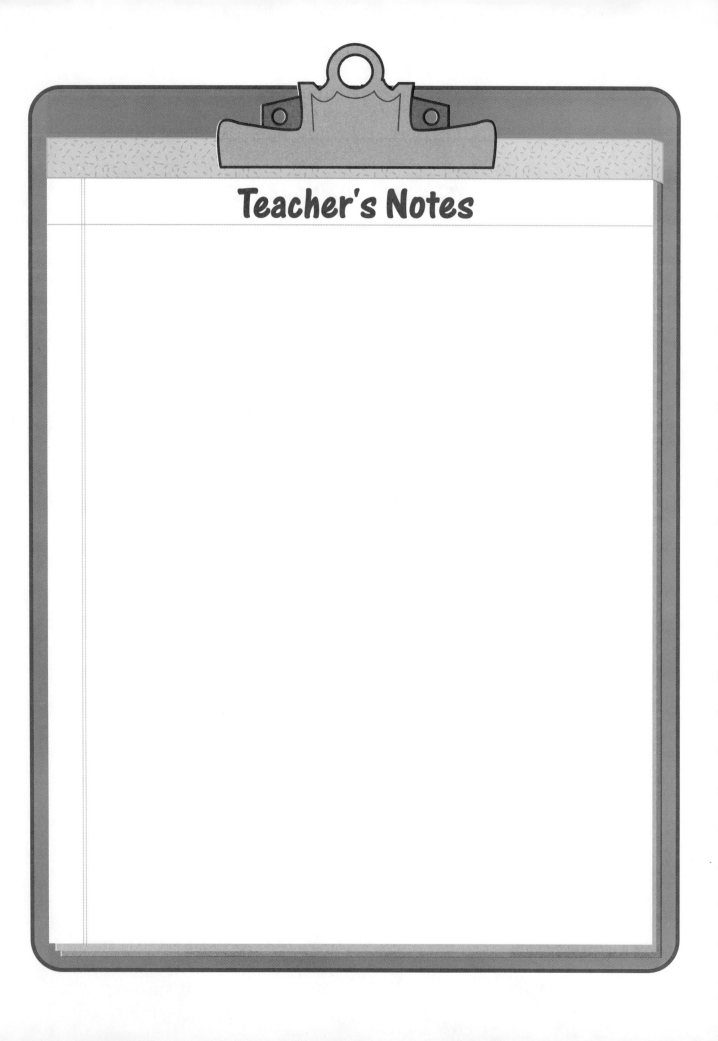

Teacher's Notes